General Experimental Psychology

General Experimental Psychology

AN INTRODUCTION TO PRINCIPLES

LAWRENCE M. BAKER
Purdue University

New York · OXFORD UNIVERSITY PRESS
1960

To My Wife and Three Daughters

PREFACE

Several years before beginning this book, the author selected topics, and, in collaboration with another psychologist, wrote illustrative experiments upon what were believed to be the most fundamental problems in experimental psychology (1).* Most of the problems were the same as those worked upon by earlier experimenters. The methods and procedures, while shortened and simplified, remained closely parallel in other ways to some of the classical experiments. The general experimental patterns have been used over and over by many writers and teachers, so no claim was made for any degree of originality. Even after our attempts at simplification, the experiments often seemed difficult and confusing to beginning students. A great burden was placed upon the teacher in trying to give essential background so that the student would get the full meaning and significance of the experiments. Without such assistance the task could easily result in frustration for the student, and there was an ever-present danger that the experiment would be reduced to what would seem to the student to be a bit of tedious busy-work of no vital consequence.

The paragraph above is a necessary explanation for the preface to the present book—the second task to which we set ourself. Our motive was to relieve the teacher of at least part of the burden that we have mentioned and to be of use to the student in integrating the work of the course. It was the intention of the author to write a book dealing with experimental psychology, in which each chapter would be chosen in the first place because it was typical or representative of a group of problems. The literature that is relevant to each experiment varies greatly, and this fact became a threat to our original plan. Certain compromises have been forced upon the writer. For example, only a small percentage of

* References appear alphabetically according to author at the end of each chapter. The number in parentheses corresponds to the number before the intended reference.

the excellent experimental work on vision and hearing has been mentioned. On the other hand, some of the chapters include a considerably higher proportion of the available material in print. A sufficient coverage to make each experiment meaningful seemed to be a more desirable goal than to treat every topic according to current knowledge of that topic.

In the end there was not a strict adherence of one chapter for one experiment. Even with these modifications, it was still apparent that the original manual and the book were not sufficiently integrated. In cooperation with two other psychologists (each had made use of the earlier manual), a revision has been carried out (2). In anticipation that teachers may feel that some of the topics deserve more attention than others, a few additional or alternate experiments have been included in the manual.

In spite of the practical difficulties encountered, it is believed that the original intention had merit and we do not think that the basic purpose has been seriously compromised. The hope survives that along with performing his experiments and reporting the results, the student will be studying about the ways earlier psychologists viewed the problems, adapted methods and techniques, handled results based upon what they found, and, finally, made interpretations and drew conclusions.

The approach that was thought to be of greatest use to the student was not one involving extended presentation of detailed material, for this has been well done in more exhaustive publications, including those of a handbook nature, but one in which brief statements were made with the purpose of helping the student in his attempt to comprehend the significance of what he is doing when he performs the experiments. It was our intention to stress in textbook and manual, both directly and by implication, that successful psychological experiments are very demanding in the use of sound methods and techniques if the data are to be dependable, and, furthermore, that great care must still be exercised in thinking about the results before defensible generalizations can be drawn.

This book was written for students, not colleagues. It is hoped that it will lighten the work of colleagues, but students are the ones intended to use it. Furthermore, it is intended for the student who has had a one-semester course in psychology before starting laboratory work. There was a time when the very first course in psychology was structured with a view to laying a foundation for those who were planning to specialize in the field. Such a purpose has long since ceased to motivate the majority of elementary textbook writers, or to determine the way most first courses are taught. It was, therefore, one of our aims to prepare material that might be used with conscious intention of laying a foundation for the future psychologist. The book might be used as a supplementary text where the beginning course is more than three semester hours, including laboratory. On the other hand, it is scarcely sufficient in detailed description about how to carry out experiments to stand alone without the use of a laboratory manual or other material intended to serve the purpose of directing the student as he goes about the task of experimenting.

We have necessarily not covered a great deal of material beyond that found in some of the elementary psychology books, for some of the authors cover a staggering amount of content. A more definite historical slant has been used than is common in elementary books and emphasis has centered upon the process and results of experimenting. We intended to serve those students who want to major in psychology, those who will use the background of knowledge and laboratory experience in preparation for studying other sciences, or those who consider a basic course beyond the usual elementary course in psychology as essential to them in obtaining a sound general or scientific education. Nevertheless, the content of this book, it is recognized, remains not completely adequate for these several purposes; therefore considerable use of the carefully chosen readings is urged.

It was necessary to make a definite decision regarding the demands to be placed upon the student in comprehending the book, carrying out each experiment, and reporting the results. Because of the educational level of the student expected to be served, no statistical demands are made beyond what should be possible for a student with the usual high-school courses in mathematics. A course in statistics is not a prerequisite, just as it is not demanded before taking a laboratory course in one of the other sciences. We leave most statistics, as well as tests and measurements, to be handled elsewhere. In these matters, we take a departure from the content and procedure of many beginning experimental courses in psychology. It is granted that more general statistical competency might well be required before further experimental work is attempted. Another bothersome decision had to do with definitions of psychological words, terms, and concepts. Obviously some space must be devoted to giving definitions, so discussion may proceed in a meaningful way. However, the student who elects to take the course in which this book is to be used is assumed to know the meaning of the most common terms in psychology, and he is further assumed to be sufficiently interested in the subject to obtain access to a psychological dictionary, or, at the very least, an unabridged dictionary.

It is thought that the student who seriously considers choosing psychology as a basis for a career could best gain proper perspective by studying early and simultaneously the most essential psychological facts and principles along with the methods and techniques required in laboratory procedures. Perhaps there is little glamour associated with beginning laboratory work in any science, but we can at least hope that fruitful interest may be kindled and that scientific comprehension may be extended.

L. M. B.

Lafayette, Indiana
December 1959

REFERENCES

1. Baker, Lawrence M., and Holmes, William E. *Laboratory Experiments in Psychology*. St. Louis: Educational Publishers, 1949.
2. Baker, Lawrence M.; Weisiger, Carroll; and Taylor, William M. *Laboratory Experiments in General Psychology*. New York: Oxford University Press, 1960.

ACKNOWLEDGMENTS

In a brief acknowledgment it is impossible to express appreciation to all those who have made direct and indirect contributions. First of all, we would mention the hundreds of psychologists whose names do not appear any place in the book but who have, nevertheless, made their work felt. We are grateful to those who remain nameless because of the unintentional but dangerous implication that exclusion means an adverse value judgment. Having lived much with the work of two psychologists over several years, we can only hope that we have not unconsciously and unfairly taken material from their writings without due notation. How can anyone write in the area of experimental psychology without great risk of plagiarizing from the works of Woodworth and Boring? We can hope that unfortunate distortions have been avoided; we feel that each will forgive us if we have transmitted accurately their ideas! We are indebted to Purdue University for making time available for this project, and this included one semester of sabbatical leave given when the book was being planned and gotten under way.

CONTENTS

General Experimental Psychology

1 | GENERAL PROBLEMS, METHODS, AND TECHNIQUES

INTRODUCTION

PSYCHOLOGY AND SCIENCE

Psychology is still in the process of becoming a better defined, a more unified, a mature science. While a given science is set off from another by the content covered, it has been said that science is to be distinguished from other areas of knowledge by methodology rather than content. The methods and techniques described in this book have a great deal in common with those used in science generally; the subject matter is, of course, almost exclusively psychology. It is, therefore, first and primarily, the purpose of this book to acquaint the student with scientific principles and methods; secondarily, to show how these are applied in studying specific problems in psychology. In order that the reader may be sure to orient himself to the intentions of the writer, he is urged to read the preface at this time, if this has not already been done.

The student who is expected to use this book has already become acquainted with some of the general content of psychology. While there will remain the continuing need to increase his knowledge of factual information, it is the intention of the writer that the student now begin to turn more of his attention to a study of the ways in which facts, principles, and concepts are discovered and used. It is hoped that an experimental course will enable the student to begin to evaluate the adequacy of methods and techniques used by a given scientist, and that he will develop in ability to think critically about interpretations and conclusions drawn from scientific data. Thus, he will be preparing himself to scrutinize with skill and intelligence the conclusions set forth by psychologists. The well-trained scientist knows that his methods and techniques are very

3

important determiners of the results he obtains. Without a thorough knowledge of essential controls and acceptable procedures, no person is in a position to evaluate satisfactorily the conclusion drawn in a given science. The scientist must necessarily give close attention to methods and procedures if he is to perform well for society in the field for which he has assumed responsibility. It is largely because he is expected to have knowledge in these matters that his judgment about scientific subjects is accepted more readily than the opinions of the layman.

THE INDIVIDUAL AND THE SELECTION OF A SCIENCE

An individual may become a scientist by studying any one of several subjects that have been organized into formal disciplines. These include physics, chemistry, biology, and, along with other sciences, psychology. Becoming well acquainted with the content in some one of these fields is essential to becoming a scientist; yet, all through the years emphasis has been placed upon the importance of original observation and experimentation in the making of a scientist. It is only through pursuit of these last activities that much progress is made in a given science.

This book is devoted in part to describing how early investigators went about studying psychological problems; then it presents some of their most important findings; and, finally, it tries to indicate how the beginner may master the methods and techniques that have been proved to be fruitful. It is assumed that such study must be accompanied by actual participation in laboratory activities if the learning is to be thorough. Although it is true that learning by doing can be carried to ridiculous extremes, there are many skills that cannot be developed merely by reading about what to do. No amount of reading about the game is likely to prevent the individual from making a poor showing when he tries to perform on the tennis court for the first time. It is assumed that optimum efficiency in learning experimental psychology requires some kind of division of time and effort between reading about the work of others and first-hand experience in performing experiments and reporting the results of those experiments.

There are many excellent sources for obtaining background material for each of the experiments that are to be performed in the first experimental course in psychology. For convenience some of this material has been assembled in this book. More of it can be found by following up the recommended reading and turning to the references that are cited. The energetic student will certainly want to pursue the subject matter of several experiments by reading articles in the numerous psychological journals. It might well be a requirement in the course that each student select one topic for extensive outside reading.

EXPERIMENTING IN PSYCHOLOGY

In the strict sense of the word, few, if any, of the experiments written for the beginning student are genuine experiments. Rather, they tend to be demonstrations based upon experiments that have been performed in the past. The same condition holds to some extent in all of the sciences. The student will not get too bored while collecting his data, even though the experiments may seem rather obvious, if he is continuously thinking of them as models that can be imitated in designing and carrying out more extensive experiments of his own. The author considers it desirable for each student to begin planning an original experiment early in the course. If such an experiment is a course requirement, much of the outside reading might well be related to that experiment. If this procedure is adopted, the student should read Chapter 17 when beginning to think about the project. It is believed that he will find useful suggestions there, although for several reasons the material is placed near the end of the book.

Perhaps there can be no better measure of the success of the course than the originality the student can display in finding a problem; his resourcefulness in selecting a suitable design; and his skill in carrying out his own experiment. While the creative student, if lucky, may think of a good psychological problem and be able to invent an ingenious technique for attacking it, this is not ordinarily to be expected of the beginning student. It is the usual order of events, even for brilliant students, that laboratory techniques first be reduced to routines; that experimental designs tend to become familiar patterns before creative imagination can be freed to operate effectively with problems of science.

It is not an unreasonable expectation that by the end of the course the student will have a knowledge and understanding of what constitutes an experiment and how to design and then perform one. Furthermore, he should become well acquainted with the basic problems that are a preoccupation of professional psychologists, and he should know something of how they go about solving these problems. This should not be taken to mean that only those expecting to be professional psychologists can find anything of interest or use in the course. It is true that not many psychologists will be dealing directly, and only, with the type of problems presented in this book. Few, however, will fail to work with very similar problems and to make almost constant use of the methods introduced.

SCIENTIFIC VIEWPOINT AND ATTITUDE

While the mastery of methods and techniques is important in the development of a scientist, one is unlikely to become a first-rate scientist without what is called scientific curiosity, and, along with that, a well-alerted scientific attitude. For these reasons, we have tried to combine and integrate information about scientists, and the way they work, with the discussion of scientific problems and their solutions. Hence, there has been some attention given to the presentation of historically important discoveries, plus comments about the individuals, along with discussion of problems, apparatus used, controls, and procedures. Familiarity in all of these things is thought to be essential in the making of a careful scientist.

It is interesting to see how the solution of one problem in science has so often enabled the investigator to state several other problems. At the same time, other investigators may be stimulated to carry the work forward into ever-expanding areas. The scientist does not work himself out of a job. The more developed a science, the more mature a science, the more endless the possibilities for new experimentation appear.

In science there is no authority generally accepted save that of repeated observation and verification. For example, every time a microscope is developed that enables the observer to see smaller particles, every time a telescope is improved to enable him to see farther, the question must be asked again, "What can be seen now?" There is no longer an obligation to adhere to what some recognized expert may have reported when he was using an inferior or more limited instrument. The right and privilege of the scientist to question, and to observe again, is an essential condition for his best work.

DESCRIPTION IN SCIENCE

In science, there are two main approaches to the description of a phenomenon—qualitative and quantitative. The first is concerned with a difference in kind; the latter a difference in amount. In chemistry, a study of qualitative differences led investigators to name a large number of elements. Whether further study and measurement will eventually prove that there are more elements, or, on the other hand, only different aspects of fewer elements, remains to be seen. There are qualitative differences in psychology, such as those obtained from use of different sense modalities, for example. There is great difficulty in comparing what can be seen with what can be heard, what can be smelled with what can be tasted; for these are differences in sensory quality. In general, where it has been possible to measure, with the result that more or less of a given characteristic or trait was found, investigators seem to make faster progress. When using this approach it becomes possible to speak of quantitative differences. Studies of intelligence enabled psychologists to determine that one individual has more ability than another and, hence, a comparison could be made between people. There are many other areas in psychology where people can be rated, or some performance quantified, so that comparisons can be made between individuals. Quantitative measurement becomes basic to personnel selection and has many other uses where it becomes necessary to differentiate between people.

It will be seen that language tends to become more precise, usually mathematical, when measurements are made that can be stated in exact amounts. Measurement makes possible better understanding, and comparisons can then be extended to include more universal principles. Thorndike has said that whatever exists must necessarily exist in some amount and that the scientist should be able to take a measurement. Finding a way to measure human characteristics and behavior has not always seemed possible. Difficulties are apparent when attempting to measure some abstract quality, such as the influence of a symbol or the strength of an attitude. It is not easy to measure the intensity of a person's feeling toward a given religious doctrine or the emotion experienced upon hearing the name of an enemy. Means have yet to be developed for taking exact measurements in dealing with many of the most vital problems in psychology. It is due to these limitations that psychology may seem to lag behind the other sciences.

If attempts at quantification in psychology have but a short and somewhat discouraging history, it should be kept in mind how relatively inaccurate the attempts to quantify in some other areas of science were at one time. Babylon and Egypt had the beginning of science at the dawn of history. They had rough means of quantifying. On the other hand, they were deficient in the use of hypotheses, except in the realms of religion and mythology, and in these the nature of their hypotheses is not readily distinguished from mere superstition. Psychology seems to have made relatively good progress in generating many hypotheses for scientific exploration. If there is a tendency to become discouraged about difficulties in quantifying data so that hypotheses can be adequately tested, encouragement may be taken from the unreliability of measuring procedures practiced by ancient people, who, nevertheless, found their efforts beneficial. Freedman (2), in discussing this situation, has the following to say: "In Babylon, about 2500 B.C., there were already standard units of length, volume, and weight. These units, while arbitrary,

were based on what appeared to be the most reliable and readily repeatable observations. Thus the unit of length was the finger, equal to
about ⅔ inch (breadth)—twenty fingers to one foot and 30 fingers to a
cubit." The variations in the units of measurement in psychology today
are certainly not always greater than the variations in the thickness of
fingers!

One of the first applications of measurement in psychology has to do
with time—the time between the reception of a stimulus at one of the
sense organs and the response of a given muscle. This kind of measurement becomes the subject matter of the next chapter in this book. In
psychology, even after having described something well and having
taken a precise measure, one may still find it difficult to furnish an explanation of the phenomenon described. Then, with or without completely satisfactory explanations, the psychologist or other scientist may
seek to predict and to control. It is because the experiment meets so well
the demands for description, explanation, prediction, and control that
this method is held in such high esteem by scientists. In the laboratory,
events can be made to happen over and over while the experimenter
makes careful observations, systematically turning from one aspect of his
problem to another, until he comes to what he thinks is adequate comprehension.

The experiment, or, more often, a group of experiments, dealing with a
given problem around which each chapter in this book has been organized, is believed to be of basic importance. Extension of these experiments directly, or by combining old methods and techniques with new
ones, will continue to be the primary business of a psychologist whether
he is to label himself an academic psychologist or an applied psychologist.
In short, the task in this book has been to outline problems and subject
matter; indicate methods and procedures; touch upon the most important
results and conclusions; and, when possible, to suggest the implications
for future study and research.

BECOMING AN EXPERIMENTAL SCIENTIST

It has been implied that the basic purpose of this book is to enable
the student to take a first, or additional, step toward becoming a scientist.
Pavlov (3), the world renowned Russian scientist, shortly before his
death and after a long and fruitful life of scientific endeavor, had the
following advice to offer:

What can I wish to the youth of my country who devote themselves to
science? Firstly, gradualness; about this most important condition of fruit-

ful scientific work I can never speak without emotion. Gradualness, gradualness, gradualness . . . Never begin the subsequent without mastering the preceding . . . But do not become the archivist of facts. Try to penetrate the secret of their occurrence, persistently searching for the laws which govern them. Secondly, modesty . . . Do not allow haughtiness to take you into possession. Due to that . . . you will refuse useful and friendly help, you will lose your objectiveness. Thirdly, passion. Remember that science demands from a man all his life. If you had two lives, that would not be enough for you. Be passionate in your work and your searchings.

There are many useful books and articles that may help the student to orient to what can reasonably be expected of him before he can lay claim to being a scientist. Perhaps never before has there been need to sound a note of caution. Scientists have always been in short supply, although they may have remained poorly rewarded in money and prestige. There is no early prospect of too many competent scientists now, but there might be individuals drawn into the field who are not particularly well-suited to the work of a scientist by either ability or temperament. In periods of the past there may have been ten times as many adolescent boys hoping to become physicians as training facilities or the need for physicians could justify. More important still, many of these hopeful candidates did not have the necessary ability and, worse than that, many of them lacked knowledge about the work and responsibility that burden the conscientious physician. Rather, they were impressed by the prestige and income that was often bestowed upon the famous surgeon. They were, no doubt, interested in the position of the great physician, but were they aware of the work necessary to arrive at and to retain that position? These things are said because the present great stress upon the need for scientists could lead some to assume that the path to fame and fortune as a scientist is to be traveled without much effort. Certainly, those who are both capable and properly motivated are to be encouraged to become scientists. However, now that becoming a scientist promises to be, as never before in history, "the thing to do," there is an obligation to present a clear picture of what is entailed in becoming and remaining a contributing scientist.

More is said about the requirements for becoming a scientist in a later chapter, but it is necessary that the student keep constantly in mind the basic goals of the course. The particular task of the student, if he is to be a scientist who works in the field of psychology, is to master the fundamental methodologies and to extend his knowledge of the scientific information now available in his chosen field. The writer tends to agree with Bancroft (1) that "In physical science the discovery of new facts is open to any blockhead with patience and manual dexterity and acute senses." Or again, we may accept as basically true his further statement: "Accurate and minute measurement seems to the nonscientific imagination a less lofty and dignified work than looking for something new; yet nearly all the grandest discoveries are made this way." Thus it is seen that Bancroft and Pavlov make similar statements about what is involved in becoming a scientist and then in living a life dedicated to scientific work. Certainly there is no lack of very dramatic discoveries that have been made by a few fortunate scientists. Enough of these incidents have occurred for scientists to appreciate the fascination that seems to grip the incurable gambler. There is inspirational reading to be found among the biographies and autobiographies of famous scientists (some of them psychologists) and such material should be part of the reading of the student who is ambitious to become a scientist.

While it is important to become informed about past experiments and the people who performed them, it is even more important to help the individual to become an experimentalist himself. The success or failure of a course in laboratory psychology is to be judged mainly in terms of this objective. Not only in the realm of science, but in everyday living there are ample opportunities for improving the solutions to numerous problems by using the experimental method. Experimenting should not be limited to the laboratory. Every person will have many occasions to use this method with profit to himself and to others. It has been a major characteristic of the people living in all important cultures of the world that many individuals showed a great willingness to bring the experimental approach to bear upon the problems of living. Questioning and reëvaluating the old, plus creating and testing the new, have seemed to be necessary to usher in all the great achievements—social, religious, artistic, or scientific in cultural development.

BASIC METHODS

This section is intended to set forth the general methods, procedures, and techniques that have the greatest historical interest and current usefulness for experimenting in psychology. These will be elaborated upon in later chapters, along with the presentation of additional information having to do with the more specific topics and experiments in the various areas of psychology.

Even though the student may be familiar with most of the terms and concepts to be mentioned, it is felt that some time can be used profitably to review those most pertinent to our purposes. At the same time, content, methods, and techniques thought to be most essential for working and thinking in the general area of experimental psychology will be discussed. The student need not be alarmed if he reaches the end of the chapter with a lingering feeling that not everything has been thoroughly understood. While materials that are *not* to be learned at this time are not deliberately set forth, the writer does realize that complete comprehension of all that is mentioned or implied in this chapter might well justify a question as to whether the student still needs to study the rest of the book, or if there would be good reason to do the experiments that might go along with the study of this book.

DEVELOPMENT OF PSYCHOPHYSICAL METHODS

While modern psychology is usually said to date from the establishment of the laboratory at Leipzig in 1879 by Wundt—and the writer has no inclination to challenge the importance to general psychology of that event, because present-day experimental psychology descends directly from the tradition started then—at the same time it is important to trace two other developments that are now recognized as also having great importance in furthering the work of the experimental psychologists. First, the reader is referred to the development of *psychophysical methods,* which in the early years was mainly due to the work of Weber and Fechner. The purpose that these men had in mind was to discover a means by which they could study the relationship or interaction between the psychical and physical worlds. They were trying to discover scientific laws that governed the relationship between mind and body and to express that relationship mathematically. They were undoubtedly influenced by Descartes' dualistic philosophical system. This system is often referred to as one in which psychical events and physical events are supposed to move along separate but parallel lines. It has been said that Descartes succeeded in separating mind and body in his speculations and that investigators have been busy ever since trying to get them back together. Many have assumed that there must be a continuous interaction between the two, while others have postulated a variety of possibilities, including the assumption that only one is a reality, the other fantasy.

While it is true that early interest was focused primarily upon the philosophical and metaphysical problems that seemed vital to scholars of the period, it was not long before more concrete and specific problems came under investigation. The practical approach to the more abstract problems appeared to be possible by systematic study of how changes in stimuli resulted in changes in sensations. Eventually, investigators became concerned more with variations in responses. That is, they observed the subsequent overt behavior rather than attempting to analyze sensation alone. It was soon learned that predictable changes could be brought about in the response if the amount of energy (stimulus intensity) applied to the sense organ was systematically varied. While problems of sensation are, no doubt, of lasting interest and importance in psychology, eventually many workers despaired of investigating the problems involved in sensation by use of desirable objective methods. It will be seen that an increasing number of investigators turned to a study of overt behavior because they considered this line of research more fruitful. Nevertheless, subjective measurement and the rendering of judgment based upon sensation continue to have great usefulness in research.

It is probably safe to say that, to this day, the original philosophical problem has not been resolved to the complete satisfaction of any investigator. Psychologists have not only tended to shift their interest to observable behavior, but they have become more concerned with everyday problems of living. For example, they may try to find out why it is that hundreds of thousands of the citizens of the nation must be confined in mental hospitals because of disorganized and confused behavior, or placed in prisons because of socially unacceptable behavior. This state of affairs seems to them a fantastic waste of human and economic resources. They would like to bring science to bear upon such problems and to make these unfortunate personal and social consequences unnecessary. Many of these investigators do not assume that they must first answer all the abstract and philosophical questions before they move on to the solutions of numerous practical problems. It is readily seen that a shift in the problems that were raised for study influenced the methodology to be used. Even so, some of the most pressing social problems are attacked at present by psychophysical methods that have much in common with those first put into use.

Psychologists, as well as other scientists, must necessarily continue to be interested in theoretical concepts if their science is to advance systematically. Broadly speaking, psychologists now hope to comprehend how stimuli that arise in environmental conditions operate to produce various behavior patterns and personality characteristics. An understanding of what is implied by this statement should enable them to make predictions about behavior, and ultimately to set up situations to produce the desired behavior. Laboratory techniques are used in the hope of reaching a better understanding of the whole process and to improve success in making predictions and, hence, in determining what factors must be manipulated, and how, in order to produce a given type of behavior. Thus, instead of persisting with the broad abstraction of the mind-body relationship—and this is surely one of the general concepts in psychology that cannot be totally ignored—experimenters today usually strive to state their problems in terms that are more specific and detailed; fraction them into answerable questions; and hopefully try to resolve the problems by scientific procedures reproduceable by succeeding generations of investigators. Because of the assumptions that psychology should help people to live more effective and pleasant lives, there is great eagerness shown by people in a multitude of professional positions to grasp hastily the various principles of behavior advanced by psychologists.

Historically, there are many examples of the enthusiastic application of well-publicized psychological principles far in advance of adequate scientific validation. While popularly advocated principles of behavior that were eventually found to be unsound were not usually the product of trained psychologists, it is nevertheless true that a great deal of research time and effort has gone into obtaining evidence to counteract false claims. Psychology is not a science unique with regard to this situation. Sound theory is of great help in evaluating new claims as well as in serving in its primary function of facilitating new hypotheses.

THE EXPERIMENT AND PSYCHOPHYSICAL METHODS

It might be said that the traditional psychological experiment is primarily a procedure whereby the investigator sets out to manipulate the stimulus (here the independent variable) systematically and then to observe how behavioral changes (dependent variable or variables) are brought about. The concept of the whole stimulus-response situation is, of course, extended to include internal bodily conditions as well as the surrounding environment and impinging stimuli. Consequently, biological and physical factors involving the organism, such as sense organs, neural tissue, and muscles, necessarily come under examination by the psychologist, for he needs to understand all the mechanisms that are involved in behavior. These structures, and their functioning, are judged to be of importance, for they constitute the connecting links and modifying agents that stand between stimulus and response. In the aggregate these structures are usually referred to as *the organism.*

In some manner, not yet well understood, the organism is capable of modification in structure or function as a result of experience, so that previously learned information and established habit systems are always to be taken into account if the immediate and complex behavior of man is to be understood. How experience is stored by the organism and then brought into appropriate use when the individual is responding to stimuli, or, especially, when dealing with new problems, continues to be a basic concern among psychologists. It will be necessary to return to this topic when discussing learning, a topic that was of relatively little interest to those who initiated psychophysical investigations, and yet these scientists were clearly initiating experimental procedures that would ultimately have relevance here.

All of Weber's work and most of Fechner's preceded that of Wundt. While these investigators may have lacked equipment, apparatus, and space in a building that could be dignified by the word "laboratory," they still performed experiments. Neither of these men considered himself to be primarily a psychologist, but others who *were* experimental psychologists soon followed their leadership. Psychophysical methods were developed further and used extensively by Titchener, an Englishman who studied under Wundt, and who later came to America and worked at Cornell University. More recently, these useful techniques have served many investigators in working with a great variety of psychological problems.

BEGINNING OF STATISTICAL PROCEDURES

The other important development in psychology was the use of *statistical procedures,* or the mathematical treatment of the data collected, so that the investigator could first analyze his findings and then present them in an effective and meaningful way. The objective of this book with regard to statistics is to present no more than a minimum of procedural and technical information, and to encourage a maximum of statistical thinking. Nearly all scientific thinking in psychology seems to demand the use of some of the more general statistical concepts, but it is believed that we can dispense with all but the simplest techniques in beginning experimental work.

Galton, a general scientist, appreciated the usefulness of statistics as a means of studying individual differences among people. Karl Pearson was also an early contributor who showed how statistics could be a useful tool in the hands of the psychologist. Although Pearson was primarily a mathematician, he was greatly interested in the way mathematical principles might be applied in order to gain a better understanding of biological and social phenomena. He is perhaps best known in psychological circles for the development of a mathematical formula for determining the degree of relationship between two sets of data. What is known as the Pearson r is used in an equation for expressing the correlation coefficient between variables. More will be said about the meaning of correlation later in this chapter.

A statement in his book, *The Grammar of Science* (4), further endeared Pearson to psychologists, who were having great difficulty in defending psychology as a science at that time. He said that any field of knowledge is a science if it consistently employs scientific methods. Others have emphasized that a science must include an organized and well-established body of knowledge, but presumably Pearson was assuming that such knowledge could come into existence only as a result of systematic investigation, and hence he emphasized the methodology as primary. In Pearson's way of thinking, the free use of mathematical concepts and techniques was essential for a sound methodology in most sciences. It is certain that in present-day psychology, mathematical procedures are used extensively. Probably research workers in psychology use statistics as persistently as workers in any area of science. Consequently, in this and in other ways, it no longer seems debatable that psychologists use an acceptable methodology and thus qualify their field as a science.

Perhaps Spearman deserves credit for being the first man fully identified with psychology who made regular use of statistics. His work and publications date back to around the turn of the present century, but much of his contribution was summarized in *The Abilities of Man, Their Nature and Measurement,* published in 1927 (5). Other names that have become familiar because of their work in measurement and statistical techniques are Fisher in England and Thurstone in America. The latter is particularly noteworthy for our purpose, since he and his students engaged in many studies which gained them the reputation for employing careful experimental procedures, precise measuring devices, and refined statistical techniques.

Psychophysical methods and statistical procedures have had a great influence upon the way psychological data are collected. The requirements demanded by each have helped to determine the controls considered to be essential when performing most experiments in psychology. When writers speak of "experimental design," they usually refer to the way observations are made and data are collected, as well as to the statistical treatment that is involved in analyzing the data.

PSYCHOPHYSICAL METHODS

"Psychophysics is that branch of psychology which is concerned with subjective measurement. Obviously a unit of measurement is required. Psychophysical theory is concerned with the logic of subjective measurement, and psychophysical methods are concerned with experimental procedure." In this way, Thurstone (6) once started a discussion of what was meant by psychophysical methods and how these techniques were used by psychologists. He indicated how application is made of these methods in dealing with a great variety of problems of a psychological nature. In order to make use of each method, a subjective unit is required, and the one that has perhaps served most widely has been the *just notice-able difference* (j.n.d.). This is the way we indicate the smallest amount of difference that the subject can detect between stimuli with a con-sistency greater than one produced by chance. The usual criterion in psychophysical procedure is set at the 50 percent level. There are situa-tions in which another criterion may be used, such as the 75 percent level, or midway between what guessing would give and 100 percent accuracy. The limen is that stimulus magnitude that can be distinguished by the subject in half of the trials.

THRESHOLD

Then in establishing *absolute threshold,* the stimulus is sensed by the subject in half of the trials attempted; stimuli of greater strength are recog-nized more than half of the time; those that are weaker less than half of the time. It is obvious that a unit of measure must also be used if accurate description is to be used to indicate quantity changes in the stimulus value. These units are well known, for the most part, since they may in-volve inches, millimeters, grams, decibels, and so forth.

Because of the fact that there is some overlapping in the different methods used in psychophysical procedure, and especially because there is a lack of consistency among writers as to what is covered under the name of a particular method, it is not easy to make a satisfactory list of psychophysical methods. The following list is not intended to be a com-plete one, but it should be recognized that some of these methods are modified in application so that several procedures that are slightly dif-ferent may still be appropriately grouped under one of the special meth-ods.

SPECIAL METHODS

Rank Order

Here the words used are descriptive of the process. However, this is a method that can be used with varying degrees of sophistication. The general principle is easily understood, and almost everyone makes some use of the procedure in everyday life. The farmer may *rank order* his melons so that a higher price is scratched on the more choice ones and descending prices indicated down to the lowest price for the poorest one in the lot. The teacher may *rank order* her pupils with regard to what she believes to be their fund of knowledge before she begins to dispense final grades; the employer *rank orders* applicants for a job before he fills the position. Use may be made of other psychophysical methods to refine and improve the ordering process.

Paired Comparison

It is the usual procedure in *paired comparison* that every item is compared with every other item. The procedure becomes long and cumbersome if the number of items is great, and rarely is this method carried

Fig. 1.1. This apparatus enables either the subject or the experimenter to set it for light equality or difference. A dial on the back of the apparatus allows the experimenter to read the settings for light intensity on the window. This is a simple but convenient apparatus useful for certain studies in which psychophysical comparisons are made. (Courtesy Lafayette Instrument Co.)

out to the bitter end if more than fifteen or twenty items must be dealt with. It is not unusual for judges to make use of paired comparison procedures in preparation to making a rank order of objects with regard to some quality, or as a beginning step if research data are to be put into rank order. If a full record is made of each comparison rendered, the total choices for each judge can be summed and the results from the different judges can be combined for final ranking. Such a procedure is believed to improve accuracy in reaching conclusions about the presence, absence, or amount of a given quality.

Method of Limits

The method of limits is a relatively simple procedure that is often used for establishing the absolute threshold, as well as for determining the difference limen. This method is frequently spoken of as the *method of minimal change*. There is an appropriateness in the use of this name, for the essential problem is that of detecting the smallest change in the stimulus that can be detected with a stated degree of confidence.

First, consider the way this method may be used in determining the *absolute threshold*. Suppose that the experimenter wants to determine at what distance his subject can hear the ticking of a watch. The physician may use this as a rough test of the hearing acuity of his patient, but he does not pursue the process to the extent necessary in most experimental work. The experimenter first places the watch at a distance too great to be heard at all, then moves it slowly toward the subject. At designated intervals of distance (and these can be made appropriate to the refinement sought in the experiment) the subject is asked to report if he hears the ticking. Eventually the subject reports "yes," and this indicates that the threshold has been crossed. It is known that a single observation of this sort is not highly reliable, so the process is typically repeated several times before the average distance for all observations is calculated. However, an unexpected factor is also to be taken into account. The subject will be found to have a higher threshold if the observations are always taken by approaching the threshold from below. The usual procedure is to take an equal number of observations approaching from above the threshold. Thus, the watch would be brought within easy hearing distance and gradually moved farther away from the subject. It is better to alternate trials from each direction. Finally, the threshold is considered to be the average that is determined by combining all observations.

The procedure for determining the *difference limen* is essentially the same, except that there is an upper and a lower limit to be established, which means that two or three readings will be taken in both ascending and descending order as applied to a given type of stimulus. Suppose the subject is given the task of comparing a variable tone as to intensity with a tone of constant or standard intensity. Then the standard is sounded as one of the pair along with the variable. The latter, so to speak, is at first clearly lower in intensity. The intensity of the variable tone is gradually increased until it approaches the standard, and finally the subject no longer says "lower" but answers with "same" or "higher." In order to eliminate the probable constant error, both ascending and descending presentations are used as previously explained, and the midpoint between the results from the two approaches is used as the difference limen.

The Constant Method

Somewhat better results are obtained in working with some types of problems if the subject does not know which stimulus is the standard and which is the variable one. The experimenter keeps a record of the results of the judgments that are made as stimuli are presented at random but in pairs, without the subject knowing which is the standard. During each trial he must render his decision as to which stimulus has more of a particular quality. In the case of tone, he might be required to decide which has the higher intensity or the higher pitch. In weight discrimination he would not know which was the standard, but he would render a judgment as to which of the pairs of weights was heavier for each of a large number of trials. In the procedure used here, elements of both the paired comparison and the method of limits are seen.

Method of Equal-Appearing Intervals

The purpose in this method is to assign stimuli along a psychological continuum so that the intervals between them are subjectively equal. One is reminded of what the waitress is trying to do when she attempts to divide a pie into five equal wedges, or of the task before the mother who tries to break a large stick of candy into equal parts so that each of her four children will be satisfied that he is getting his fair share. Should the teacher decide that she would give an equal number of her pupils grades of A, B, C, D, and F, she might try to sort essay papers into piles of equal quality, although it could scarcely be hoped that the quality intervals would be exactly an equal distance apart. Considerable use is made of this method when setting up specimen scales, such as in handwriting, drawing proficiency, or levels of skill as revealed in handicrafts. Subjectively, equal-appearing intervals may not coincide perfectly with physical units having equal magnitude difference. That is, a sound of ten decibels may not seem to be twice as loud as one of five decibels. Again, the relationship of changes in the sensory experience to changes in stimulus magnitude that holds in the middle range of sensory reception may not hold at the extreme ends of the continuum.

What has just been said about the relationship between changes in the stimulus and changes in the sensation has been carefully studied since the time of Weber. Fechner's famous formula, $S = K \log R$, covers the basic relationship, but this formula does not stand up very well when applied to data obtained from the extreme ranges of sensory experience. Thus, pitch discriminations may follow rather closely with frequency changes in the tone of the middle range of hearing, but the curves do not fit closely when pitch approaches the upper capacity of human hearing. It should be noted that the letters used by Fechner in his formula can be misleading. The S stands for subjective continuum or *sensation* and *not* stimulus. The R denotes the physical continuum or *stimulus* and comes from the German word *Reiz*, which is translated *stimulus*. It is probably less confusing if the formula is stated as Sensation = Constant Log Stimulus. The sensation is roughly proportional to the logarithm of the stimulus. Sensation refers to the number of "sensation units," or, perhaps more accurately, the "perception units" that are equally well perceived.

PSYCHOPHYSICS IN DAILY LIVING

It is certainly true that psychophysical methods can involve much tedious work and that such work may be directed toward solving problems that are abstract and seemingly far removed from daily living. The writer believes the use of space to illustrate how the process itself is used in common situations is justified. Let the reader follow a woman as she goes shopping at the grocery store and see what she does as she surveys shelf after shelf and chooses items.

Suppose the shopper decides to buy potatoes instead of one of the other vegetables because these, for the moment at least, give promise of making the most pleasant appeal to the members of her family. She has already at this time made a choice upon the basis of imagined goodness, or of the assumed *subjective judgments*, of the members of her family. Now review what she does at the potato bin: one by one, the potatoes are selected upon the basis of some *criteria* she uses. Perhaps she wants large potatoes so that each will make a generous helping after it is baked. Those below a certain judged size must be rejected. She has set a lower limit of acceptability with regard to size and her task should be a relatively simple one. However, this may not be quite the case, for she at once becomes aware that some of the potatoes are large enough but she does not like them for other reasons. This one may be knotty, another was cut when being dug, the next one appears to have been exposed to the sun too long and is discolored. She begins to be concerned that one of her children will get to the table late, already cross, and his bad humor will be aggravated by the fact that only a poor potato is left for him. In the end, she decides to abandon her earlier objective of choosing potatoes with primary consideration given to size and thinks that she had better take into account several desirable qualities of the potatoes so that she will have a happy family at the dinner table.

It will be seen that our shopper could take several different approaches in selecting the potatoes and each might involve some kind of a procedure that fits within the framework of psychophysical methodology. Suppose she makes a new start and reaches the conclusion that she will first select a relatively ideal or standard potato—one that has such a combination of qualities that she can find others that do not deviate too far from it in any one particular quality. Obviously, she will have to compromise with regard to size. She takes one of medium size, smooth, not cut or bruised, of good coloration and firmness. Now she begins the task of picking the rest of the potatoes, and at once she makes use of one of the most familiar variations of psychophysical methods—*paired comparison*. Each potato is compared with the standard and those that deviate too much from it are rejected, while those that are similar are kept.

If the shopper is a relaxed and conventional one, she is likely to put the potatoes in a bag, have them weighed, pay for them, and go on her way. However, for the purpose of a further elaboration upon what she might do to illustrate the use of psychophysical methods, suppose that she is endowed with an unlikely combination of personality traits. Perhaps she is very compulsive and is so concerned with doing a good job of selecting the potatoes in order to avoid conflict at home that for the moment she becomes indifferent to custom and convention in her shopping. Never mind that she is about to indulge in peculiar behavior that will attract the attention of other shoppers. She finds space on a nearby shelf and places the potatoes out in a neat row. She has already noticed blemishes upon one or two and closer inspection is required. She decides to place the potatoes in *rank order* for she thinks she must reject some of the poor ones and find better substitutes. She quickly makes a mental comparison between all of them and arranges the best potato to the left and the poorest one to the right. Before returning the two least desirable ones to the bin she is intrigued by the fact that her original choice, or the standard by which all the others were judged, ended up in second position rather than first. Another potato turned out to be more nearly perfect for her purposes. She carries the newly selected standard with her to the bin and repeats the paired comparison procedure until two acceptable potatoes are found. They turn out to be better than one that was left on the shelf but she decides that she is well enough satisfied, so she does not again shift the potatoes into a new rank order.

Since some assumptions about the woman's personality have already been made, it might be interesting to further assume that she has a tendency to vacillate and to perseverate. On her way home she begins to wonder about all the factors that entered into her choices. Should she arrive at home with time on her hands, she might make a further check upon her skill and again arrange the potatoes in *order of merit*. If so, perhaps she now finds that the two potatoes that had originally been used as standards are shifted further toward the less desirable side and thus she sees that her procedure has not been very consistent from trial to trial. By making a careful record of all comparisons and repeating the process, it becomes possible to determine how reliable her technique has been. But that would lead into the use of statistics before it is time to discuss that aspect of experimental work.

It could be that the intellectually curious woman notices that there is a closer resemblance between some of the potatoes than others and, hence, she wonders whether some other potato might not have been found that would have meant a smaller gap between two or three of the potatoes. The specialist in the use of psychophysical methods would say that the choices had not been made to fit *equal-appearing intervals*. The shopper might be persistent enough in her deliberations to become conscious of the fact that a narrower range of differences might have resulted. In other words, the *differential threshold*, or her ability to make finer discriminations, has not been fully tested. It is clear to her that, with greater effort and more time, she could have chosen potatoes of greater uniformity without use of any other measuring device than subjective judgment. The *just noticeable difference* is less in amount than is reflected by the differences between the several potatoes. While in this illustration several qualities might have been involved and none of them was systematically controlled, nevertheless a close parallel between the shopper's discrimination and experimental studies set up to determine the ability of subjects to observe a difference between stimuli upon the basis of any quality or quantity can be seen.

PSYCHOPHYSICS AND SOCIAL PROBLEMS

Self-examination might lead the shopper to see that she was influenced to buy at a particular store because she was a friend of the owner, rather than because she had a chance of getting better groceries there. In this case, she might conclude that she allowed personal factors to enter her choices. These factors, too, might be studied and evaluated by psychophysical procedure. Some of the most intriguing studies in which psychophysical methodology has been used have had to do with attitudes regarding political, economic, and social problems. Thurstone (6) undertook to measure the attitudes of individuals regarding a variety of socially undesirable activities, ranging from bank-robbing to begging. Then, after scaling the attitudes as to how objectionable each was for his particular subjects, the group was exposed to a movie in which the unfortunate consequences of gambling were dramatized. A repeat of the same measuring procedure then revealed that the attitude toward gambling had shifted. The first measurement indicated that gambling stood in the middle range among several undesirable types of behavior; now it had shifted a considerable distance toward the more objectionable end of the continuum. The difference in attitude at the two testings was readily measurable and the difference was statistically reliable.

Many illustrations of how choice is made by people following use of a rough psychophysical procedures might be given. Politicians can be rank-ordered for their vote-getting ability; the house-painter mixes paint by adding different colors in order to reproduce the subjective color value of previously used paint; the professional food or drink-taster tries to see that standards are maintained. Interestingly enough, the taster is said to be able to detect differences that remain well beyond distinctions that are possible by present methods of chemical analysis.

It is beyond the purpose of this book to give detailed direction that can be depended upon to enable the individual to use the many different variations of psychophysical methods. In later chapters further explanation will be found as to how these methods are used in the study of sensory processes. Fuller description of each method and essential information for their use can be found in the suggested readings. Some of the methods call for fairly elaborate statistical treatment of the data if refined analysis of results are to be obtained. Not much space can be devoted in this book to showing how psychophysical methods may be used in the study of attitudes, esthetics, and social phenomenon, but it is probable that the most energetic use of psychophysical methods in research work during recent years has been made by those working in industrial and social psychology. It seems safe to say that the basic concept of measuring subjective phenomena, which grew directly out of classical psychophysics, is of fundamental importance in dealing with many current problems in social psychology.

SIMPLE STATISTICAL PROCEDURES

As has been stated, this book will dispense with as much technical and specialized information about statistical procedures as seems expedient. Statistics are used to serve several important purposes in experimental psychology, and it becomes essential to convey some information about the process. If data are to be effectively presented to others or thoroughly understood by the investigator himself, statistical analysis is frequently necessary. Statistics, in this case, means the collection and classification of facts on the basis of relative frequency, or occurrence, primarily for the purpose of making inductions and deductions. Thus, the statistical worker devotes his time to making systematic compilations and calculations so that inferences may be drawn concerning facts and their relationship to general or scientific truths.

It will be assumed that a number of relevant mathematical and statistical concepts are already familiar to the reader, but it is recognized that skill in the use of all of these may not extend to every unique situation. Reference is now made to the meaning of such terms as average (or mean), median, range, mode, and the distribution of scores. An understanding of these is essential to a meaningful discussion of other statistical concepts and the writer makes use of them on several occasions.

In order to communicate to others about his results, the experimental psychologist has almost constant need to make use of at least two additional statistical functions. The first of these has to do with how sets of data may be described with regard to similarity or difference. The question might be asked: How can one know if sets of data are alike? Or if the data are different one may want to know how much difference exists between them and whether the difference can be accounted for by chance, that is, whether a "true" difference is to be postulated.

Suppose the psychologist has the idea that he can introduce a new method of learning that will enable the student to learn more in a given time than by the old method that has been used. Then he is confronted with the problem of setting up systematic controls so that irrelevant factors may not operate to the advantage of one method. He must collect, classify, and analyze data before he is in position to make a meaningful comparison between the two methods. It is not enough to determine that the average amount learned by the subjects using the new or "experimental" method is greater or less, for this could readily occur in the first experiment, only to be reversed in the next experiment. To be sure, one way is to replicate the experiment over and over. This is laborious and is no longer necessary, as dependable statistical procedures have been invented that enable the investigator to predict in advance and with great accuracy about the outcome of such a procedure. Information of this kind is discussed under the topic dealing with the *reliability of differences.*

The other statistical function that seems to be indispensable to experimentalists, even in beginning work, has to do with the relationship between data. Without an analysis of how data are related, or, as the statistician says, "correlated," we are not in a position to understand and to describe how events are associated. In the case of the experimentalist, his usual problem is to predict about how much change can be expected in the dependent variable if the independent variable is manipulated in a given way.

The psychologist is all but helpless, his science largely futile if he is not in position to predict with some degree of accuracy what conditions will lead to what outcome. Always, but possibly in the background at times, is the basic problem of controlling behavior. The main research obligation, implied but not always explicitly stated by psychologists, with regard to their work is the discovery and explanation of how conditions may be manipulated to bring about behavior that is considered to be constructive in the culture. *Correlation techniques* are among the most important tools that are used to serve these purposes. In the following pages a brief introduction is given to some ways that the experimentalist might want to treat his data.

THE MEAN

In a normal probability curve, the bell-shaped curve familiar to almost everyone, the mean, median, and the mode are all found to stand at the same point on the base line. Great use is made of the mean in statistical analysis and we shall proceed with a discussion of how this fulcrum or balance point is of use in describing data. The symbol used in discussing the mean, as well as certain concepts about the mean, are carried on to consideration of other and more complicated statistical concepts and functions. These less familiar, and harder to understand, procedures are less baffling if a gradual approach is used in leading up to them.

Statisticians often use the capital letter X to stand for any score or measurement, and the mean may be identified by the symbol $\overline{X}$ (read "X bar"). The formula for finding the mean then becomes:

$$\overline{X} = \frac{\Sigma X}{N}$$

While this formula may look strange to some, it simply indicates what is well known. The mean is found by taking all scores, adding them together, and dividing the sum by the number of scores involved.

In the interest of logic and consistency, perhaps, the deviation from a mean is frequently referred to by statisticians as a small x. Its value is

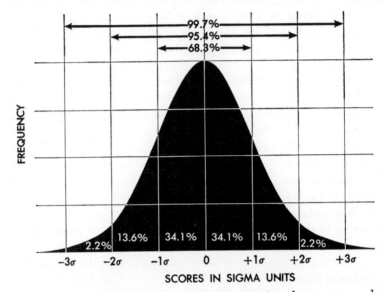

Fig. 1.2. The normal probability curve. By counting the squares under the curve, a close estimate can be made of what percent of scores will fall within a given distance from the mean.

found by subtracting the mean from any given X score. When negative and positive deviations are added, the sum is zero. If the distribution is a "normal" one, the mean is the point about which scores deviate the same distance in either direction.

Most of the time, statisticians deal with data in which scores have been grouped into intervals. By taking the midpoint of each interval and ignoring the actual spread within the interval, a very close approximation of the true mean is found. In this case the formula for the mean of grouped scores is as follows:

$$\overline{X} = \frac{\Sigma f X'}{N}$$

It is common practice to let X' constitute the midpoint of each interval; this is multiplied by f (the frequency at each respective interval) and then the products are added to obtain a grand total before dividing by N.

VARIABILITY

One of the primary uses of the mean is to furnish a stable point so that data may be described with regard to how they deviate from it. The way scores are distributed about a mean is important. The statistician usually makes use of the mean if he wishes to describe his data completely, or if he hopes to make predictions about similar data. *Average deviation* or *standard deviation* are among the most widely used terms to indicate how data are distributed. It seems that average deviation is easier to understand, but certainly greater use is made of standard deviation. The latter term refers to a more stable score and, in general, it has advantages over average deviation in statistical analysis.

Average Deviation

Average deviation (AD) means what the words would seem to imply. The deviations from the mean are calculated and then averaged. The algebraic sign of the deviation, whether plus or minus, is ignored. The formula is

$$AD = \frac{X - \overline{X}}{N}$$

Fifty percent of the scores stand within the distance of one AD of the mean. The average deviation can be calculated from the median, and this is sometimes useful. However, it is more common in statistical practice to use the mean as the point of departure in figuring deviations.

Standard Deviation

Standard deviation (SD) is defined as the square root of the mean of the squares of the deviations from the mean of the distribution. This sounds like a complicated sentence, but it becomes more comprehensible by illustration and explanation. Unfortunately for the beginner, at least three different symbols may be employed in referring to standard deviation—SD, s, or σ (the Greek letter sigma). One standard deviation includes 34.13 percent of the scores, either above or below the mean, in a normal distribution. Thus, one SD below the average plus one SD above the mean includes slightly more than two thirds (68.26 percent) of all the scores. Consequently, if the SD is large, the distribution is widely scattered; if small, the scores tend to cluster closely about the center, or the mean, of the distribution. The same situation prevails with regard to the relative size of the AD.

Continuing to use the symbols already given in calculating means, the formula for figuring standard deviations is as follows:

$$s^2 = \frac{\Sigma(X - \overline{X})^2}{N} = \frac{\Sigma x^2}{N}$$

$$s = \frac{\sqrt{\Sigma(X - \overline{X})^2}}{N} = \frac{\sqrt{\Sigma x^2}}{N}$$

The reader will often find in print a different formula used in determining standard deviation. This is especially true in the older literature, where the reader is likely to see the familiar formula

$$\sigma = \frac{\sqrt{\Sigma f d^2}}{N}$$

Since f stands for frequency, d indicates the deviation from the mean, then the formula produces the same result when used as that found by applying the one listed earlier.

STANDARD SCORES

Individual scores may be turned into standard scores by finding where each score is located in the distribution with regard to all other scores. There are several standard scores, but all have in common the fact that each gives information about how the individual score stands in relationship to others in the distribution. For example, it can be determined by use of little effort that a student has earned a score that stands a given distant in terms of standard deviations above or below the mean. Let us suppose that the student has answered 85 questions right when the mean of the class is only 65 and the SD is 10; his score is then two standard deviations or sigmas above the mean. It will be recalled that approximately one third of the scores will fall between the mean and one SD above it. Tables have been worked out and published that make it easy to determine how many individuals in a sample of one hundred would make a higher score than two sigmas. Approximately 95 percent would fall within two sigmas above and below the mean. Half of the remaining 5 percent would be at the lower end of the distribution so that we ascertain that only 2.5 percent have earned a better score. This is strictly true only if there is a normal distribution of scores; yet no more than a small difference of a few percent can be expected in a distribution that is markedly skewed. In a curve that has a general similarity to the bell-shaped curve, the difference will always be slight. Also corrections can be made for skewedness so that dependable predictions are still possible.

One of the most commonly used standard scores is the percentile. Here all scores are divided into one hundred cells, a procedure not readily applied unless there is a large number of scores involved. If a given individual earns a score that places him in the 90th percentile, that means that 10 percent of the scores are higher than his, the rest lower. If few scores are in the distribution, then deciles (groups making up 10 percent of the total) or quartiles (25 percent) may be more practical than percentiles.

Obviously, such standard scores have nothing to do with what percentage of questions have been answered correctly, but they are determined by the individual's standing as determined by relationship to the rest of the group. Standard scores can be added together without doing violence to logic. On the other hand, it would be no more legitimate to combine a student's raw scores earned respectively in history, English, and algebra, and then speak of a single score that is fully meaningful, than it would be to try to add pigs, calves, and chickens together for a meaningful total. Yet, standard scores can be combined, so that the total or average scores of one student can be compared with those of another. It is possible to weight scores if those in certain fields are conceived of as more important than those in another area. Thus, if algebra is assumed to be a third more important than history, this judgment can be incorporated into the statistical treatment.

RELIABILITY OF DIFFERENCES BETWEEN MEANS

Most of what has been said so far about the mean has little practical use to the experimentalist, except as the knowledge may be used in other calculations. However, the *reliability* or *unreliability* of *differences* between two or more means has many uses in experimental work. Essentially, the problem is that of determining the *probability* that repeated experiments will result in data showing that one of two means will continue to be higher. The way data are distributed is of fundamental importance here. Two averages may be very close together in terms of difference in the respective score and yet confidence can safely be placed in their retaining their relative positions. On the other hand, a wide spread in terms of score units between means might not be stable. When the distribution about each mean reveals great scatter, the difference between the means must be a great one; otherwise a reversal in relative position might occur by replication of the experiment.

Sometimes the formula that is used for determining the reliability of the differences between averages is as follows:

$$\sigma_{\text{diff.}} = \sqrt{\frac{\sigma_x^2}{Nx}\frac{\sigma_y}{Ny}}$$

It will be seen that the sigma difference is dependent upon the variability of the two measures, x and y. Once this value has been found, the

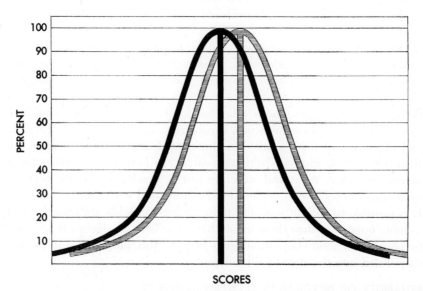

Fig. 1.3. Reliability of difference between means. Statistical procedure enables the investigator to determine whether the difference between the averages is a "significant" one.

difference between averages is divided by the sigma difference to establish an experimental coefficient. The formula for this is as follows:

$$\text{Experimental Coefficient} = \frac{\text{Difference between Means}}{\text{Diff.}}$$

Tables can then be used to see what the chances are that the difference is a significant one. "Significance" is ordinarily set at a particular level, say at the 1 percent level or the 5 percent level. By this it is meant that the chances are one in a hundred (or five in a hundred) that repeated observations will result in data that will be consistent in showing that the group with the higher mean in the first experiment will continue to earn higher scores.

CORRELATION

The degree of relationship between variables can be stated in terms of a single number. This number is referred to as a *correlation coefficient*. It is found that a coefficient may stand any place between a perfect

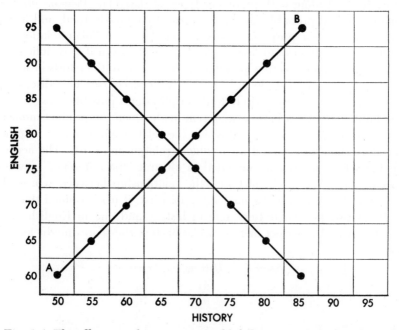

Fig. 1.4. This illustrates how scores would fall on a straight line for either perfect negative (−1.00) or perfect positive (1.00) correlation. The line from A to B is the positive relationship.

negative relationship, which is given as −1.00, to a perfect positive correlation, which is 1.00. If there is no systematic relationship between two variables, this is expressed as zero or 0.00. Prediction from knowledge of one variable to the other is possible for either negative or positive coefficient of correlation. If the relationship is a perfect one, prediction can be made with complete confidence. Knowledge of either variable will enable the investigator to know exactly what the second variable will be.

Except in the case where very few measurements have been taken, or in exclusive phenomena, perfect correlations are rarely found. By mutually exclusive data we mean that if one condition prevails, by definition, perhaps, the other condition cannot exist. The problem of establishing criteria may be difficult, but once this is determined, classification may proceed in such a way as to set the data into a perfect negative relationship. For example, the number of cloudy days in a year is necessarily inversely related to the number of sunny days; wet days are exclusive to dry days; wise men exclusive to stupid men; and so forth.

A variety of correlational procedures may be used and several of these are useful in dealing with particular types of data. The Pearson *product moment* method probably has been the most commonly used, and it will serve well here for purposes of discussion. This is a *linear* relationship and it is relatively easy to describe and illustrate, even if it is difficult to explain. Explanation as to why it works will be left to the efforts of teachers of statistics, or to study in a more advanced course. This discussion will be confined almost entirely to description and possible uses.

As implied above, a basic assumption made when the product-moment method of correlating is applied is that the relationship is linear. Another procedure should be used if a curvilinear relationship exists. The accompanying sets of figures are intended to illustrate the difference between types of data. We might illustrate the relationship between scores obtained by students in two school subjects. First, if it is assumed that the results in two particular tests, one in history and one in English, happened to reveal a perfect negative relationship, the scores might look as follows:

Subjects	History	English
1	94	65
2	92	76
3	90	80
4	87	87
5	80	90
6	76	92
7	65	94

It will be seen that the student who stood first in history was last in English and that the position of all students in the English test have been reversed from the standing on the history test. The correlation would turn out to be a −1.00. Here it can be seen that the teacher of English might have saved herself the trouble of giving the test. She could have predicted from the history test exactly what each student would do on the English test.

An illustration of a perfect positive correlation, again making possible prediction accurate to one hundred percent, would mean that the scores were as follows:

Subjects	History	English
1	94	94
2	92	92
3	90	90
4	87	87
5	80	80
6	76	76
7	65	65

In both of the distributions, a scattergram would reveal that scores fell on a straight line. In the negative correlation, the subjects would have fallen on a diagonal line extending from top left to bottom right;

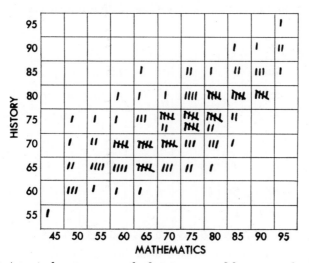

Fig. 1.5. A typical scattergram of what is expected between school subjects. By inspection it can be determined that the scores fall along a diagonal axis and this would give a positive correlation.

the positive correlation would reveal scores distributed along a straight line from bottom left to top right.

In order to figure correlation, we build upon the information given in the discussion of the reliability of differences between two means. The most common formula involves use of the same symbols:

$$r = \frac{xy}{N\sigma_x\sigma_y}$$

In the formula the small r stands for the coefficient of correlation; x and y are the deviations of two sets of scores (X and Y scores); N is used in place of the number of subjects involved; the sigmas are those obtained from each of the distributions. Take an imaginary problem involving 20 scores in which the mean of the X scores is 85; the mean of the Y scores is 83; the summation of xy is 1157; σ_x is 8.11, and σ_y is 8.07. Then by substituting we get the following results:

$$r = \frac{1157}{20 \cdot 8.11 \cdot 8.07} = .88$$

In approximately the same general procedure as indicated earlier about reliability, it is now possible to go a step further and determine what the chances are that repeated observations will produce correlation coef-

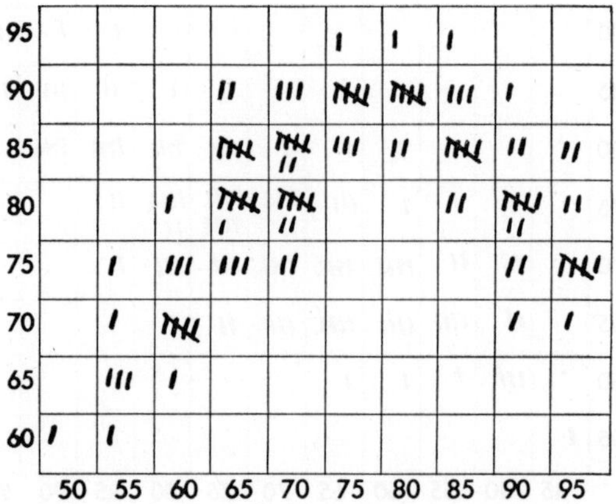

Fig. 1.6. If a distribution is found to be like the above, the relationship is curvilinear. A line that connected the mean point in each column would be a curved one. This kind of a relationship is rarely found between academic subject scores.

ficients ranging within a given distance of .88. Variability about this figure, if many observations and calculations are made, will tend to take on the general appearance of the normal probability curve. In other words, it is a good guess (two chances in three) that the mean of all correlations of data obtained in the same way and upon the same population will be within one standard deviation of the obtained figure, roughly, therefore, between .80 and .96, if we base our estimate upon the deviations reported in the two distributions involved here.

SUMMARY

Briefly stated, statistical analysis is made so that greater precision is possible in organizing and summarizing data and in communicating factual results to others. An additional, and very important, use is in extending and enhancing interpretations of phenomena. Inferences may be drawn and predictions made. Not only can predictions be made, but the accuracy of such predictions can be estimated statistically and then checked by experimental verification. Often specific questions can be answered, such as: how much difference must there be between the averages of experimental and control groups before it can be considered that a "true difference" exists? Or again, to what extent will a deliberate change that is made in the independent variable be expected to be reflected in the dependent variable? There are various levels of refinement in statistical analysis, so that the beginning experimentalist can quickly master a few elementary procedures that will serve him effectively. Careful research work involving fine measures, numerous variables, and complex analysis may call for extensive statistical knowledge.

SCIENTIFIC OBSERVATIONS, LAWS, AND LOGIC

The collection of scientifically useful data in psychology depends primarily upon the use of a consistent and orderly process so that a clear description can be given of how each observation is made. It is a basic operational tenet among scientists that the whole process of experimentation be carried out and reported so that another person can replicate the procedure. Otherwise it may be held that essential objectivity has not and cannot be demonstrated to the degree required of science.

In their enthusiasm to divorce their work from the bonds of philosophy, metaphysics, and subjectivism, scientists have sometimes seemed to place themselves in a position of opposition to philosophers. Philosophers are reputed to be fond of logic and many of them do like to engage in deductive reasoning. Yet science is certainly not illogical, nor can it very well dispense with the deductions that are derived from assumptions that must be made. No doubt, scientists make relatively more use of inductive reasoning, especially in a new science, than do philosophers. However, the scientist realizes that philosophical assumptions do underlie all scientific principles and laws. It is part of his business to fit his observations into an acceptable and logical system.

The extreme empiricist may manipulate a variable with scarcely more than a vague hunch as to what the outcome of his experiment may be, but he does not hold an attitude that causes him to proceed by pure trial and error. He must make certain assumptions; then he formulates hypotheses; next, he makes predictions upon the basis of the principles and generalizations that he believes to underlie events; finally (and this is critical in the work of the scientist), he must constantly verify step by step as scientific development takes place. Thus, the scientist assumes that events are not capricious, that there is order in the sequence of events. It is his major task to discover scientific laws that govern events and then to state these in precise language.

Some scientists emphasize the importance of an empirical approach more than others, and these individuals may feel that relatively little time should be spent in the development of theory until after a mass of properly collected data has been gathered and analyzed. Others may devote more time to evolving general theories to guide them before they go about collecting data. It is sometimes claimed that the strict empiricist may waste time and effort because of lack of better guideposts and that, in the end, his findings may remain chaotic and meaningless. This criticism may have validity, but a more theoretical approach does not necessarily enable the worker to avoid all pitfalls. It is possible that those who take a definite theoretical position may overlook significant data if these do not fit within the framework of the theory that has been embraced. Again, the ardent theorist may become the victim of wrong interpretations resulting from emotional investment and the biases that usually accompany strong feelings.

Scientists tend to resist accepting most assumptions except upon a tentative basis or where they may be accepted as "operationally" useful. This may mean that a particular scientist takes the position of assuming that a given concept will ultimately be found to be true, although convincing evidence is not yet at hand; therefore he goes ahead with his observations, working as though the concept had already been established as a scientific law. He may hold that even widely accepted scientific laws still fall short of having been proved absolutely; that it is practical and fruitful to assume that scientific truth is relative; at least, he cannot wait until all evidence has been collected. Then he may feel secure in accepting a so-called scientific law while proceeding to make his observations and continuing his efforts toward interpreting the events under investigation. How can it be determined when, or if, all relevant data have actually been collected? The scientist tends to say that there is no certainty with regard to this. He operates in a world where the "final" evidence can never be assumed to be assembled. But this tentative or questioning attitude does not paralyze him! A clear understanding of how the scientist views his world and then takes steps to deal with the problems with which he is confronted is important for the would-be scientist.

It is hoped that the student will be in a better position to profit from a discussion of this general topic after he has practiced more of the methods and procedures used by scientists. For that reason it is considered desirable to return to this basic theme at various and seemingly appropriate places in the book. Finally, an attempt will be made in a later chapter to summarize and to synthesize the materials that deal more definitely with broad problems common to those working in all fields of science.

SUGGESTED READINGS

NOTE: Readings have been arranged, in part, according to difficulty or complexity, but the writer would not want to defend their relative positions. The first listed are ordinarily elementary or general psychology textbooks; those toward the end of the lists are more advanced, technical, or specialized. It is assumed that there will be variation from student to student with regard to the material that has been covered and learned in a previous or beginning course. It is believed that there will be something new and worthwhile for each student. Some regard has been given to the books that are likely to be available and there is no intention to pass an unfavorable judgment upon the many excellent books that have not been included. Journals have been avoided (it is hoped for sound reasons); nevertheless, a few students can make effective use of them, and references to the journals are abundant in the recommended readings.

GENERAL READINGS

Morgan, Clifford T. *Introduction to Psychology*, pp. 1-24. New York: McGraw-Hill, 1956.

Munn, Norman L. *Psychology* (3rd ed.), pp. 127, 500-505. Boston: Houghton Mifflin, 1956.

Bugelski, B. R. *A First Course in Experimental Psychology*, pp. 3-13, 38-50. New York: Henry Holt, 1951.

Andrews, T. G. (ed.). *Methods of Psychology*, pp. 1-22, 124-157. New York: John Wiley and Sons, 1948.

Woodworth, Robert S. *Experimental Psychology*, pp. 392-449. New York: Henry Holt, 1938.

REFERENCES

1. Bancroft, W. D. *The Methods of Research.* Rice Inst. Pamphlet, XV, p. 167.
2. Freedman, Paul. *The Principles of Scientific Research.* Public Affairs Press, Washington, D. C., 1950.
3. Pavlov, I. P. "Bequest to academic youth," *Science* (AAAS, Washington, D. C.), 83, 1936, p. 369.
4. Pearson, Karl. *The Grammar of Science.* London: Adam and Charles Black, 1911.
5. Spearman, C. *The Abilities of Man, Their Nature and Measurement.* New York: Macmillan, 1927.
6. Thurstone, L. L. "Psychophysical Methods," p. 124 in *Methods of Psychology,* ed. T. G. Andrews. New York: John Wiley and Sons, 1948.

2 | MEASURING TIME FOR RESPONSES

INTRODUCTION

The study of reaction time is an old problem, yet a new problem; a simple problem, yet a complex and difficult problem. Every psychologist is confronted with the necessity of knowing something about reaction time; every competent psychologist will know many principles associated with the topic. He will have many and varied uses for this knowledge. In one way or another reaction time is involved in a wide variety of important problems in psychology. Thus, it is required that the serious student inform himself concerning this subject. When and how did the study of reaction time have its beginning? What were the methods used at first and what today? What apparatus was used and how has that been improved with time and effort? Who were the men that studied reaction time and why did they consider the subject important? What did they learn? After several hundred experiments extending over a period of about a century, why must we still do experiments to learn more about reaction time?

A set of questions similar to this might be asked at the beginning of almost every chapter of this book. We shall refrain from asking them in this exact form since the reader might become tired of their repetition. However, we shall assume that many questions will arise in the reader's mind. Those anticipated, even if not stated, may still furnish the basis for much of our discussion.

THE MEANING OF REACTION TIME

In its simplest form, reaction time (RT) means the time interval between the presentation of a stimulus to the sense organ and a muscle response. Perhaps it can be assumed that the very simplest reaction is the one requiring the least time following a stimulus. The time interval in so-called simple reactions varies with several factors. For example, there is a different average reaction time found by use of each sense modality. RT is longer for a pain stimulus than for a visual stimulus; it takes longer to respond to salt on the tongue than for pressure on the skin; longer to react to a visual signal than an auditory one. The factors making for variation in RT are both numerous and subtle. They will be taken up in considerable detail later. It is well to keep in mind the essential meaning of RT—the time interval between reception at the sense organ and muscle response.

ORIGIN AND DEVELOPMENT OF REACTION TIME STUDIES

Apparently the first man to use the term "reaction time" was Exner, a physiologist. Exner lived in Vienna, where he was busy experimenting upon physiological problems that soon became of even greater interest to psychologists than to physiologists. Most of this work was reported between 1870 and 1880. However, his contribution was neither the first, nor necessarily the most interesting to psychologists. Interest in the subject goes back much earlier, and even clearly conceived experiments upon the problem date several years before Exner used the term "reaction time."

It seems certain that the first clear concept of RT arose accidently from an interesting, although otherwise somewhat trivial, historical incident occurring at the Greenwich Observatory, England, in the year 1795. Maskelyne, head of the observatory, discharged an assistant because he had ". . . fallen into some irregular and confused method of his own" (Boring, 3) and failed to read the transit of a star across the meridian at the same time as that observed by Maskelyne. Maskelyne was a trained astronomer and naturally enough assumed that his own readings were accurate. The task involved observing the star in transit. At the instant the star passed over the middle line in a vertical grid, the time had to be read. While it is not part of the story, as usually told, to include any account of what happened to the professional future of the unfortunate assistant, Kinnebrook, we do learn that many years later another astronomer in Germany, Bessel, read the Greenwich report and the incident caught his attention. In 1823 Bessel compared his readings with those from another astronomer, Argelander, and found a difference of 1.223 seconds. Bessel soon determined that one astronomer might give consistently slower or faster readings than another astronomer. He found that no two agreed precisely on the time of a given star's transit. While skilled observers agreed within less than a second, still the difference was of great consequence in astronomical calculations, and hence the term "personal equation" came into use. This was the label given to the newly discovered variable and was the forerunner of a large number of problems generally grouped under the heading of individual differences by modern psychologists. The Greenwich Observatory incident was very important in stimulating scientists to pursue the task of determining how and why people are different.

Astronomers have long since perfected a device for recording automatically when a moving hair line crosses the meridian. Now the task for the observer is simpler and reduces the error to relative insignificance. The use of vision is still necessary to read the record and to make a discrimination. It should be noted that the human observer has not been entirely eliminated nor can he be. It is, as always, that the grossness of the error can be reduced by the application of better apparatus and techniques; variation due to the human factor is not totally eliminated. Psychologists, economists, political scientists, sociologists, and businessmen continue to be vitally interested in the "personal equation." It cannot be said that apparatus, methods, or techniques have reduced the errors of observation to anything approaching insignificance when dealing with most of the problems confronting these professional people.

The work of Helmholtz around 1850 to 1860, while not dealing directly with reaction time as his central problem, was extremely stimulating to investigators. Also, his contributions are important on both theoretical and technical grounds. Helmholtz was trying to measure the speed of the neural impulse. This was a very live issue at that time. Some scientists said that the neural impulse was instantaneous; others estimated its speed at a few feet per second. In his first attempts, Helmholtz used a frog's leg and tried to determine the time elapsing from stimulus to response and then measure the distance the impulse would have traveled, and in this way calculate its speed. Later he stimulated the human arm at different levels, still timing the interval as he tried various stimulus points from lower to upper arm. Eventually, through the use of differential RT and measuring the distance between the closer and more remote point of stimulus origin, he concluded that the nerve current must travel at a speed of about sixty meters per second. He had assumed that each neural impulse would complete a circuit to the brain and back to a given muscle requiring the same distance except for the variation at the starting points. The rather great variability of RT from trial to trial, even when applying the stimulus to the same point, finally led Helmholtz to doubt his results. However, his procedure of taking repeated observation and then using an average of these turned out to be a better safeguard against wrong conclusions than he had assumed. His estimates were not far from the correct speed. Furthermore, the regularly obtained variability in the psychologist's observations has led later investigators to use averages and the deviations about these as a means of statistically determining the confidence that may be given to collected data. Again, it must be granted that a satisfactory statistical control does not entirely eliminate the error; it does help to prevent the investigator from drawing faulty conclusions from inadequate observations.

With improved devices the speed of neural impulses in man has now been determined to be roughly seventy meters per second. Several factors give rise to considerable variations within the same organism, and the speed is markedly different for different animals. Some cold-blooded animals have been shown to have a neural impulse speed as slow as ten meters per second. Most of the variation which confused Helmholtz was not due to a difference in neural transmission speed, but was a result of other factors making for variation in RT. Concerning these, Helmholtz could have little or no knowledge at that time. These factors have been discovered and described since then but it is safe to assume that experimenters have not completed the task of accounting for every last variable of some significance.

We have seen that the reaction-time problem was introduced through studies in astronomy and that Helmholtz, a physicist and physiologist, made further contributions. Now we come to the first man to consider himself as a psychologist who was interested in the problem. About 1860, Wundt became interested in the "personal equation" and physiological psychology. Wundt, a favorite student of Helmholtz, was a physiologist before he was a psychologist and his RT studies were important in his transition over into the field of psychology. Among the many famous students who worked under Wundt, several did experiments upon RT. Cattell is of particular interest, for his investigations expanded and led him into an intense and prolonged interest in individual differences. Cattell was to become the first man in America to be made a professor of psychology. He had a part in the early establishment of psychological laboratories at both the University of Pennsylvania and Columbia University. He directed attention to individual differences and their great importance relative to many psychological problems and, furthermore, he displayed ingenuity concerning experimental attacks upon these.

It is found that Wundt's interpretation about reaction time was much influenced by Donders, a Dutch physiologist. Donders extended reaction studies to include choice before making a response. This involved what has come to be regarded as *complex reaction time*. In this way Donders was hoping to isolate and study central neural activity or so-called mental processes. The number of variations that can be introduced in both stimulus and response are, of course, many. Examples of this include responding with the left hand for a green light; right hand for a red light; index finger for one color and the thumb for another, etc.

After many years of intensive work, Wundt finally came to the conclusion that simple reaction time included a sequence of three processes: (1) sensory impression coming into the field of consciousness, (2) entrance into focus of attention, and (3) the volunteer release of the signal movement. (Woodworth, 9) He took exception to Donders' belief that the time necessary for choice could be isolated and measured separately from the sensory and motor aspects of the process. His ideas in this matter, no doubt resulting from his great prestige, came to be the accepted one. This view was a great disappointment to those who hoped to isolate the so-called mental process for further study by this means. Whether future refinements in measuring devices will again make investigators accept Donders' view remains to be seen. There are still those who believe this approach to have promise of fruitful results. However, as much as the enthusiasm and industry of the early investigators may be admired, it is now clear that they expected too much; that they were overly optimistic in hoping that they would soon unlock the secrets related to the thought processes by studying reaction time. Even today knowledge is extremely limited as to exactly what takes place in the nervous system when man thinks.

THE CHRONOSCOPE

Very closely tied in with the research upon reaction time was the development of a device which would measure short intervals of time with a high degree of accuracy. The problems in this undertaking were indeed great one hundred years ago. It is difficult for people with easy access to electric clocks, electric motors, electronic devices, and other precision instruments to realize how hard it was to get an apparatus that would start without delay, afford calibration, and then be capable of stopping without a lag. It is true that clocks were invented long before that time and the principle of the pendulum was quite well understood. However, these were of no use without special adaptation. This process of having to adapt apparatus to his needs has a long history for the psychologist. Few instruments have been invented for the direct and only use of psychologists so they have had to borrow and improvise.

Again, the needs of the astronomer came to the fore and a Swiss, Hirsch, working in collaboration with an engineer, Hipp, invented what ultimately became known as the Hipp chronoscope. The development of more modern chronoscopes took place in the early eighteen sixties. First used to check upon the astronomer's calculations about the speed

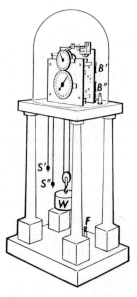

Fig. 2.1. THE HIPP CHRONOSCOPE

The clockwork of this chronoscope is driven by the weight, W, which is raised by a key fitting in the center of the lower dial. The chronoscope is started by pulling S' and stopped by pulling S". The two recording dials are divided into hundredth parts. The hand on the upper dial revolves ten times every second, each division on the dial corresponding to a thousandth part of a second. The hand on the lower dial revolves once every ten seconds, each division on the dial corresponding to one tenth of a second. Reaction time is calculated from both dials, the units and tens from the lower and the hundredths and thousandths from the upper dial. The speed of the dial hands is controlled by a small steel tongue which is accurately tuned to vibrate 1,000 times per second. B' and B" are electromagnets which control the starting and stopping of the dial hands. F is a binding-post. Various control instruments have been devised to check the accuracy of the readings given by this chronoscope. (From Garrett, Henry E. *Great Experiments in Psychology*. New York: Appleton-Century-Crofts, 1951.)

of light, chronoscopes were later used for determining the speed of rapidly moving objects such as the velocity of bullets fired from guns. After many modifications and refinements, Hipp's chronoscope proved to be the forerunner of scores of devices for helping the investigator to determine time required for events to take place or to determine the speed of moving objects.

Various inventions and improvements have been made in timing devices. The main problem to overcome in RT studies has not been that

Fig. 2.2. This reaction time apparatus made use of lip keys for both experimenter and subject. (Courtesy Ralph Gerbrands Co.)

of obtaining rapid or constant speed since electric motors were invented. However, engaging a clutch to start or stop without important errors has been very bothersome. Helmholtz made use of the deflection of the needle of a galvanometer in his RT studies. By using a current of constant intensity the swing of the needle could be calibrated to indicate time.

As indicated earlier, measurement is of fundamental importance in nearly all sciences and the development of the chronoscope became a general landmark in the progress of science. It becomes a fascinating story to trace the development of accurate timing in terms of seconds,

Fig. 2.3. An apparatus used for measuring braking reaction time. The stimulus can be variable involving visual, auditory or cutaneous cues. The response is a relatively complex one, or at least one involving many muscles. (Purdue Psychological Laboratory.)

Fig. 2.4. Reaction time apparatus with modern electric timer. Keys allow for multi-choice responses. (Courtesy C. H. Stoelting Co.)

tenths of seconds, hundredths, thousandths, and finally, by modern electronic and photographing devices, to millionths of seconds. Much of the
history of science could be written without going very far afield from
the story of man's struggle to measure more precisely the passing of
time. Even the geologist and the botanist find it important to establish
the sequence and date of important events in their sciences.

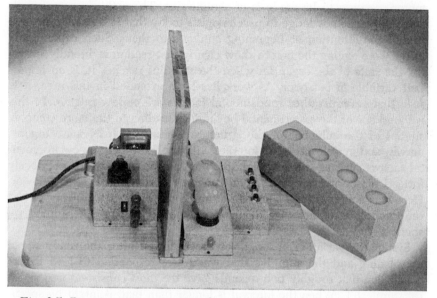

Fig. 2.5. Reaction time apparatus that provides for four light stimuli which
might be different in position or color and four keys for responding. (Courtesy
Lafayette Instrument Co.)

FACTORS IN SIMPLE REACTION TIME

While doing research in an attempt to learn more about the functioning of sensory equipment, neural impulses (including central nervous
activity or mental processes), and muscle responses, it soon became
apparent that many factors operated to produce the variation in RT. This
gave investigators the problem of isolating and systematically varying
these if they were to do a good job in describing and explaining. It turns
out that these factors making for differences in RT also have important
practical significance in administering certain psychological tests or
"mock" performances in which results are greatly influenced by skill in
sensory-motor coordination. For convenience we have grouped the fac-

tors which increase or decrease reaction time under the following head-ings:

The Factor of Readiness

Experimentation revealed that the way instructions were given to the subject and the time interval of the readiness signal influenced the quickness of reaction. Even directing attention to the stimulus instead of the motor response to be made is of significance. These things are of such commonplace knowledge to psychologists today that it is easy to neglect to call the attention of beginning students to them. Such experiments in RT were among the first to show clearly that readiness, broadly speaking the state of the organism when the stimulus reaches it, is an important variable in behavior. As work has been extended in this area, it is seen that several rather fundamental factors are closely related. In this is found one of the experimental beginnings leading to the more complex studies of the influence of the structural factors, such as sense organs, nerves, and muscles as these interact with the more definite environmental factors such as learning, conditioning, or the presence of previously formed biases or prejudices, as all converge to determine total behavior. Here was a suggestion of how to attack those problems growing out of the interaction of heredity factors and "mental set" in determining responses.

Systematic variation in length of time allowed after the ready signal or warning and the stimulus that was to be responded to lead to the conclusion that roughly two seconds gave the most consistent and shortest simple RT. When the interval is longer than that, it might be speculated that the effect of the warning is lost by the influence of surrounding stimuli acting as distractors, or by what might be considered normal deterioration of attention with the passing of time. When the interval is much less than two seconds perhaps there is not time for adjusting senses and muscles or possibly a lack of time to mobilize fully the organism for response.

The problem of providing a warning signal and at the same time preventing the subject from making his response to the warning rather than to the intended stimulus became apparent. In other words, while the two-second period is close to optimum, if this length interval is always used the subject soon comes to anticipate and respond to the warning signal itself although by delayed reaction. This fact can be ascertained by observing the subject "jump the gun." If he is responding to the readiness signal, he can be tricked into responding when only this signal is given. In order to avoid this difficulty in establishing reaction time, the experimenter resorts to varying the time interval, but still makes the average or median time come close to two seconds. This treatment may fail to prevent some anticipated responses; however, it does allow the experimenter to deal effectively with the error. The error theoretically should be distributed largely according to chance instead of the response being systematically too soon. Without some such control the subject may come to time himself and the reaction is then almost simultaneous with

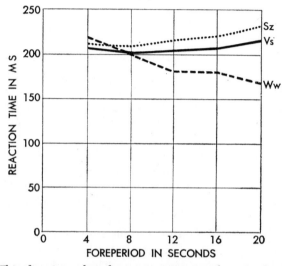

Fig. 2.6. This drawing taken from an experiment by Woodrow (1916) reveals how reaction time varied for three subjects when the warning signal was given at different intervals. (From Woodworth, Robert S., *Experimental Psychology.* New York: Henry Holt & Co., 1938.)

the stimulus, giving a false impression that training can eliminate reaction time.

A common procedure used to overcome the difficulty mentioned is to divide trials into series, say of ten trials, and keep checking for false reactions. Each series in which a false response has been made is eliminated in the final data. If a given subject continues to "try to cheat" all data from that subject is considered to be worthless. What is considered as a "false" response must be arbitrarily set in advance. However, the subject sometimes does not respond for several seconds and the response, if made then, is certainly not RT and should not be counted when figuring an average. On rare occasions a subject will fail to respond altogether unless reminded to do so. Any selection of data from a given subject or the removal of all data from a subject is, of course, a serious and doubtful procedure in science. However, the experimenter upon RT seems to have no desirable choice here. It is certainly more serious to average in responses made after long delays—these not being a reflection of RT at all, but rather of forgetting by the subject—than to use some consistent procedure as a correcting device. Any known procedure with regard to the specific problem being raised here remains imperfect, but by combining both experimental and statistical control the experimenter can still arrive at fairly satisfactory results.

Magnitude of Stimulus

The intensity of the stimulus and the length of time it is continued are both factors making for variation in RT. A number of experiments have been performed with systematic changes made in the intensity of the stimulus. When the subject is barely aware of the stimulus, the responses vary widely and average slower. The RT decreases as the intensity increases above the threshold level. However, it must not be assumed that this relationship will hold indefinitely. Investigators seem to be forced to conclude that most of the experimental work suggests an optimum intensity for reaction that is somewhere within what is called "medium" intensity. Thus, both Wundt and Pieron took the position that RT would decrease as intensity is increased beyond the threshold up to a given point and would then tend to increase again. Extremely intense stimuli would consequently give a somewhat longer RT than mild stimuli when applied to the same sense organ. This would give a curvilinear relationship. In describing Berger's (1) extended studies upon this problem, Woodworth (10) indicates that the relationship remained linear. Woodworth concluded that Berger must have failed to increase the intensity beyond the optimum level when collecting his data.

At first thought it seems to be illogical that the duration of the stimulus should have anything to do with the RT. Presumably the subjects respond to the starting of the stimulus. The results, then, are peculiar in that RT is affected by how long the stimulus is continued. Continuation of a sound, for example, beyond 3 ms (ms = mille seconds or thousandths of a second) gives decreased RT. If the sound is continued beyond about 50 ms, no further reduction in RT is observed. Similar findings for the other senses lead to the generalization that here again there is an optimum duration for the stimulus to be applied if the objective is to obtain the shortest RT. There is not evidence of reversal, as is the case for intensity, but eventually no further reduction in time for the respond is obtained by use of a more prolonged stimulus.

Satisfactory explanation for these findings in regard to intensity and duration are not readily at hand. Possibly there is a summation effect which operates up to a certain level and beyond that there is a loss of attention, or in the case of some stimuli, the activation of another sense modality. Either a light or sound may become sufficiently intense to be painful. When this occurs RT might shift from that typical of vision or hearing to that typical of pain, which is longer than either. If the transi-

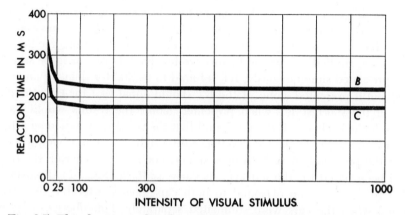

Fig. 2.7. This drawing, taken from Berger (1886), shows how simple reaction time decreases as the light stimulus increases. However, the RT soon stabilizes with no further significant change for the intensity used. (From Woodworth, Robert S., *Experimental Psychology*. New York: Henry Holt & Co., 1938.)

tion were sudden, it might be considered that this explanation is very acceptable. No report of a systematically controlled experiment for determining whether the results are really due to transition to another sense modality has been found in the literature. It would not seem difficult to design an experiment to clarify the point.

Not having disposed of the difficulties just mentioned, yet further complications soon arise because the optimum level of intensity or duration for one subject is unlikely to be the same as that for the next subject. This may be due to the fact that the sensations that arise from subject to subject vary because of sensitivity differences of the sense organs involved. When equal light energy strikes two sets of eyes, one person may have good acuity of vision while the other does not. Knowledge about such variables is such as to enable experimenters to set up reasonable controls for practical purposes. An arbitrary intensity or duration of stimuli can be agreed upon and consistently used throughout the experimentation upon a given problem and for all subjects. This, of course, means that conclusions can only be stated within the limitations stipulated about variations about an average. What might be expected of one individual is, then, in terms of probability about the average found for a given population.

Summation and Facilitation

It is altogether possible that the factors discussed in the previous section help to give rise to summation and facilitation effects. However, in most RT experiments where the influence of summation and facilitation are being studied, additional factors are involved. If two or more stimuli are presented simultaneously, RT is found to be shorter than for any one of them if presented alone. If the RT should equal that for the stimulus giving the shortest RT when presented alone, the results would seem more logical. That is, if it were found that the response was sooner when light is presented to the left eye than to the right eye then it would seem that the presentation to both eyes should not result in shorter RT than had been found for the left eye. As early as 1893, Bliss (2) discovered that the presentation of sound to both ears gave shorter RT than was found when the ears were stimulated separately. Poffenberger (7), in 1912, demonstrated that RT for either of the eyes was longer than when both eyes were used.

When stimuli are presented to two or more sense modalities simultaneously, there is difficulty, as subjectively judged, in maintaining attention upon either one as "the stimulus" and thus an additional variable is encountered. The result is that RT is less consistent and does not take a time pattern characteristic of that expected from any one of the stimuli used. The tendency is for RT to be most like that for the sense which averages shorter RT.

In view of what has just been said, it is perhaps not surprising to find that the selection of two stimuli is possible which if presented at the same time will facilitate speed; also that it may be possible to produce longer RT under some conditions. In 1913 Todd (8) found that giving the subject an electric shock preceding a light stimulus by less than a second interval prolonged the RT. Thus the appearance of antagonistic stimuli or making additional demands upon the organism may inhibit rather than facilitate response. In some ways this procedure resembles the conditions set up when multiple choice is demanded in selecting an appropriate response, and is therefore like complex reaction time.

RT for Different Senses

RT differs markedly as a result of the sense that is being stimulated. This could result from several factors. In the first place care must be taken that timing is accurate at the instant the stimulus acts upon the sense organ. There may be important experimental errors due to the instruments that are used. The experimenter is forced to use instruments giving a different kind of energy in order to activate each sense modality. If timing is from the initiation of the stimulus instrument such as a bell, or the flash of a light, it may well be that there is considerable time lost while the mechanism of the bell operates and also some time is necessary for the transmission of the sound wave to the ear. In the case of light bulbs, the ordinary incandescent light bulb is slow to reach its maximum illumination. It would be unwise to assume that such variables will be equal and so cancel each other. A satisfactory or completely reliable difference between averages in RT for the various senses, therefore, has not been established.

Some of the more common problems that are encountered in determining RT differences have been stated in the preceding list of variables. While it might appear to the beginning experimentalist that adequate controls could be set up quite readily, there are at present only rough controls. For example, it has been learned that intensity of the stimulus is an important factor, and of course an optimum intensity may be established. On the other hand, it may be desired to know how intense a light to pair with a sound of given value. While a great deal of thought and work has been done upon this deceptively simple-appearing problem, the experimenter is confronted with a conflict that is suggestive of the difficulty arising if he should want to add sheep and pigs together and come out with a meaningful total. Language does at least allow him to speak of so many animals. Quantification of light into foot candles and sound into decibels is very satisfactory when one light is to be compared with another light, or one sound with another sound; crossing the qualitative boundary from light to sound is an entirely different matter. In their dilemma psychologists have sometimes approached the problem by first trying to establish a threshold for seeing a dim light and then determine each successive point of increased intensity that can be discriminated from the one below. A similar procedure is then used for locating points in the hearing scale. Finally, it is possible to choose and compare two points at an equal number of discrimination intervals from the threshold, say the fifth or tenth point above the threshold for both vision and hearing. This may be useful, but the sceptical individual may still question that a meaningful comparison between RT for vision and hearing can be made through any such maneuvering. The presentation of wholly convincing evidence is not now possible. The psychological intervals arrived at in this way are called "just noticeable differences."

In spite of the unreliability of measures for comparative purposes, the differences in RT found for the various senses are so great as to be very convincing that there is a genuine difference. Thus, doubts arise in deciding how much difference rather than being convinced that no real difference may exist. Results are quite consistent in showing that RT is greater for visual stimuli than auditory; greater for pain than hearing, etc. Only by an indefensible manipulation of the variables that have been described is it likely that a reversal in the direction of results would be obtained. The following range of values cover the results from almost all the studies that have been reported:

Pressure	.112 to .118 seconds
Hearing	.120 " .140 "
Vision	.130 " .160 "
Cold	.150 " .170 "
Warmth	.170 " .180 "
Smell	.190 " .220 "
Taste	.280 " .310 "
Pain	.350 " .450 "

Other Factors in RT

There is perhaps no point in attempting to go into detail regarding all the factors that have been shown to influence RT. We shall only add a few miscellaneous but interesting findings. Pearson (6) measured RT for thousands of people in England of all ages and from many occupations. He found that RT tended to decrease up to early adult life and then gradually increased with age. Thus one reason is seen why fighter pilots are selected and trained intensively with a view to have them ready for combat at an age when their RT is at its shortest during their early twenties. High level motor skill in most work or sports follows closely the pattern for RT. No prize fighter can come to the maximum of his earlier potential in this matter after he has reached the age of thirty. While the fighter might gain in strength or strategy as he grows older, he will inevitably lose speed.

All kinds of conditions that tend to impair the body may be expected to increase RT. There is an adverse effect from fatigue so that the auto driver is much less efficient in his reactions after several hours of driving. The RT will be longer as he becomes drowsy. Pilots not only may suffer loss in RT from fatigue or sleepiness, but there are additional hazards at high altitudes. Keeping warm is too obvious a factor to need discussion since everyone is aware of how difficult it is to make quick finger movements when cold. However, the pilot may suffer a RT loss that is more subtle but nevertheless very important if he gets into atmosphere that is thin and he does not get enough oxygen. It is reported that the pilot may even think that he performs more efficiently under these conditions so that he has a false notion about his skill.

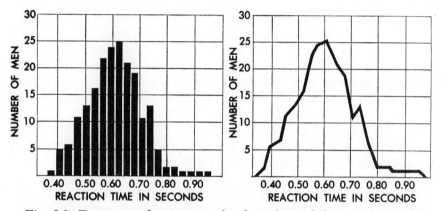

Fig. 2.8. Two ways of presenting the data obtained from 30 men when using braking reaction time apparatus. A few individuals were conspicuously slow, requiring more than twice as much time as the fastest ones. (From Morgan, Clifford T., *Introduction to Psychology*. New York: McGraw-Hill, 1956.)

Several drugs increase RT. This not only includes narcotics but also alcohol. Here again, the subject is not a good judge of what happens to him. Most experimentally naive subjects tend to overestimate their skill and speed of response after taking alcohol. It has been shown that a small amount of caffeine is an exception. However, the body soon adapts to the drug unless a greater amount is used. In general, there is no lack of drugs to slow responses but relatively little success can be expected of drugs to speed up performance. Yet it must not be assumed that RT cannot be influenced by motivation factors, reward, or punishment, as the results taken from the experiment of Johanson (4) clearly illustrated.

CURRENT RESEARCH ON RT

While reaction time may not enter directly into very many present-day psychological experiments, yet it may underlie many complicated problems. To whichever field or area of psychology one turns, some aspect of simple or complex reaction time is likely to arise. For example, in clinical psychology it is seen how this enters into answering questions in most diagnostic tests. The time from the presentation of a Rorschach card until the first response is made may be used as an index to emotional disturbance or to guarding by the individual. Short RT is sometimes interpreted to mean a lack of intellectual inhibition or control, especially if the response is also found to show evidence of poor form discrimination or to contain content material not typical of the normal subject. In industrial psychology, not only does reaction time have great significance in a variety of tests used for selecting employees, but also becomes one of the focal points in analyzing time-motion problems. The investigator will want to know how long it takes to initiate a motor response, and even more important, how segments of motor activity become woven into a smooth pattern of appropriate responses—one leading into another with fine timing and coordination.

Tests of reaction time have been used as a part of many aptitude types of tests. Certainly the baseball coach would not want to waste his time coaching the individual who must start striking at the ball before it leaves the pitchers hand. The longer he can wait and still get the bat around in time to meet the ball, after he has been able to watch the ball part of the distance, the better chance he will have to hit it. He will want to continue to modify the direction his bat takes until it comes into contact with the ball. This involves an intricate feed-back system which is a part to the sensory-motor combination that makes for good or poor performance.

Every worker in the assembly line in a factory must work within the limits laid down by his combination of sensory-motor equipment. In some jobs only relatively little improvement can be expected with practice. That improvement usually comes after a small amount of training and then levels off. Naturally we do not mean to imply that the average worker performs at a level anywhere near his actual upper physiological or psychological limit. However, it is not unreasonable to suppose that those who must approach the limit in order to do satisfactory work must push themselves more. Sustained great effort would be expected to give rise to accumulated fatigue with a tendency for the individual to become discontented and unhappy with his work. In these matters writers are willing to accept the idea that morale and good motivation is of primary importance in making a good worker. Just exactly what conditions, what characteristics of the individual, what demands of the job have important bearing in achieving high morale is not easy to determine. Research intended to uncover all these factors of morale might well be directed to relating together as many basic processes as possible, especially those that can be accurately measured. These would certainly include sensory equipment, motor strength, and coordination, simple and multiple reaction time of the individuals.

CONCLUDING REMARKS

Even though the use of electronic equipment now enables the instrument maker to construct much more satisfactory apparatus for measuring RT, it is nevertheless true that research having to do directly with RT stimulates relatively less enthusiasm than was the case a century ago. The range of problems that are now attacked by psychologists is many times greater than it was then. Also, most investigators attempt to build upon these earlier experiments. There is an attempt to advance to more complex problems not only of theoretical significance, but also to everyday problems where great demand is placed upon psychologists to help with solutions. Yet experimenters still find occasions for doing research on simple or complex RT not unlike that done a century ago. For example, the unbelievable demands made upon the pilot of the jet plane for quick and coordinated motor responses require that knowledge concerning RT be reviewed and that refinements in research procedures be made in order to obtain even more dependable information.

SUGGESTED READINGS

Postman, Leo, and Egan, James P. *Experimental Psychology: An Introduction*, pp. 239-274. New York: Harper, 1949.

Garrett, Henry E. *Great Experiments in Psychology*, pp. 312-330. New York: Appleton-Century-Crofts, 1951.

Woodworth, Robert S., and Schlosberg, Harold. *Experimental Psychology*, pp. 8-42. New York: Henry Holt, 1954.

Boring, Edwin G. *A History of Experimental Psychology*, pp. 147-153. New York: Appleton-Century-Crofts, 1950.

Dennis, Wayne. *Readings in the History of Psychology*. Cattell: "*The Influence of the Intensity of the Stimulus on the Length of the Reaction Time*," pp. 323-325; "*The Time It Takes to See and Name Objects*," pp. 326-328. New York: Appleton-Century-Crofts, 1948.

Woodworth, Robert S. *Experimental Psychology*, pp. 298-338. New York: Henry Holt, 1938.

REFERENCES

1. Berger, G. O. *Philosophical Studies*, 3, pp. 88-98. 1886.
2. Bliss, C. B. *Yale St. Psychology*, 1, pp. 1-55. 1893.
3. Boring, Edwin G. *History of Experimental Psychology*, p. 134. New York: Appleton-Century-Crofts, 1950.
4. Johanson, A. M. *Archives of Psychology*, 54 (1922).
5. Morgan, Clifford T. *Introduction to Psychology*. New York: McGraw-Hill, 1956.
6. Pearson, K. "On our present knowledge of the relationship of mind and body," *Annals of Eugenics* (1925).
7. Poffenberger, A. T. *Archives of Psychology*, 12 (1912).
8. Todd, J. W. *Archives of Psychology*, 25 (1912).
9. Woodworth, Robert S. *Experimental Psychology*, p. 304. New York: Henry Holt, 1938.
10. *Ibid.*, p. 317.

3 | GENERAL SENSITIVITY AND STRUCTURAL CONSIDERATIONS

INTRODUCTION

Having finished with a chapter on reaction times, which is clearly within the domain of psychology, it may seem to some that we are now retreating into physiology. However, the material of the next few chapters is considered to be a necessary basis for obtaining a sound orientation to experimental psychology. It is particularly relevant for the experimentalist but useful to all who would work in any area of psychology.

There was a time when it was thought appropriate and logical to begin the study of psychology by taking up the senses first of all. This material was the focal center for the first course in psychology. It was not uncommon for half or even three-fourths of the first course to be devoted to sensory processes. This approach was no doubt due in large measure to the fact that much was already known by physicists and physiologists about the senses and the energy that activates them before psychology became a separate discipline. Some think that a study of the physical mediators of behavior—sense organs, nerves, and muscles is a dull but necessary part of psychology. A very few believe that such material may be eliminated without seriously handicapping the student. The assumption is made here that the material is not necessarily boring and that a knowledge of it is essential to the making of a competent psychologist.

It is, of course, possible for a student to learn a great deal about psychology and at the same time to learn little about the organism itself. This area of knowledge might in that case be left to the anatomists and the physiologists. To be sure, the chief concern in psychology is with the behavior of the whole organism. Thus, much of the detailed research directed toward studying the structure and functions of the several organs (including sense organs) might be left to other specialists.

It is equally true that the efforts of psychologists are not directed primarily to studying the relationships between groups of people. Here there would be danger of encroaching upon the preserve of the sociologists. However, it appears that the psychologist must know something of the fields of knowledge that surround him if he is to know well his own domain. The boundary between psychology and these other subjects has not been sharply drawn and it appears safe to assume that much is gained by allowing free intellectual traffic across the frontiers.

In presenting the material of this book, and pointing out experimental problems, we may be somewhat closer to the physical sciences than to the social sciences. A book to be used by students taking a more advanced course in experimental psychology might shift the emphasis with a stronger orientation to the social sciences. Most investigators would probably agree that leadership in scientific methodology was captured by and has remained with the physical scientists. Considering the overlapping of psychology with both physical and social sciences it is reasonable to expect that the advanced student of psychology should feel at home in both broad fields of science. Certainly he needs to know much about the organism and the way it functions in a social environment. This chapter is devoted to presenting some of the broad generalities about the physical equipment and the way it functions to enable the individual to survive and to adjust in his surroundings. Later chapters will appear to be more closely associated with content of the social sciences.

IRRITABILITY AND DIFFERENTIATION OF TISSUE

Irritability of living tissue is one of the fundamental facts of life. All living tissue is irritable. That is, it responds when energy is applied to it. Differentiation of tissue into specialized structure and function is of similar fundamental importance. Specialization of the tissue determines what type of energy will be responded to with greatest efficiency.

There is only the slightest hint of specialization in the receiving and responding mechanism in the lowest forms of animal life. This would be true of all one-cell animals, like the amoeba. As the animal world is surveyed, a fairly consistent relationship is found between specialization in sense organs, nerves, and muscles and the level of development of the animal. This is one of the indices that is used in classifying animals with regard to the extent of development. There remain some striking exceptions to the rule that the more primitive animals have less specialized tissues. Certain insects and most birds have excellent vision, yet these are classified as relatively primitive animal types. In neither insect nor bird does the degree of specialization in structure and function extend, in a comparable way, to the nervous system. The relative enlargement of the nervous tissue into the brain, therefore, is also important in determining the evolutionary status of the animal.

THE SENSES: "DOORS TO THE MIND"

The sense organs are the mechanism for receiving energy from the outside world. They are the means of maintaining contact with the conditions about the organism. The senses represent the end result of a long process of development and extension of the principles of irritability and specialization of tissue. Each sense in man may be thought of as an extension of the specialization process: eyes respond to light waves; ears to sound waves; nose to odors; etc.

Wundt began considering himself a psychologist while he was mainly concerned with the subject of sensation. As we have previously indicated, he was first a physiologist and later became interested in sensation as a result of his careful study of the structure of the sense organs and the way these organs functioned. However, he used the introspective method to study sensation and that was at least as closely akin to philosophy as to physiology. Thus he was already losing to some extent his identification with physiology before he became primarily a psychologist.

Wundt set the pattern for breaking sensations down into their various attributes by using trained introspectionists who described their experiences. This procedure, greatly extended by his student, Titchener, had much in common with the work of the chemists of that day. Chemists spent most of their time describing, identifying, and labeling the elements of the physical world. It might be said that the content of psychology of that time was primarily philosophical and that the methods used to attack the problems were borrowed in large part from physics and chemistry. However, it was only in the isolation and analysis of small parts or fragments of experience that psychology was imitating these sciences. The use of introspection or subjectivity had no place in chemistry or physics. Early psychologists thought that the subject matter of psychology forced them into using introspection as a method.

We wish to make clear that sensation psychology was derived at least as much from philosophy as from physics and physiology. It had been held for centuries that the senses were the gateways to the mind; that it was only by means of the several senses that man could experience the external world. In the fifth century B.C., Heraclitus (3) made the statement, "through the doors of the senses," when trying to explain how information got into the mind and how ideas were formed. It was not long afterwards that the notion of *tabula rasa* came into wide acceptance and the meaning of this was that each sensory experience produced an imprint on the smooth blank surface of the brain. Experience was believed to be the cause of all the fine wrinkles on the cortex.

Many centuries later a group of English scholars built a system of knowledge based upon associationism. They called themselves empiricists, and that implied that they considered sensory experience the building stones for ideas and concepts. These writers were opposing the notion that ideas came innately, or that people were born with certain fundamental concepts. It was a basic premise of philosophers and theologians who opposed associationism that man inherited certain ideas and beliefs. They held that a man would innately know right from wrong, for example. The associationists were, on the other hand, laying the foundation for those who were to place great stress upon the environmental influences that came to play upon the individual in determining whether he would be saint or sinner; gangster or law-abiding citizen; industrious and productive or a parasite upon society. After repeated sensory experiences ideas were thought to emerge. Then by adding ideas and compounding them, concepts of great complexity might be developed. Consequently, building upon the simple sensations as the foundation, thinking might be extended to the most lofty concepts of which man was capable.

MIND-BODY PROBLEM

At the time of which we have been speaking, scholars were already deeply involved in the mind-body problem. Some had thought to escape the need to resort to mysterious reference to what went on in the mind or soul. They did not find a solution to the relationship between bodily structures and modification of behavior resulting from experience. There are still many problems to resolve in these matters. One of the weaknesses of the associative system was that clear evidence for an important premise could never be obtained. It could not be established that a new sensation actually produced a new groove in the brain. The man of wide experience and great wisdom did not necessarily have more wrinkles on his brain than did the moron. In fact, *post mortem* examinations of the brain might not enable, even the expert, to determine which had belonged to genius and which to feeble-minded. The doctrine of *tabula rasa* became discredited as an explanation of how the organism stored experience so that it might later be used in the form of memories.

A great amount of the work of the associationists remains useful and it was perhaps unfortunate that so much that has later been proved to be of such great scientific worth was temporarily cast into doubt. The sponsors had embraced an erroneous doctrine about structural changes that they thought should be directly related to changes in mental processes. The postulated relationship between experience and wrinkles on the brain was not established. Yet the empiricists had contributed an extremely fruitful approach to problems of science. For a time their work became controversial and bitter criticism (at least partially justifiable) was directed at them, resulting in a partial eclipse of what had been a brilliant hope for the improvement of man by environmental manipulation.

Now in modern guise, the old mind-body problem is still very much with investigators. It continues to be grist for controversy among philosophers and also the subject of psychological and medical research. The neurologist, physiologist, or the psychologist who does experiments in which he tries to relate bodily changes to psychological phenomena is preoccupied, in part, with this basic problem. The methodology now used has better scientific status than did earlier subjective speculation. Psychiatrists and clinical psychologists busily do research and write books and articles that have to do with problems in psychosomatic medicine. This becomes a central issue for those who believe that physical illness must be expected to have important impact upon mental and emotional reactions and that mental illness may be expected to have a basis in neural, glandular, or other physical mal-functioning. Many, in fact, believe that mental and emotional distress may bring about physical imbalance of important consequences. Further discussion of these relationships will be undertaken in later chapters.

DISCOVERIES IN NEUROLOGY

An important turning point in regard to relating neural activity to behavior was brought about by the discoveries of Bell and Magendie shortly after 1800. The two men, Bell an Englishman, and Magendie a Frenchman, worked independently but came to similar conclusions. Through experimentation and clinical observations, they came to realize that the spinal cord might be divided into two types of nerve tracts. There were sensory nerve fibers which carried the impulses toward the brain and these were found along the dorsal side of the spinal cord. The ventral tracts were made up of motor nerves and these carried impulses to the muscles.

Forward Action

The discoveries of Bell and Magendie made a further implication clear —the neural impulse traveled on a one-way track. Then, if this should be the case, every sense organ must be attached to a sensory nerve that carried the neural impulse toward the brain. The search was soon on for the multitude of sensory nerves having origin at every point over the body.

At present it is known that there are more sensory nerve fibers than there are sense organs. There are thousands of so-called "free" nerve endings which act to receive stimuli much in the same way as the specialized sense organs.

The discoveries referred to above gave new impetus to physiologists. Not only did they carry out investigations to establish the connections between sense organs and sensory nerves, they extended their interest into the sensory process mediated by the brain. They threatened to invade a province held by the philosophers. They could proceed with some confidence toward explaining what happened in the process of getting ready to think. The question remained as to how far they could go in understanding what happens when man thinks. The *tabula rasa* had been a false doctrine, but was it wrong in principle or wrong in detail?

At an earlier period, phrenology had held out the hope that personality could be interpreted from the size and shape of the head. It was largely in the process of establishing evidence against this doctrine that Bell and Magendie had come upon their discoveries. There was no longer a question about phrenology. It represented a wrong approach to understanding the development of personality traits and characteristics. Arguments about the usefulness of studying the nervous system in order to solve psychological problems continue until today. However, it has not been mysterious since the time of Bell that a cut on the leg might prevent all sensations of pain from arising at a certain point on the foot, or that another similar but slightly different cut might leave the individual able to sense pain from the foot but render the muscles incapable of contracting as needed for moving the foot. A more detailed discussion of these interesting discoveries can be found in the second chapter of Boring's book "A History of Experimental Psychology."

SENSATION, PERCEPTION, BEHAVIOR

It may be seen that the hopes of the early investigators, when trying to achieve certain goals in the analysis of sensation, resulted in frustration and failure. Part of the reason lies in the fact that the organism is an integrating mechanism. Sensation cannot be fenced off sharply from perception. Nor is it possible to separate behavior completely from these other processes. Those who would avoid all reference to sensation and perception in order to concentrate upon behavior or response psychology also have their difficulties. When does response begin? Is response limited to muscular contraction? Is the sense organ not responding when it receives stimulation from outside energy and transmits that to the nervous system? What has been transmitted to the nerve to set up the neural impulse? What does the motor nerve transmit to the muscle that makes the muscle contract? Has the nervous tissue been responding as surely as the muscle responds? Is not the interpretation of the meaning of a sensory experience a response?

An arbitrary distinction has sometimes been drawn between sensation and perception. Sensation was said to be without meaning. The instant that interpretation is made it might be said that the individual is perceiving. A sound that is recognized as the shot of a gun or the blow of a hammer has already been interpreted. Perception may even take place before the individual can attach an accurate label. Misinterpretations are, nevertheless, perceptions. If the easily frightened individual hears the backfire from the exhaust pipe of a truck and believes he has heard a gun fired, he is perceiving regardless of how wrong he may be.

The early investigators held, if they followed the tradition of Wundt, that sensations must be reduced to their attributes before psychology could become a true science. Only after the problem of sensation had been solved, it was held, should psychologists attempt to study perception. Some of Wundt's followers, Titchener being one, seemed to think that most of the difficult problems confronting psychologists would be resolved when sensation was thoroughly understood. Eventually there was a rebellion staged by young men in the field. They took the position that it was futile to try to understand the most important problems in psychology by introspecting upon sensory qualities. These investigators asserted that workers could never hope to make a science of psychology until they confined their efforts to observing and recording behavior. This was a rebellion within psychology, but the primary goal was to make a complete break with philosophy. To a very great extent, the rebels won the argument, and psychology became more objective in the way advocated by those who were interested in the individual as a functioning organism rather than as an absorber of experience. Emphasis in psychology shifted away from sensation and the sensory processes toward response psychology, or the study of behavior.

Currently, a rather vocal group of psychologists take the position that the revolution was carried too far. There is no strong movement afoot for psychologists to return to an unqualified introspective method, but there is a revival of interest in the study of both sensory and perceptual processes. An important impetus for return to the study of perception was initiated by those interested in measuring personality traits. While this renewal of interest in perception would have been gratifying to the introspectionist, they had once assumed that personality would not be suitable for scientific psychological study for many years. Projective tests are based in part upon the assumption that perceptual distortions and projections may be used as indices to personality characteristics. Another important reason for returning to a study of the senses had to do with a different kind of practical problem. For example, it has become important to know more about the eyes and ears and other sensory equipment of individuals who are to be selected and trained for certain military or industrial tasks. The tremendous demands placed upon an individual to respond to sensory stimuli with speed and precision is continuously being increased because of scientific and technical advances. Today few investigators are greatly concerned about trying to draw a fine distinction between sensation, perception, or response. There is more interest in how integration takes place and how this culminates into action by the individual. Yet in presenting the content of psychology it seems necessary to indulge in a certain amount of segmentation as a means of simplifying and to eliminate unnecessary confusion.

CLASSIFICATION OF THE SENSES

Traditionally, writers have spoken of five senses. These are vision, hearing, taste, smell, and touch. It becomes necessary to divide touch into several senses and then, in order to be complete, some additional senses must be named. The number of senses to be listed for animals, including man, is still an open question. Among investigators there will be satisfactory agreement for pressure, heat, cold, pain, equilibrium, and kinesthesis. When these are added to hearing, vision, taste, and smell ten senses have been listed. There is a fairly extensive list of doubtful senses: contact, deep pressure, dizziness, movement, appetite, hunger, thirst, nausea, sex, tickle, itch, vibration, wetness, suffocation, and several varieties of pain. Subjectively, distinction is possible between aching pain, prick pain, deep pain, shooting pain, sharp pain, and dull pain.

The problem of classification, or the enumeration of the senses, might be approached from at least three viewpoints: (1) the stimulus or physical energy that will activate the sense; (2) the qualitative or sensation derived; and (3) the structure of the sense organ. While none of these approaches is necessarily wrong, the last is a strict criterion. Wherever there is a well identified anatomical structure for a given sense, investigators will probably accept this as satisfactory evidence for a separate sense. If there is a willingness to overlook a certain amount of ambiguity and disagreement as to which sense organ goes with what sense among the skin senses, structure has been identified that is associated with each of the ten senses listed.

There has been lack of convincing identification of structural organs for the senses given in the doubtful list. At present there is only a psychological basis for considering some of these as special senses. It may be that all are derived from sensations coming from one of the named senses or from a combination of several of these. It may seem peculiar that psychologists will accept a classification dictated by anatomical rather than one premised upon psychological grounds. Actually, it is the intention here to speak with confidence concerning those senses that meet the criteria from all viewpoints. We have placed in the doubtful list those senses that may not meet all the requirements. Question can be raised as to whether we are giving due regard to the first criterion, the stimulus or type of energy applied. It would not be easy to defend the proposition that there are really ten different kinds of energy that match the senses. Anyway, there is at least a difference in the way the energy is applied to the sense organ, or in the medium by which it is conveyed to the organ. The three criteria are closely associated with three disciplines: energy with physics, sensation quality with psychology, and structure with anatomy and physiology. No doubt conclusions that one makes in psychology should be in harmony with those derived from careful observations and thought in related fields of study. Fortunately, there is much consistency especially where objective methods have been employed. This kind of consistency which crosses conventional boundaries of science is one of the best types of scientific validation.

SHERRINGTON'S CLASSIFICATION OF SENSES

Sherrington (6), a physiologist, introduced a very different kind of classification of the senses. His approach has been widely accepted by physiologists. The classification was based upon the source of the stimulus, the location of the receptor, the projection of the sensation, and the main biological function of the particular type of receptor. While recognizing the senses, as they had previously been named and described, he grouped them under *telereceptors, proprioceptors, exteroceptors,* and *interoceptors.* The telereceptors gave information about the distant environment, and included seeing, hearing, and smelling. The proprioceptors gave information about movement and position of the body or parts of the body. The end organs were those scattered through the muscles, about the joints, and in the tendons. The exteroceptors were used to give information about the immediate environment and included the skin senses. The interoceptors were those receiving stimuli from the visceral organs of the body.

LIMITATIONS OF THE SENSES

All senses are limited with regard to the type of energy or stimuli that will activate them. They are further limited as to the range of intensity receivable. In the case of vision and hearing, at least, reception of energy

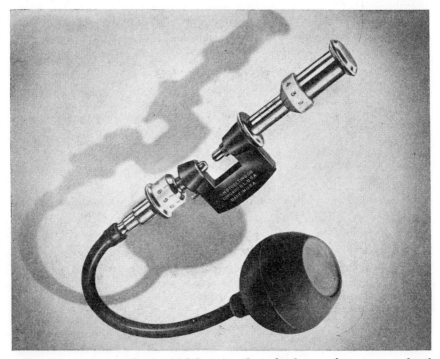

Fig. 3.1. Galton Whistle (Edelman). The whistle can be set at a level beyond the hearing of man but within the range for a dog. (Courtesy C. H. Stoelting Co.)

is to only certain wave lengths. The eyes respond partially, if at all, to ultraviolet or infrared; the ears do not detect very short sound waves that may be air-borne. Radio waves are not responded to at all by the ears. It is necessary to use devices to transpose radio waves into suitable sound waves in the air before the ears become sensitive to them. Not all animals will respond to identical bands of energy, for the dog hears sound waves of higher pitch than that possible for man. Galton made practical use of this knowledge by making a whistle (known as the

Galton whistle) that can be used to call a dog without nearby people being able to hear the sound. The presence of infrared and ultraviolet has been well established and many uses have been made of these light waves.

Many forms of energy exist that make little or no impression upon man's sensory equipment and some of these types of energy are dangerous to him. There is not intention to imply that there should be a parallel between energy forms and sensory equipment. However, one very important function of the senses is to help warn the organism of dangerous conditions. This use continues to be of importance to man although it might well be that the relative value of the senses for survival is less for modern man than is the case for lower animal forms, or than was true for primitive man. The senses do fairly well in detecting dangers from most of the "natural" phenomena to which man is exposed. They do not cope very well with many of the obnoxious and even very dangerous conditions created by man. The sense of taste may fail to warn against the poisons of modern chemicals; smell fails to enable man to detect monoxide poison in the air. No sense warns against radioactive particles in the environment. A Geiger counter may be used for this purpose so that the warning signal becomes sound. Supersonic sound waves may also be capable of damaging tissue without the sensory mechanism giving a satisfactory warning.

There seem to be adequate grounds for accepting the basic truth of evolution. If so, the efficiency of the senses should tell something about the things and conditions that have been most hazardous to man—that the senses would be atuned to the most prevalent threats to life. It might be expected that some sense would be able to detect and thus give warning of a particular danger that has been encountered frequently during the long struggle for racial survival. Furthermore, it would seem reasonable enough that energy that has been converted from one form into another by modern discoveries and inventions might leave mankind dangerously exposed. The recent controversy over the causes of cancer testifies to these possibilities. There have already been several tragic accidents involving radioactive exposure. It would be interesting to determine how well, if at all, the individual could be trained to use his senses to detect these various new dangers in man's environment.

ADAPTATION AND FATIGUE

All of the senses become adapted or fatigued after extended exposure to stimuli. Fatigue and adaptation are not quite synonymous terms but as they apply to the sense organs it is very difficult to distinguish between them. Adaptation is more often used in connection with a modification in the capacity of the sense organ to respond, while fatigue is often used to indicate a loss of efficiency in muscular reactivity. It is not immediately clear whether only one or two basic phenomena are to be dealt with. The problem is further complicated because it is not known how much of the manifest change in functioning of sense organ or muscle is due to changes associated with connecting nerve fibers.

There is a lack of consistency among writers in the meaning intended to be conveyed by both adaptation and fatigue. We shall try to stay with the meaning of increased threshold level for receiving stimulation when using the word adaptation. It is harder to pin down a satisfactory meaning for fatigue. Along with other interpretations, the word has been used to refer to decreased muscular output, loss of skill in motor performance, and a subjective feeling of tiredness. When discussing changes in the sensory mechanism, thought to be brought about by continued stimulus exposure, we may do well to stay with the word adaptation. It should be kept in mind that we attempt to offer little, if anything, in the way of explaining what happens in the sense organ or sensory nerve as adaptation takes place. The term is used for purposes of description rather than explanation.

There is a marked variation in the speed with which adaptation takes place among the several senses. It usually takes the sense of smell only a few minutes to adapt to a given odor. After this initial period there is a tendency to lose awareness of the odor and awareness may not come again unless there is a conscious effort to sense the odor. While this kind of loss of attention to a stimulus is not unusual, it is especially noticeable with regard to smell, taste, and the cutaneous senses. The sense of pain adapts very slowly. A toothache may continue with apparent unabated severity for hours or even days.

Adaptation and aftereffects lead to many complications when experimenting upon the senses. For example, it is necessary to control in some way the odor that has just been sensed before applying the experimental odor. How is the tongue wiped clean from the previous taste effects before the subject tastes the experimental substance? To some extent the same kind of problem is present for the less adaptable senses. It makes an important difference whether the subject has been looking at a green surrounding before he is called upon to make discriminations between shades of greens, or between reds and greens. What we have been saying has to do with the preparation of the subject for the experiment that is to be performed. This is a broad and complicated problem that plagues the psychologist in many situations. He encounters a similar sort of difficulty when experimenting with learning. He must describe and try to standardize conditions during the period which the rat has been deprived of food before any general idea of the strength of the hunger drive can be obtained. When the human subject is called upon to learn a list of nonsense syllables, it makes a difference whether he has just been sleeping, or has turned immediately from learning a previous list of nonsense syllables. If constancy cannot be achieved when trying to control factors of the kind reviewed, at least the sophisticated experimentalist will carefully describe the conditions under which the data were collected.

If it can be assumed that all nervous tissue is of the same nature, the implication seems clear—adaptation can be identified with the sense organ. There are occasions where the process of adaptation or fatigue can be partially controlled voluntarily. The purpose in the use of an anesthetic is to reduce the efficiency of the pain sense or else to prevent awareness of the pain. However, if adaptation is confined to the sense organ itself, it is interesting to speculate upon why effort to reduce pain has been directed almost entirely to blocking the neural impulse in the sensory nerve. Drugs are frequently used to induce unconsciousness. Presumably the latter condition is brought about by the effect produced by the drug on the brain. While blocking of the neural impulse in the peripheral fibers or within the brain are both effective in relieving suffering, a suitable drug that acted directly upon the sense organ should also be useful, especially if only a highly localized area needed to be involved. Furthermore, those drugs that are used to knock out consciousness very frequently have undesirable side effects.

The physiologist, Ruch (5), has made an interesting statement about the rate of adaptation of the different senses. We can do no better than to quote his statement.

> Adaptation is not equally rapid in all sense organs. . . . Certain types of end organs adapt very little after the initial few seconds of response, but are able to maintain discharge for minutes and hours. In the class of slowly adapting end organs come the muscle spindle, tension receptors at the root of the lung, pressure receptors of the carotid sinus, and the pain receptors of the cornea. Pressure receptors adapt somewhat more rapidly but not so rapidly as touch receptors, especially those associated with hairs which give rise to a burst of impulses largely ended within half a second. Adaptation to this degree would obviously unfit an end organ for serving long sustained postural reflexes or for recording the pressure of blood within the carotid sinus. Similarly, if pain end organs were to cease generating pain impulses before the noxious stimulating agent is removed, pain would lose much of its protective function. On the other hand, the

rapid adaptation may be an advantage to an exploratory sense such as touch. Contacts are perceived, then the slate is wiped clean by adaptation and made ready to receive a new impression.

It will be seen that Ruch relates the way the senses function to the biological purposes to be served. The student may or may not find the above speculative explanations to his satisfaction. However, it is hoped that the student will not become engrossed with accumulating facts and forget to raise interesting questions. The acquisition of facts should serve to whet the curiosity. It is by raising questions, when trying to furnish explanations for observed phenomena, that the scientist is able to generate hypotheses for further investigation and experimentation.

NEURAL CORRELATIONS

Every sense organ is connected with a nerve ending. Thus the senses are all tied in with the most important integrating agency of the body. This makes interaction possible. It is assumed that somewhere and somehow the organism records and stores every experience that results from a stimulus crossing the sensory threshold. Many of these impressions are exceedingly faint and soon fade beyond much usefulness. There is today only slightly less mystery about how this process takes place than there was centuries ago.

In spite of the truth of the above statement, investigators are not totally ignorant of some interesting activities within the nervous system. We shall present three important principles in neural conduction. It is still unknown whether these three laws are going to be of much use in understanding how the nervous system stores experience so that the individual may bring the events of the past to bear when solving problems of the present. These principles could be little more than a beginning upon this difficult problem. They are called the "law of specific nerve energy," the "all or none law," and "local sign." These principles are discussed because they are of general interest and educational value, even if they have somewhat limited usefulness at present in understanding most psychological problems.

SPECIFIC NERVE ENERGY

The law of specific nerve energy was first stated by Johannes Muller. The idea was later greatly extended and clarified by Helmholtz. The law of specific nerve energy originally implied that a given nerve fiber, attached to a particular sense organ, carried only the neural impulse specific to that sense. Thus a nerve that had its point of origin with a pain

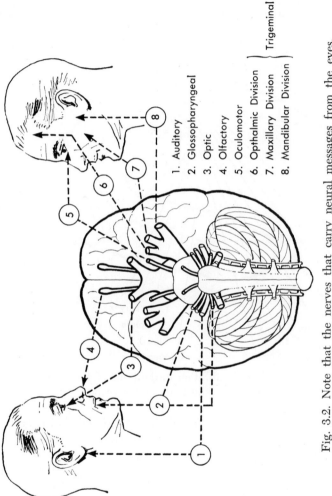

1. Auditory
2. Glossopharyngeal
3. Optic
4. Olfactory
5. Oculomotor
6. Opthalmic Division ⎫
7. Maxillary Division ⎬ Trigeminal
8. Mandibular Division ⎭

Fig. 3.2. Note that the nerves that carry neural messages from the eyes, nose, tongue, ears, face, and vestibular apparatus go directly to the brain, i.e., not via the spinal cord. The nerves that carry impulses from the skin, muscles, and joints of the rest of the body enter the brain via connections in the spinal cord.

end organ would not transmit an impulse that gives rise to sensations of heat, cold, or pressure. It is true that pressure upon the eyeball may give rise to two or more kinds of sensation, such as pressure and visual image, but more than one nerve becomes involved. The optic nerve continues to serve the purpose of vision and the subject gets the impression of flashing lights, dots, various shades of gray, and so forth as a result of me-

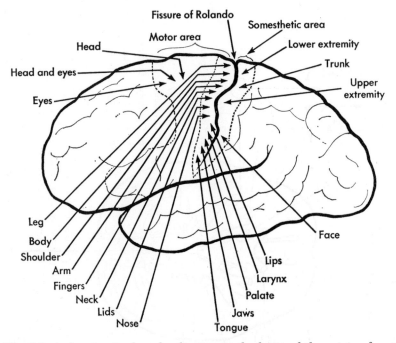

Fig. 3.3. A drawing to show localization in the brain of the origin of motor nerve fibers which extend to the several parts of the body.

chanical stimulation of the retina. Helmholtz considered that specificity was the basis for discrimination in vision of the various colors—particularly end organs in the retina for receiving each color that could be discriminated. Also, he held that pitch discrimination was possible because there would be a receptor for each pitch that was in turn attached to a specific neural fiber that carried the appropriate impulse that enabled the subject to identify the pitch.

The number of nerve fibers from senses like pain, heat, cold, or pressure run into many thousands. It is generally accepted as fact that there are one or more nerve endings for each sense bud regardless of how numerous these may be. The nerve fibers do not borrow work from each other but each carries its own impulse from the sensory origin over connecting fibers to the terminal destination in the brain. Complete information about specific nerve energy phenomenon is lacking. In recent years,

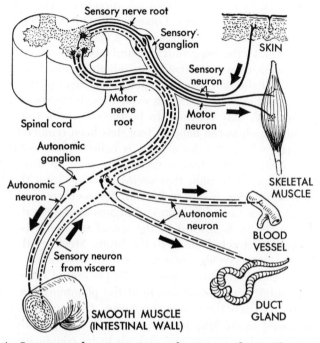

Fig. 3.4. Sensory and motor nerves showing pathway that completes a neural arc. Both skeletal and autonomic neural fibers are shown. Note that all sensory fibers enter the cord on the dorsal side; motor nerves leave cord by dorsal side. (From Morgan, Clifford T., *Introduction to Psychology*. New York: McGraw-Hill, 1956.)

some doubt has been expressed that sufficient importance has been attached to the location of the terminal point in the brain. Specification might be determined more by the terminal fiber location in the brain (as the Gestaltists insist) than by the point of origin in the peripheral parts of the body. The evidence is clear enough that something depends upon what part of the brain is activated by the incoming impulse and the awareness of sensations. Space does not allow for the presentation of the abundant research bearing upon the broad implications of these matters.

LOCAL SIGN

Closely related to the phenomenon of specific nerve energy is the principle of *local sign*. By this term it is meant that a sensation arising in consciousness has reference to some particular part of the body. This doctrine was advocated by Lotze, who took occasion to criticize some aspects of the specific nerve energy theory. Lotze held that it was because identification of the sensation with stimulation at a specific point that the individual is able to make the numerous discriminations involved in keeping oriented. Confusion does not arise as to whether pain is coming from the hand instead of the foot, from the stomach instead of the eye.

There is a persistence in localizing even though the sense organ has been destroyed. This may continue to be the case even though a large anatomical unity, such as the hand or foot, has been removed. There are many individuals who suffer from what is called "phantom pain" after losing a limb. Years after a foot is gone there may be times when the individual will experience pain that seems to come from the lost foot. Presumably this situation is due to specific nerve energy and local sign. The nerve that was attached to pain end organs in the toe remains alive and intact from the stub upward to the spinal cord and then connects with fibers in neural tracts leading to the brain. Mechanical stimulation anywhere along the nerve fiber may give rise to sensation.

It is assumed that irritation, or pressure at the end of the nerve where scar tissue is found, is the usual source of the phantom pain. The uninformed victim may draw the wrong conclusion. He may think that something is happening to the long lost foot or hand. The pain that seems to come from the hand or foot is real enough to be convincing to him. A person was once known by the writer to demand that a lost leg, which had been buried in a box that the victim had been told was too short for it, be dug up and reburied in a more suitable box. The unfortunate man then reported that his leg felt better! Part of his reaction may have been due to suggestion, but no doubt the gradual growth of tissue over the stub where the leg had been amputated was the most important reason for the reduced pain. The whole experience no doubt seemed mysterious and without adequate explanation to this man, for he was without much information concerning the structure and function of the nervous system. Once facts are known about the way the nerves and sense organs function, a reasonable explanation is at hand.

ALL-OR-NONE LAW

By the "all-or-none law," is meant that the neuron (structural unit of the nervous system) discharges with full force if at all. It is said to be like all protoplasm substance in this regard. If a stimulus is adequate to activate the sense organs and to set up a neural impulse, an increase in the intensity of the stimulus will not result in a stronger discharge. The nerve acts much like dynamite or gun powder when discharging. It does not make a partial explosion. Adrian (1) was able to show that a nerve impulse that was partially blocked by an anesthetic at a given point would, if it did cross the blocked region at all, come back to full strength upon reaching the unaffected tissue beyond the place where the anesthetic had its effect.

WHAT DETERMINES INTENSITY OF PAIN?

A question may be raised about how the subject obtains stronger and weaker pain sensations. One injury, it is obvious, may be more painful than another. There are two important means for obtaining variation. The intensity of a pain is primarily in proportion to the number of end organs for pain that are activated. Then the larger the surface of mutilated skin, the more painful the injury may be expected to be. This statement must be qualified in order to take into account the uneven distribution of pain end organs over the body.

Increased intensity of a sensation, such as pain, may also be brought about by an increased rate of neural discharges. The neural current is not a continuous flow, but moves in waves with one impulse following another. There is a measurable amount of time between each impulse. Adrian (2) was able to isolate a single nerve fiber from the larger bundle and to photograph cathode waves that are assumed to represent discharges as these pass over the neuron in rapid succession. By this means he was able to demonstrate that there is a refractory period between each discharge, a brief but measurable pause before the nerve can receive the next impulse.

There appears to be no way of closing the gap between one neural impulse and the next. It is as though the nerve must observe a rest period to regain energy for the next discharge. However, there is some flexibility regarding the time interval between the passing of succeeding waves. It seems that the nerve gradually regains energy after discharge, and that a stronger stimulus will fire the nerve fiber again sooner than will a weak stimulus. The necessary stimulus for response occurs when the two variables come together—another firing occurs when the adequacy threshold is crossed. This means that a more closely packed succession of impulses will move along the nerve fiber when the intensity of the stimulus is increased.

While there are many fascinating facts and principles known about the nervous system, the most intricate and complex mechanism known to man, we must content ourselves with only a brief sketch of the most important findings. Here no more can be attempted than to give a bare minimum of information that is rather directly related to the problem of trying to understand the way the senses function. At any rate, it can be seen that the senses do not serve their complete purpose in isolation. Their usefulness to the organism is premised upon the way they are tied in with the nervous system and the conscious processes that are brought to bear with the muscular responding mechanism of the body.

CONCLUDING REMARKS

Further discussion about the structure and functioning of sensory equipment may be presented in connection with other topics. Additional implications will appear as each sense, in turn, is described more fully. Investigators today are likely to agree with the ancients who considered the senses to be the "gateways to the mind." All that is of much importance in learning about the world must come via one or another of the senses. It is true that direct stimulation of brain tissue with an electric current may produce a muscular response. This is a unique condition and is of limited importance except in research. In other words, with regard to experiencing, there appears to be no access to the brain of practical importance except through the senses. If there are defects of the senses, inevitably the subject obtains distorted, incomplete, or inadequate information. He is forced to use this unsatisfactory material when thinking, making decisions, choosing what to believe, and taking action. To be sure, excellent sensory equipment does not guarantee that thinking will be profound, or that adjustments will be skillful. The most crucial problem-solving activity undoubtedly takes place within the brain. However, at the present time, man is largely excluded from examining directly this process, and certainly today the scientist is handicapped in trying to observe, to direct, or to modify what takes place there. On the other hand, thousands of people get off to a bad start in dealing with the problems of life because of limitations in their sensory mechanisms. They are deprived of accurate, vivid information about the world that surrounds them. Within limits, there are means of giving aid to those with faulty eyes, ears, and other defective sense organs. In so far as this is true then, others may direct and control, to some extent, the psychological development of the individual by providing him with appropriate sensory aids. It may also be of great value to the individual that he be made aware of any sensory deviations that he suffers even though corrective procedure is impossible. Such knowledge would help him to make a better adjustment to the realities of his world. At present, for example, it is not known how to remedy most color blindness but it might lead to great tragedy if a man should become a truck driver although he could not distinguish between red and green signals on the highway.

In his recent book "The Human Senses" Geldard (4) is concerned primarily with so-called "pure science," but he pauses to give a brief review of the recent stress that has been placed upon the functioning of sense organs in the development of human engineering. The second world war gave impetus to psychological studies having to do with the relationship between weapons systems and human capabilities, sensory and motor. The rapidly expanding field of human engineering, now assumed to be more concerned with peace-time pursuits, is not leading to neglect of sensory processes. To the contrary, this aspect of psychology long associated with, and largely limited to, laboratory work, and which was often thought of as "ivory tower" psychology, has taken on the complexion of being indeed very practical and down to earth. Stevens (7), in speaking of the demands placed upon sense organs during the second world war, said: ". . . it was fought largely on margin—sensory margin—where the battle hangs on the power of the eyes or the ears to make a fine discrimination, to estimate a distance, to see or hear a signal which is just at the edge of human capacity." Stevens was writing in the war period and the rapid onrush of events over the past decade to usher in the "age of automation" has certainly served to substantiate the implication of his words: ". . . the paradox of it is that the faster the engineers and inventors serve up their 'automatic' gadgets to eliminate the human factor the tighter the squeeze became on the power of the operator." In short, we might conclude that automation does not eliminate the need for great care in making sensory discriminations; that push-button controls might mean that a mistake in discriminating between the buttons that are to be pushed could lead to rapid and great catastrophe.

SUGGESTED READINGS

Ruch, Floyd K. *Psychology and Life* (3rd ed.), pp. 237-277. New York: Scott, Foresman, 1948.

Morgan, Clifford T. *Introduction to Psychology,* pp. 531-557. New York: McGraw-Hill, 1956.

Munn, Norman L. *Psychology,* pp. 393-417. Boston: Houghton Mifflin, 1956.

Boring, Edwin G. *A History of Experimental Psychology,* pp. 24-94. New York: Appleton-Century-Crofts, 1950.

Boring, Edwin G. *Sensation and Perception in the History of Experimental Psychology,* pp. 3-91. New York: Appleton-Century-Crofts, 1942.

Fulton, John F. *A Textbook of Physiology.* Ruch: "Somatic Sensation," pp. 292-344. Philadelphia: W. B. Saunders, 1949.

REFERENCES

1. Adrian, E. D. "The all-or-nothing reaction," *Ergelin. Physiol.* 35 (1933), 744-755.

2. Adrian, E. D., Cattell, McK., and Hoagland, H. "Sensory discharges in single cutaneous nerve fibers," *J. Physiol.* 72 (1931), 377-391.

3. Boring, Edwin G. *Sensation and Perception in the History of Experimental Psychology,* p. 4. New York: Appleton-Century-Crofts, 1942.

4. Geldard, Frank A. *The Human Senses,* p. 25. New York: John Wiley and Sons, 1953.

5. Ruch, Theodore C. "Somatic Sensation." In Fulton, John F. (ed.). *A Textbook of Physiology,* pp. 293-315. Philadelphia: W. B. Saunders, 1949.

6. Sherrington, C. S. *The Integrative Action of the Nervous System,* chap. 3. New York: Scribners, 1906.

7. Stevens, S. S. "Machines Cannot Fight Alone," *Amer. Scientist,* 34 (1946), 389-400.

4 | EXPLORING CUTANEOUS SENSE FUNCTIONS

INTRODUCTION

The cutaneous or skin senses are far more important for the comfort and survival of the organism than is immediately apparent. Such a statement undoubtedly has more significance for the biologist than for the psychologist. Nevertheless, the psychologist cannot very well ignore the basic facts having to do with survival. Many subtle psychological reactions are necessarily premised upon this consideration, for the ever-present threat of injury and death are very pervasive. It must be supposed that the detection of conditions dangerous to the organism is one of the main functions of the senses.

HOW SKIN SENSES SERVE

The skin senses warn against dangers to the organism growing out of intense cold, heat, or the mutilation of tissue. They are of further use in examining the world or in making discoveries. The composite sense of touch has sometimes been referred to as the exploratory sense. It is used in the examination of objects to determine their size, shape, and other characteristics like temperature or smoothness and softness. If the individual is handicapped in the use of vision, touch may be of primary use in motility. It is possible to "feel our way" around.

There are three rather distinct types of responses that may follow stimulation of the senses of the skin. In the first place there are reflexes under the control of the autonomic nervous system. Then there are reflex movements that are mediated by the central nervous system. Finally, voluntary action may be taken after perception of the condition under which the sensation arose.

We shall try to illustrate how the senses may initiate these responses.

If the stimulus is cold, then the heating mechanism of the body is set to operating automatically. Quite a series of events may take place, such as contraction or dilation of the blood vessels, changes in blood pressure, and speeding up of metabolism. As heat builds up, the cooling mechanism may be triggered in order to keep the temperature of the body within a narrow range of change. The two senses, heat and cold, are of vital importance in helping the body maintain balance under variable temperature conditions.

Reflexive withdrawal is well illustrated by what happens if a hot stove is touched. This response is made by the striped or skeletal muscles of the arm. The subject does not have to stop long enough to think that the tissue will be damaged before the hand is jerked from the stove. Voluntary behavior involving decision may result from various sensory experiences. If the individual decides that he must have warmer clothes so that he may not freeze, or that he should put a salve on a burn, he executes appropriate responses by conscious behavior.

It seems to be futile to argue over which kind of response is more important. In some situations, man cannot survive very long without making all these responses. If there is failure of reflexes of the first type that involve activity of the autonomic nervous system and the vital processes of the body, survival may be brief. The skin senses are important in triggering some of these senses but these are scarcely the same kind of purposes served by such senses as vision and hearing. As essential to the organism as these last senses seem to be, they do not affect directly very much of the essential regulatory mechanism of the body. They do not feed in vital information to nerve centers and brain, second by second, that must be acted upon immediately.

In view of what has just been said, it seems strange that some of the skin senses are as limited in their functioning as occasionally found. For example, it is not unusual for an individual who is exposed to dry cold to have both the sense of cold and the sense of pain fail to give essential warning. Exposed parts of the body such as nose, ears, or extremities may become frostbitten without the individual becoming aware of much discomfort. Under this circumstance, the chances are that the heating system did respond, but the heat loss was too great for the circulatory system to keep pace and prevent tissue damage. Since cold reduces the speed of the neural impulse, this may account, in part, for the senses failing to give an alarm consistent with the danger that is present. Perhaps man has not lived long enough in cold dry regions for satisfactory biological adaptation to this kind of an environment!

LOSS OF SKIN SENSES IS RARE

In one way nature has done very well in regard to the skin senses. There is practically no such thing as an individual suffering total loss of all skin senses over a large part of the body. This fortunate condition is due to the widespread end organs and to the ingenious neural connecting system. The nerves for the several senses are gathered into bundles which then go to the spinal cord. The nerves enter the cord at various levels and then an interesting strategy is observed. Part of the nerve fibers cross to the opposite side immediately, others filter across before reaching the top of the cord, and still a very few others do not cross at all. An injury must be widespread and severe over a large portion of the surface to produce anything approaching total cutaneous sensory loss, and it is unlikely that cuts or lesions will interrupt all sensory nerves.

Regarded from the evolutionary viewpoint, the skin senses are much more primitive and less specialized than are vision and hearing. Serious loss in vision and hearing is common, and of course very conspicuous, for the individual is immediately handicapped in learning the things to be transmitted by cultural processes if these senses are defective. However, it is only in terms of meeting the obligations imposed by culture that seeing and hearing can be thought of as being more important than the skin senses.

EXPERIMENTS WITH SKIN SENSES

While there have been many experiments in which one or another of the skin senses has been used as the independent variable, the beginner does not ordinarily perform experiments upon them in the usual meaning of that word. A great deal of the factual material was originally obtained by exploration and examination of the skin senses that scarcely involved experiments. It does not seem that the objective in experimental psychology is lost if similar explorations of these senses are made and demonstrations used rather than formal experiments performed. By this procedure, essential factual material may be learned rapidly and the results presented in a convincing way. By this means necessary background information is obtained that is desirable before attempts are made to do experiments. Yet there is certainly no lack of possibilities for experimenting upon the skin senses. In some ways they have been rather seriously neglected in recent years. Much of the earlier work needs to be repeated now that better equipment can be utilized. There remain many practical and theoretical problems that might be attacked.

STRUCTURE OF THE SKIN

We have indicated that one useful criterion of a sense is an identifiable structure, an end organ. It is difficult to apply this criterion in the case of the skin senses. There is no lack of sufficient variety of sensory end organs in or just under the skin. The trouble arises mainly because of

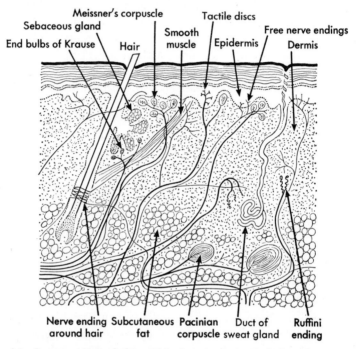

Fig. 4.1. Cross section of skin. This drawing is intended to be a composite picture of the various structures of skin and sense organs. It is not an exact reproduction of what is found in a single cross section. (From Gardner, E., after Woollard, Weddell and Harpman, *Fundamentals of Neurology.* Philadelphia: W. B. Saunders Co., 1947.)

difficulty in determining which end organ goes with which sense. While some investigators have been firm in their convictions about the type of end organ to associate with each sense, other authorities have been less confident. Careful study of Fig. 4.1, which shows a cross section of the skin, will be helpful in understanding many of the problems of identifying the end organs. It should be kept in mind that this is a drawing. No actual cross section might reveal all that is shown here unless it happened to be a fortunate selection.

There is great variability in the distribution of the end organs on different parts of the body. Marked differences are to be expected between the skin of the hairless portions of the body—palms of the hands and soles of the feet—and the rest of the body where hair follicles are found. The lips and mucous membranes present still a different picture.

The skin is usually described as having three layers. These are the epidermis, dermis, and subcutaneous tissue. The boundaries are not sharp between them and there is constant growth from underneath. The surface cells lose their nuclei and become hard and are eventually sloughed off. Unlike the snake that sheds the whole of the exterior skin at one time, man gradually sheds his in small particles.

The end organs of the skin are buried at various depths. The endings are close enough together so one small object may stimulate more than one sense. There is a fringe area round the point of greatest sensitivity for a given end organ. This helps to give the impression that there is overlapping of the senses. Again, the way reception takes place in the fringe areas may be an important reason for the apparent shifting of the location of the skin senses. The point that appears to be the exact center for a cold spot today may be a fringe area tomorrow.

TYPES OF END ORGANS

About half a dozen types of end organs in or under the skin have been identified and named. Some of these end organs have been named for the individuals who discovered or made a special study of them. We present the following list of end organs with the sense that is believed to belong with each:

1. *Krause End-bulbs.* These are thought to be the receptors for cold. According to Fulton (1) Von Frey is given credit for first establishing that these spherical-shaped end organs are the receptors for cold. Von Frey observed that the margin of the cornea was sensitive only to pain and cold. There are two types of receptors present at this location. The first is free nerve endings and these can be identified with pain. Thus, Von Frey concluded that the Krause end-bulbs were the receptors for cold. However, not all cold spots over the rest of the body seem to lie directly above a Krause cell. Therefore, it is not clear that this is the only end organ that is capable of sensing cold.

2. *Meisner Corpuscles.* These are found on the hairless portions of the body and are believed to be the mediators of the pressure sense. These have been called "touch" corpuscles.

3. *Ruffini Endings.* These lie rather deep in the skin and are believed to be the receptors for heat. They may be activated by external warm

objects, or by changes in skin temperature brought about by the dilation of the capillaries. The individual can often determine that he is blushing —presumably these end organs are stimulated giving a warm, glowing sensation.

4. *Pacinian Corpuscles.* These end organs are deeply embedded in the subcutaneous tissue and they are generally associated with deep pressure.

5. *Hair Receptors.* These constitute nerve endings that are wrapped around the roots of the hairs. The movement of the hair is the usual stimulus that arouses them. In a way, it might be said that they are like extensions of the pressure sense. They may be activated without the external object touching the skin directly. Upon actual contact with the skin, there is usually a masking of the sensation from these endings. The sensation of pressure from the other end organs in the skin readily becomes dominant.

6. *Free-branching Nerve Ends.* These are the most widespread of all the end organs if, indeed, they should be called end organs. They do not seem to be highly specialized in their function. As previously indicated, they certainly receive stimuli that provoke pain. They may have additional functions.

It may be difficult for the student to understand why there is so much uncertainty about which sense goes with a given end organ. In order to establish the relationship between the function and the structure there is need to observe, under a microscope, the end organ while it is intact and functioning. Even when this is done there is a very bothersome problem in trying to stimulate a given sense and not another that has a sense organ close by the first. The prick of a pin can be used to elicit pain—at the same time pressure is almost certain to be stimulated. In fairly recent experiments upon heat and pain Hardy and others (3) have used radiant heat. By this means they have improved the technique in isolating pain for study. Perhaps new methodology or techniques can be brought to bear that will, in a similar manner, lead to greater success in identifying the relationship between structure and function of all these senses.

DISTRIBUTION

The skin senses are distributed in what is called punctate fashion. This has already been implied by what has been said regarding their structure. Yet, most people seem to be in the habit of thinking of the skin sense organs as though they covered the entire surface of the skin instead of being closely packed. As a matter of fact, some of the senses are quite widely scattered on certain parts of the body. Only in the case of the free nerve endings is there a close approach to a solid sheath of receptors in or under the skin.

The punctate distribution is easily demonstrated in the case of end organs for cold. By taking a cold temperature cylinder and moving it along on the surface of the skin a point of high sensitivity is crossed and then there is only a dull impression of cold separating the next end organ and again heightened sensitivity. The same sort of demonstration can be carried out for heat, pressure, and pain. There have been a great number of experiments on pressure in which determination of the two-point threshold has been the objective. Much of the methodology that is spoken of as psychophysical was worked out in experiments of this kind. It is the usual practice to use an aesthesiometer in the experiments and two points are stimulated simultaneously. The variable is a systematically changed distance between the two points.

While the sense organs of the skin appear closely intermingled and overlapping in their coverage, it is doubtful if the surface point of greatest sensitivity ever coincides exactly for two different senses. If one sense organ were directly superimposed above the other this might result in reduced efficiency for the one underneath, and result in diffusion. The more deeply buried sense organ could not be expected in that case to be highly sensitive to surface stimuli. More will be said about the distribution of the skin senses when discussing each one separately.

PAIN

PAIN AS A SENSE

To modern investigators it seems strange that pain was not separated out as a definite sense by the very first people who engaged in the work of classifying the senses. Psychologically, pain is so completely undeniable that primitive man would have been forced to recognize it. However, pain was not one of the original five senses as given by Aristotle, who spoke of it as a "passion of the soul." It is only fair to say that Aristotle did speak of pain. He included it with the other senses as a part of touch. An aching muscle or joint must have been difficult to accept as a part of touch. It is possible that these were the pains actually referred to as "passion of the soul." Aristotle's partial neglect of pain was unfortunate, as subsequent writers for several centuries were greatly under his authority, and hence the inaccurate limitation of the number of senses to five.

CONTROL OF PAIN

Effort to overcome pain by means of various drugs, heat, cold, alcohol, hypnosis, and mystical incantations goes back earlier than any dependable history of man. In some parts of the world powerful drugs derived from plants were sometimes very effective in the temporary relief of pain. Lack of knowledge of the nature of the drugs used, the pain mechanism involved, and especially the lack of experimental methodology for evaluating their effects left much room for abuse. If we may judge from conditions found more recently among tribes having primitive cultures, dangerous trial and error practices were indulged in by the users. In many instances there would not have been enough knowledge for people to avoid disastrous consequences from continued use, or overuse of drugs. Often the choice was one of desperate extremes. Major operations were sometimes performed, such as amputations, without any sedative. This might have been a better choice from the viewpoint of survival than the use of a drug of unknown reactions when great quantities were required to induce anesthesia.

Slightly more than a century ago, with the discovery of ether and chloroform, dramatic success in the temporary suppression of consciousness of pain was achieved. Immediately before these discoveries there had been a marked increase in the use of hypnosis for this purpose. These two drugs quickly supplanted almost all use of hypnosis in surgery, for they held many advantages over hypnosis.

There has never been a lack of great motive to avoid pain. Man has been lacking in knowledge of a safe way to achieve this goal. Partial suppression of pain is now so widely practiced that even small children are aware of the use of aspirin and other mild sedatives. One might say that the sense of pain has a uniqueness all its own—man's efforts are directed toward avoidance of the use of this sense. Anyone who comes to enjoy pain, and does things to obtain this sensation, is considered to be abnormal. People go to tremendous effort and expense to block the neural transmission of the pain impulse, or to prevent events which bring about this sensation. Much of the work of the doctor and dentist is directed to helping the individual get over suffering pain or to avoid pain before it arises. The performance of surgery or the filling of decayed teeth may cause temporary pain, but the person involved hopes to have less total pain in the end.

Blocking or suppression of pain may be either in the brain or at lower levels in the nervous system. Spinal blocks have been used rather widely in recent years for certain kinds of operations. Cocaine and some other drugs are frequently applied around the nerve endings to help "kill pain."

It is difficult to determine how much drug addiction is due to the attempts of individuals to avoid pain. Among well-educated people the consequences of the use of drugs to avoid pain is well enough understood that this is probably of relatively little importance. However, here we speak of physical pain only. Many experts think that the basic reason for persons becoming drug addicts is that they seek to avoid "psychological pain."

DISTRIBUTION OF PAIN END ORGANS

There is probably a wider distribution of pain end organs than any other sense. While this may be true, yet it is found that there is great variability in the closeness of the end organs. There are some areas almost without pain sensitivity. Portions of the skin of the mouth have few pain endings, and it is said that the uvula is completely insensitive to pain over the lower half. There is a close relationship between the closeness of the end organs and the sensitivity for pain within a given region. The thickness of the skin that overlays the end organ affects the sensitivity. A small grain of sand placed inside the eyelid is extremely painful but if placed in the hand with the same pressure exerted upon it, there is not likely to be any pain.

Attempting to standardize the stimulus to elicit pain, Von Frey explored many parts of the body for purposes of mapping the areas for pain sensitivity. In 1924, Strughold (8) obtained the results given in the accompanying table. His studies include many additional areas of the body but these results will suffice to indicate the great range of variability found.

DISTRIBUTION OF PAIN SENSITIVITY

Skin Region	Pain "points"/cm^2
Back of knee	232
Neck	228
Shoulder blade	212
Back of hand	188
Eyelid	172
Ball of thumb	60
Sole of foot	48
Tip of nose	44

In contrast to the distribution of pressure end organs, there are fewer pain points toward the extremities of the limbs.

It seems clear that pains which have their origin in muscles, joints, or vital organs differ psychologically from skin sense pains. The latter has sometimes been described as "quick," "bright," or "burning" pain, while deep pains tend to be dull, nagging, or aching. The internal pains are likely to be more persistent, although this may be due to the continual presence of noxious substances which are not likely to be sharply localized. There are numerous pain points in the covering of the bones and sensation arising from these may give the impression of being rather definitely localized.

Referred pain is an interesting phenomenon. By this it is meant that the pain does not appear to originate at the point of infection or tissue mutilation. The victim is led to believe that the pain is arising from some other place. There is some regularity in the way pains would mislead the victim so that the skilled physician may still be able to locate the real difficulty although his patient describes the position of the pain as elsewhere.

ADEQUATE STIMULUS FOR PAIN

A great variety of stimuli, if intense enough, may cause pain sensations. This is true for pressure, heat, cold, some chemicals, or electric shock. The fact that intense application of various types of energy could produce pain may have been the main reason for the long delay in giving pain status as a separate sense. Some investigators in the past thought that pain arose with overstimulation.

PAIN ADAPTATION

We have previously indicated that all of the senses are adaptive. Pain, especially, may persist over a long period of time. Some writers have read biological purpose into the fact that pain is persistent while the pressure sense, for example, is quick to adapt and is thus ready to function again in exploratory activity. It is known that nerve tissue continues to carry impulses with little change in efficiency after repeated stimulation. There is little reason to suppose that a sensory nerve that carries an impulse from a pain end organ would differ greatly from the fiber that connects with one of the other skin senses. The search for an explanation for differential adaptation appears to narrow down to the sense organ or to the way the stimulus is applied. There is some ground for believing that the latter is responsible for most of the variation.

It is recognized that taste, smell, heat, cold, and pressure are senses that are readily adaptable. On the other hand, vision continues to be efficient in receiving light stimulation after hours of activity. However, if the stimulus is applied constantly on the retina, clearness in vision is lost within a minute or two. This is readily convincing if a person focuses upon a given point, does not shift the eyes and inhibits the eyewink. It appears that eye movement or the eyewink tend to wipe the visual field clean so the image is again vivid. It is suggested that there may be a similar constant change around the pain end organs which keeps renewing their sensitivity. There is sometimes awareness of how the pain comes and goes with the pulse, if a cut or a headache is the source of the pain, but of course this could be due to pressure changes around the injury. A painful infection might have accompanying tensions, congestion, and so forth about the affected area.

In trying to compare the senses concerning these functions the investigation is again confronted with difficulties growing out of any satisfactory measurement that applies equally well in the different sense modalities. It becomes necessary to introspect upon the sensation and submit a report. The fact remains that in usual life situations the several senses do not continue to activate conscious sensations over a prolonged period in the same way that pain does. But it would seem improbable that the basic adaptive process would be entirely different for the various senses.

EXPRESSION AND REPRESSION OF PAINFUL EXPERIENCE

As previously indicated, one of the ways of studying pain is by subjective report. Another way is to observe the expressions that accompany or follow the application of painful stimuli. For ages, people have been asking whether some individuals are more sensitive to pain than others; whether some suffer more acutely if the tissue is equally mutilated. A similar question has been raised in regard to the differential of pain among higher and lower animals. Much of the problem is a matter of definition of pain, a semantic problem that we may do well to avoid at this time. By definition we might insist that only such animals as we conceptualize as being endowed with consciousness can experience pain. Most of us have been hard pressed in answering the child's question about whether the fish "feels" pain when the hook penetrates its mouth. We can be reasonably sure that neural impulses are sent along to such small brain as the fish possesses. On the other hand, the range of awareness of the fish, if there is awareness at all, is presumed to be so limited as to make a very great difference between man and fish. Having failed in the past to give a very satisfactory answer to the child's question, we must still leave the reader to his own devices in trying to get off this hook!

It is known that one person will complain much more than another when the mutilated tissue appears to be equal. Again, it is certain that some chemicals or drugs decrease sensitivity while other chemicals may enhance pain. Strychnine, if taken in a small amount, does not usually kill the human subject, but may make him much more sensitive to pressures and irritants on the skin. Again, factors such as chemical balance, attention, muscular tensions, and attitude are suspected of giving rise to some variation within the same individual. It is not unreasonable to suppose that the same individual may be, day after day, in such condition that the pain threshold is lower than that for another person. However, there is little ground for thinking that the person who is most vociferous in expressing his suffering is necessarily the one experiencing the greatest amount of pain.

There is a good chance that tolerance for pain is premised upon both physiological and psychological factors as well as an interaction between these. Some of the famous fakirs, who made their living by doing punishing things to their bodies, may have had large areas of the body that were insentive to pain because of deficiencies in pain organs or nerves. It is also possible to learn to inhibit external expression of pain. The American Indian was famous for his ability to avoid any expression of pain. This was a personality trait encouraged within the culture. Their children were carefully taught that they must not show emotions as a result of experiencing pain. In other cultures, a different emphasis may be found, even an assumption made by psychotherapists that freedom in the expression of emotions leads to better mental health.

CONCLUDING REMARKS

There is good reason to consider pain as a separate and important sense. It serves the organism in initiating withdrawal activity, and serves to trigger body mechanisms associated with responses needed in emergencies. The individual does not have to learn the first withdrawal responses, and once learning has enabled him to anticipate pain, he is strongly motivated to avoid stimuli that are expected to be painful. A great deal of the story of psychology might be presented within the framework of trying to describe all of man's activity that has been motivated by his suffering or anticipation of pain. It seems natural and somewhat inevitable that man divides sensory experiences into the painful and the not-painful—unpleasant and pleasant. Directly or indirectly, the goal of most research upon pain is to learn about its nature in order to know how to prevent its occurrence, or to suppress awareness of pain without doing damage to the individual while he is being shielded from the conscious experience of pain. Thus the manner of handling pain is a fundamental issue in the life of each individual. The adequacy of the individual in managing himself under the reality of pain or the threat of painful experiences, psychological and physiological, becomes an important index to character and personality.

TEMPERATURE

INTRODUCTION

We shall discuss the senses for heat and cold under the general heading of temperature. This does not mean that they are considered to be one sense. It does mean that we think of these two senses as operating very much as a team in helping to regulate certain body mechanisms. It is only by efficient operation of these two senses that man can range so widely in the world and stay alive. He can explore in tropical lands, for he has a marvelous cooling system that will start operating by reflex when there is a threat that body temperature will rise too high; he can go to the arctic and his warming mechanism will help to protect him while there. Perhaps no other animal can do so well in such a variety of climatic conditions. Of course, it is recognized that most of man's advantage over other animals is due to conscious effort in obtaining clothing, building fires, and providing shelter for himself. It is also true that other animals are not likely to place such great demand for quick adaptation upon their bodies. Airplanes, especially, frequently transport people from one extreme to the other in a matter of a few minutes. Man's great motility stands in sharp contrast to that of most other animals. Even the migratory birds, while sometimes caught in sudden weather changes, do, nevertheless, tend to move along with temperature changes.

DISTRIBUTION OF END ORGANS

Probably the best evidence in support of two temperature senses instead of one is that there is a marked difference in the distribution of receptors for warmth and cold. Strughold and Proz (7) took great care in mapping out different areas of the body for the receptors for the two senses. They attempted to standardize their procedure so that time difference in contact, intensity variables, etc., would be minimized. Depending upon the part of the skin chosen, there might be ten or twenty times as many receptors for cold as for heat. A few spots, like the tips of the fingers, have almost an equal number of warm and cold spots. However, the total difference over the whole of the body seems to reveal a marked imbalance. In mapping, care must be exercised in keeping uniformity in pressure, time, and size of the contact points. There may be other important sources of error. Nevertheless, in spite of the unreliability of tests, there is undoubtedly a very great preponderance of cold receptors over warm ones, for investigators have repeatedly and uniformly found this general result in their observations.

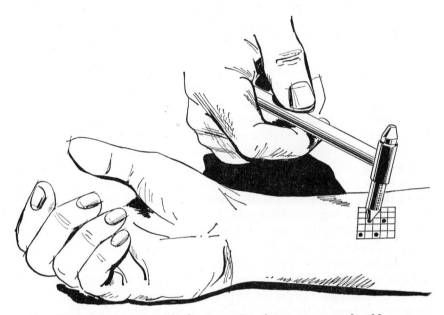

Fig. 4.2. A temperature cylinder is used to locate warm and cold spots on the arm. A grid is printed on the skin so the position of each end organ can be indicated. Some shift in the most sensitive point is usually found after a few hours or days. More refined controls are desirable for research purposes. (From Munn, Norman L., *Psychology*. Boston: Houghton Mifflin Co., 1956.)

ADAPTATION AND PHYSIOLOGICAL ZERO

We have already spoken of adaptation of sense organs in general but we need to mention this again with regard to a special kind of phenomenon known as *paradoxical cold* or *paradoxical warmth*. The first is relatively easy to demonstrate or to experience, but the latter is less conspicuous. If a cold spot is stimulated by a warm object the sensation will be cold if there is any sensation of temperature. This observation is, of course, in keeping with the specific nerve energy principle. Paradoxical heat can be obtained in a similar manner. When using both kinds of stimuli, the heat transfer phenomenon is important. There is naturally a spread of the heat by conduction and radiation from the warm object. According to the first law of thermodynamics, transfer always takes place from the warmer to the cooler object. Thus the direction of transfer, if a cold stimulus is used, is from the hand to the object; then reversed if the stimulus is warmer than the hand. The stimulus value of an object is greatly influenced by the material involved, depending upon its conductibility. Wood and metal of the same temperature will not give rise to the same sensory reaction.

It may well be that a study of paradoxical heat and cold and the search for stimuli of neutral temperature value led to some of the first experiments upon sensory adaptation. One of the oldest experiments in psychology is that in which it was demonstrated that a difference in sensation could be obtained from left and right hand when both were immersed in water of uniform temperature. This result is achieved by first placing one hand in cold water, the other in hot water and allowing them to stay a few minutes. Then both hands are plunged into the same pail of water. If the water is near the physiological zero point, roughly ninety degrees F., under average room temperature conditions, the sensations are likely to be cold from one hand and warm from the other. In any event, the sensations will differ for the two hands. Awareness of a difference will be observed regardless of the absolute temperature of the water so long as there is a substantial difference between the water in the first two pails. It is to be noted that physiological zero for the skin is not body temperature. Ordinarily neutral temperature level for the skin is found to be eight or ten degrees below body temperature. However, this will vary greatly with the surrounding temperature. Several factors such as adaptation, contrast effects, air temperature, and humidity will influence the zero point.

INSTABILITY OF RECEPTORS IN THE SKIN

A very bothersome problem in studying the skin senses is that points of greatest temperature sensitivity shift on successive trials. This is not very noticeable unless tests are placed several hours apart. It is probable that most of the instability reported in early studies can be explained upon the basis of inadequate controls and experimental errors. However, this does not seem to explain all of the mobility of the sensitive spots. It is possible that the results are due in part to adaptation, contrast effects, or even suggestion. Jenkins (5) has shown that repeated stimulation will yield variation in the subject's report as to whether the sensation is strong or weak. He used a scale of four, ranging from strong to neutral, and then added all the judgments together to obtain a composite score. As a result of his studies, he concluded that he would have to postulate a much larger number of end organs than had once been considered necessary. The number would appear to exceed all the encapsulated endings. As a result of his findings, Jenkins raised a question about the possible use of the free nerve endings in receiving stimulation from heat and cold. If these should turn out to be receptors of somewhat less efficiency than the Krause end-bulbs for cold and the Ruffini corpuscles for warmth, but still able to mediate these two stimuli, a number of difficulties might be clarified. However, some writers already complain that the free nerve endings have been somewhat of a catch-all, having to account for too much of the poorly understood phenomenon of skin reception. Yet, it is not unreasonable to suppose that these endings are capable of receiving a variety of stimuli. They stand somewhere between ordinary live and irritable cells that make up nonspecialized tissue, and the more specialized skin senses in their structural appearance. Perhaps they represent tissues that have not yet become highly specialized, but are on their way to this as the evolutionary process takes place.

CONTACT AND RADIANT HEAT

There has been an increase in the use of radiant heat in recent years as a means of studying problems having to do with comfort under variable temperature conditions. Hardy and Oppel (2) found different results when radiant and contact heat were used for stimulation. It appears that radiant heat must be spread over a larger area for the sensation of heat to rise prior to pain. The surface that would be exposed needed to be several hundred times larger than necessary for heat to be experienced when contact stimulation was used. Presumably this phenomenon is brought about in some way by the difference in heat transfer. Under either condition there would be necessarily simultaneous stimulation of the cold spots and this might give rise to new problems of figure-ground relationships. With radiant heat there is not a ready means of heat transfer away from the body except by radiation. Where contact is made with the skin by any material, conduction is added to radiation. Moving air across the skin may constitute a problem. Presumably, pressure sensations are an additional factor in the total situation when contact is used in studying temperature sensitivity. Thus several different problems arise in trying to compare the results from radiant and contact stimulation.

CURRENT PROBLEMS

Many of the theoretical and basic scientific problems continue with regard to these senses. Most of the remarks that follow are devoted to somewhat practical considerations. Not all of them have to do directly with man's sensory processes but are directed toward the manipulation of the environment which provides the stimuli for the temperature senses.

There is currently strong interest in research upon a variety of problems related to space heating and cooling. Part of this research stems from engineering problems and the new industry of air conditioning.

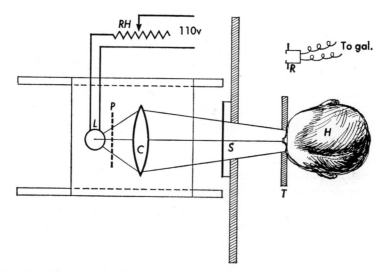

Fig. 4.3. The use of radiant heat as a means of studying pain threshold is possible by use of the apparatus as diagrammed above. L is a heat lamp and the rays are focused by the lens C through shutter S to the forehead of the subject. An automatic shutter at P allows for control of exposure time. Intensity is regulated with a rheostat RH. Calibration in terms of energy units applied is done by placing radiometer T in position of forehead. (From Wolf and Wolf, after Hardy, Wolff, and Goodell, *Pain*. Springfield, Illinois: Charles C Thomas, 1948.)

There has been some experimental work dealing with the relationship between physical heating or cooling of houses and the comfort of the people who live in them. It is entirely possible to have a heating or cooling system that keeps the air in a room at the theoretically correct temperature level and still have the individual report discomfort. The solution to this paradoxical problem seems to revolve around heat transfer and no doubt this includes differences in humidity. For good cooling, an attempt is made to obtain a condition where there is a rapid transfer of the heat away from the body; the opposite situation is sought for comfortable heating. The absolute temperature of the surrounding air is by no means the only factor in achieving this result. It is probable that one room might be comfortably warm at well below seventy degrees while another may not be comfortable until the temperature is at least seventy-five. This fact may have great economic significance when viewed from the total heating and cooling provisions for the people of a nation. Conceivably, equal physical and psychological comfort might be achieved although millions of tons of fuel were saved.

Military organizations are very much interested in research upon temperature and the numerous physiological and psychological factors involved. The anticipation of possible military action in either arctic or tropic regions, strange to the soldier, poses many problems. Not only are the hazards of survival great, due directly to the extreme temperatures, but there are also attitudes and psychological reactions to take into consideration. Fear is said to be an even greater hazard than cold to the man trying to survive in a strange, unfriendly, and barren wasteland of ice and snow. Pilots go into regions high above the earth where temperature is extremely cold and dry and the pressure is low; submarine crews go below the ocean's surface where pressure, humidity, and temperature may all rise to uncomfortable levels. More knowledge is needed to cope with many problems involved in this.

High industrial efficiency can only be expected under favorable temperature conditions. It has been demonstrated that individuals work more efficiently if the temperature is carefully matched with the type of work that is to be done. The sensory reaction and the muscular coordination must both be taken into consideration. Where gross bodily muscles are used, the optimum temperature is considerably lower than if the work involves a sedentary operation of the kind associated with white-collar jobs. In all cases, the attitude of the worker plays an important part. Unfortunately, subjective judgment or choice is not necessarily a safe guide to the best work condition in all cases.

Even those in an industry such as cosmetics must interest themselves in the heating and regulating mechanism of the body. Sweat glands are said to be the chief offenders in producing body odors. Some of the deodorants are said to destroy or reduce activity of the sweat glands. Whether this leads to a net gain in the reduction of body odors or merely a transfer of the odor to some area where the sweat glands continue to operate in a normal and healthy fashion is still a question. It does not seem likely that the destruction of a few sweat glands would lead to a serious loss of efficiency of the cooling mechanism, but it is conceivable that excessive destruction over large areas of the body might be a hazard to health.

PRESSURE

STIMULUS AND END ORGANS

There is little doubt that light pressure was more closely associated with the old label of "touch" than any of the other skin senses. There seems to be good grounds for separating pressure into two types. Not only are they different psychologically, but there are at least two fairly different types of end organs involved. It might be better to speak of three kinds of end organs—the Meisner corpuscles for light pressure on the hairless parts of the body; the nerve fibers around the hair follicles, which receive stimulation even when there has been no actual contact with the skin but a movement of the hair; and more deeply buried Pacinian corpuscles believed to receive deep pressure sensitivity. In addition to these the free nerve endings may be of use in receiving light pressure. There are small tactual discs near the surface that some think are the receptors for tickle and itching.

The time factor in the presentation of stimuli may be an important factor in the separation of light pressure and deep pressure. In the sequence of energy application the senses near the surface would be stimulated first and then the more deeply embedded endings would be reached later. Light pressure tends to be masked out as deep pressure emerges.

It can be seen that the discussion must deal with two basic variables, and each may have subfactors—one of the variables having to do with the presentation of stimuli and the other with structure of the end organs. As the stimuli are applied to most areas of the body first there may be contact with the hairs of the skin, then later contact is made with the surface, and finally pressure is exerted to activate the deep and encapsulated corpuscles. There appears to be continuity from the free nerve endings to surface discs and on to the well encapsulated larger corpuscles. To a considerable extent these various endings serve the same purpose. Some writers think we would do well just to describe one sense and then indicate how there is a range of both stimuli and endings involved. There is a degree of variation among the end organs of all senses. It is by no means certain that there is a necessity to include a greater variety of end organs under a sense such as pressure than is demanded for vision and hearing. In dealing with vision it is recognized that rods and cones have rather distinct functions and at the same time extend over a wide range of difference in structural appearance. Yet vision is still spoken of as being one sense although thousands of discriminations for color and form are possible and undoubtedly a wide range of cells of various structure are brought to function in each visual experience.

TWO-POINT DISCRIMINATION

Careful investigations of two-point threshold were among the earliest in psychology. Weber and Fechner both made many studies in which pressure was the sense modality used in formulating their concepts of psychophysical relationships. Their work was eventually formalized into what is known as the Weber-Fechner Law. The "just noticeable difference" (j.n.d.) of historical significance was perhaps more closely associated with lifting weights, but even in this there is a combination of muscle sense and pressure sensitivity involved in making the discriminations. It was soon learned that holding the weight constant and varying the size, either with the eyes opened or closed, gave rise to a difference in the estimates when comparing weights.

The general problem of discrimination is more appropriately dealt with when discussing perception. However, there are some interesting facts about perception in which pressure is of primary importance and a few remarks are not out of place here. Most people think of visual and auditory problems when considering experimental contributions upon perception. Actually all of the senses are used in receiving stimuli that are later used in perception. The usual identification of perception with vision is no doubt primarily due to the greater abundance of research upon that sense modality.

The perception of two points as distinct from one has been given much systematic study. One of the interesting findings to keep in mind is that the distance apart that two points must be in order for a discrimination to be made has a close relationship to the structural closeness of the end organs involved in pressure. Thus the number of nonstimulated end organs between the points that are being activated may help in the perception of the difference which is recognized as two points. Since there is a marked difference in the distribution of pressure end organs over the body, it follows, theoretically, that there should be a great difference in two-point threshold discriminating on various parts of the body. This is found to be the case. In general there seems to be better discrimination at the extremities and on the more exposed parts of the body. This stands in contrast to the receptors for pain, at least in regard to the receptors on hands and feet. Discrimination can be made between two points that are very close together on the lips, tongue, finger tips, and face. In order to discriminate two points on some portions of the body, say the back for instance, two stimuli may have to be spread almost an inch apart.

If a normal subject is blindfolded and the skin is touched, and then he is asked to touch the same spot again, he does it with great accuracy. This finding is, of course, consistent with what we would expect if local sign holds. An interesting and not very well understood fact is that error for this kind of reproduction is less than the necessary distance required in making two-point discriminations. It might be thought that correction could only be made when the subject could detect the not-right-stimulus which would mean stimulating a different end organ.

TEXTURE

It is mainly by use of the pressure end organs that the subject is able to appreciate texture. Man's ability to sense differences in roughness is remarkable. Actually, the use of modern measuring devices often fails to meet the standard of exactness in the discrimination that is possible by use of the pressure sensations. The tips of the fingers are far more sensitive to roughness of a surface than is vision. Rubbing the fingers over a board enables the individual to detect how well the material has been smoothed by sandpaper. Bumps that have height in terms of thousandths, maybe millionths, of an inch are readily felt. An ordinary hair laid on a piece of glass and covered by ten or twelve sheets of typing paper may still be felt if the fingers are rubbed over the paper above it. Here it is assumed that there is little change except a slight rise in the paper. Katz (6) made a systematic study of the individual's ability to discriminate between the smoothness and roughness of paper and found that subjects were remarkably accurate in identifying and ranking fourteen different roughnesses ranging from glazed paper to linen paper. This would suggest that several hundred discriminations might be made from the smoothest of material to moderately rough sandpaper.

ADAPTATION

Pressure adaptation is considered to be very rapid. It is certainly true that the individual soon loses awareness of the hundreds of pressure end organs that are activated by the clothing. Movement of the clothes or movement of the body may bring about awareness. There is some similarity in this process and the discrimination made by the finger tips in detecting smoothness. If the fingers are placed upon the object, with no rubbing, discrimination of smoothness is very poor. A garment lying at rest upon the skin may not be adequate to cross the threshold of awareness, but becomes an adequate stimulus with the slightest movement. Most people become quite unaware of their garments except when new, the fit is poor, or in some way attention is called to the clothing. These various cues and others apparently may be enhanced for the highly self-conscious adolescent. This serves as a reminder to investigators that social interactions and other very abstract factors may have an influence upon the sensory processes. Again, what would at first seem to be a simple psychological problem, that might be attacked and readily resolved, actually comes to involve not only the whole organism, but extends to cultural considerations.

VIBRATION AND MOVEMENT

It is not very well understood as to how vibration is sensed. Psychologically this is a very distinct sense and most investigators think that the sense organs that mediate it are the pressure end organs. High frequency of variable intensity is stimulating to the surface of the body. Detection of vibration of wide range is possible by the fingers. They are sensitive to the violin that is being played, to a running motor, or to the walls of a room that is filled with intense sound waves. Vibrating machinery, of previously unknown high frequency, has been developed in recent years and this has given rise to a need for experimental work to determine the effects of these machines upon the organism. Supersonic wind tunnels, jet motors, rockets, and so forth are a part of the environment of many people at present. It is known that sound waves may be produced at such rate and intensity that animals die of exposure to them. Small animals, such as mice, have been killed in laboratory experiments of this kind. It cannot be assumed that man's sensory equipment will give him adequate warning about these "artificial" stimuli. People usually report unpleasant sensation arising from exposure to high frequency instruments but again it may not necessarily be that they are aware of such exposure. Prolonged exposure to supersonic vibration may well have undesirable consequences to health. Individuals have complained of mounting nervousness under extended exposure but present knowledge about these matters is largely confined to casual comments and these may have little scientific worth.

The subject may get an impression of movement by use of the pressure end organs. This is possible by the transmission of an object over the surface of the skin within certain limits of speed. This sensation is aroused by moving the object so it stimulates one end organ after the other in time sequence. However, a similar impression may be obtained by discrete application of points to the skin and use of proper timing. If a row of pointed objects like small nails are brought into contact with the skin one after the other in rapid succession there will appear to be an object moving across the skin. This sensation will arise whether or not withdrawal of each nail is made after it was brought into contact with the skin. This phenomenon is an example of "apparent" movement. There has not actually been physical movement of a stimulus object across the skin but separate stimuli presented in time succession. A row of discrete light flashes also give the impression of movement as experienced by vision. It is well known that the ordinary movie is made by presenting a large number of similar, but slightly different, still pictures in rapid succession.

Continuity in time and space has broad significance in psychological problems because of the necessity of the individual to keep oriented in each if he is to adjust well to life situations. Effort goes on continuously to gain a better understanding of space-time phenomena, and especially to integrate the findings into sensory and perceptual processes. Progress has not been rapid. Man lives in an increasingly dynamic world of movement in which the stimuli that come to him are in motion, or the man himself is moving through space. Emulating living conditions in the laboratory relative to these conditions is often difficult. The scientist is called upon to make observations and interpretations about objects in rapid motion while he is stationary; about objects that are stationary while he is in motion, or in circumstances when both are in motion. There are differences, perhaps important ones, that arise in the sensory and perceptual progression as this applies to stationary conditions versus what takes place in the world of whirling movement that characterizes what is experienced by the pilot in the jet plane. The relatively near prospect of man being hurtled through space in a rocket will increase the need for knowledge of much that is now vague or confused. Perhaps too much of the burden of orientation has been placed upon vision. It is said that we must expect darkness in outer space with the sun resembling the light from a flashlight. There appears to be many possibilities for use of other than the sense of vision when many signals are to be mastered and responded to in manipulating the ever increasingly complex machinery that man creates.

APPARATUS

The aesthesiometer has been the time-honored apparatus for studying two-point threshold. This is a simple and easily used instrument. At the same time it must be granted that most aesthesiometers are crude instruments when viewed for research purposes. If manual application is used it is scarcely possible to exert the same pressure on each of the points. One point is likely to touch the surface before the other, giving rise to time differences as an unintended factor. It is important that better apparatus be developed that would enable the investigator to exercise more refined control over these variables.

In order to determine the amount of pressure that must be exerted to cross the threshold, von Frey (9) measured the energy that must be exerted upon the end of a hair 1.0 cm. long. It was found that 0.4 ergs was more than sufficient energy to cross the threshold of sensation. Wolf (10) used improved apparatus and was able to show that somewhat less

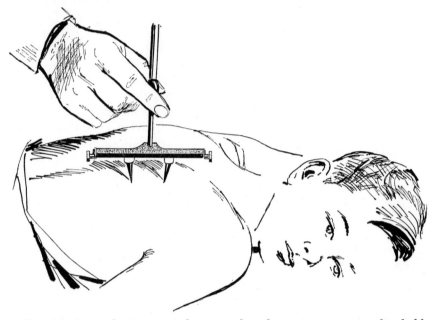

Fig. 4.4. An aesthesiometer is being used to determine two-point threshold. The points can be moved and calibration along the bar makes reading of distance easy. (From Munn, Norman L., *Psychology*. Boston: Houghton Mifflin Co., 1956.)

energy than this amount would activate light pressure sense organs. He found considerable variation for different spots on the body. In comparison with the necessary energy to activate the receptors on the retina of the eye for visual stimulation this is a great deal of energy. It has been estimated that it may require as much as 100 million times as much energy applied to the skin to produce sensation as that required to activate the retina.

CURRENT RESEARCH

Research upon the skin senses in terms of the number of published reports has failed to keep pace with that in many other areas of psychology. It seems that there are relatively few practical problems that present themselves and theoretical problems have usually been attacked by using some other sense modality. There has been a small amount of research directed to determine whether individuals might successfully use vibratory sensations as a substitute when hearing has been lost. It

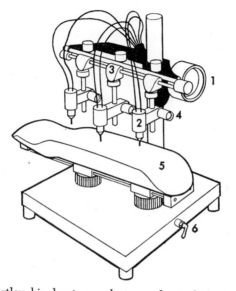

Fig. 4.5. A Bartley kinohapt—an electromechanical device for contracting the skin with tiny styli, with precise pressures and time relations. Item 1 is the knob for adjusting the whole carriage vertically; 2 is one of the solenoids activating a stylus; 3 is a solenoid carriage adjustable horizontally; 4 is a knob adjusting a single solenoid vertically; 5, the arm rest, adjustable in all directions; 6, the arm rest lock. (From Bartley, S. Howard, *Principles of Perception.* New York: Harper & Brothers, 1958.)

might be that apparatus could be invented that would amplify the effects of the vibrations and that patterns could be made comprehensible so that they would serve the purposes of language. Some deaf individuals are able to improve their comprehension of the spoken word by holding their fingers on the throat of the speaker. This is a rather conspicuous and awkward procedure. There has been little exploitation of the skin senses for constructing psychological tests and selecting personnel. Recently there has been some interest in the tactual type of responses in projective tests when using these tests as an approach to personality. The relationship remains speculative. In the use of ink blots or pictures in projective tests, if texture responses are given in excess, the subject is thought to be reflecting certain kinds of unfulfilled needs. It has been assumed that ungratified love and affection needs may find expression in this way. At first thought this is likely to strike the reader as farfetched and without foundation. Nevertheless, there is awareness that the infant is cuddled and stroked by the fond parents. Thus it may well be that affection, security, and the feeling of general comfort might get associated with tactual perceptions, and hence there may be a meaningful connection between simple sensory experiences and the subtle complexities of personality. Recent studies by Harlow (4) have shown that young monkeys respond much more favorably to a synthetic mother-figure in which the surface that may be touched by the young is soft. Visual impressions were not judged to produce a difference in the responsiveness of the young monkeys. It is so difficult to find fruitful approaches to personality that investigators eagerly follow any promising cue. Perceptual reactions have been greatly stressed in recent years as a promising approach to personality. Although this has usually meant visual perception, there might be great advantage found in extending studies of personality to include perceptions mediated by the more primitive senses. Considered relatively, it might be surmised that the cutaneous senses are far more important to the individual in establishing his contacts with his environment in infancy than is the case during later life. Furthermore, it is the assumption of most investigators that basic personality characteristics are largely determined during the very early years of life.

SUGGESTED READINGS

Postman, Leo, and Egan, James P. *Experimental Psychology*, pp. 33-50. New York: Harper, 1949.

Andrews, T. G. (ed.). *Methods of Psychology*. Jenkins: "Studying Skin Senses," pp. 250-267. New York: John Wiley, 1948.

Geldard, Frank A. *The Human Senses*, pp. 158-232. New York: John Wiley, 1953.

Stevens, S. S. *Handbook in Experimental Psychology*. Jenkins: "Somesthesis," pp. 1172-1190. New York: John Wiley, 1951.

Woodworth, Robert S., and Schlosberg, Harold. *Experimental Psychology*, pp. 267-296. New York: Henry Holt, 1954.

Boring, Edwin G. *Sensation and Perception in the History of Experimental Psychology*, pp. 463-522. New York: Appleton-Century-Crofts, 1942.

Best, Charles Herbert, and Taylor, Norman Burke. *The Physiological Basis of Medical Practice*, pp. 921-934. Williams and Wilkins, 1950.

REFERENCES

1. Fulton, John F. *A Textbook of Physiology*, p. 302. W. B. Saunders, 1949.
2. Hardy, J. D., and Oppel, T. W. "Studies in temperature sensation III. The sensitivity of the body to heat and spatial summation of the end organ responses," *J. Clin. Invest.*, 16 (1937), 533-540.
3. Hardy, J. D., Wolff, H. G., and Goodell, H. "Studies on pain. A new method for measuring pain threshold: observations on spatial summation of pain," *J. Clin. Invest.*, 19 (1940), 649-657.
4. Harlow, Harry F., "The nature of love," *The American Psychologist*, 13 (1958), 673-685.
5. Jenkins, William Leroy, p. 1175 in Stevens, S. S. (ed.). *Handbook in Experimental Psychology*. New York: John Wiley, 1951.
6. Katz, D. "Der Aufbau der Tastwelt," *Z. Psychol. Ergbd.*, 11 (1925).
7. Strughold, H., and Porz, R. "Die Dichte der Kaltpunkte auf der Haut des menschlichen Körpers," *Z. Biol.*, 91 (1931), 563-571.
8. Strughold, H. "Ueber die Dichte und Schwellen der Schmerzpunkte der Epidermis in den verschiedenen Körperregionen," *Z. Biol.*, 80 (1924), 367-380.
9. Von Frey. "Ueber die zur ebenmerklicher Erregung des Drucksinns erforderlichen Energiemenge," *Z. Biol.*, 18 (1932), 115-120.
10. Wolf, H. "Exakte Messungen über die zur Erregung des Drucksinnes erforderlichen Reizgrössen," Inaugural dissertation, Jena, 1937.

5 | # POSITION AND MOVEMENT SENSITIVITY

INTRODUCTION

The ability to make coordinated movements and to maintain postural balance is due primarily to the functioning of two senses. These senses have been given various names. Kinesthesis and equilibrium do about as well as any labels. Without these senses, the individual would be reduced to a remarkable state of helplessness. Walking would be a skill very likely impossible to master. The kinesthetic sense is essential in recognizing the position of the foot and how far and how fast it must be moved in taking each step when walking. In effect man falls forward each time he takes a step. The sense of equilibrium furnishes needed additional information about the falling. Through good coordination by use of the remarkable feed-back system of sensation, muscle movement, and new sensation, the foot is moved forward just enough to catch the body before it really falls. By repeating the process over and over, the individual completes one step after another as he walks.

There are many gaps in existing knowledge regarding these senses, but enough is known about them to attest to their importance. Other senses have some part in helping to coordinate movements and to make the individual aware of the positions of all parts of the body and thus help in maintaining posture. Vision, especially, is used when there is sufficient light to see. Individuals who have suffered some loss in the use of the kinesthetic sense may still do reasonably well in making gross bodily movements during the day. They become much more helpless in darkness. Of course, it is common to look at hands, feet, and other parts of the body when making fine coordinations and the individual is handicapped in darkness. Most of the language used in describing movement and position relates to visual experience.

By means of careful experimental studies and supporting clinical evidence, investigators have come to know something of the end organs that mediate the kinesthetic sense. The receptors for equilibrium, or the static sense, give no great difficulty. The vestibular and semicircular canals form part of the inner ear and have long been recognized as the seat for the sense used in maintaining postural balance. This sense is distinct from hearing, although the semicircular canals are referred to as part of the inner ear, which might suggest a closer relationship than actually exists. Not infrequently an accident or disease that produces deafness will also impair the sense of equilibrium.

The complete separation of kinesthesis from equilibrium insofar as they affect motor responses has not been possible. Taken together, they initiate and direct many reflexes as well as voluntary motor responses. It is therefore in part due to our inability to deal with each separately that has led us to take them up together in this chapter. Before turning to historical background regarding the way we have come by knowledge of these senses, we wish to present the following recent and striking quotation from Jenkins (9).

> Kinesthesis—the sense of position and movement—is probably the most important sensibility man possesses. Without kinesthesis a person could not maintain erect posture, let alone walk, talk, and engage in other skilled activities. Yet the existence of kinesthesis is not popularly appreciated, and the word has no counterpart in common language.

Unfortunately this remarkable statement is followed by scarcely more than two hundred words of discussion in a handbook of experimental psychology which emphasizes the basic processes and which extends in length to nearly fifteen hundred double-column pages of closely packed factual information. While asserting the importance of the subject, and then so quickly dismissing it, the implication is inescapable that the fund of dependable knowledge is very limited.

Why can so little be said about a sense that psychologists are in agreement is so important in the survival and well-being of the organism? How does the kinesthetic sense operate? Is it really a sense at all, or is it a combination of several senses? Where are the end organs located? What apparatus is used to measure or test this sense?

Our incomplete knowledge of kinesthesis still permits us to state a few facts and principles. However, unlike the problem in this book in regard to several of the other topics where we must try to select only a very few of the most important findings for presentation, here we must search diligently and discuss almost everything that has been contributed in order to give the student a reasonable orientation to the subject. The writer is in agreement with Jenkin's statements of the importance of kinesthesis and consequently the discussion has been expanded to the limits of discretion. We hope that we have not gone beyond the dictates of good judgment in trying to set forth the importance of this sense and to give useful information. In a very recent (1958) publication Bartley (1) has the following to say when introducing a discussion of perception and muscular mechanisms:

It might be said that we live in our muscles. This is true with certain qualifications. We largely gauge body positions and limb movements and the like through sensory mechanisms in the muscles and tendons. We likewise perform most of our self-appraisals of body state through the way the muscles and joints feel. We may feel weak, limp, inert, achy, "tired," etc., owing to some conditions of muscle tension, or to tone or possible changed internal state of muscle cells. A great deal is yet to be explored and found out about muscle conditions and metabolic conditions by study of the sensory mechanisms in muscle. In fact, it will not be until we succeed in delineating the relations between muscle condition, muscle activity, and muscle sense-organ activity that we will understand the organism-as-a-person very well. The door is wide open for this vast territory of inquiry.

KINESTHESIS

TYPES OF END ORGANS FOR KINESTHESIS

Apparently there are at least three types of sense organs of importance in giving rise to sensations that indicate position and movement of parts of the body. These include (a) muscle spindles, (b) tendon organs, and (c) joint end organs. The muscle spindles are scattered through the muscles and are spiral in shape. They give rise to sensation only when the muscle is stretched. On the other hand, the tendon end organs are spiral-like fibers fastened around the tendons near where the muscle is attached and they are stimulated by contraction of the muscle. The sense organs around the joints are of a more general type and are widely distributed through the body. They are usually known as Pacinian corpuscles and these were discussed when reviewing their part in sensing deep pressure. There are naturally changes in pressure about the joints with each movement. There is much variation in these corpuscles, with those around the joints and bones having at least very different shape from those typically found in the muscles.

The problem of locating and verifying these sense organs having to do with kinesthesis, or the muscle sense as it was usually referred to in earlier days, has been a long and tedious task. There are still those who question the adequacy of the three types of end organs in account for kinesthesis. It is no doubt true that under special conditions any or all of the skin senses furnish cues of movement or position that are of considerable importance. This is made easier if clothes are worn that will rub and bind as movements are made. As indicated previously, vision can and does play a role in motor coordination that must be taken into account.

HISTORICAL NOTES

In reviewing the historical background of kinesthesis, Boring (3) indicates that interest and some knowledge of this sense can be traced back as far as Descartes. While Aristotle is claimed by some to have implied such a sense, it is also true that the list of five senses as promulgated by him excludes kinesthesis along with several other senses.

In 1637, Descartes explained how a blind man becomes aware of distance by the use of two staves, one held in each hand so that he can "feel out distance." He also made note of the sensations coming from the eyes when the two eyes were focused upon an object. Berkeley, again, included muscle strain in the eyes as one of the means of perceiving distance as early as 1709.

Boring gives credit to Charles Bell in 1826 for establishing the muscle sense as the "sixth sense." However, end organs now believed to be identified with this sense were not discovered and associated with kinesthesis until sometime later. Others had argued for a sixth sense and it was usually referred to as the muscle sense. This idea was not generally accepted, with confidence, until Bell had made his discoveries about the sensory and motor tracts in the spinal cord. Bell went on to explain that there must be sensory nerves in the muscles which enabled a person to judge small differences in the weights of objects, perceive distance, size, form, hardness, and roughness. He assumed that this sense was often supplementing the skin senses in helping the individual to perceive most of these things. The following quotation from Boring (4) gives a short summary:

> Bell also described—and this instance was crucial to his argument—a case of a woman with an insensitive arm. She could hold her baby to her breast only so long as she looked at her arms; when she looked away, the arm would drop and the baby start to fall. The case was probably one of *tabes dorsalis*. In the later part of the century many such cases were cited as indication of the important function of kinesthesis in directing movement. For instance, in *locomotor ataxia* the patient cannot walk without

leaning forward slightly in order to use vision for correct placement of his feet. This is exactly the point Bell was making about the "nervous circle": precise movement depends not only on motor innervation which originates in the muscle—the brain can make the muscles move correctly only because it has from them a continuous report as to how the movement is getting on. Bell's argument about this nervous circle finds itself amply sustained today in our knowledge of proprioceptive reflexes and of the reflex circle, where kinesthesis is necessary for correct movement unless vision be substituted for the kinesthesis.

While it is obvious that Bell had available considerable information, aside from his own discoveries about sensory and motor neural equipment that could be used in his thinking, it does not appear that he connected the spindles found in the muscles directly with his conclusion about sensitivity. These had previously been described but as indicated in the next section most of the discoveries about the end organs had not yet been made.

SEARCH FOR END ORGANS

As early as 1741, Vater described the spindles in the muscles, but it seems his discovery was neglected and ultimately forgotten. About one hundred years later, in 1835, Pacini rediscovered these sense organs and described them more fully. Subsequent writers have referred to them as Pacinian corpuscles; on rare occasions Vater-Pacinian corpuscles. Pacini described the corpuscles as they appear along the stringy muscles of the fingers. Later it was shown that these are mainly distributed along the tendons and ligaments of the joints. While Helmholtz, Lewes, Muller, Wundt, and others were at one time or another interested in kinesthesis, the significance of this sense in coordination of movement and general neural integration was more fully expounded by the physiologist, Sherrington, around the beginning of the present century.

While it is difficult to be sure of the persons who should have credit for discovering muscle spindles, it is certain that Kuhne described them as early as 1863, but was very cautious about claiming that they were receptors for the muscle sense. In 1892, Ruffini identified the spindles as neural tissue. Shortly afterwards Sherrington was able to show definitely that they were sensory fibers for he cut the nerve roots at the spinal cord and produced insensitivity. Mathews (12) was able to isolate a single muscle fiber and spindle and found that stretching the muscle activated a neural current.

The tendon receptors were described by Rollett in 1876, according to Boring's account, and then they were more fully described by Golgi in 1880. These fibers have often been referred to as Golgi spindles since that time.

In order to simplify the discussion of sense organs associated with the kinesthetic sense, a recent designation of the endings has been A_1, A_2, B

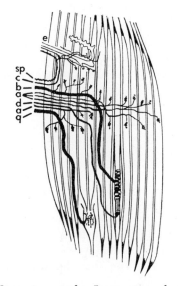

Fig. 5.1. Nerve endings in muscle. Innervation, both motor and sensory, of a group of muscle fibers. Motor neurones are those marked a. Three kinds of sensory fibers subserving kinesthesis are shown: Matthews' Type A_1 ("flower spray" endings) at the termination of fiber d; Type A_2 (annulospiral endings) at the end of b; and Type B (Golgi tendon organs) terminating g. The structure labeled e is a small blood vessel innervated by sensory fiber c (pain?) and a sympathetic plexus, sp. (From Fulton, J. F., *Physiology of the Nervous System*. New York: Oxford University Press, 1943.)

and C. Active muscular contraction or stretch stimulates A_1 while A_2 has been used to indicate the end organs associated with passive muscle stretch. Type B endings are those associated with muscular tension and the sensations that result from the activity of the end organs located around the tendons and muscle junctions. The threshold of stimulation for the B endings is said to be higher than that for the type A endings. The C type endings, found in muscles and tendons are perhaps the same as Pacinian corpuscles. Bartley (2) has made a comparison between the new classification and the older designation for these endings.

PSYCHOPHYSICAL METHODS AND KINESTHESIS

The period during which psychophysical methods were being worked out coincided rather closely with the discoveries of the end organs for the kinesthetic sense. However, the men busy with these methods were concerned with sensory qualities and they used introspection. This was not a useful approach to studying the structures involved in receiving stimuli. Psychophysical methods were more fully worked out by means of weight lifting than any other procedure. Apparently Fechner and others assumed that the muscle sense was what enabled the individual to make the discriminations. His attention was directed toward working out the mathematical relationship between stimulus and sensation and subsequent judgment. It was necessary to standardize the procedure in lifting the weight since accuracy was greatly improved by lifting the weight up and down before rendering a judgment in making comparisons.

EARLY MEASURES OF KINESTHESIS

In a number of systematically controlled experiments, Goldscheider undertook to measure sensitivity to movement in several joints. A general conclusion was that kinesthesis was more precise than cutaneous space perception. At a rate of .3 degrees per second, the threshold for passive movement of the shoulder, was found to be crossed by moving between .2 and .4 degrees. The shoulder was the most sensitive joint that he measured.

Laidlaw and Hamilton (10) in recent years confirmed most of Goldscheider's results. There was a tendency for the larger joints—shoulder and hip—to be more sensitive than the smaller joints such as ankle, wrist, and fingers, according to the results from both studies. This conclusion is one that may seem contrary to expectation. It might have been supposed that mass or weight of the part of the body involved would be important, but it would have seemed reasonable that the greatest accuracy would be found where the weight of the body unit involved was least—that a finger would be superior to the arm.

Goldscheider also determined that active voluntary movement resulted in greater sensitivity than passive movement. By this he meant that in passive movement the limb was moved by a force outside the individual's own energy. Goldscheider injected cocaine underneath the skin to anesthetize the skin senses and found that this had little effect upon the sensitivity of movement. On the other hand, by passing faradic current through the joints he produced a partial anesthetized condition which greatly reduced sensitivity to movement. Thus he collected evidence that the skin senses were of little importance in movement. By paralyzing the end organs in the joint he produced marked change in accuracy. Hence, a satisfactory association was established between kinesthesis and the mediating sense organs about the joints and tendons.

Woodworth was interested in the kinesthetic sense at an early date and published two papers reviewing the small amount of research up to the time and setting forth some of the problems and probable significance of this sense. The first of these publications was the thirteenth number of the *Psychological Monograph,* (15) which came out in 1899. The other paper was in French *Le Mouvement* and bears the publication date of 1903.

THE TERM PROPRIOCEPTORS

In a number of experiments in the late eighteen-hundreds, Sherrington gathered data upon sensory reception and organized them into a system for which he used the word proprioceptors to indicate the senses involved. Mott and Sherrington showed that sensory impulses from the muscles are necessary for accurate voluntary movement. Proof of this was obtained by sectioning the posterior roots of the spinal cord in animals. If the incoming nerve from the leg was cut, then the animal was unable to make much use of that leg. With the shift of psychology from introspection to overt behavior the word proprioceptors gained in popularity. For a time it appeared that the word kinesthesis might fall into complete disuse. It had been used first by Bastian nearly a century earlier. Still, psychologists cannot very well continue to ignore sensation, and especially perception, so the older term still persists and possibly has gained in usage during the more recent years. Since kinesthesis has been used in both introspection and behavior psychology, the connotations go beyond simple bodily movements. Thus, kinesthesis has proved to be a difficult term to discard. Perhaps investigators are unable to invent a better term to take its place.

KINESTHESIS AND ATTITUDES

Titchener proposed that conscious attitude be substituted for the long-debated problem of whether thoughts must be composed of images. He often resorted to description in terms of kinesthesis: "Introspective protocols on the thought processes were filled with sensory accounts of what the observer's body was doing." It became very popular to list attitudes and describe what bodily sensations were aroused by each. Titchener was a devoted student of Wundt, and Wundt had used the sensations arising in the muscles to postulate one of the dimensions in his theory of feelings. Earlier Wundt had accepted and used the older idea that convergence of the eyes furnished kinesthetic cues for depth perception. His tridimensional theory of feeling included (1) pleasantness-unpleasantness, (2) excitement-calm, (3) relaxation-tension. The third dimension was clearly associated with the sensations coming from muscles and joints while it might be wondered if excitement-calm could also reflect to some extent these sensations.

One of the most elaborate attempts to relate attitudes to sensations arising from the body was made by Clarke (7) and published in 1911. In this study, fifty-nine "conscious attitudes" were described in terms of their relationship to sensory modality. There was an attempt to localize the sensations for a number of attitudes. For example: pride was said to give rise to "slight tendency to straighten up my neck and smile." Irritation was associated with "sensation from frowning; visual image of frowning face; tendency to lower and shake the head; hot sensation in head and back." Disgust became "organic sensation throughout the body." According to Boring (5), who counted the mental processes described by Clarke, the sense modalities used had the following distribution: kinesthetic or organic 113; verbal (kinesthetic, auditory, visual) 21; visual 18; tactual 9; auditory 5.

While it is accepted today that attitudes are extremely important in personality, Clarke's approach has not been judged to be fruitful by most investigators if the number of experiments reported means anything. There has been almost no follow-up work that is closely similar. Wundt's theory of feelings has given way to other theories of emotions and little use is made of this kind of introspective analysis when trying to measure personality traits. Undoubtedly one of the greatest weaknesses of the method is that each individual uses his own set of descriptive adjectives and there is little way of quantifying the data. Comparisons between persons remain on a qualitative basis and there is no good way to standardize results, so communication remains a problem. In spite of these difficulties, there are some techniques that are closely reminiscent of these earlier attempts to understand attitudes and personality. Among these techniques are the expressive movement tests in which the subject is asked to perform some motor task such as drawing a person, house, or tree. The "draw a person" task was used by Goodenough as a means of estimating the intelligence of children and has later been elaborated upon by Machover and others as a useful item for diagnostic work. The Bender Gestalt Test requires the reproduction of several configurations made of dots, small circles, and lines. Claims are made that this is a useful test for identifying individuals with neurological damage—perceptual ability being reflected by the individual's inability to perceive the figures, while involvement of the motor nerves would make it difficult or impossible to execute the required hand movements to reproduce accurately the figures. Interpretations go beyond this and many implications about personality are set forth by some of the more enthusiastic users of this test.

The analysis of handwriting or other expressive movements such as Mira's "Myokinetic Test" have considerable usage. Handwriting is more seriously studied by a number of qualified psychologists in Europe than is true in this country. While graphology has tended to be pursued by charlatans in this country it remains a possibility that some interesting psychological phenomenon may be studied by analysis of handwriting. The written word becomes a recorded segment of behavior and reflects ability to coordinate the muscles and the way these follow neural commands that appear to be initiated by the dictates of the kinesthetic sense. Thus if we take seriously the statement of Bartley "that we live in our muscles," then important information might be squeezed from such samples of behavior. The question, of course, must be raised about how much useful information can be obtained; how dependable it is, and how much time and effort must be expended in order to render it scientifically useful.

Mira has developed a personality test that makes primary use of motor activity. In this test which is known as the "Myokinetic Test" the subject is required to perform a number of tasks such as drawing parallel or vertical lines while blindfolded. An experiment by Reid (13) is of interest in this connection. Reid was able to demonstrate that the subject tended to draw lines of unequal length when trying to reproduce them as the same, and when working blindfolded. There was a constant error that seemed to be related to the direction that the lines were drawn relative to the position of the subject's body. Reid spoke of his findings as being suggestive of an illusion that operated in producing lines in the horizontal and vertical planes.

Verification and standardization are difficult problems with tests of the kind just reviewed. The difficulties compare in some ways to those encountered by investigators who use introspection to study sensations and attitudes. Attempts to meet the exacting demands required of science in these approaches to personality have been only partially met at the best.

SEMICIRCULAR CANALS AND EQUILIBRIUM

What we have said so far about sensitivity for movement and position has been almost entirely confined to kinesthesis, largely excluding the so-called "static sense." The static sense, contrary to what the word might seem to imply, is not stimulated by remaining still but rather the sensations arise only with movement. Other labels than the static sense include "sense

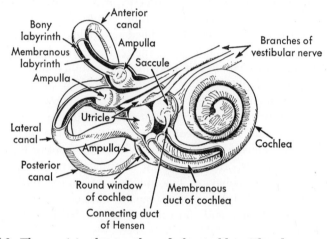

Fig. 5.2. The semicircular canals and the cochlea. The three semicircular canals stand at approximately right angles to each other. (From Geldard, Frank A., *The Human Senses*. New York: John Wiley & Sons, 1953.)

of equilibrium," "vestibular," "balance," or "labyrinthine" sense. The end organs for this sense are located in the semicircular canals.

An interesting peculiarity of equilibrium is that the sensations are not subjectively localized as coming from the area where the sense organs are located. Stimulation, or it might better be said, overstimulation of the semicircular canals gives rise to rather general bodily sensations of dizziness, nausea, and vague but unpleasant visceral sensations. The experience is too common to need much description. All people with normal semicircular canals, who have gone to sea, have experienced overstimulation and probably resulting seasickness. Rotation of the body, riding in airplanes, autos, roller coasters, merry-go-rounds, and elevators may stimulate this sense beyond the level of pleasantness. Most of the conscious sensations are undoubtedly secondary and it is not quite accurate to call them sensations from the static sense. The stimulation of the semicircular canals triggers reflexes to both the striped muscles of the body and to the smooth muscles of the vital organs. It appears to be the neural reporting back to the brain of the changes brought about among the involuntary reflexes and processes of the body, such as the stomach, that makes the individual aware of unpleasantness.

EARLY STUDIES

The physiologist, Purkinje, studied the sense of equilibrium and published several descriptive papers around 1820. His work was largely confined to describing what happened to the individual when rotated. He determined that if the person were rotated at a steady rate that the sensations of movement ceased, only to be newly aroused if the movement became slower again. By quick change in speed and slowing down to a stop, the individual would have a sensation of going in the opposite direction. This phenomenon of aftereffect is experienced for many of the senses but it is most commonly noticed by the layman in the after image of vision. Another illusion may be experienced when visually observing a moving object while the observer is not having clear sensations of bodily movement. Most people have sat in trains and found it difficult to decide whether they were moving or whether it was the train on the next track that was in motion. Consequently they may find themselves alternately attending to the sensations of vision, equilibrium, skin senses, and those of a kinesthetic nature in an attempt to determine the true situation.

During the same period that Purkinje was making his studies, Florens, another physiologist, began a series of studies of great importance to both physiologists and psychologists. He developed the technique of sectioning brain and nerves to determine what effect this would have upon motor responses. For the most part, he used animals in his studies, but was sometimes able to compare his results produced by ablation in animals with clinical cases of persons injured in accidents or who had to undergo surgery. A final check on these cases usually required an autopsy.

Relevant to the present topic was Florens' series of experiments in which he systematically sectioned the semicircular canals of pigeons and observed the effects upon their activities after the wound had healed. At first it was believed that the loss of hearing caused the incoordinations. It was these studies that helped to establish that equilibrium and hearing were different senses. Eventually it became clear that dizziness, vertigo, and these various symptoms were, for the most part, independent of hearing and that stimulation of the semicircular canals was the real source for the sensations. One case of prolonged dizziness was cured by the accidental removal of the semicircular canals which by some circumstance were attached to the external meatus, all of which was removed in the operation. This observation was a later one and made by Toynbee and it served to clinch the evidence indicating the crucial part played by the semicircular canals as the receptors for these sensations.

EQUILIBRIUM AND GEOGRAPHIC ORIENTATION

Many investigators have considered the sense of equilibrium important in geographic orientation of animals to the world. The maintenance of

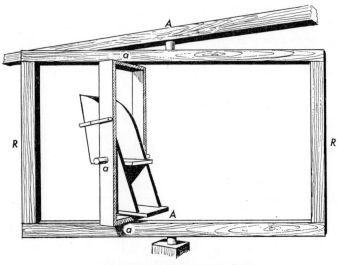

ROTATION FRAME: MACH (1873)

Fig. 5.3. The subject sat blindfolded in the chair, whose angle could be changed about the horizontal axis *a*. The back and sides protected him from air currents on rotation and he could also be boxed in with cardboard. He could then be rotated by hand about his own vertical axis, *aa* or about the eccentric axis, *AA*. In later models the radius *aA* could be altered and there were counterweights on the frame *RR* to balance the subjects. In the original instrument *RR* was 4 m. long, built of 4- x 4-in. timbers.

directional orientation to north and south, for example, which seems to be a part to the migrations of birds and the homing capabilities of various animals may be possible as a function of this sense. Clear evidence for this conclusion is lacking, but it may also be said that investigators are still lacking in a complete understanding of how animals and birds find their way back home over great distance.

The invention of the airplane has forced interest and research in the senses believed to be of use to the pilot in maintaining a sense of direction of movement in all dimensions of space and with regard to geographic orientation. Most people have heard of the Link Trainer, a device for whirling the individual in all planes to test the subject's ability to avoid sickness. Beyond avoiding incapacitating illness, the pilot needs to be able to orient as to direction and also to coordinate movements involving both gross bodily activities and the fine skills required in using his instruments. Between 1870 and 1875, Mach carried on an experiment that was a direct forerunner of the devices in current use for testing these abilities of pilots. He made a large rotating chair where the individual was seated. Then after being blindfolded the subject could be rotated at various speeds. The subject reports his sensations and estimates about movements and directions. A summary of the findings and opinions held by Mach are given by Boring (6):

> In 1873, Mach developed this idea by showing that rotation might be expected to create in any canal a pressure which varies in amount according to the component of the rotation that lies in the plane of that canal. Horizontal pressure would affect only the horizontal canals. Rotation about a transverse horizontal axis would affect all four vertical canals, since they lie at about a forty-five degree angle with the plane of rotation. But Mach went further. He pointed out that the principle of inertia would operate, not for rotation, but only for a change in speed of rotation, that is to say, for acceleration or deceleration. Thus his theory made angular acceleration the stimulus to the pressure pattern upon the nerve endings in the ampullae of the canals. This conception explains, of course, why rotation is perceived during the acceleration of starting rotation from rest, why there is adaptation (no perception of rotation) when speed is steadily maintained, while deceleration or stopping arouses the negative after-image (perception of reversed rotation).

Since the three canals lie in all three planes, movement in any direction is expected to give rise to movement of the fluid in at least one of the canals. The work of Mach did not prove that there was actual movement of the fluids in the semicircular canals, but he made the assumption that there would be such movement. His work was later supplemented by that of Breuer and Brown and ultimately the theory became known as the Mach-Breuer-Brown theory.

DISCOMFORT ASSOCIATED WITH VESTIBULAR AND CANAL DISTURBANCES

Various people had observed that vertigo was less common among deaf-mutes than normal individuals. In 1882, William James rigged a simple apparatus for comparing the sensations experienced by deaf-mutes and normals when spun around rapidly. He used two ropes and a seat, similar to the ordinary child's swing, and then twisted the ropes so the individual when seated in the swing would be whirled around rapidly as the ropes unwound. Of the two hundred students all but one reported dizziness; of 519 deaf-mutes, 199 were dizzy, 134 others somewhat dizzy, and 186 not dizzy at all. He and other investigators also noted that many individuals who have lost their sense of hearing have difficulty in keeping oriented in water.

It was during the first world war that the interpretation of the results about the vestibular sense became so important in trying to understand all the problems encountered by the pilot in flying the newly invented airplane. Not much that could be called new was discovered at that time, but there was an intense effort made to apply the knowledge obtained earlier. The rather sudden intensification of requirements to be met by many pilots produced great pressure for quick applications of all the basic knowledge then available. While instruments have made it almost unnecessary for the pilot to "fly by the seat of his pants" (referring to all the bodily sensations that come to him) there is still lively interest in research oriented toward problems in this field. The research is now more directed to coordination problems, influence upon efficiency of different motor skills, attitudinal changes associated with the visceral reactions, etc. Under certain conditions the pilot is not only instructed to substitute instrumental information for his sensations and impressions; he may even find it necessary to suppress his own sensations and perceptions, for these have been known to lead individuals into disaster.

At first it was the assumption that the individuals who never suffered vertigo, or airsickness, should make the best pilots. This is not necessarily true. To be sure, many of the experienced pilots were undisturbed by being rotated in the various training devices. The important point eventually became clear. It was the side effects that were eliminated by experience. Most individuals can be conditioned so that they are no longer upset by the reflexes set to functioning by stimulating the semicircular canals. The desirable situation is for the individual to have his senses intact but to learn to ignore the sensations that may lead to dizziness and convulsive responses. It is the learning or, better, the unlearning of the responses, so deplored by the person who habitually becomes seasick, that is important in differentiating the individuals. Native equipment might make this learning harder for one person than another.

KINESTHESIS AND LEARNING

While it is often important to suppress certain reactions when adjusting to the sense of equilibrium, kinesthesis is ordinarily to be used in a much more positive way. There was an extreme emphasis upon motor behavior with the rise of the behavioristic school in psychology. The experiments of Watson (14) and Lashley (11) were fairly typical of these experiments. Many experiments were attempted in which there was a study of the relative importance of the several senses in the learning process. Isolation of the kinesthetic sense is naturally difficult because of the widespread end organs. It is not much of a problem to cover the eyes or plug the ears, but the elimination of kinesthesis altogether is practically impossible. Some learning experiments were made with the use of *curare,* a drug capable of paralyzing the muscles, but which leaves the sensory equipment intact and functioning. The neural repetitive circle is thus broken for no sensations of movement can arise since no movements are made. The total situation is so altered, however, that there remains a question of whether this is a satisfactory way to control the effect of the kinesthetic sense in learning. There can be no question that failure to make the completed motor response, whatever the explanation may be, has a marked detrimental effect upon learning. On the other hand, rats still learn to run a maze quite well after an attempt has been made to immobilize each or all other senses including vision, hearing, smell, and the skin senses.

The relationship between kinesthesis and the learning of artistic and social skills is very close. Fantastic demands are made upon the feedback system involving the sense end organs, nerves, muscles, and again, the reflex circling of this process when the individual is trying to get all the fine shadings of tone out of the violin or his vocal organs. It is due in part to the fine motor coordinations and adjustments that the expert is distinguished from the amateur. The artist who is trying to make fine differences in lines and color to give the best meaning to his picture is also making demands upon this same feedback system. In the use of these bodily mechanisms and sensory appreciations, the fields of sports and fine arts have much in common.

KINESTHESIS AND SOCIAL SKILLS

The social significance of good motor coordination associated with kinesthetic sensitivity must surely be important in the development of personality. The physical and social awkwardness of the adolescent is at least partially a matter of the lack of good balance and coordinated muscular movements. The individual who spills his cup of tea or stumbles over the chair, or again steps on the toes of his dancing partner can scarcely be expected to show social poise and to respond with an air of confidence in the social situation. There is a considerable capacity for most individuals to improve their motor skills by practice. By practicing skills the adolescent may take an important and practical approach to the development of the more positive personality traits. Incidentally, such a procedure is generally neglected by the backward or withdrawn individual who might still insist that he is interested in improving his personality. He may not know a practical way to go about achieving the desired results.

APPARATUS AND TESTS

Occasion was taken to mention the measurement of kinesthesis made by Goldscheider, but he did not use better than a very simple procedure for measuring the distance that a limb might be moved, either by the individual, or by the experimenter rotating the passive limb through a short arc. This involved a ruler for measuring distance and a platform upon which the arm or leg might be rested and swung around. Mach built the rotating chair and the idea was later to be used in constructing rather complex power-controlled seating devices like the Link Trainer in which the individual could be whirled around in various directions under regulated speeds and directions. These devices have more application to equilibrium than kinesthesis.

It is perhaps not far from the truth to say that there is no satisfactory apparatus or test for measuring the sensitivity for making fine discriminations in movement. Thus the investigator is handicapped in comparing the results from one person to those obtained from another. There is no widely recognized test of kinesthesis on the market. This is in sharp contrast to the variety and accuracy of testing instruments and devices for obtaining comparative data for studying the senses of vision and hearing. A similar dearth of instruments for studying the sense of equilibrium exists. It may be expecting too much to hope that the experimenter can have comparable devices for use in kinesthesis as those in use for vision and hearing. For example, devices like microscopes, telescopes, or ordinary eye glasses are used as aids to vision. A variety of hearing aids enable the individual to hear better, and highly sensitive electronic devices enable man to extend the range of hearing enormously. While the problems are different in the various senses, it does seem that measuring devices for kinesthesis and equilibrium would enable workers to do a good job of picking out those individuals having superior and inferior senses. There may be no way of using corrective devices where these senses are poor in the individual, although crustaceous animals have been able to adapt a technique of interest. They sometimes attach pebbles to themselves when balance has been upset by the loss of a pincer! Again, there is some reason to believe that careful training in the use of kinesthesis and equilibrium may lead to greater modification in the use of these senses than has been the case for eyes and ears. In reality relatively little is known about the limitations and potentialities of these senses for receiving training. Many suppositions are made about improvement in motor skills in athletes, artists, musicians, and industrial workers while not much is known about the part played by the senses most immediately involved in these skills. Important research is scarcely possible until better techniques and tools are invented.

SUGGESTED READINGS

Geldard, Frank A. *The Human Senses,* pp. 249-269. New York: John Wiley, 1953.

Bartley, S. Howard. *Principles of Perception.* "Perceptions Based on Muscular Mechanisms," pp. 314-324; "Vestibular Sense," pp. 325-336. New York: Harper, 1958.

Boring, Edwin G. *Sensation and Perception in the History of Experimental Psychology,* pp. 521-573. New York: Appleton-Century-Crofts, 1950.

Best, Charles Herbert, and Taylor, Norman Burke. *The Physiological Basis of Medical Practice,* pp. 921-934, 948-973. Baltimore: Williams and Wilkins, 1950.

REFERENCES

1. Bartley, S. Howard. *Principles of Perception,* p. 314. New York: Harper, 1958.
2. *Ibid.,* p. 315.
3. Boring, Edwin G. *Sensation and Perception in the History of Experimental Psychology,* pp. 524-535. New York: Appleton-Century-Crofts, 1942.
4. *Ibid.,* p. 527.
5. *Ibid.,* p. 533.
6. *Ibid.,* p. 539.
7. Clarke, H. M. "Conscious Attitudes," *Amer. J. Psychol.,* 22 (1911), 214-249.
8. Goldscheider, A. *Physiologie des Muskelsinnes: Gesammelte Abhandlungen, II.* 1898.
9. Jenkins, William Leroy, p. 1185 in Stevens, S. S. (ed.). *Handbook of Experimental Psychology.* New York: John Wiley, 1951.

10. Laidlaw, R. W., and Hamilton, M. A. "A study of thresholds in perception of movement among central subjects," *Amer. J. Psychol.*, 49 (1937), 469-475.

11. Lashley, K. S., and Bell, J. "Spinal conduction and kinesthetic sensitivity in the maze habit," *J. Comp. Psychol.*, 9 (1929), 71-105.

12. Matthews, B. N. C. "The response of a single end organ," *J. Physiol.*, 71 (1931), 64-110.

13. Reid, R. L. "An illusion of movement complementary to the horizontal-vertical illusion," *Quart. J. Psychol.*, 6 (1954), 107-111.

14. Watson, J. B. "Kinesthesis and organic sensations: their role in reactions of the white rat," *Psychol. Monogr.*, 33 (1907).

15. Woodworth, R. S. "The accuracy of voluntary movement," *Psychol. Monogr.*, 13 (1899).

16. Woodworth, R. S. "Le Mouvement," *Doir*, Paris (1903).

6 | CONTRIBUTIONS AND EXPERIMENTS ON HEARING

INTRODUCTION

This chapter is designed to help the student orient himself to the broad scientific problems involved in hearing; to further his knowledge of facts and principles about hearing; and, especially, to direct his attention to the auditory problems most relevant to the work of psychologists. As will be the case for vision, it is easy for the student to become confounded by the tremendous amount of scientific knowledge centering around audition. Care must be exercised in selecting and organizing the material most important to psychologists. It is necessary to by-pass many, if not most, of the findings and problems which physicists, physiologists, and musicians find intriguing. Possibly the literature dealing with audition is somewhat less voluminous than that for vision, but all the appropriate and relevant material cannot be sampled under the time and space limitations that must be exercised here.

In many ways, hearing is the sense of greatest vigilance. It is used defensively. Eyes and ears are thought of as distance receptors, but, under many natural conditions, vision is greatly limited. At night, vision is reduced; the eyes are closed during sleep. The ears continue to function twenty-four hours a day. Recordings indicate that auditory neural impulses are set up while the individual remains asleep, and, perhaps more than any other sense, hearing acts to bring the person out of sleep. Consequently, man is less able to withdraw from a world filled with sounds than one filled with light. This follows, not only from the fact that he has nothing comparable to eyelids to close the ears, but also because noises continue after sundown when the chief source of visual stimulation is removed. Many people find it difficult to stay awake for any length of time when put in a soundproof room. Sleepiness soon develops, although it may not be time to retire. Furthermore, extended time in a soundproof room leads to much more than the normal amount of sleep.

It is not the intention of the writer to de-emphasize the highly technical problems in hearing, such as those studied by the physicist whose knowledge of the properties of sound is fundamental to his science. Problems of aesthetics in hearing are left as the primary concern of the musician. The psychologist is mainly interested in the part contributed by hearing to the individual in his struggle to survive; in the way this sense is used to learn about the world; in how it helps the individual to make personal and social adjustments. In order to understand these functions, it becomes necessary to have some background information about the nature of sound as a stimulus, and to know something of the anatomy involved in hearing. However, the main business of this chapter lies in the study of how this sense serves in receiving stimuli that lead to perception and finally to behavior. In a way, all our senses are in competition. Our attention and awareness shifts from sensations breaking through to consciousness via the nervous system, now by this sense modality, and now by that. There will be more said here about masking effects in dealing with hearing than for any other sense. To some extent, phenomena similar to masking can be generalized with regard to all the senses. Intense stimuli applied to any sense, may, for a time, serve to mask all others.

RELEVANT PROBLEMS

In psychology, it is important to find answers to such questions about hearing as the following: How can the individual's hearing be measured? Is there a relationship between hearing disability and a child's achievement in school? How important is hearing in the performance of various jobs? Do individuals who are handicapped in hearing tend to develop more personality problems than others? If so, would knowledge enable the sufferer to avoid such pitfalls? It is assumed that verbal language is the principal means of daily communication. What are the ramifications of a hearing loss? What effect does a slight hearing defect have upon general linguistic ability? Are such limitations confined to speaking and listening ability, or do they extend, as well, to reading and writing?

An answer to how the eyes and ears are to be used by the school child might structure rather completely the methods of teaching, and even help to determine the content of what is to be taught. Visual defects, if such disabilities as color blindness are ruled out, are more likely to be detected in a child than are hearing difficulties. This may be due, in part, to obvious behavior, such as stumbling over objects that are not seen, or inability to catch a ball. However, there is also a much greater social awareness of defective eyes than of defective ears. In addition, it has been found that the eyes are much more likely to cause pain if they are not functioning well. Rarely, except during acute infection, do the ears cause pain. It is known that many children continue in a classroom unaware that they do not hear the teacher as well as the other children. Such a child may miss important information and be puzzled about his failure to recall when examination questions are asked. The child may have always been hard of hearing, and, therefore, have no standard of judgment, except that based upon his own defective hearing.

It is not the immediate business of psychologists to become involved in many of the present-day scientific and engineering problems having to do with the application of stimulus material for vision and hearing. However, they cannot completely avoid the impact of much of this work in modifying the psychological environment. A large part of the environment of many people has been created by radio, television, and other modern inventions. Thus it is important for every citizen to gain knowledge of these things. It is also true that those who specialize in psychology and come to know a great deal about sensory and perceptual processes often enter the fields of telephone, motion picture, phonograph, radio, or television research. This is not so strange as it may seem at first. There is usually a large body of common knowledge that must be mastered by any person who would become an expert in any one of several branches of related sciences. In the auditory fields there has been, among other things, a great deal of manipulation of the stimuli, having commercial value, to be sure, that is to be presented to the sense organs. In television, both sound and light energy must be converted and transmitted and then reconverted for consumption by the individual on the receiving end. It is too obvious to need mentioning that a long progression of discoveries were made before these present-day remarkable uses and adaptations in sound and light were possible. The end objective remains though—to enable the distant receptors of man to become still more distant receptors. Psychologists may find it necessary to resist going too far afield in studying all of these technical matters. However, mankind is being called upon to adjust to a rapidly changing world of sights and sounds, and the individual does not waste his time if he tries to orient to these influences as well as he can.

HISTORICAL ANTECEDENTS

In the historical beginnings of scientific work on hearing it is no more surprising to find the names of famous physicists, than it is in the case of vision. The pattern is the same—important first successes usually had to do with the nature of the stimulus. And, if the details concerning discoveries and individuals were gone into, many of the same names would be repeated: Galileo, Newton, Helmholtz. Here and there, names of recent people, such as Edison or De Forest, would be added. However, in the case of hearing, another list of no small importance would be found. These are the musicians who studied sound over many years, not strictly for scientific purposes, but in order that more pleasing sounds might be made. They were forced to learn about sound so that musical instruments could be made which would produce the desired effects. It would appear that there has often been only a narrow gap between artistic work in music and the scientific interests of mathematicians and physicists. Each has dealt with sound in his own way.

The writer can do no more than mention the names of a few musicians who have contributed to the science of sound. Some of the names are familiar—Pythagoras, Bach, Shore, and Koenig. Koenig made a great variety of musical instruments and improved others. John Shore, a musician who worked in the early years of the nineteenth century, invented the tuning fork. This became a basic instrument for the physicists and served many useful purposes in the study of the nature of vibrations. To some extent, modern inventions have displaced it, for now there are electronic and other more refined instruments for research.

PHYSICAL NATURE OF SOUND

The ear responds to vibrations or waves set up in the air. Transmission is by the compression of air. A vibrating body, such as a violin string, produces alternate phases of rarefaction and condensation in the air. When these waves, which are the stimuli to hearing, strike the eardrum, the various mechanisms of the ear are set into motion and, eventually, a neural impulse is started on its way to the brain.

Air is not the only means of transmitting sound waves, but it is the usual media for activating the ears. Sound waves are carried through water at about twice the speed of air and in various metals at roughly four times the air speed. Some of these materials are excellent conductors of sound, while some are poor. That sound is not transmitted through a vacuum was one of the early wonders of physics. A sound, such as the ticking of a clock, gradually weakens and disappears as air is pumped from a bell jar.

Sound waves are usually illustrated by a sine curve. While this is a satisfactory way to represent sound waves, it may be easier for the person without a knowledge of physics to understand the transmission by using an analogy of waves produced upon smooth water when a pebble is dropped. Concentric waves move in all directions in rapid succession. Since sound waves travel in all three dimensions, this is difficult to illustrate by a drawing.

Speed of Sound

If there are no obstructions, sound waves radiate in all directions with approximately equal speed. The earth, of course, becomes a barrier. If the sound waves strike a distant barrier, such as a mountain, they will bounce back and sometimes produce an audible echo. In fact, the echo was one of the first ways of measuring the speed of sound. By careful timing between the onset of the sound and its return, and measuring the distance to the reflecting object, Mersenne determined the speed of sound at 1038 feet per second. This was done before Newton arrived at the slower rate of 968 feet per second by theoretical calculations. Over a period of more than a hundred years prior to 1740, different investigators came up with figures which varied by more than several hundred feet per second. Most of the variability was due to the limitations of the techniques available. Finally, after more refined measuring devices were invented, it was established that the speed of sound changes with temperature, moisture, and density or pressure of the air. Now the speed is not likely to be stated except in round numbers, unless these qualifications are added. (The speed of sound in dry air at 20 C. at sea level is about 1128 feet per second.)

The facts about the speed of sound in air become of vital importance in a world where man has moved faster than sound, or where an enemy may attack and pass before the sound of his approach reaches the ears. It is said to be a weird experience to have bombs drop nearby before the plane that carried the bomb has been heard passing overhead. However, the significance of such things is not limited to war activities, for more and more people must learn to live in a world where traditional sequences and relationships are violated. In general, the adaptive processes of the organism are slow, and there is likely to be a great lag before any modification of the organism comes to man's rescue.

Wave Frequency

The frequency of waves generated per second determines the pitch of a sound. Since sound waves travel at the same speed through a given medium and under constant conditions, there is a direct relationship between wave length and frequency. The wave length of high frequencies will be short. There are some qualifications to this statement, but they are of little practical concern here.

The normal human ear responds to sounds between 20 and 20,000 vibrations, or cycles, per second. There is some variation between persons of more or less normal hearing, especially at the upper limit. However, little practical use is made of the upper three-fourths of this range band. Most human communication can be carried on by use of frequencies between 100 and 1000 vibrations per second. The range of the human voice and of most musical instruments extend over only a few hundred cycles; however, the richness of overtones would be largely lost without the additional higher frequencies. Thus, there might be aesthetic loss even though little difference occurred with regard to accuracy in communication.

Galileo was able to measure the length of the sound wave and relate it to pitch by scraping a brass plate with an iron chisel. High pitch was produced when the scratch marks were accompanied by numerous parallel streaks as a result of the chisel's work. Pythagoras learned about the relationship of longer strings to lower pitch. Finally, the relationships between length of string, size of string, and the amount of tension upon the string could all be written into a mathematical formula. When this became possible, investigators could work with greater speed and skill, for they could readily make changes to produce exactly the sounds they chose to study. Much of the research upon these problems was done by Mersenne who built upon the discoveries made by Galileo.

Amplitude

Amplitude of a sound wave determines the loudness or intensity. There is greater displacement of air molecules when the amplitude is great and, of course, greater energy has been involved. The relationship between amplitude and energy is not a simple one, for frequency is a factor as well. Sounds of high frequencies possess greater energy than those of low frequency if the amplitude remains the same. It should be kept in mind that there is a difference between amplitude, or the energy level involved, and loudness. The former term has to do with the physical properties of energy while sound is a psychological term referring to the reception by a listener. If one shifts backward and forward from physical characteristics of the energy to the psychological factors involved, one must be cautious in the use of terminology in this discussion, or else much confusion can arise.

Two tones of unequal cycles per second may be matched as equal in pitch by the subject if the experimenter carefully manipulates the intensity levels. This might be thought of as an auditory illusion. Stimuli that are known to be different in physical characteristics are sometimes judged to be the same by the subjects. This is more or less parallel to the misinterpretation in such visual stimuli as the Muller-Lyer illusion.

ANATOMY OF THE EAR

An effective way to become acquainted with the structure of the ear is to make use of a cross-section figure of the ear while attempting to trace the successive events that take place from external source of sound until an auditory perception has emerged.

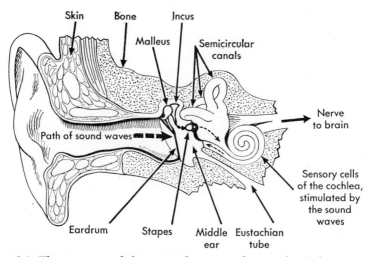

Fig. 6.1. The anatomy of the ear and semicircular canals. (After Davis, H., *Hearing and Deafness: A Guide for Laymen.* New York: McGraw-Hill, 1947.)

A sound wave reaches the external ear and travels along the opening to the eardrum. The wave in the air then sets the eardrum, which is a thin, tightly stretched membrane, to vibrating. This, in turn. mechanically moves the three bones of the middle ear. The handle of the hammer (malleus) is attached to the eardrum and the other end of it makes contact with the anvil (incus). The stirrup (stapes) extends from the anvil to the oval window. The oval window is the partition between the middle ear and the inner ear. Here, again, there is a flexible membrane stretched across a small opening in the bony structure. Mechanical vibratory pressure continues on to the fluid found in the coil-like structure of the cochlea. In the inner ear, many intricate parts are to be found. Stated briefly: embedded in the basilar membrane that extends along a bony shelf which helps divide the cochlea into two long channels are small hair-like fibers which float in the fluid. Movement of the fluid in the

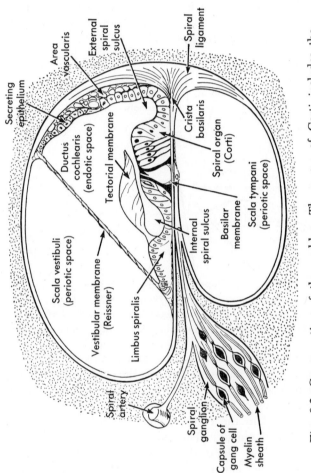

Fig. 6.2. Cross section of the cochlea. The organ of Corti includes the wedged-shaped central portion. The receptors for hearing are the cells within this area. (From Rasmussen, A. T., *Outline of Neuro-Anatomy*. Dubuque, Iowa: William C. Brown Co., 1943.)

cochlea moves the hair-like particles, and this activates the nerve-ending cells about their roots. Then the small nerve fibers that originate with the nerve-ending cells are gathered up into the auditory nerve. This nerve

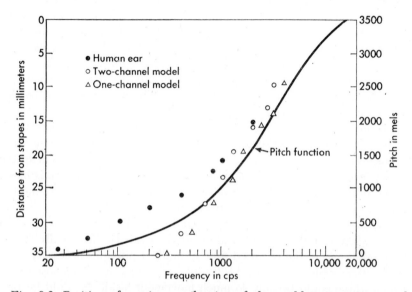

Fig. 6.3. Position of maximum vibration of the cochlear partition, as observed in ears and in models (Bekesy, 1942). The curve relating pitch frequency (Stevens and Volkmann, 1940) is drawn for comparison. The form of this curve is in agreement with "maps" of the basilar membrane derived from several sources: (1) position of maximal electrical activity (Culler et al., 1943); (2) impairment of cochlear microphonic by localized lesions (Stevens, Davis, and Lurle, 1935); (3) degeneration in human cochleas associated with deafness (Crowe, Guild, and Polvogt, 1934); (4) integration of pitch jnd's (Stevens, Davis, and Lurie, 1935); (5) width of critical band in masking (Fletcher, 1940); (6) contribution of various frequencies to total loudness (Fletcher); (7) contribution of various frequencies to speech intelligibility (French and Steinberg, 1947. From Stevens, S. S., *Handbook of Experimental Psychology*. New York: John Wiley & Sons, 1951.)

forms connections that lead to the cerebral cortex, or more specifically, to the auditory center located in the temporal lobe. This would seem to be the location at which sensation begins to arise. Perhaps a clear auditory perception only emerges after the neural impulse has traveled to the frontal lobe which is believed to be the center for memory. Thus, before a sound can be identified, or the name given to a particular sound heard, an extremely elaborate mechanism is involved. The whole process, however, may require only a small part of a second.

What has just been said is an obvious over-simplification, but it does serve to give the major steps encountered in the process of hearing. In particular, the numerous possible happenings that take place in the complex mechanism of the cochlea, or in the even more complex brain, were not dwelled upon. There remains some doubt that all the events mentioned do actually occur in the way indicated. Important considerations, such as indicating where and how pitch and intensity discriminations are made, have been left out. Such questions will be returned to in the discussion of theories of hearing.

Certain interesting characteristics of the structure and function of the ear have yet to be mentioned. It was not known for a long time what purpose was served by a small round opening close to and similar to the oval window. The cochlea, coiled in about two and a half turns, is like a double tube formed by a partition extending the length of it. At the top of the cochlea is a small duct between the two canals. This part of the cochlea is known as the helicotrema, and is an opening about the size of a pin. The round window, while near the oval window, really stands at the other end of the enclosed tube of fluid. It provides necessary flexibility in the cochlea. Without this flexible membrane to the enclosed tube of fluid, there could be only so much movement inside as could be produced by compression of a fluid.

If the inner ear remains intact, hearing by bone conduction is possible. In other words, mechanical devices can be made to substitute for all the essentials that take place before the inner ear is reached. Fortunately, most ear defects are due to ailments in the middle ear, so that corrective devices are feasible. The middle ear is a place of great vulnerability to infections. It is sealed in from the outside ear, but there is an opening into it from the nasal passage. The middle ear is an air chamber, except for the bones that have been mentioned. Efficient hearing is possible only when air pressure is approximately the same on each side of the eardrum. If a person moves rapidly from one altitude to another, as when taking off or landing in an airplane, the air pressure may become unbalanced. Temporarily, there will be greater pressure on one side of the eardrum than the other, and this will lower the efficiency of hearing and probably produce a roaring in the head. Normally, equilibrium of air pressure is restored by swallowing.

There are apt to be unpleasant auditory sensations any time an individual has an infection that causes congestion of the Eustachian tube leading into the middle ear. This tube opens slightly when the individual swallows or sneezes. Thus, there is a ready approach to the middle ear for bacteria during throat infections. With the discovery of modern drugs, such infections are more effectively treated. It has been said that as many as a third or a fourth of the people in the British Isles, in earlier days, had experienced a ruptured eardrum. Many had continuously running ears, since the eardrum did not completely heal, because of repeated infections. Nearly always, such a condition is accompanied by some hearing loss.

It should be recognized that the structure of the inner ear is extremely difficult to study when intact and functioning in the living animal. In fact, the tissue is even complex and difficult to study after being removed and placed under a microscope. At such time, it is nonfunctioning and only certain information remains available. The inside of the cochlea cannot be very satisfactorily observed directly without puncturing the walls and consequently allowing the fluid to drain and collapse the mechanism. The mechanism is extremely delicate, in the first place, and deterioration takes place rapidly with the passing of time. Much of the early theorizing about hearing was relatively fruitless and was, no doubt, set forth by sorely frustrated investigators who were unable to make the kind of observations essential to a real understanding of the process involved in hearing.

AUDITORY THEORIES

Nearly all the theories of hearing can be divided into two types. These two types have often been referred to as the "resonance theory" which was stated by Helmholtz, and the "telephone theory," formulated by Rutherford. Nearly all investigators align themselves with one or the other of these general approaches. The fundamental difference between them is that in the resonance theory, pitch is thought to be determined by the sympathetic resonance of fibers in the basilar membrane, while pitch or tonal analysis, in the telephone theory, is assumed to take place in the brain. The theory of hearing has been built almost exclusively upon the way pitch discrimination is made. It is just possible that relatively too much attention has been given to pitch in developing auditory theory. Of course, no complete hearing theory could be constructed without explaining pitch, but it is also true that other discriminations, such as intensity, are important.

Both types of theories, presumably, could be subjected to proof or disproof if one could be certain of how the structures, described in the previous section, function. Research on hearing, therefore, has been directed largely toward establishing the relationship between the parts of the inner ear and the various attributes of hearing.

Boring (1) gives a very satisfactory review of the earlier theories of hearing and states the advantages and limitations of the better-known ones. He concludes: "We have noticed, and reviewed as space permitted, twenty-one theories of hearing. The scientific progress made is disappointing." If this last sentence is justified, the student can scarcely be expected to want a detailed account of all the theories in a beginning experimental course. Not all the theories and supporting arguments will be stated here.

Boring, the persistent and meticulous historian of psychology, turned with renewed optimism to a discussion of research, which started about 1930. He believed that recent research has been based upon much more observation and experimentation, and proportionally less speculation. Modern devices and techniques have been helpful. Experimenters have been able to push the bounds of factual information further before turning to subjective speculation. It has, by now, become clear enough that not all the claims made for any one of the older theories can be supported. A few dependable facts have been established. For example, repeated experiments have shown that there is an association of pitch discrimination with location in the cochlea. Evidence makes it possible to construct, with considerable confidence, Fig. 6.3 which is reproduced from Stevens (6). Loss of hearing can be produced experimentally and autopsies reveal damage of predicted segments of the cochlea. Individuals who have been observed to have tonal islands are found, upon autopsy, to have deteriorated portions of the cochlea.

Such evidence seems to be in general support of the Helmholtz theory. This experimental result was anticipated by him, although he did not have evidence for it. He would have arrived at such conclusions from the assumption that the fibers in the basilar membrane would be set to vibrating in such a way as to produce this correlation between structure and function. Few, if any, investigators today will subscribe to Helmholtz's notion about the vibration of the fibers in the basilar membrane being closely comparable to the vibrations of the strings in a piano. One of his conclusions seems to be supported, but the explanation for it is rejected. Geldard (4), after explaining how Helmholtz's suggestion is not and cannot be the case, makes the following statement: "The place idea, then, we do well to preserve, while rejecting the crude notion of resonance through sympathetic vibrations. Withal, the modern form of the Helmholtz theory seems capable of embracing the major facts of hearing, and with its fruitfulness in pointing to new discoveries there can be little dissatisfaction."

In a final statement about hearing theories, Geldard (5) implies that elements of both theories may have to be accepted. Present knowledge would seem to prejudice one toward a place theory for high tones and a frequency theory for low ones. The *volley* theory advanced by Wever and others is an attempt to reconcile the conflicting points into a more comprehensive theory allowing for the observed facts.

Surely, the point need not be labored that an adequate theory or explanation of how hearing takes place is important in psychology and other sciences. It is immediately apparent that the establishment of a correct general theory would have bearing, not only upon auditory perception and how the various parts of the ear operate to bring about sensation, but also upon the determination of exactly what the auditory nerve carries. This, in turn, would be likely to reveal something about the capabilities of any nerve. Further, it would establish, with greater certainty, what does or does not happen in the brain. A rather complete understanding of all the factors involved in the use of one sense is likely to enable the psychologist to make rapid progress in the study of all senses and the nervous system. Going beyond these important scientific matters, there might be many implications for all kinds of sound sources and media used in communication. The point is that fundamental discoveries in science have the most surprising range of subsequent applications. Perhaps nothing is more striking in the history of science than the discovery of a principle, which seemed abstract and remote from the needs of man when first discovered, but which is put to good everyday use years later.

Instead of having to stumble upon certain useful facts by more or less trial and check methods, it is hoped that as many principles as possible can be arrived at by systematic progression. If certain facts and general principles are known, there are often valuable deductions that can be readily made. As an example of this, it was anticipated from theory that it would be possible to save time in communication by cutting out part of the sound of words, still leaving them intelligible. But effort, more or less on a trial or error basis, was required before satisfactory verification was obtained, and there still remained developmental work upon techniques before practical usefulness could be made of the discovery. Knowledge of the facts and principles of shortening or lengthening a speech now enables those who record it for radio or television to reproduce the speech so that it will conform to the necessities of exact time intervals. The speaker does not have to keep repeating the speech until he manages to come out at the end by using, so to speak, exactly twelve minutes and twenty seconds. He does not have to repeat at all, if the speech is anywhere near the correct time, for the condensations or expansion of time needed to fit the interval can be done by mechanical means, without serious distortion. Cutting or adding the time factor is done as required, within a considerable range of time.

LOCALIZATION OF SOUND

The problem of localizing sound is primarily a problem in perception. In some ways, it is unique to hearing. Aside from rare and relatively insignificant refractions of light, and misperception in the use of local sign because of mutilation of skin sense organs or nerves, there is not an equivalent problem for any of the other senses. One might raise a question about determining direction and distance by smell. In man, at least, this cannot be done without other means of checking, such as vision; or by moving toward and away from the source of the odor; or by use of knowledge or memory of the source. Localization is a psychological problem which has relatively little interest for scientists other than psychologists. The physicist, of course, might become concerned about the reflection of sound as it goes from one medium to another. Psychologists are interested in sound reflection which may readily lead to a misperception. Unexpected interference in the stimulus between the point of origin and the point at which it reaches the ear produces an auditory illusion. However, most of the psychological problems in determining direction and distance remain, even though the stimulus has not been interfered with in any special way.

Then, with regard to judgment of direction and distance the psychologist has a problem for which he is almost exclusively responsible. This is an important part of hearing, for it has bearing upon discriminations that may be critical for adjustive behavior in the vicinity of friends or enemies. Psychologists share interest and investigative effort with regard to such problems as pitch, timbre, and fusion with musicians; pitch, intensity, and other physical characteristics of the stimulus with physicists; sensory and neural processes with physiologists. There is little chance to shift to other scientists responsibility for scientific progress in understanding the perception of sound.

Concerning localization, the question to be asked is: how does the organism distinguish the relative position and distance of sound? Early writers were extremely interested in determining whether the listener could make these discriminations natively, or whether learning was the only means of acquiring ability to localize sound. A line was drawn and a position taken, again, as usual, between the nativists and the empiricists. At first, the problem was attacked largely by philosophical argument.

More than a century ago, Johannes Müller noted that a perception of direction must be due to intensity difference at the two ears. This could be due to two factors: first, "the thickness of the head"—greater distance to the ear opposite the source of sound; and second, the shape of the external ear, which is structured to catch better the sound waves on the side toward the sound source. The first explanation might be of some importance if proportional distance is considered for close sounds, but it could scarcely be expected to be above the threshold of discrimination for distant sounds. The second conclusion appeared to be supported by the experiments in which localization, as determined by the listener when under water, was only possible by gross determination of right and left. Also, experimenters produced evidence of serious loss of ability to localize sound by the physical manipulation of the external ears. By bending the ears forward or tying them close to the head, it was possible to get judgments of direction that were so wrong that even the opposite direction might be given as the source of the sound.

Some years later—in 1876—Polizer reported that a man with a hearing defect always located sound in the direction of the more sensitive ear. Presumably, this individual had not learned to compensate or to correct for the unequal reception in the two ears. This kind of misjudgment is not very common among people, but a difference of sensitivity between the ears in the same individual is frequently encountered. It is very likely that Polizer's report, or other current interest at that time, led Lord Rayleigh in the same year to perform a crude, but still useful, experiment. He had people stand in a circle on a lawn and then placed a blindfolded subject in the center of the ring. In turn, the individuals forming the ring would speak and the blindfolded person had to point out the position of the speaker. The subject was able to do this rather well. The errors could be quantified in terms of degrees from the true direction. Basically, the principle and procedure are not different from those used in the sound helmet which was made by Preyer about ten years later. All sound cages built before 1900 seem to have made use of the same general technique.

Rayleigh experimented upon listening to the human voice, tuning forks, and, possibly, other sounds. It is amazing how many correct conclusions he was able to draw, simply by applying a basically good, but not refined, scientific methodology. Boring (2) says: "Thus he demonstrated altogether (a) that noises (voices) are better localized than tones, (b) that high tones are better localized than low, (c) that binaural intensity ratio is crucial for localization, (d) that there is confusion between front localization and any symmetrical position in back, and (e) that there is no confusion between right and left." Under special conditions, some of these conclusions would not hold, and slight modifications, or qualifications, would be necessary for all of them.

There was a tendency to overemphasize intensity differences between the two ears, and there was a neglect of phase difference. There would, of course, have been no way of studying phase difference with the methodology used by Rayleigh, since the individual is unable to report consciously a phase difference. The invention of the "pseudophone," while helping to usher in a study of phase, also helped to strengthen the notion that intensity was the most important cue. The "pseudophone," invented by Thompson, is an apparatus which catches the sound waves on one side of the head and leads the sound to the opposite ear. A sound, with its source to the right, would be led to the left ear. Thus there would be greater intensity in the left ear since the pick-up would be turned to receive from the right.

It is interesting to note that the investigators of this early period got off to a number of false starts. Sometimes there is a temptation to think that scientists spend more time disproving some hunch or claim than establishing the truth in a positive way. It was necessary to prove that the semicircular canals were not the organs that enabled an animal to localize a sound. Interestingly enough, the skin senses about the face and ears were once thought to help the person to localize sound. It was necessary to prove that "touch" was not the explanation for localization.

Following the development of the sound cage, and after there was a better awareness of the necessity for strict controls, many facts about sound localization have gradually been accumulated. In the use of the sound cage, a great many cues, other than the sound intended by the experimenter, may be used by the subject. For example, the movement of sound equipment from front to side may give away completely the new location before the intended tone is presented. Various kinds of clicks in closing switches, rubbing of metals, and so forth may be used as cues by the subject. The "bugs" were gradually taken out of the apparatus and necessary precautions described. In the decade following 1930, a number of careful experiments were made which had definite bearing upon different aspects of localization. Investigators were able to demonstrate that the localization of pure low-pitched tones, produced on a raised platform out in the open where reflected sounds are reduced, was very accurate in contradicting the belief held by Rayleigh.

Recent work has shown clearly that phase difference and time difference are both of importance, while relative intensity is not as much emphasized as formerly. Furthermore, it has been shown that the different factors combine, so that the relative influence that each has is not uniformly consistent over all levels of pitch and intensity. Intensity may be at a maximum of usefulness at one level, and phase at another.

NOISE

Noise is a term that has both scientific and common speech meaning. People are inclined to speak of any unpleasant sound as noise. This might be applied to the bang of a hammer, or to the notes coming from a violin played by a skillful artist. In other words, mood and circumstance may lead to choice of whether the word *noise* or *sound* is applied. The request to turn off the "noise" coming from the radio is the consumer's reaction to the musical program for which someone else is paying. The musician responsible would surely use a word other than "noise" to describe his productions.

Noise, or better still, "white noise," has come to have a very precise technical and scientific meaning. Theoretically, it includes a mixture of all sound waves, analogous to white light. Fundamentally, there is no tendency at present to contrast harmonious sounds and noise. There was a time when investigators considered that pleasant sound—or, in other words, music—stimulated one part of the sense organ, and noise another. There was once an attempt to set forth a duplicity theory of hearing; that is, sound activated the end organs in the cochlea, while noise was received by the vestibule of the ear.

However, a special situation exists: what is called noise becomes a personal and social problem in cities and around large industrial plants. This problem is not directly related to the scientific problems of concern to the physicists and, once more, we are in a province largely reserved for psychologists, or social scientists. It is usually found that those interested in these matters are trying to learn what effect is produced upon the listener. Thus, noise becomes a human and social problem. If the solution is to be one of changing the stimuli, then the physical scientists may need to be called in to give technical assistance. If stress is to be placed upon enabling the individuals to adjust to the physical condition, then the psychologists or social scientists are confronted with the whole problem. It is possible to use scientific methodology to achieve either goal. It is an exceptional circumstance if those who are engaged in a campaign to combat noise go beyond identifying someone, or some condition, to be blamed. This limited procedure appears to be a rather futile one. A scientific approach, either of changing the people or changing the conditions, should prove to be of greater usefulness.

MASKING

It is commonplace knowledge that a loud noise will "drown" out or "mask" a less intense one. Ordinary conversation cannot be heard above the noise of clanging machinery; thunder masks the patter of raindrops on the roof. It is scarcely less obvious that another fundamental of masking can be observed—that there will be greater interference in hearing someone speak if the tones of the surrounding noises are similar to those of the voice. Sounds of similar characteristics cause a great amount of interference. If this were not true, much greater difficulty in verbal communication would be experienced in noisy situations. It remains true that on the battlefield or in the boiler factory, where the decibel rating is very high, the human voice may still get through for some reception.

At one time, it was believed by scientists that lower pitch tones could mask higher ones but not the other way around. The evidence is clear now that lower tones do more effectively mask the higher frequencies, but masking can take place in either direction. Masking effect is ordinarily greatest when the pitch of two tones is near together. However, a reservation must be made if they blend into beats.

As in so many psychological phenomena, there is trouble in avoiding a dualism. There are two kinds of conditions to be explained. One has to do with the physical characteristics of the stimuli, and the other with the reception and use of the stimuli by the organism. When competing or complex waves strike the eardrum and these are mechanically transmitted to the cochlea, a certain amount of distortion takes place. The mechanism of the ear does not follow accurately the sine wave because of the great demand placed upon it. Aside from this, there is modification in the masking effect by the way the subject attends. A sound that has come to have more vital meaning is more likely to be sorted out and heard than a meaningless one. Presumably this is due to learning, attention, and set. Then, it appears that there is a degree of voluntary control over the auditory threshold. The expected sound or the one being "listened" for is heard at a lower intensity level than are other sounds.

An analogy might be drawn between masking effect experienced in the competition for attention of a given sound as it comes from a complex ground of noise, and what happens in daily events. The listener tries to distinguish between the important and the unimportant in order to retain orientation to figure in a ground of complex social relationships. Or it might be supposed that it is one of the primary purposes of science to sort out and focus upon the scientific truths from a broad field or ground of speculations made up of half-truths or false notions. By careful verification, the scientist is able to identify the correct and useful principles from a chaotic ground of conflicting opinions.

AUDITORY FATIGUE AND INJURY

There is every reason to believe that the process of adaptation in hearing is of the same general nature as that found in vision and the other sense modalities. However, it must be granted that the auditory sense is relatively slow to fatigue. It was once seriously held that fatigue did not take place. It is wondered if those holding such a belief had not ever experienced roaring in the head after an exciting day at the fair or carnival. Individuals regularly report disturbing auditory sensations after a prolonged period spent in a situation where sound, or noise, is intense. It may also be that, if there is an accompanying state of tension, or emotionality, residue sensations are more conspicuous.

An explanation for the difference in the conscious awareness of tiredness relative to eyes and ears can surely be premised, in part, upon the difference between sensations arising around each sense organ. In the case of vision, there is much muscular activity and eventually pain from what appears to be overwork. In fact, the complaint of fatigue is almost unique to vision, for complaint is rarely heard from anyone concerning tiredness or pain associated with further sensory experience with the other senses. The external muscles of the eye, the ciliary muscle, and the pupilary reflex are active while the individual is seeing. There is no comparable muscular activity associated with sensory functions in the other senses. There is a small amount of muscular activity involved with the adjustment of the small bones in the middle ear, but this would seem to be of minor significance compared to the remarkable demands placed upon the eye muscles for coordination and adjustment.

There are many unpleasant sensations of fatigue in the gross body muscles which might constitute an exception to what has been said about fatigue of the eyes. However, these sensations seem to be more directly related to muscular functions and less a matter of further sensory activity. It may well be that chemical changes that take place within the muscles do give rise to pain sensations and that the kinesthetic sense is also involved. Some writers have speculated that an additional sense must be postulated to account for these gross bodily sensations that arise after prolonged muscular activity. It is interesting to note that those senses that adapt, or, if preferred, that fatigue more rapidly, may cause the least suggestion of awareness of pain and fatigue. There is little awareness of changes of this sort in the adaptation of taste, smell, heat, or cold, and these are the senses that adapt most readily.

SENSORY DAMAGE UNDER EXPOSURE

There is no longer a doubt that prolonged application of intensive auditory stimulation will injure the ear mechanism. The intensity does not have to rupture the eardrum nor necessarily become recognized as painful. All hearing can be destroyed in animals by the use of sound waves. The high incident of partial, or even near total, loss of hearing among persons engaging in certain kinds of industrial work makes it completely convincing that intense and prolonged noise does harm the human ear. It has been demonstrated that hearing loss for some persons can be associated with noise situations that are common in the environment. Damage can occur in noisy offices, restaurants, or near radios, without the individual necessarily experiencing discomfort. Presumably, visual damage is no less appropriately associated with occupations and poorly lighted situations. The difference in awareness when damage is being done must be part of the reason that more damage suits seem to arise from auditory damage presumed to be due to occupation than is the case for visual loss. The individual who is doing fine work on the assembly line or in watchmaking may suffer from eye strain, but perhaps since he is more aware of prolonged visual distress, he is held more responsible for his own acts. He has experienced a warning in the form of pain from the eyes. The individual who has hearing damage may be oblivious of the progressive changes, until suddenly he becomes aware that he has a serious hearing loss.

SENSORY LOSS AND SOCIAL PROBLEMS

It will be seen that this discussion has progressed to problems somewhat beyond a usual or reasonable boundary of experimental psychology. Nevertheless, it may be acceptable to take the viewpoint that this is an interesting frontier of experimental research, where the laboratory psychologist meets the social worker, the economist, or the lawyer. In some occupations, insurance rates must be high in order to take care of the incident of loss of capacity to earn because of physical and sensory detrimental effects associated with the work. Hearing loss constitutes one of the better recognized changes presumed to result from the job. In order to establish the relationship between bodily damage and occupations, better measuring devices than exist at present are needed. Also, it would be important to trace what might be called "normal sensory loss with age," and to distinguish between this loss and that associated with the job. Altogether, the problem is complex, and many confusing factors arise. Armchair speculation can scarcely be expected to furnish particularly valid answers, so an experimental approach is greatly needed.

It may well be that the experimental approach will have to be extended into what is at present an even more ambiguous area of human problems. For example, the question will have to be raised as to how much of the sensory change is due to an actual modification of the structural mechanism and how much to functional factors. What part of a hearing loss is to be charged to the fact that the individual is unhappy in his work, so that the noise becomes unpleasant, and hence the individual is motivated to escape the whole situation? What part, if any, is played by the promise of financial reward if sensory damage is determined? Malingering or hysterical reactions might be anticipated in some cases. Must various personality characteristics be considered before drawing conclusions about hearing losses? What responsibility can be placed upon the individual worker for using protective devices that are furnished to him? In other words, if he chooses to make no use of earplugs, goggles, or masks that have been provided, what should be the evaluation of any subsequent sensory loss? Such questions inevitably raise other questions about rights and privileges that may be extended to both worker and employer.

Usually, damage suits arise long after the sensory loss. Thus, legal authorities and scientists may be trying to evaluate a capacity that has already partially disappeared. They will then be trying to determine the cause of the loss after the fact. Obviously, accurate measuring devices are needed and it is quite probable that norms are needed in order to know what is the usual speed of deterioration with the aging process under assumed normal conditions. Thus, pre- and post-measurements might have to be taken if an analysis is to be scientific. Consequently, a wide variety of physical, sensory, and psychological tests administered before any worker begins on the job could be of great protection to the employer against unfair damage claims. Firm knowledge should be a protection for the worker, so that he may get justice. There are many interesting, if rather forbidding, problems that must be attacked experimentally before some of the tests that might be anticipated are constructed.

SPECIAL AUDITORY APTITUDES

There are numerous hearing tests for various aptitudes and purposes. Among the better-known ones are those intended to measure musical aptitude, such as the Seashore test. Most of these tests will obtain an index of the individual's ability to discriminate small differences in pitch, intensity, and time. These abilities are assumed to be primarily of native origin. Yet, tests reveal some improvement if training is given. It is, of course, true that the subject must learn to label properly the higher of two tones, or the louder of two, before his answers are meaningful. The difference between tones might be perceived without the proper labels being attached. An example is recalled of an individual who consistently called the higher pitch of two tones lower because he had not previously learned what was meant by high and low pitch.

There are also tests to indicate the person's preference between what are considered by experts to be good and poor choices of rhythm, timbre, and harmony. These choices, it will be recognized by the psychology student, are greatly influenced by cultural factors. Then tonal memory, motor skills, etc., may be of further importance, and these will be expected to relate to some extent to the intellectual capacity and the neural and muscular equipment of the individual. Most often the indices of skill used in these are largely due to achievement. It is certain that if an individual possesses a given skill, he has the native endowment to make the achievement possible. However, many individuals may possess all the basic requirements for learning musical skill but lack motivation. Thus, a test that samples achievement is often desired, since this may become at least an indirect approach to motivation where there has been some opportunity to learn music. It would be rare that an individual would be wise to begin a musical career, for commercial or artistic purposes, if he had made no achievement in music during childhood. The study of music for appreciation and personal gratification is a different matter.

Aptitude test items for hearing ability that are to be used in selecting industrial personnel are usually directed toward measuring acuity. Sometimes it may be desirable for the individual to make tonal discriminations in his performance on the job. Tests of hearing to be used upon pilots and others engaged in critical communication tasks will need to allow for assessing the subject's ability to perform under stress conditions. It is especially important that the pilot be able to respond to the intended signal in a ground of irrelevant and masking noises.

It is not the writer's purpose to discuss psychological tests in detail. It will be noted immediately that tests of sensory processes, such as those for vision and hearing, were directly derived from methods and techniques developed in the laboratory. Laboratory training is essential if these tests are to be skillfully used and wisely interpreted by the psychologist. Other psychological tests may be more definitely patterned after educational or achievement types of tests and stem less directly from the laboratory or "ivory tower science."

Experimentation with hearing, as with other psychological phenomena, involves the psychologist in difficulties if he goes from the laboratory to the normal operating situation. In the laboratory, he may attempt to freeze all variables except one. In the more complex and dynamic situation where the individual functions daily, many variables are encountered in the subject as well as in the stimulus source. Hence, it is not enough to experiment in the relatively static condition of the laboratory and then try to deduce about what will happen in the highly kinetic situation. To be sure, abundance of observational data and good theory are of great help. However, it must be remembered that four close walls about a laboratory may involve variables that are amazingly different from those of the pilot in the cockpit of the powerful airplane, or, again, those the individual meets if he must descend under a parachute. In general, available information about vision tends to be more exact, more detailed, and more extensive than that concerned with hearing. This is especially true with regard to application in the natural, or work, situation. No doubt, need has furnished the impetus to research on vision directed to dynamic situations. Scientists must of necessity, continue to learn about how the ears serve in a world ever devoted to increasing speed.

SUGGESTED READINGS

Dashiell, John Frederick. *Fundamentals of General Psychology,* pp. 250-258. Boston: Houghton Mifflin, 1949.

Morgan, Clifford T. *Introduction to Psychology,* pp. 480. New York: McGraw-Hill, 1956.

Munn, Norman L. *Psychology,* pp. 362-378. Boston: Houghton Mifflin, 1956.

Postman, Leo, and Egan, James P. *Experimental Psychology,* pp. 51-84. New York: Harper, 1949.

Woodworth, Robert S., and Schlosberg, Harold. *Experimental Psychology,* pp. 323-361. New York: Henry Holt, 1954.

Boring, Edwin G. *Sensation and Perception in the History of Experimental Psychology,* pp. 312-436. New York: Appleton-Century-Crofts, 1942.

Geldard, Frank A. *The Human Senses,* pp. 94-157. New York: John Wiley, 1953.

Davis, H. (ed.). *Hearing and Deafness.* New York: Rinehart, 1947.

Hirsch, I. J. *The Measurement of Hearing.* New York: McGraw-Hill, 1952.

Stevens, S. S. (ed.). *Handbook of Experimental Psychology.* Davis: "Psychophysiology of Hearing and Deafness," pp. 1116-1142; Békésy and Rosenblith: "The Mechanical Properties of the Ear," pp. 1075-1115. New York: John Wiley, 1951.

REFERENCES

1. Boring, Edwin G. *Sensation and Perception in the History of Experimental Psychology*, p. 418. New York: Appleton-Century-Crofts, 1942.
2. *Ibid.*, p. 384.
3. *Ibid.*, p. 385.
4. Geldard, Frank A. *The Human Senses*, p. 151. New York: John Wiley, 1953.
5. *Ibid.*, p. 157.
6. Békésy and Rosenblith: "The Mechanical Properties of the Ear," p. 1098 in Stevens, S. S. *Handbook of Experimental Psychology*. New York: John Wiley, 1951.
7. Wever, E. G. *Theory of Hearing*. New York: John Wiley, 1949.

7 | FACTS, PROBLEMS, AND EXPERIMENTS IN SEEING

GENERAL CONSIDERATION

Vision is undoubtedly the most specialized, the most intricate, the most thoroughly investigated sense of man. Much of man's general scientific inquiry seems to have been initiated by questions that arose concerning the explanation of how it is that man can see.

The retina of the eye is sensitive to a remarkable degree. It is said that under some conditions a man might see the flame of a match two hundred miles away. The energy coming from a match at that distance is obviously very little. The energy required to activate a neural impulse on the retina is believed by some investigators to approach one quantum, which is the smallest postulated unit of energy. The sensitivity of the retina far exceeds that of the finest camera, with which the eye is often compared. There are similarities in structure and function between eyes and cameras, but there are also important differences. The camera is but a poor imitation of the eye, and is far from complete in being capable of doing many of the important things involved in vision. Beyond the eye proper, it must be remembered that the neural and muscular systems are closely interconnected. Thus, the retina, a crucial structure in vision, and everything beyond that and including the brain, has no counterpart in the camera.

In gathering information about the world the sense of vision easily stands first among the senses. The more civilized man becomes, the more cultural knowledge each generation must try to transmit to the next, the more important vision seems to become. Perhaps the only serious threat to this state of affairs developed with sound recording and radio transmission. However, even without the subsequent invention of television the relative predominance of the eyes might not have been successfully challenged. Thus, vision may be considered first among the senses for

serving the purpose of cultural learning and as a means for social interaction. While in primitive man vision as a distance receptor must have
been of importance in detecting enemies or in finding sources of food,
the greatest use, and stress upon the eyes, is now associated with near
activities. These include reading, making fine discriminations in lines or
color, and identifying and adjusting small objects, as when working on an
assembly line. The burden upon the eyes in performing these many
intricate tasks becomes ever greater and, as a result, a high percentage
of people must now wear glasses as a necessary aid to vision.

VISION IN DIFFERENT SCIENCES

Much was known about vision before psychology became a recognized
discipline. Perhaps there is no topic in psychology that overlaps so much
with other recognized fields of science. Optics is a major subject in
physics; the anatomist devotes much time to studying the intricate mechanism of the eye; the physiologist has a big task in determining how the
eye functions and coordinates with the other parts of the body. Even
the chemistry of vision is complex and of great importance in research
for several professions. Aside from people working in these sciences, who
may do research having a bearing on problems of vision, there are many
thousands of people who devote their professional lives to therapeutic
work serving those who experience visual difficulties. They are kept busy
treating eyes or applying devices for the protection or improvement of
vision. This type of work is carried on by ophthalmologists, oculists, and
optometrists, and in addition there are a great number and variety of
occupations associated with optics in one way or another.

LIMITATIONS IMPOSED UPON PSYCHOLOGISTS

Without necessarily assuming that psychologists have overemphasized
vision, we have chosen to give less space to this subject than most of our
colleagues when they have dealt with experimental or laboratory psychology. We are trying to present only the most relevant material of wide
scientific, as well as psychological, significance. This means that we shall
extract only a very small amount from the voluminous research literature.
We run a calculated risk of leaving an area having an abundance of well
authenticated research data for the somewhat less certain and more
speculative material dealing with other aspects of psychology. Our defense, if one is needed, is that we may well leave many problems in vision
to people devoted to professions other than psychology, who have better
training for working on some of these problems than can reasonably be
expected of the psychologist. The field is so vast that one easily gets lost

in the mass of details. Very long books have been written about vision and yet they cover only a tiny portion of all that is known about the subject.

GROSS STRUCTURE OF THE EYE

Perhaps the quickest and best way to get a knowledge of the structure of the eye is to study a picture or drawing of the eye. Figure 7-1 has been reproduced in order to make this possible.

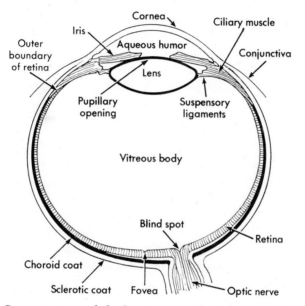

Fig. 7.1. Gross structure of the human eye. The fovea is to the side of the optic nerve nearer to the nose. (From Munn, Norman L., *Psychology*. Boston: Houghton Mifflin Co., 1956.)

Assuming that many readers will already have some familiarity with the parts and function of the eye, only a brief review is given. The walls of the eye are made up of three layers. The covering or outside coat is called the sclera. It is a tough fibrous layer of tissue which has as its main function the support and protection of the eye mechanism. The middle coat, choroid, has much the same function as the covering of a camera. It prevents light from filtering through the walls of the eye and prevents reflection from within the eyeball which would produce a diffuse and vague image on the retina. It is within this layer that much of the nutrient mechanism of the eye is to be found. There is a rich blood supply passing through the capillaries. The iris serves as an extension of the choroid coat, but is different in that this portion is mobile—allowing the size of the pupil to change according to the intensity of the light. The opening, or pupil, is reduced in bright light and is enlarged under semi-darkness conditions.

The inner layer of the wall of the eyeball is called the retina. It is here that the end organs for vision are to be found. The fovea (or macula) is considered the center of the retina because this is where the rays of light entering through the pupil are most sharply focused. The retina is pinkish in color and is made up of rods and cones. The cones are predominate in and around the fovea while the rods prevail in the peripheral part of the retina. Rods and cones have different functions, and are so named because of their shape, although there are many in-between cells that cannot be readily identified as belonging to either class.

The Blind Spot

The function of the retina in receiving the stimulus for vision was not known until this fact was arrived at by discovery of the blind spot by Mariotte in 1668. The explanation of the blind spot made it obvious that the retina contained the end organs for vision. It was determined that light rays that fell upon the connecting neural tissue making up the optic nerve, as it entered the eye, did not initiate any sensation. The blind spot is a point not far from the focal center of vision. Light waves falling upon the zones where the end organs (rods and cones) are located do initiate a neural impulse. This knowledge firmly establishes the retina as the receptor for vision.

The pupil is the opening which is surrounded by the iris. The pupil looks dark because most of the light is excluded from inside of the eyeball by the iris and the choroid coat. The impression is much like looking into the mouth of a cave. By use of a suitable retinoscope, a sharply focused light ray can be projected through the pupil so the retina can be observed. The pupil enlarges with relaxation of the iris, since the structure is composed of circular fibers. If the iris does not respond adequately with changes in light intensity, vision is impaired. In albino animals there is a deficiency of pigment in the iris and the choroid. These animals usually have poor vision. The pupil of an albino appears to be pinkish. This is true because the observer is able to see through the pupil to the retina, which is not well shielded from outside light.

The lens serves to focus the light waves sharply on the fovea. Much philosophical debate developed concerning how it was that man could see things right side up when the image on the retina, following passage of the light waves through the lens, was upside down. Only slowly did it dawn upon investigators that the individual learned to respond, in the first place, with the image in this position and thus no confusion ever

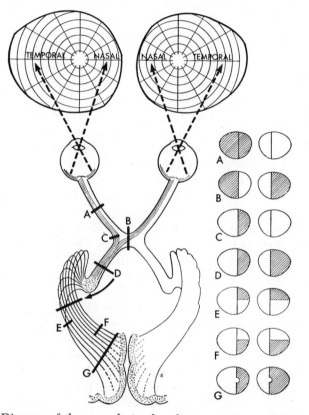

Fig. 7.2. Diagram of the central visual pathways passing to left hemisphere. Shaded areas in inserts indicate visual defects resulting from lesions at point indicated by corresponding letter on left-hand figure. For convenience, the visual fields for two eyes are shown separated, but actually they superimpose so that the vertical meridians coincide; A, complete blindness of left eye; B, bitemporal hemianopsia; C, unilateral nasal hemianopsia; D, right homonymous hemianopsia—interruption of either optic tract or geniculocalcarine projection; E and F, right upper and lower quadrant hemianopsias; G, right homonymous hemianopsia from a large lesion of occipital lobe. (From Homans, A Text-book of Surgery (5th ed.), 1941, after Fulton, John F., A Textbook of Physiology. Philadelphia: W. B. Saunders Co.)

arose. No other position has been experienced in the natural environment since birth.

The lens changes in thickness as the eyes are rotated to focus from distant to close objects. This change in the lens is called *accommodation*. The ciliary muscles control the thickness of the lens through contraction or relaxation. Earlier investigators were greatly intrigued by the lens and several erroneously thought that it contained the receptors of vision.

The eyeball is filled with a thick fluid which serves to keep the eye from collapsing. It is slightly yellowish in color but is sufficiently transparent for light rays to pass through. The fluid in the main chamber of the eyeball is called vitreous humor and that in the cornea aqueous humor. The fluids are chemically similar.

The optic nerve and connecting fibers transmit the neural impulse to the occipital lobe in the brain. Reference to Fig. 7.2 will enable the reader to get a clear idea of the pathway of the nerve fibers. The crossing of half of each of the optic nerve fibers as they extend back to the lateral geniculate body and finally to the occipital lobe is an arrangement giving rise to a number of interesting phenomena. Knowledge about the pathway of the nerve fibers makes comprehensible several visual defects. Many variations in partial blindness have been found among clinical cases. Verification of the effect upon vision of a lesion or section, as indicated in the figure, comes from both experimental cutting of the fibers in animals and in cases where surgery has been necessary in people. Damage resulting from disease or accident reveal the same conditions.

While we shall have occasion to mention other details regarding the structure and general functions of the parts of the eye, for more thorough description the reader should turn to the material listed among the references. It can be assumed that ancient man would have examined the eyeballs from animals that he killed for food so that some knowledge of the eye probably predates historical records. Yet it took a long progression of scientific investigation to establish the present fund of knowledge and there remains much to be done regarding the anatomy and physiology of the eye.

THE STIMULUS

The adequate stimulus for vision is the light wave. While pressure, rubbing, etc., will give rise to sensations of flashing of light and vague forms, this is of little concern in the main problem of vision. Historically, it is found that acceptable knowledge about the energy that serves as the stimulus preceded most of the discoveries about vision itself. This was perhaps necessarily the sequence of scientific discovery, for little understanding of the problems of vision seems possible without taking into account the nature of light. Nevertheless, the motivation for research upon light certainly stemmed primarily from curiosity about vision.

The eye is sensitive to a narrow band of wave lengths lying between infrared on the side of the longer waves and ultraviolet on the side of the shorter ones. The length of the light waves, in part, determines hue or color. Between the limits that activate receptors man can discriminate an estimated 350,000 colors, which includes variations in hues, saturation, and brightness. As might be expected, there is tremendous variation between people in making these discriminations.

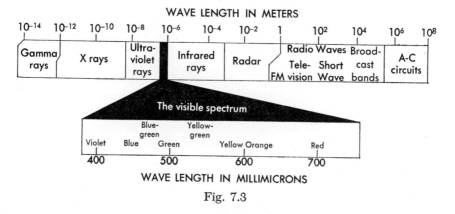

Fig. 7.3

While it is known that Roger Bacon used lenses as an aid to vision in the thirteenth century, not much progress was made in studying problems of vision before Newton made his important discoveries about the nature of light in the seventeenth century. Newton, a general scientist making many important discoveries, found that light waves could be separated by means of a prism. By use of the prism, sunlight could be broken into the colors of the spectrum. This means that all the colors with their wave lengths between red and violet, to which man's eyes were sensitive, could be reproduced at will for study. Newton's book, *Opticks*, published in 1704, laid much of the groundwork for research on vision.

Many of the problems of vision had already been studied by the middle of the eighteenth century. William Porterfield published *A Treatise on the Eye, the Manner and Phenomena of Vision* in 1759. In this he assembled information for discussion under such titles as retinal image, accommodation, convergence, perception of distance, binocular vision, adaptation, and color vision. This outline does very well today. In fact, writers do not ordinarily depart very much from such a list of topics in dealing with vision, although many contributions concerning each have accumulated since Porterfield's time.

LIGHT SOURCES

Complete knowledge concerning the nature of light is still not at hand and remains a topic for study among physicists. Some phenomena, it is said, are better explained by wave motion or undulatory theory, while others fit better with the notion that light is a barrage of emissive particles—a central point in the quantum theory. We are not in a position to discuss meaningfully these fundamental theories concerning light, although it might well be of great advantage to psychologists in planning their research if they could proceed with complete confidence about the nature of the stimulus. Confidence in these matters must await further progress in the field of physics.

Light comes from two types of sources: incandescent bodies (hot sources), and luminescent bodies (cold sources). In discussing these sources of light Geldard (3) is led to state the opinion that the future may witness important uses of luminescent sources of light. The relative efficiency is said to be about five times as high as that expected from tungsten filament lamps. Luminescent light is a different kind of light from that coming from the sun. While the human eye presumably has been adapting to sunlight over thousands of generations, this might but does not necessarily mean that a different kind of light will be harder upon the eyes. Evaluative studies will be needed, for commercial lights are already being made by use of short-wave radiation. In the case of fluorescent materials, light is due to the glow during activation; in phosphorescence it is a continuing effect after cessation of activation. These materials are finding wide use in advertising and warning signs.

A high degree of accuracy has been achieved in measuring light. Units have been referred to as foot-candles and millilamberts. It was necessary to quantify the intensity of light before a very fruitful attack could be made upon such a basic problem as visual acuity. Visual acuity is so dependent upon the intensity of the light coming to the retina that it becomes essential to describe the intensity in meaningful terms before the results can be communicated very well to others. It has been found that visual acuity increases with brightness up to an amazing intensity, which is far beyond the level of what is commonly thought of as a well lighted room or even bright sunlight. However, there is some tendency for extremely bright lights not only to be more fatiguing, but actually to produce pain before the maximum of acuity is reached. Consequently, determining the optimal intensity of light to be used depends partly upon the purpose to be served. Establishing optimal levels of lighting for greatest efficiency becomes a complex problem involving more than just finding the illumination for greatest visual discrimination.

MEASURING VISUAL ACUITY

Most people are acquainted with the physician's procedure in measuring the acuity of vision. There has been standardization of what the individual *ought* to be able to see. It is said that the individual's vision is "average" if he has 20/20 vision. This means that he is able to read printed material of a given size at a distance of 20 feet. This standard has not been determined upon strictly statistical grounds. It seems to be somewhat of a compromise between a statistical norm and a norm of assumed adequacy. If the individual has 20/20 vision or better, he is not judged to need glasses or any corrective devices because of poor vision. If a person can read only at 20 feet the size of letters that others can see at a distance of 40 feet, he is said to have 20/40 vision. There are several other ways of rating the individual regarding his visual acuity, but all of them will be based upon some means of comparing one individual's vision with norms or assumed norms among people. These ratings and procedures have to do with practical problems, such as fitting the individual with glasses so he can read printed material or do fine tasks without eye strain. It is, of course, recognized by the person who examines the eyes that he must keep certain physical conditions under careful control. In a half-lighted room, for example, the individual's vision would not be up to 20/20, although he actually had average or usual visual ability.

RESEARCH MEASUREMENT OF VISUAL ACUITY

Laboratory methods of measuring visual acuity are elaborate and the accurate measurement of absolute and differential threshold become fundamental problems. Many attempts have been made to determine the minimum of energy necessary to elicit a visual sensation. Only in recent years has this been very satisfactorily done. Hecht (6) and co-workers were able to work out techniques and to do an excellent job measuring the energy required to stimulate the rods. Since the rods and cones have a different threshold level, control of the spot on the retina that the light rays strike becomes important. On a given light patch these investigators held the exposure time constant at 0.001 second and repeated many exposures, each time having the subject report whether or not he was able to see the light. It was determined that the average flash necessary for the individual to respond positively when the light was projected from outside to the fovea was between 21 and 57 hundred billionths of an erg for different observers. After calculating the probable loss of light through the refraction of the various mechanisms of the eye they concluded that it took, on an average, about seven light quanta to stimulate the retina enough to initiate a neural impulse. The exact amount of light necessary varies with the size of the stimulus and with the part of the retina that is stimulated. The peripheral points of the retina where the rods are found is far more sensitive to light than is the fovea. This was a finding that was at first surprising to some investigators, since it seemed reasonable that greatest sensitivity would be in the center of the visual field.

By differential threshold is meant the increased amount of light that is necessary for the individual to perceive a difference. The problem of discriminating letters or numbers from the background is one of differential threshold, for there must be discrimination of the light coming from the black letter as distinguished from a white background. Without an appreciation of this difference the letter could not be read. In some ways letters are not very satisfactory for laboratory measures for there is a difference threshold for the various letters themselves. This is due to their different shapes and the thickness of the lines in them. The enclosed white space is a variable related to visibility and, of course, the problem of discriminating one letter from another because of more or less similarity presents a problem. It is much easier to discriminate between o and l than between o and e. For these reasons letters are almost never used in research upon vision unless the problem has to do specifically with letter or word discrimination or recognition, as in research upon reading problems.

There have been a number of standardized procedures used for laboratory visual stimuli. Two lines drawn with variable white space between them is one procedure. The subject is required to judge whether there is one line or two. A convenient and very satisfactory device is to use a circle with a small opening or gap in it like the letter c. In presenting the stimuli, various sizes can be used for whatever distance is desired. These circles, usually known as Landolt rings, can be systematically or randomly presented as to whether the opening is at top, left, bottom, or right. The subject answers in terms of the position of the opening. This allows for a nice statistical treatment, as guessing—a continuously bothersome problem in many types of psychological research—can be dealt with very readily.

FUNCTIONING OF RODS AND CONES

The retina is made up of rods and cones, but many of the end organs are not distinctly shaped like either. The rods make possible night vision and enable the subject to make discriminations of light-dark, form, and movement. The cones have these same functions plus that of color vision, but there is a difference in efficiency of the two for different stimuli.

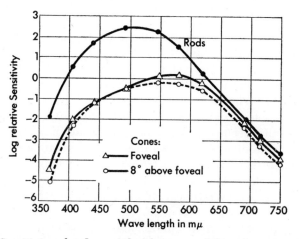

Fig. 7.4. Sensitivity of rods, peripheral cones and foveal cones to light wave lengths. The rods are more sensitive than the cones to the short waves. Sensitivity was defined in terms of 1/threshold with the foveal threshold at a wave length of 555 m taken as unity. (After Wald, G., "Human vision and the spectrum," *Science*, 101 (1945), 653-658.

What is known as the "duplicity theory" of vision refers to rod and cone vision.

As early as 1866 Shultze concluded that the eye is an organ not for one sense but two. His conclusion seems to have been a recognition of some of the conditions now associated with rod and cone functions. Later, in 1881, Parinaud used the idea of the double retinal function to account for night blindness, which had been discovered in a number of people. In 1885 von Kries assembled the literature dealing with the subject and presented evidence of his own in support of what became known as the "duplicity" theory. Von Kries held that the rods function only at low light intensity and did not initiate neural impulses resulting in color sensations. He concluded that they enabled the individual to see form and movement, and to make discriminations of different shades.

In general, present evidence still supports his major conclusions concerning the function of the rods. The cones were believed to operate only at high light intensities and to enable the individual to see color. How much of the function of rods may be carried on by the cones has been the subject of long debate. It may be of interest to the student to know that most of the supporting evidence for the duplicity theory advanced by von Kries and others in the earlier days was based upon the anatomy of the retina and the histological development. This evidence turned out to be less convincing with closer study and subsequent clear proof that many of the cells could not readily be classified as either rods or cones. However, while this line of reasoning became weaker, the theory scarcely suffered from a loss of faith by investigators. The division in function between the rods and cones became more definitely indicated with further research.

The concept of a continuum with distinctive rods at one pole and cones at the other seemed to be more appropriate than the concept that the cells could be divided into two distinct and separate groups. It has become evident that two spectral visibility curves must be plotted: one for daylight or high intensity spectrum and one for twilight or dim spectrum, if we are to reconcile the data obtained from observations made through various levels of light. These curves have become known as photopic, or color vision curves, and scotopic, or colorless vision curves. All colors disappear eventually as the subject passes from bright light into total darkness. Actually no animal is able to see anything in absolute darkness, hence the complete disappearance of form at a given low illumination. Naturally the level for either color or form varies from type to type of animal and also between individual animals of a given family.

The fact that colors have a different brightness in early twilight was observed by Purkinje more than a century before von Kries formulated his theory of duplicity. Purkinje's discovery has become known as the "Purkinje Phenomenon." That certain colors disappear before others in twilight vision was one of his observations. Colors of long wave length at the red end of the spectrum disappear into blackness faster than those of short wave length. When two colors are matched for brightness under intense illumination, one will lose brightness faster than the other as the light is reduced. The reverse is true with the change from darkness to light, so that the colors emerge in an orderly way, those that disappeared first being the last to reappear.

The above facts have both theoretical and practical implications. It is from established facts of this kind that investigators are able to formulate general laws in science and make predictions that can be verified as true. From a practical viewpoint the facts indicated are useful to the costume designer, the interior decorator, the man who puts up warning signs along the highways, or any one who may be using color with the expectation that these colors must retain contrast value under variable light intensities. It is useful to know that yellow retains brightness, for example, and becomes a good background color for danger signs that must be read at night. The costume designer will no doubt be working under bright light conditions when doing his designing and may find that what was harmonious under this condition becomes drab, or the colors may clash, giving the impression of poor artistic taste when the costume is worn in the usual dimly lighted banquet or dance hall.

There are many uncertainties about the details of how rods and cones function together but the basic principle of the duplicity theory is perhaps safely established. Animals noted for nocturnal vision have either only rods or a strong predominance of rods. These include owls, rodents, bats, and those birds that migrate only at night. Some animals have only cones, and vision is poor for them under partial darkness. These animals include pigeons, chickens, many birds, and most reptiles. Other animals, of which man is one, have both rods and cones with variable proportions of each. The proportion of rods to cones seems to bear a consistent relationship with the animal's ability to discriminate colors or to see in twilight.

Knowledge of the functioning of the rods and cones is essential for understanding light and dark adaptation, night blindness, day blindness, color blindness, and a number of other phenomena that would be most confusing in the absence of this information.

ADAPTATION

Adaptation is of two types. The increased sensitivity of the retina due to lack of light stimulation is known as dark adaptation. By this it is meant that a much less intense light can be seen after the individual has stayed in darkness than if he has been exposed to light for some time. The decreased sensitivity of the retina brought about by prolonged stimulation by light is called light adaptation. The individual will do better at some tasks after dark adaptation, better with others after light adaptation. If the person is hoping to see a plane or ship at night he improves his chances of accurate observation by first becoming dark adapted. On the other hand, if the task is to discriminate between colors, a certain amount of light adaptation is essential. The individual does not see well either when first stepping from the dark room into the brilliant sunlight or when first coming in from bright light to the dark room. Those who have gone into the theater and out again during the day have become conscious of both kinds of difficulty.

Of such great practical importance are these facts that during World War II pilots who might be required upon a moment's notice to man their planes, and scramble to seek enemy craft in the darkness, were kept dark adapted while on duty. It was learned that by wearing red goggles the pilots could be kept partially dark adapted and yet see enough to do most of the things required in routine activities.

Dark adaptation was described by Auber in 1856. There can be no doubt that people at a still earlier date recognized the phenomenon. Primitive man could not have been oblivious to his visual difficulties when stepping from bright firelight into darkness, or from the cave into sunlight on snow. He would have realized that his vision gradually cleared and that the outline of objects became more distinct after he remained for a time in the darkness or light, as the case might require.

The course of dark adaptation has been found to depend upon several factors. Wave length is important, for if the individual has been exposed to red waves instead of the shorter ones he will begin twilight vision with a lower threshold and regain faster. Length of time and the intensity of the light to which the person has been exposed are both important variables. If there has been a long period spent in a bright light, dark adaptation takes a long time. Thus, if a person steps into a brightly lighted room from darkness and returns to darkness within a few minutes recovery is rapid.

THE DISCOVERY OF RHODOPSIN

There is every reason to suppose that light adaptation is the obverse of the dark adaptation process. Belief in this idea led to a search for a common factor operating in both. The common factor is visual purple, or rhodopsin, which is found in rods. According to Bliss (1), it may also exist in small amounts in the cones. The isolation of rods and cones for making a chemical analysis is difficult in those animals having both. Rhodopsin is a reddish pigment, first discovered by Ball in 1877. When exposed to light, rhodopsin is found to bleach; in the absence of light there is recovery of the pigment. Thus there seems to be a photochemical process taking place which is intermediary between light wave and nerve impulse. While much is known about rhodopsin and the way it serves in vision, a great deal remains to be learned about the basic process.

The photochemical process is more rapid for some wave lengths than others. This has been found to be directly related to the speed of light and dark adaptation. In what is known as Draper's Law it is stated that the photochemical effect of a given wave length is proportional to the degree to which that wave length is absorbed. Absorption is most rapid within the middle range of waves that are visible and less rapid toward the extreme ranges.

SLOWNESS OF ADAPTATION

The length of time required for light and dark adaptation has been found to be quite long—much longer than the layman might suspect. It seems reasonable that adaptation takes place within a few minutes. The individual is not conscious of changes for very long, yet under some conditions it has been found that adaptation may continue for at least eighty minutes and it probably extends well beyond that. Approximately sixty percent of dark adaptation can be expected within five minutes. After the first rapid adjustment, adaptation becomes slower but may still be of some importance for a long period. For most practical purposes little change in acuity is to be expected after the subject stays in a condition of level illumination for fifteen or twenty minutes. Individuals vary considerably and the factors previously reviewed must be taken into account in determining the total time required. A difficult experimental problem is encountered because of the influence of repeatedly testing the eye and thus changing the light condition. This obviously introduces an artifact of some importance but fairly satisfactory controls have been worked out. The individual must be tested on repeated occasions—after five minutes, ten minutes, and twenty minutes at different experimental periods. A single occasion in which the test would be made in succession at these intervals will not give the most refined research data.

NIGHT BLINDNESS

It has been mentioned that some people are handicapped by night blindness. At least two major causes are indicated. Some individuals appear to have a congenital or hereditary deficiency in rhodopsin. This is considered to produce a permanent condition since at the present time effective treatment is not known. The other condition associated with night blindness, as Hecht (6) and others have shown, is vitamin A deficiency. This produces temporary night blindness, which can be remedied by administration of vitamin A. There is some question about whether prolonged deficiency may cause irreversible damage.

While it has been clearly demonstrated that night blindness can be produced in animals by depriving them of vitamin A, it is not known how widespread such a deficiency is among people. There is no evidence that an overabundance of vitamin A has a beneficial effect upon night vision. There is little question but that many carrots, consumed during World War II by anxiety-ridden pilots hoping to improve their night vision, were wasted carrots! People having a reasonably adequate diet are unlikely to have a vitamin A deficiency great enough to handicap them in night vision.

In some ways the investigator is better able to study the process of adaptation in vision than in the other senses, and adaptation must be thought of as a fundamental problem having broad significance. Not only is there need to come to an understanding of adaptation in order to know more about the functioning of the various senses, but fatigue and recovery from fatigue appear to involve similar phenomena. Thus the concepts that are worked out in this might be extended to help explain changes in neural and muscular responses that are due to activity, and the recovery that takes place with rest. It is interesting to speculate upon the nature of recovery of sense organs, nerves, and muscles taking place during sleep. Sleep is a compelling urge of almost, if not complete, universal biological range and relatively little is known about its physiological and psychological significance. While rhodopsin, for example, is bleached and recovered in rapid succession under ordinary visual fatigue, eventually a more prolonged period for recovery is required if visual exposure has been prolonged. In the latter case a certain amount of general bodily chemistry must presumably take place, including utilization of vitamin A and other metabolic processes. This is but one example of a restoration which occurs, along with the many others, in the homeostatic or rebalancing processes that take place during sleep.

AFTERIMAGES

The individual may experience both positive and negative afterimages. The positive afterimage can be experienced by looking intently at a bright light and then quickly shifting the focal point to a smooth dark surface. For a very brief period the subject can "see again" the light at which he had been gazing. The assumption is that the photochemical process that was initiated by the bright light continues briefly before coming to a complete stop, or else neural activity has been started that has not yet completed its cycle in the brain. It is much like a moving object that may continue motion in the direction it was going even after the application of all external energy has been cut off. The lag in the visual process is not great enough for the phenomenon to be easily observed. In a way this is very fortunate. If the afterimage should last very long, or be vivid, there would be the risk of its overlapping with the new image when the eyes are shifted quickly. This could conceivably give a kaleidoscopic effect of superimposed images which would be most confusing.

The negative afterimage is experienced much more frequently than the positive afterimage. It is vivid only after the eyes have been kept fixed upon an intense stimulus for several seconds. The eyewink or shifts of the focal point, either while looking at the original stimulus or when trying to revive the afterimage, tends to dissipate it. However, there are some situations in which the afterimage can be unpleasant and can even endanger the individual's life. Most people have faced an oncoming car having brilliant lights and found two dark smudges in front of them at the instant they pass the other car. These afterimages rather quickly fade and disappear, but if the driver happens to be driving fast on a crooked road there is risk that he may be confused long enough to have an accident. Some of the effect of the afterimage can be avoided by focusing the eyes on the edge of the road rather than at the two lights of the oncoming car. Then when the car is past and the eyes are focused on the road again visibility will not be greatly hindered. The afterimages of the lights, if present, will be off the side of the road where they will not bother the driver. This is an example of the bright light having fallen on the peripheral part of the retina away from the fovea and, presumably, affecting only the rods in a small retinal patch. If the eyes have been focused as suggested above, not much is required of these particular rods for the next few seconds.

The explanation for afterimages seems to be essentially the same as that for light and dark adaptation. It is supposed that the brilliant light leads to rapid light adaptation and when the stimulus is quickly removed some time is required for recovery in the eye. The afterimage has been systematically studied for many reasons, but the support or refutation of theories of color vision often has been the primary concern. No theory of color vision can be satisfactorily established until it can be reconciled with observation upon afterimages, color contrast effects, color blindness, adaptation, and other similar visual phenomena. Hence we shall have occasion to mention afterimages when discussing the next topic, dealing with color vision.

COLOR VISION

There are three older and widely known theories of color vision. These are known as the Young-Helmholtz, Hering, and Ladd-Franklin theories. It is perhaps discouraging that these remain theories; that no one of them can be considered well enough established that it can be spoken of as the *law* of color vision. Neither are there grounds to reject any one of the theories as of no possible use in interpreting the research data currently available concerning color vision. The oldest of the three theories was formulated in part by Young about 1807. He assumed that all colors may be reproduced by the suitable mixture of but three primary colors—red, green, and violet. Violet, which is in the spectral region of blue, has most often been referred to as blue in the discussion of the three primary colors.

Young's theory was expanded almost a half century later by Helmholtz and has been known as the Young-Helmholtz theory since then. Helm-

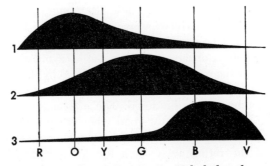

Fig. 7.5. Excitation curves of the Young-Helmholtz theory (1860). The curves were constructed by Helmholtz and intended to indicate how the "red-sensitive fibers" distributed in the top curve; the middle curve was for green-sensitive fibers, and the lower is for violet-sensitive fibers. (From Boring, Edwin G., *Sensation and Perception in the History of Experimental Psychology.* New York: Appleton-Century-Crofts, 1942.)

holtz tried to make the theory consistent with the assumptions of specific nerve energy. Color vision was assumed to arise from the degree of excitation occuring in each of three kinds of nerve fibers when stimulated by light from each wave length across the spectrum. It will be seen from Fig. 7.5 that maximum excitation of part of the fibers is at the end of the long waves.

Modern investigators who have held to the idea that the Young-Helmholtz theory remains the most adequate one conceive of three sets of cones each having sensitivity and absorption characteristics of its own. Perhaps it is safe to say that a majority of research workers in this field still cling to the Young-Helmholtz theory as the most promising theory. If the cones could be separated and studied individually this might furnish a definitive answer to the question. However, a technique for leaving the cones intact and functioning while studying them is a complicated matter. Promising attempts by Granit (5) have been made by means of microtechniques in recording electrical changes accompanying activity of single retinal elements in animals capable of color vision. The cones are so closely packed in the fovea that stimulating one by a light beam that does not spread to excite others has been an important stumbling block. Some believe there is supporting evidence for distinct end organs for the different colors because of the arrangement of six different layers of nerve fibers in the lateral geniculate body through which the connecting optic nerve fibers pass before reaching the occipital lobe. Degeneration in this area has been found to correlate with tissue destruction of local areas in the retina.

The Hering theory, which postulates that there are three substances in the retina, seems to furnish a ready explanation for certain color vision phenomena. For example, the lack of a red-green substance would appear to explain why color blindness is nearly always in this pair of colors. However, there are other combinations of colors sensed by observers which seem to depend upon these colors as well, and there is usually no difficulty in other visual abilities. A total lack of a substance accounting for a third of color vision would be expected to be more handicapping than is the case with color-blind people. The three substances were supposed to be a black-white substance, one for red-green, and the other for yellow-blue. Then it was hypothesized that one color of the pair would be experienced when the chemical reaction was one of anabolism and the other for catabolism. If the red-green substance were being torn down (catabolism), red sensations would be produced; when built (anabolism), green would be seen, etc.

Two very important conditions that might bolster Hering's theory have not so far been established. No one has identified the three substances in the first place. While there are certain similarities to what is known about rhodopsin and light-dark adaptation, this is far from sufficient to embrace all that is implied in the Hering theory. Another consideration has been raised by physiologists. They have not been able to accept the idea that metabolic reactions can be initiated and carried on by external stimulus, as demanded by the theory. Such a notion seems to them inconsistent with established knowledge about metabolism.

The Ladd-Franklin theory is to some extent a compromise theory. This theory is not stated as an independent theory that is expected to displace either or both of the older theories. The proposals set forth in the Ladd-Franklin theory are intended to furnish an explanation for color blindness and for the color zones. It has been referred to as a genetic theory, because the essential difference between it and the other theories is that it attempts to give an explanation of color vision in evolutionary terms. Ladd-Franklin believed that dark-light discrimination was an older visual capacity, considered from an evolutionary viewpoint, and that yellow-blue discrimination developed next and last came the capacity to see red-green. Thus red-green vision would be expected to be less universal and less stable than the other abilities. It is true that color blindness is far more common for red and green.

An evaluation of color theories is not without difficulties. None of them explains satisfactorily all color vision phenomenon. Refutation of the Young-Helmholtz theory appears more difficult than for either of the other older theories. It is also true that a few well-established observations are consistent with the assumptions in it. However, it is also true that certain modifications are clearly indicated. One of the most difficult criticisms to escape with regard to the Young-Helmholtz theory is the problem of accounting for the several hundred thousand color discriminations that have been empirically determined as possible for some individuals to make.

COLOR ZONES

By use of a perimeter it is possible to plot the areas in the visual field where color discriminations can be made. The results from the procedure reveal that all colors are discriminated in a relatively narrow field about the focal center of vision. Then, correspondingly, it is assumed that all receptors for color are located in or near the fovea of the retina. If the stimulus patch is moved from the focal center it is found that red and green soon disappear as colors. Then beyond where these colors can be seen there is a more or less circular area where yellow and blue can be discriminated. Further away still, only form, movement, and light discriminations are possible. There is a close relationship between the extent of the color zones and the distribution of cones in the retina. In the peripheral portions of the retina are only rods, and thus the rod functions are the only ones that can be activated in this part of the retina. The boundaries of the fields for the different colors vary considerably from a perfect circle and are usually quite irregular. Color adaptation, contrasting colors, and light intensity level are factors that probably give rise to some of these variations. Fundamental theory regarding these conditions, if based upon a knowledge of structure, is quite generally consistent with empirical experimental evidence.

DEFECTS OF VISION

The common defects of vision are often used as a means of checking upon the experimental findings about vision and thus help to support or refute theorizing about vision. Irregularities of the lens or retina of the eye are associated with astigmatism. The person having astigmatism experiences difficulty in obtaining a sharp image. The irregular lens causes a diffusion of the light rays as these strike the retina. Thus, glasses that are ground to compensate for the uneven lens are used to correct astigmatism.

Nearsightedness and farsightedness are conditions that are due to the light rays not being focused properly upon the retina. If the lens is thick, refraction will be too great and the focal point is between the lens and the fovea. Thus there will be a crossing of the light rays making up the image. This results in eyestrain for the ciliary muscle tends to contract in order to bring the lens into shape for focusing on the fovea. In the case of farsightedness the focal point, if projected, is behind the retina. Both of these conditions, if not extreme, can be cared for very readily by glasses with lenses made to increase or decrease the refraction, as the case may require. When people grow older there is a tendency for the eye mechanisms to become rigid and slow in accommodation. This condition is known as presbyopia.

Where there are difficulties in focusing the two eyes on the same object then the external muscles attached to the eyeball are the source of the trouble. If these muscles are not in good balance the individual may have the eyes cross, as is the case if the muscles on the nasal side are too short or too strong. If the external muscles are too strong the eyes may diverge. In both cases there is a tendency for the images from the two eyes to be so different that fusion of the images cannot take place. In a few people one eye will tend to focus on a higher plane than the other. Much of the discomfort that people experience after prolonged use of the eyes is due to muscular fatigue in the external muscles of the eyes. Muscular imbalances of the kind mentioned are referred to as phorias.

CONCLUDING REMARKS

There have been many important discoveries about the complexities of vision and the contributions have been scattered over a wide range of years. This makes it easy to neglect current work on the subject. There is at present an exceptionally large amount of experimenting upon vision and much of it may well deserve mention even in a book like this that cannot attempt to review very much of the highly specialized material. However, reading and reference material that deals with vision is likely to be easy to obtain. Also, there is such a close relationship between the topics covered in this chapter and those to be discussed in the next chapter, where problems of perception are to be related, that we are not taking complete leave of important problems in vision at this time.

SUGGESTED READINGS

Dashiell, John Frederick. *Fundamentals of General Psychology*, pp. 258-269. New York: Houghton Mifflin, 1949.

Morgan, Clifford T. *Introduction to Psychology*, pp. 449-479. New York: McGraw-Hill, 1956.

Postman, Leo, and Egan, James P. *Experimental Psychology: An Introduction*, pp. 105-146. New York: Harper, 1949.

Bartley, S. Howard. *Principles of Perception*, pp. 97-170. New York: Harper, 1958.

Garrett, Henry E. *Great Experiments in Psychology*, pp. 297-310. New York: Appleton-Century-Crofts, 1951.

Wenger, M. A., Jones, F. N., and Jones, M. H. *Physiological Psychology*, pp. 190-226. New York: Henry Holt, 1956.

Boring, Edwin G. *Sensation and Perception in the History of Experimental Psychology*. New York: Appleton-Century-Crofts, 1942.

Woodworth, Robert S., and Schlosberg, Harold. *Experimental Psychology*, pp. 362-397. New York: Henry Holt, 1954.

Geldard, Frank A. *The Human Senses*, pp. 14-93. New York: John Wiley, 1953.

Stevens, S. S. (ed.). *Handbook of Experimental Psychology*. Bartley: "The Psychophysiology of Vision," pp. 921-984. New York: John Wiley, 1951.

Poloyak, Stephen. *The Vertebrate Visual System*. Chicago: The University of Chicago Press, 1957.

REFERENCES

1. Bliss, A. F. "The chemistry of daylight vision," *J. Gen. Physiol.*, 29 (1946), 277-297.
2. Boring, Edwin G. *A History of Experimental Psychology*, p. 102. New York: Appleton-Century-Crofts, 1950.
3. Geldard, Frank. *The Human Senses*, p. 15. New York: John Wiley, 1953.
4. *Ibid.*, p. 28.
5. Granit, R. "The retinal mechanism of color reception," *J. Opt. Soc. Amer.*, 31 (1941), 570-575, 580.
6. Hecht, S., and Mandelbaum, J. "Dark adaptation and experimental human Vitamin A deficiency," *Amer. J. Physiol.*, 130 (1940), 651-664.

8

FACTORS IN PERCEPTION: FORM, DISTANCE, MOVEMENT

INTRODUCTION

The capacity to see or perceive form is a primitive one. As indicated in the last chapter, either rods or cones in the retina can act as the mediating receptors for perceiving form. The perception of form seems to require discrimination of lines or edges. Thus the difference between the light from an object, or some part of that object, and the background must be raised above the threshold for discrimination to take place. These threshold differences can be in color or light intensity. For objects in the peripheral field of vision, discrimination would be due largely to light variations and hence mediated by the rods.

Interestingly enough, there has been a tendency for theoretical interpretations of form perception to be localized in the brain rather than in the retina. The opposite approach tends to prevail in theorizing about color vision. Each of the three major theories of color vision is based upon an assumption that something takes place in the retina that determines the color sensation. Some investigators, notably the gestaltists, have insisted that too little attention has been given to brain processes in formulating color vision theory. Others will tend to think that space perception is a step beyond the sensory phase with which we deal in discussing sensations of color. Ordinarily, we do not speak of sensing space but of space perception. Meaning is implied beyond elementary sensation.

Perhaps in no area of knowledge has the issue of nativism vs. empiricism been more sharply drawn than upon the origin of space perception. Kant and others advanced the doctrine that visual space perception is native; it comes as an *a priori* intuition. In this view he was in agreement with many of the philosophers and scholars ranging from Descartes to Hering. Some of the present-day psychologists who identify with the gestaltist school of thought take a position close enough to nativism for their opponents, at least, to accuse them of holding to a nativistic doctrine.

Most psychologists have identified themselves with some brand of empiricism. Beginning with the English associationists who laid the philosophical groundwork for modern psychology, there is an easily traced development in thinking upon this problem from Locke to Wundt, and then on to the position currently held by all strict environmentalists. In general, the nativists have fought a losing battle about the origin of ideas. However, in perception we find a last stronghold that has not been easy to crumble. A kind of primitive unity in the perception of form is difficult to explain away as being due to learning or experience. Thus it may be argued that there is a crucial, even if limited, native function or process that serves as a beginning for more complicated psychological processes. The nativists are willing to say that such native capacity is small in its scope, but still insist that its importance is difficult to exaggerate. It has been reported by Senden (9) that patients who have had congenital cataracts and, therefore, had no vision until they were adults were able to perceive figures at once after the removal of the cataracts. The identification by name of a triangle, square, or ball was, of course, not possible until the individual had been drilled to know what object or form went with what label. This, of course, is a matter of language acquisition.

FIGURE AND GROUND

While figure-ground relationships appear to exist to some extent for the various senses, this distinction is of greatest importance in vision, or at any rate has been discussed more thoroughly with regard to vision

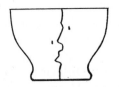

Fig. 8.1. A very simple reversible figure in which each figure shifts rapidly to ground and back to figure.

than other senses. On occasions the individual becomes conscious of figure-ground in hearing. The advertiser who broadcasts music and, simultaneously makes a speech about a given product, is trying to frame his words by giving a background of music. Figure-ground phenomenon is not readily perceived in sense modalities other than vision and hearing.

In a painting the artist usually hopes to present a persistent figure on a background. This effect is likely to be achieved by (1) the more distinct lines; (2) the location in the center of the picture; (3) having the figure superimposed upon objects that disappear behind the figure; (4) having lines converge upon the figure; (5) the use of color differences; (6) a number of other minor techniques and the blending of all factors together into a well-conceived unity. The artist is interested in capturing and holding the attention of the viewer upon the object chosen as the most important in his picture. In a somewhat analogous way, each figure that emerges in the field of vision as the subject focuses upon it tends to stand out from the background. Probably the same sort of condition exists in the whole visual field before a person as that identified in the composition of a picture as outlined above.

Competing objects having approximately the same characteristics can be drawn by the artist so that a rapid shift takes place. What is first figure and ground reverses so the original figure becomes ground and the old ground is figure. While the semi-illusory characteristics of a picture that leads to easy shift from ground to figure that has been spoken of is not often reproduced in nature, there is reason to suppose that such a process could, and does, take place more or less continuously as vision shifts from focal point to focal point. Where the whole field of vision is made up of more or less uniform units, there is still this emerging figure-ground phenomenon taking place and the observer becomes distinctly aware of this if he analyzes carefully. This process takes place when gazing intently at an area of sand upon the beach—now one grain of sand becomes the center of the visual field and the focus of attention, then another grain becomes the center of vision and attention. These relationships appear to emerge whether or not the observer wishes them. Avoidance of the emergence of figure and ground is difficult or impossible if the eyes are kept fixed on any given point.

PAST EXPERIENCE IN FIGURE AND GROUND

While it is apparently subjectively clear to the observing person, under almost all conditions, as to what is figure and ground, exactly the difference between them is hard to put into descriptive terms. This may be due, in part, to the rapid shifts that take place. Is figure-ground purely a matter of attention? That the figure is the center of attention is scarcely questioned, but is it something more than just this? On rare occasions perhaps all people have the subjective experience of gazing blankly without a sharp focusing of the eyes while attention is claimed by an abstraction, which for the moment is independent of vision. There is a sort of rivalry between intellectual attention and the things that are being observed visually. Many blind individuals report that it is easier for them to concentrate upon a given subject than for those having vision since they have so many fewer distracting influences. It is not known whether this observation has scientific worth, but the statement seems reasonable.

The phenomenal difference between figure and ground was one of the problems attacked by Rubens (8) in his extended studies of perception. He came to the conclusion that the figure had rather definite form while ground remained somewhat formless. The ground appears to extend continuously and to go behind the figure and thus the figure stands out in front. Such differences as the figure being more vivid, easier to remember, and carrying more specific meaning are closely associated with attention.

From these considerations it can be assumed that learning and previous experience will be important in determining what is perceived as figure and what as ground. A familiar object or an object carrying intense emotional associations would be expected, figuratively speaking, to leap out of the vague field and demand attention.

It is upon assumptions of the kind just mentioned that vague stimuli are used in projective tests. The preoccupations of the subject and the highly emotional content material will tend to be projected into the field. Lines may be distorted, gaps bridged, or extraneous material drawn in. Deviations in structuring are expected to be in the direction of internal needs. In effect this means that the threshold of suggestion for those things that are producing worry, anxiety, fear, and so forth is lower than percepts with other content. Therefore, out of the vagueness of the ground these will emerge and become structured by the person as he observes, interprets, and reports. It does not appear necessary to insist that there is a mysterious process or even that it is entirely unconscious. Some writers having a strict psychoanalytic orientation conclude that by the use of vague or relatively unstructured stimuli the examiner is able to tap the unconscious. This is no doubt true, but it is also reasonable to suppose that the response might result from either conscious or unconscious processes. More likely there is a continuous associative and interactive process taking place which involves material found in both the conscious and the unconscious. There seems to be scientific advantage in dealing with phenomena that are within the range of consciousness before invoking the concept of unconscious motivation. This orthodox psychological approach might still enable the investigator to go quite far in interpreting projective test results and drawing conclusions about the personality of an individual who has produced certain kinds of responses to projective test items.

PERCEPTUAL UNITS

In order that a figure emerge from the ground several characteristics are known to be of importance in giving visual perceptual advantage. While it might be generalized that these factors of advantage are due to the nature of the stimulus and to past experience, it is possible to be more specific than this. Some of the factors have their basis in the physical qualities of the stimulus, while others are more closely dependent upon modification of the organism because of past experience. A sharp separation as to whether the element of stimulus factors or of past experience is chiefly responsible is not possible, for both elements are likely to be interacting under all conditions.

As we have indicated before, in order for a figure to be discriminated from ground, there must be a lack of uniformity in the visual field, a differential threshold between figure and ground. Even where there is a recognizable difference, a pattern may not become clear unless some time for organizational activity is possible. In tachistoscopic presentation, the exposure time may be too short for grouping to take place. A quick glance at an expanse of sand, or at the stars in the sky, may be too brief for any conscious separation into patterns, or so much as to allow field and ground to be distinguished. Using time as a variable, and allowing longer and longer exposure, grouping or organization will take place—apparently in spite of the subject's effort to avoid this consequence. The factors of advantage leading to the emergence of certain patterns rather than others will be dependent upon the following considerations:

1. Nearness or Proximity. Stimulus items that are close together in space tend to be grouped into a unit. It is not difficult to observe subjectively the grouping process, on the basis of nearness, if a person gazes at the star-filled sky. One pattern after another will emerge, including the stars that are close together. The stars will fall into triangles, squares, or the outlines of familiar objects. If this last becomes very striking, stars may be organized that do not take in all the closest ones. The names of constellations, which include animals and such objects as the "dipper," must reflect these tendencies and represent the meaningful end product of perceiving by the name that is given to the constellation.

2. Similarity. Similar objects, other things being equal, tend to be organized. Two circles are seen as a pair more easily than a cross and a circle. In the illustration of the stars being formed into patterns upon the basis of proximity, the difference in size is overcome; nearness was a more potent factor than size differences. These two factors, each giving

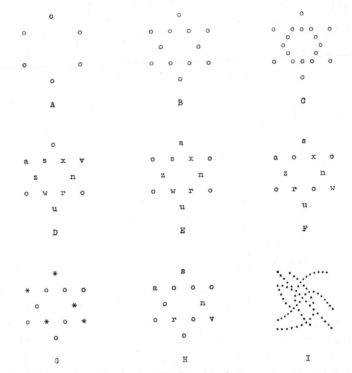

Fig. 8.2. Dot figures illustrating the factors of nearness, sameness, continuation, and good figure. The hexagon so clearly visible in A is somewhat obscured in B by the additional dots, but reappears in C as a leftover group when the addition of still more dots in close proximity to each other brings out the interior hexagon. In D, E, and F the sameness of certain items favors grouping them, and the leftovers readily fall into a complementary group, when they make a regular figure, or when, as in G, they are similar; whereas in H, where the leftover items are dissimilar and irregularly arranged, they do not get together readily. I shows the factor of homogeneous continuation, in that the dots are readily seen as lying along straight lines or fairly definite curves. (From Woodworth, Robert S., and Schlosberg, Harold, *Experimental Psychology*. New York: Henry Holt & Co., 1954.)

advantage in unifying, may be in almost constant conflict. By experimentation, it is possible to determine how much distance may be placed between objects of a different kind in order to achieve a balance with similarity. At the threshold point, perceptual shift will be rapid, and the visual field becomes unstable. Ambiguous figures can thus be made by introducing conflicting factors of advantage, such as nearness and similarity.

3. *"Good Figure."* Within a given culture, at least, general agreement can be arrived at that certain figures are better than others. Some insist that the subjects involved must learn what is a good figure before this plays any part in perceptual advantage. Others assume that there is a kind of primitive tendency to accept some patterns and reject others. Closure, symmetry, and balance have been claimed to be native. A figure possessing these qualities, so the argument goes, will be chosen over figures lacking them. A closely associated concept is that the individual, in trying to recall or reproduce, will tend to modify a "poor" figure in the direction of a "good" figure. The evidence is not clear. Some studies have supported such a conclusion while others do not. Conclusive evidence that distortion or completion will take direction toward "perfection" is still lacking. If true, it is nevertheless certain that other factors at times take precedence over this one. Should biological needs be placed in conflict with the "need for perfection," distortion will not consistently be in the direction of the latter.

MASKING OF FIGURES

If definite factors of perceptual advantage are present in a figure, the figure should be readily perceived. What happens if the factors are eliminated? It might be supposed that everything would be confused and chaotic. Then could an additional step be taken and characteristics experimentally inserted to conceal a pattern? Perhaps by this backdoor method it becomes possible to gain a better understanding of the perceptual process.

Gottschaldt (5) undertook to use masked figures to study the effect of past experience upon form perception. He made several figures in which common forms were cleverly concealed. It was his belief that a familiar figure should be no more difficult to conceal that an unfamiliar one as long as they were equally simple. The results that he obtained have not been thought to be conclusive by other investigators. His studies, and later ones of a similar nature, have revealed a number of important things about concealed figures.

Psychologists are interested in both the factors that lead to concealment on masking of a figure and also those factors which give advantage in perceiving the figure. A systematic procedure of adding lines to a geometric figure with a view to determine what causes increased difficulty is an experimental procedure that helps to fraction the problem.

Supposing a square to be drawn on a white sheet of paper, what might be done to conceal the square? An attack might first be made upon the most important ways by which the square is identified. The essentials of the square are equal lines and equal angles. Thus, lines or angles can be added that would cause confusion when trying to pick out the ones belonging to the square. By drawing six straight lines to radiate in one general direction from a given corner, Galli and Zama (3) found that the square was made very difficult to identify. It was found that filling the

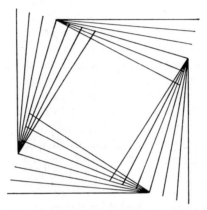

Fig. 8.3. The square is effectively concealed by the additional lines. (From Galli, A., and Zama, A., Z. *Psy.* 123 (1931), 308-348. After Woodworth, Robert S., *Experimental Psychology*. New York: Henry Holt & Co., 1938.)

corner with additional lines which projected beyond the corners also made for great difficulties in sorting out the correct square. Perhaps all nonessential lines increase the problem of making the necessary discrimination and probably add to distraction effects. Various investigators were interested in finding the type of additions that gave maximum difficulty, or on the other hand, those that had least influence. Thus, they were trying to find means of obtaining quantitative differences, or data that could be placed along the same continuum.

Lines that suggest, but do not complete, familiar figures strongly interfere with accurate perception. Thus, if the subject is trying to identify a square in a mass of lines, those lines that almost form right angles are much more bothersome than those that deviate widely. Here, the subject is confronted with two problems—one of overcoming suggestion and the other of making fine discriminations. Again, it is found that certain portions of a figure are more critical than others. A small segment of line in a geometric figure is almost worthless in trying to identify the figure of which it is a part. On the other hand, if the segment is taken from the corner so that the size of the angle can be determined, this is very helpful.

GEOMETRIC ILLUSIONS

There are many kinds of geometric figures that mislead the subject in making his judgments. One line may look longer than another when in

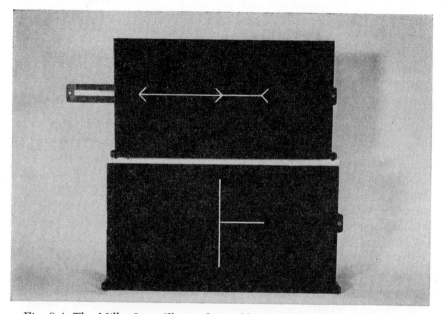

Fig. 8.4. The Miller-Lyer Illusion has calibration of length on the back and can be manipulated by either experimenter or subject. The vertical-horizontal apparatus permits setting of the horizontal line. (Courtesy Lafayette Instrument Co.)

reality it is shorter; of two figures having the same size, one may look larger than the other. Several well-known figures of this kind can be found in standard psychology books. These are spoken of as examples of illusions. If an illusion is experienced, this means that a wrong interpretation has been made. Errors in perception of this kind are thought to be due either to the characteristics of the sense organ or else to the pattern of lines in the figures.

Illusions are sometimes divided into two types: (1) those of contrast and (2) those of assimilation. A two-story building standing in the shadow of a New York skyscraper will not seem tall because of the contrast. On the other hand, a short line may seem to be longer because other lines lead to an overestimate of its length. The short line is assimilated into the pattern. This process has often been referred to as *confluxion*.

Several theories have been advanced as an explanation for illusions. These included, among others, eye movement, perspective, empathy, and pregnance. Relative to illusions, it should be kept in mind that the subject is willing to accept the fact that his judgment has been in error. However, illusions tend to persist even when it is known that there is an error in perception. Corrections can be made which prevent the subject from continuing to make the mistake, yet he may find it necessary to ignore what his eyes seem to be telling him. Eventually he comes to making allowance for what he recognizes as a constant error of impression when rendering his report.

1. Eye Movement. One interpretation of illusions rests upon the assumption that it is easier to move the eyes in one direction than another. The vertical-horizontal illusion in which the vertical line of equal length to the horizontal one is judged to be longer has been explained in this way, the assumption being that it required more effort to move the eyes upward and downward than to the sides. However, this is a doubtful explanation, since the illusion persists even if the subject is lying on his side so the eye movements involved are reversed, at least with regard to gravitational forces and the muscles in use.

The familiar Müller-Lyer illusion has been said to be due to the influence of the adjacent lines. It is claimed that these tend to lead the eyes beyond the center line, which is the one being judged for length. Just exactly what the characteristics are that one line possesses that enables it to lead the eyes along while another line does not, remains unclear. Yet, this concept is widely used by the artist in his explanations of the use of lines. Of course, he is not necessarily dealing with illusions alone. Studies in which attempts have been made to control eye movement have not been supportive of this interpretation of illusions. Voluntary control of eye movements, in which the subject fixates a point in the center of the line to be judged, does not eliminate the illusion. This procedure cannot be defended as an entirely adequate experimental control.

If two lines are to be compared in length, it is usually necessary to shift the eyes from one figure to another. However, the subject might estimate the length of each figure presented to him with the "error of estimate" used as the index to his judgment. A more satisfactory control of eye movement is possible with tachistoscopic presentation of the figure. The speed of presentation can be rapid so that the subject finds it impossible to shift his eye during the exposure of the figure. In these studies, it has also been found that the illusion persists.

2. *Perspective.* The perspective theory is not readily disposed of as having no effect. In the case of the Müller-Lyer illusion, if the four lines converge toward the center line, the line to be judged between them will be overestimated. In such a figure the subject is likely to get the impression of depth. Perception of depth brings along with it the principle of *size constancy* for which there is an abundance of supportive evidence. Size constancy presumably enables the individual to avoid a mistake in judgment when comparing two dogs of equal size, one being located twice as far away as the other. The subtended visual arc will be greater for the nearby dog but in effect this is ignored and the sizes of the two retinal images disregarded when rendering a report about the relative sizes. However, there are many visual illusions for which perspective and size constancy are inadequate explanations. A theory of illusions of greater generality would be helpful from a scientific viewpoint.

3. *Empathy.* The empathy theory appeals to those studying the esthetic effects of architecture. It is a theory, if supported when using material of neutral or slight emotional value like that of simple visual illusions, that would certainly seem to hold great promise of usefulness in trying to interpret perceptual distortions in social relationships where emotional tone may be intense. It was held by Lipps (7) and others using the principle of empathy, that a vertical line resists gravity more than a horizontal line. When this interpretation is applied to the Müller-Lyer illusion, one figure suggests expansion, giving rise to the impression of largeness, while the other appears shorter because of the feeling of limitations. There can be no question that feeling tone is associated with the shape of lines and the direction of their extension. The emotion-provoking quality of abstract lines is expanded upon when discussing emotions.

4. *"Pregnance."* The "pregnance" or "good-figure" theory advocated by the gestaltists rests upon the assumption that such factors as symmetry, closure, balance, and meaning produce some of the esthetic value of the figure. The need for these qualities may lead the organism to distort in the direction of "goodness" and hence this becomes a factor in producing the illusion. One might say that the organism resists reality and distorts in the direction of esthetically approved figures. This is an intriguing theory, but like the other theories is still lacking in wide verification.

PERSISTENCE OF ILLUSIONS

It has been well established that the extent of an illusion rapidly decreases upon repeated exposures and verified judgments. According to

Judd (6), this is true to some extent even though the subject is not given information about the accuracy of his estimates. The result given by Judd, a good many years ago, is fairly consistent with the findings of later investigators. It should be noted that Judd used the same subjects over a period of twenty-four days, during which time they had daily practice in estimating the length of lines in the illusion. It is not unreasonable to question the adequacy of controls in this and some other early experiments. For example, in this situation it could scarcely be expected that subjects would always refrain from outside checking upon a problem involving so much of their time. Outside the experimental setting, any subject might have made a quick check upon the probable accuracy of his estimates by drawing two lines of equal length upon a sheet of paper and then constructing four end lines to see what effect was produced by them. He would almost certainly have learned that one type of line led to overestimation of length, the other to underestimation. Then, he would have been likely to compensate in order to get a "better score" in the experiment. Motivation, even where there is not an obvious reward beyond being right, has been found to be very strong with some people. This effect is even strongly suspected in some lower animals. Nevertheless, there may well be some improvements without any knowledge of errors in estimates and there is certainly rapid improvement if the subject is allowed to know the accuracy of his judgments.

ILLUSIONS VS. HALLUCINATIONS

There is evidence that a visual illusion persists even though the subject learns to be very accurate in rendering good judgments. By this it is meant that the subject learns to say that two lines are equal although the visual impression is that one is longer than the other. One important distinction between the illusion and the hallucination is that the subject is readily convinced that his sensory impression is wrong in the illusion. He will make adjustments in the direction of reality, or he can be persuaded to give a different report after checking on his judgment by use of additional means. The placing of a ruler along two lines that look very unequal but which are of equal length convinces the subject of their equality. This kind of modification in the judgment or belief of the subject is not found to be the case when applied to the highly individualistic and emotionally loaded hallucination. The person who experiences a hallucination persists in his belief although confronted with objective evidence that would seem to be adequate proof to others that the interpretation had been faulty. The illusion tends to be universal among people while the hallucination is highly personal and carries with it strong emotional investment. It is often said that the illusion is normal; the hallucination abnormal. At any rate, the hallucination is something more than an exaggerated illusion; the two are probably not on the same continuum.

AFTEREFFECTS

We have discussed afterimages along with problems of color vision. There is an interesting phenomenon observed first by Gibson (4) that is similar, but perhaps also significantly different. Gibson found that a curved line if observed over a period of five or ten minutes seems to be less curved. Furthermore, if the subject is presented with a straight line at the end of the observation period, he may get the impression that the straight line curves in the opposite direction from the curved line that he had been observing. This could scarcely be exactly the same thing as the complementary color which emerges as the afterimage in color vision. Since the curve bends in the opposite direction, it seems probable that the end organs on the retina that are activated are different ones. If the curved line is presented to only one eye, it has been found that the unused eye also is affected, but only about half as much as is the case if both eyes have been stimulated by the original stimulus. This result has been interpreted to mean that the phenomenon is due to brain activity rather than limited to the retina alone. In this connection, it should be remembered that half of the neural fibers from the eye cross over on the way back to the occipital lobe. Nevertheless, there appears to be some kind of neural transfer. Studies of this kind are thought to have a bearing upon the problem of whether there are specific neural pathways through the brain for each response or whether there is a tendency for mass action in the brain. Unfortunately, the same research data have been used in supportive arguments for each position.

The aftereffect phenomenon has been found in sense modalities other than vision. There is little question that this phenomenon is but a special case of the broader problem of adaptation. Köhler and Wallach considered that figural aftereffects, of the kind found by Gibson, gave strong support to a satiation theory of perception and they believed that by means of such research a better knowledge of the dynamics of cortical fields would be forthcoming. The satiation theory is based upon the assumption of polarization of cells in the brain. Polarization of the tissue decreases the electrical conductivity, it is held, and may last in some instances over weeks. The whole system of ideas based upon satiation has been challenged and the problem cannot be resolved at present. This is a theory with broad implications and, if established by further research, will enable writers to organize much fragmentary information about perception into a more meaningful system.

DEPTH PERCEPTION

Under normal conditions, and with other senses intact, the individual probably relies more heavily upon the eyes for depth perception than all other senses combined. There are many visual cues to distance. Some of them can be used in monocular vision; others are possible only with binocular vision. The problems having to do with depth perception are of interest in both theoretical and practical research. Many occupations make great demands upon the individual for accurate depth perception. Lack of ability to perceive space accurately gives rise to very noticeable behavior deviations. While good depth perception is closely related to what is called "good vision," there are some differences. There seems to be more learning effect in depth perception than in visual acuity; the way the individual uses his eyes has an important bearing on visual perception.

The lack of good depth perception may lead the individual into inadequate motor responses, such as putting the brake of his car on too soon or too late; causing the pilot to overrun the landing strip, or to land in the trees before getting to it; causing the typist or piano player to overreach or underreach the desired key. Skill in these responses is only partially dependent upon visual space perception. We have previously discussed kinesthesis and its bearing upon coordinated movements in space. This sense is probably of much more importance in the movements of the piano player and the typist than is vision.

Vision provides the observer with cues for responding to objects in the distance as no other sense does. The sense of hearing may be of some use in judging distance and direction, as indicated in an earlier chapter. However, in hearing the subject is more easily misled than is the case in vision—as misleading as that may sometimes be. Errors in determining direction are scarcely of practical importance in vision but can be very great in hearing. Occasionally, there may be a refractory medium through which the light rays must pass before reaching the eyes and this can lead to error, as when judging the location of an object under water. Performing while looking in a mirror is a special case and requires a reversal in direction of movement from what visual perception suggests.

It is convenient to present the cues that are used in perceiving distance under two conditions—those that are present when one eye is used and those operative when both eyes are used. Another consideration to keep

in mind is that certain of the cues are primarily dependent upon the structure of the eye or eyes, while others are to be found in external conditions.
Experience or learning, of course, has an influence upon the skill brought
to bear in using all the cues.

MONOCULAR VISION

Contrary to much popular belief, the one-eyed person need not be
seriously handicapped in the perception of depth or distance. The person
who suddenly loses one eye is often very confused for a time, as he is
no longer able to use some of the cues that he had been depending upon
in the past. He can soon learn to do rather well by substituting other
cues that are available to him. It will be seen that nearly all of the important cues for perceiving distance of remote objects are still available.
In near vision, he is somewhat more handicapped. However, the loss of
approximately one-third of the visual field because of the shape of the
face and the blocking of part of the binocular field of vision by the nose
may prove very bothersome. This means that much more movement of
the body or head becomes necessary to bring objects within the visual
field. Those that have observed the boxer who has one eye swollen together will easily be convinced of the difficulties involved here.

1. Size of the Retinal Image. One of the oldest recognized cues to
distance is the retinal image. The more distant an object, the smaller the
image, or, to put it another way, the smaller the visual arc subtended
by the same object in the visual field. Interestingly enough, this cue to
distance turns out to be of relatively little use. When judging the size of
distant objects, there is a tendency, as mentioned earlier, to retain size
constancy. Thus, we tend to ignore the relative size of the image. Empirical studies reveal that judgment of distance is not greatly dependent
upon the image. Apparently past experience and memory dominate so
much that orientation to reality is not dictated very much by the retinal
image. The football tends to retain its size regardless of how far away
it may be seen; an elephant does not look to be the size of a mouse simply
because it is a mile away while the mouse is within a few yards of the
observer and, thus, the image might be about the same for both. To be
sure, some use is made of the image in estimating distance.

2. Interposition. In our discussion of figure and ground we found it
necessary to mention interposition. Interposition furnishes an excellent
cue to determining which objects are farther away. Yet, this is of little
use beyond indicating the relative distance of the objects. If the observer
had to depend entirely upon interposition, he might still find it difficult
to decide whether two objects, one of which is clearly more distant than

the other, are one hundred yards or a mile away. Nor might he have much of an idea about the distance between them. It seems obvious and logical that the nearer of two objects will blot from vision parts of the more distant one. It might easily be supposed that ability to make this kind of a discrimination is a native one. Yet, if the drawings of children, before they are able to give very meaningful verbal reports, are used as evidence, such discrimination must be the result of a considerable amount of experience and learning. Children will make drawings having what is called *transparency*. The tree intended to be placed in front of the house does not hide any part of the house. The lines of the house are drawn continuously as though the child is able to see through the tree.

The procedure, indicated above, does not seem to disturb the child in his drawing efforts, and it is doubtful that most children would correct for it without instruction. This kind of transparency is seen in most, if not all, prehistoric drawings that have been found in caves inhabited by very primitive people. Again, there is found to be a reversion to this type of drawing among maladjusted adults, and use is made of this performance in reaching a decision about the seriousness of regression or deterioration of the patient.

3. *Color.* Color is often used as a means of judging distance. Distant objects have less saturated color and there is a tendency for them to take on a bluish coloration. The short waves pass through the atmosphere better than the longer waves. While people regularly make use of color differences in estimating distance, this can be a very deceptive cue. Again, the observer finds that more dependence can be placed upon his judgment of the relative distance of two objects than of the absolute distance. Since the light waves come to the eyes through the same conditions of atmosphere, the bluer one is judged to be more distant. The person going from the eastern part of the United States to the Rocky Mountains may be very badly mislead by the distinctive outline and lack of bluish coloring of the mountain that is far away. Drawing from past experience, he may estimate that a mountain is five or ten miles away, when actually it is twenty-five miles. The difference in the higher and lower atmosphere sometimes leads to very interesting perception that is illusory in nature. It might even be possible to see the peak of a mountain that is sharp in outline but the base of it be lost in a bluish haze. In rare conditions, there may even be a continuous blue horizon below the peak so the mountain appears to be resting on the sky. Such an illusion could prove to be disastrous to the pilot of a fast plane. For example, Mt. Rainier, in the state of Washington, is seen occasionally towering above a continuous blue sky line. Is this really an illusion? At

any rate the unseen base of the mountain is there, whatever the sense organs may register at the moment.

4. *Light and Shadow.* Other things being equal, shadowed objects are usually judged to be farther away than lighted objects. This is consistent with the darker colors for great distance and with what is expected in figure-ground. An illusion can be created by painting dark and light spots on a smooth surface so that it "looks" to be rough. Knowledge of the direction of the source of light may modify one's judgment. If the sun is beyond the house, the shadow made by it is still perceived as closer than the house. The portrait painter makes use of light and dark to give the effect of wrinkles, or to make the figure stand out from the background. This is possibly the best cue to the smoothness or roughness of the surface for the distant object. Here is found a special example of depth perception, for it is a kind of miniature discrimination—a discrimination between areas that may be a fraction of an inch closer or farther, yet the whole object may be hundreds of yards away. Still, the appearance can easily be misleading, for the surface that looks farther away may be closer, depending, as indicated, upon the light source.

5. *Sharpness of Outline.* Shapes become blurred, edges indistinct in distant objects. How well these may be used in judging distance is dependent upon experience. Those who go into strange places may be misled. Even familiar objects in the accustomed environment may seem close one day and far away the next. The individual is constantly trying to compensate for variable conditions if he is called upon to give estimates. Estimating absolute distance not only involves the problem of using a standard of measurement, such as yard or mile, but also requires that allowance be made for the ever-changing conditions under which judgment is rendered. The cues that one uses may be deceptive. This is less bothersome than it might at first seem, for orientation in space is primarily a matter of relationship between various objects, and between objects and the observer. In daily activity, it is not making judgment of absolute distance that is of greatest importance but making discriminations that are accurate with regard to relationships.

6. *Accommodation.* Over a period of many years it was not known exactly what purpose the lens in the eye served. The primary purpose has now been well established, but it remains uncertain how important the lens is in helping with the perception of depth. The shape of the lens changes as shifts of focus are made from distant to close objects. The contraction and relaxation of the ciliary muscle that takes place as changes are required in accommodation may or may not give rise to kinesthetic sensations of use in estimating distance. There does not appear

to be any consciousness or awareness of such sensations. At any rate, there can scarcely be enough difference between the muscular tensions to enable the individual to determine which of two distant objects alongside of each other is slightly closer. At least, the subject does well to make much more than very general discriminations of depth by basing judgment upon accommodation.

A review of the cues used in judging depth in monocular vision leads to the conclusion that the cues that are most closely associated with the structural parts of the eye are of relatively little importance. The cues that are picked up from environmental conditions are more important. Yet these may be extremely deceptive if the observer moves from the situation in which he learned the cues to another where atmospheric and other conditions are markedly different. Relearning is rapid for the intelligent person if knowledge of errors is available.

BINOCULAR PERCEPTION OF DEPTH

Some of the most puzzling things about vision are related to how the two eyes are used simultaneously. The retinal image is always different in the two eyes because of the angle of regard. The coordination of the two eyes requires a precision that is remarkable, and sometimes movement in one eye is more rapid than in the other. One eye may move and the other "track" until it comes to the same focal point. A further complication is occasionally found wherein the image in one eye is larger than that in the other.

Considering all of these factors how is it that the images blend into a single image or perception? The answer is that fusion will take place only within certain limits of aberration. In the process of perception, it may be that one eye will dominate while the image from the other is suppressed more or less permanently. Again, there may be a rapid shift, so first perception is based upon what the left eye is seeing and next, what the right eye is seeing—the images may not be fused into a single sensation. What is perceived falls into a pattern of alternating images.

These problems have been recognized for many years. The physician, Galen, described how a column was different when viewed by the left eye, the right eye, and both eyes. Leonardo da Vinci left a number of comments upon vision and among them was a note and drawing concerning the "transparency" of objects. By this he meant that the object, if small, did not completely cut off any part of the field of vision. His drawings show that he recognized that there was overlapping of the two fields of vision coming from each of the eyes. He indicated how a small object did not obscure any part of the background when both eyes were being used. Thus, he recognized the phenomena of parallax and retinal disparity although he did not use the terminology that is current today.

Over the years there were numerous contributions to knowledge of how the eyes function together. But, as in so many scientific matters, we can point to relatively few clearcut contributions from the time of da Vinci until fairly recently. In 1775 Harris wrote a book, *Treatise of Opticks,* in which he discussed parallax and disparity. We find Boring (2)

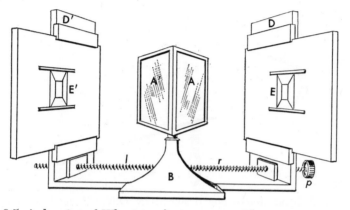

Fig. 8.5. A drawing of Wheatstone's stereoscope. The stereoscope was built about 1838. AA' are mirrors. DD' are uprights upon which EE' may be adjusted. The screw P is also for changing distances. EE' are the disparate drawings that are reflected by the mirrors. (From Boring, Edwin G., *Sensation and Perception in the History of Experimental Psychology.* New York: Appleton-Century-Crofts Co., 1942.)

quoting from that work as follows: "And by the parallax on account of the distance betwixt our eyes, we can distinguish besides the front, part of two sides or a near object, not thicker than the said distance; and this gives a visible *relievo* to such objects, which helps greatly to raise or detach them from the plane, on which they lie; Thus, the nose on a face, is the more remarkably raised, by our seeing each side of it at once."

The stereoscope was invented by Wheatstone more than a century ago. The basic principle is the reproduction of two pictures which are almost, but not quite, the same. One picture is as the left eye would view the object and the other as the right eye would see it. Thus, it could be demonstrated that any kind of mechanism that will serve to present the left picture to the left eye, and the right picture to the right eye, will enable the person to get an impression of depth. A simple stereoscope was made by Oliver Wendell Holmes a few years after Wheatstone made his rather cumbersome instrument. It became a popular parlor pastime for people to sit around gazing at stereoscopic slides. The present-day student will know about the long and expensive struggle of the movie industry to apply the principle of the stereoscope so depth perception can be obtained from the movie screen.

Retinal disparity has little value in helping to perceive depth except at close range. At distances beyond fifty or one hundred yards, the difference between the retinal images can be expected to be below the threshold of discrimination. However, binocular vision is of great im-

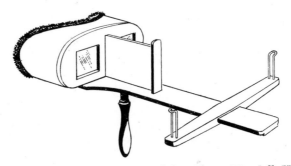

Fig. 8.6. A hand stereoscope designed by Oliver Wendell Holmes about 1861. This stereoscope became a popular item for the parlor where people used it to view travel pictures.

portance in doing many tasks close at hand. The person with one eye will have a total blanking out of part of the background by small objects. This can mean that a small object behind another, when close by, is readily seen by the individual who uses two eyes, but is invisible to the one-eyed person. The individual with normal binocular vision may see each object and around both in this situation. Thus, in such work as might be expected on the assembly line, the one-eyed person might be seriously handicapped. The use of the two eyes becomes something more than just useful in estimating distance for abstract information in that it enables the individual to move in space, exercising motor skill essential to everyday activities.

CONVERGENCE

While there is doubt about the individual's awareness of sensations from the eye muscles during accommodation, there are unquestionable sensations of tension under certain conditions when the eyes are converged. In convergence the external muscles of the two eyes bring them to focus on the same point. Where the object is extremely close to the eyes, the tension may be great enough to be painful. The kinesthetic sensations arising as a result of convergence have usually been accepted as of importance in perceiving distance. Fine discriminations between the distance of objects is probably not possible by this means. Yet, the use of convergence in discriminating between near and distant objects seems certain. However, there are also many other cues that can be depended upon for this gross distinction. Just how important is the part convergence plays in depth perception as people go about their daily activities is difficult to determine from available knowledge.

ANISEIKONIA

The discovery of an individual with a rare eye condition in which the retinal image in one eye was larger than that in the other led Ames (1) to experiment with artificially produced images of different sizes. The use of lenses that produce two different size images leads to great confusion in the individual at first, although people who have the disorder, known as aniseikonia, seem to perceive more or less normally. While this may appear surprising, probably the same explanation holds as that concerning confusion due to the inverted retinal image. If the person has never seen in any other way, he has learned to respond appropriately.

Following up the findings of Ames about aniseikonia, various investigators have built rooms in which the usual cues for depth perception have been eliminated or distorted. Lines, shadows, and so forth have been changed radically by using tree leaves or other uniform materials that lend themselves to the production of a mosaic effect on the inside of the room. The corners of the room and distances to various objects that are placed in the room do not furnish the usual depth cues. The observer is readily led into misjudgments and may feel great confusion in trying to resolve the relationships between objects in the visual field. To some extent all the visual stimuli become ambiguous and the person is a ready victim to suggestion from other stimuli that mislead him.

Aside from the novelty of these studies, they allow for interesting possibilities for isolating factors one by one so that insight may be gained to the whole process of space perception. Also, the subject who is confronted with the necessity to respond in this strange situation experiences considerable stress, or perhaps better, distress. Experiments designed to involve learning while in this visually strange situation might prove to be fruitful. The vulnerability of the subject to suggestion when subjected to this unusual and stressful condition has interested social psychologists. It is undoubtedly true that there are always many ambiguities in the social structure to which all people must try to make some kind of an adjustment. After reviewing the several studies of the kind indicated, Woodworth and Schlossberg (10) were led to the following conclusions: "We emerge from these studies with an important generalization: the less adequately a perception is determined by stimuli, the less stable it will be, and the more subject to subtle factors in O. This accounts for such diverse facts as the effect of poverty on judged size of coins (Bruner & Goodman, 1947; Pastore, 1949) and the clinical results with that most ambiguous of all perceptual stimuli, the Rorschach inkblots."

While the discovery of aniseikonia helped to initiate some new and interesting studies, the investigators were not venturing into an entirely new area of psychology when application was extended to perception and personality. We do not say this to depreciate the significance of the discovery, but rather to indicate that the results, although original in important ways, nevertheless fit very nicely into the developing science of psychology. Rorschach finished his work about a quarter of a century earlier and certainly Rorschach, with becoming modesty, did not claim that he owed nothing to still earlier investigators. He and others working with ambiguous stimuli (usually one characteristic of projective tests) drew from workers that extended back at least as far as the creative and dynamic philosopher-educator, Herbart. In ways at present not entirely clear, it is faithfully believed by many that these various investigators have laid the groundwork for a fruitful approach to the intriguing problem of the nature of personality. They believe that, by these means and other techniques that should yet be derived, investigators will be able to describe, understand, and communicate to others much more effectively concerning the dynamic characteristics that differentiate one individual from another.

SUGGESTED READINGS

Geldard, Frank A. *The Human Senses,* pp. 51-82, 83-93. New York: John Wiley, 1953.

Garrett, Henry E. *Great Experiments in Psychology,* pp. 63-82. New York: Appleton-Century-Crofts, 1951.

Bartley, S. Howard. *Principles of Perception.* New York: Harper, 1958.

Dennis, Wayne. *Readings in General Psychology,* pp. 87-110. New York: Prentice Hall, 1949.

Stevens, S. S. (ed.). *Handbook of Experimental Psychology.* Graham: "Visual Perception," pp. 868-920. New York: John Wiley, 1951.

Hebb, D. O. *The Organization of Behavior,* pp. 60-78. New York: John Wiley, 1953.

REFERENCES

1. Ames, A. "Binocular vision as affected by relationship between uniocular stimulus patterns in commonplace environments," *Amer. J. Psychol.*, 59 (1946), 333-357.
2. Boring, Edwin G. *Sensation and Perception in the History of Experimental Psychology*, p. 285. New York: Appleton-Century-Crofts, 1942.
3. Galli, A., and Zama, A. "Untersuchungen Ueber die Wahrnehmung ebener geometrischer Figuren, die ganz oder teilweise von anderen geometrischen Figuren verdeckt sind," *Z. Ps.*, 123 (1931), 308-378.
4. Gibson, J. J. "Adaption, aftereffect, and contrast in the perception of curved lines," *J. Exp. Psychol.*, 16 (1933), 1-31.
5. Gottschalt, K. "Ueber den Einfluss der Erfahrung auf die Wahrnehmung von Figuren," *Ps. Forsch.*, 8 (1926), 261-317.
6. Judd, C. H. "Movement and Consciousness," *Psychol. Monogr.*, No. 29 (1905).
7. Lipps, T. *Raumaesthetik und geometrisch-optische Täuschungen.* Leipzig: Barth., 1897.
8. Rubins, E. *Visuell Wahrgenommene Figuren.* Copenhagen: Gyldendalske, 1921.
9. Senden, M. *Raum- und Gestaltauffassung bei operierten Blindgewordenen vor und nach der Operation.* Leipzig: Barth., 1932.
10. Woodworth, Robert S., and Schlosberg, Harold. *Experimental Psychology*, p. 491. New York: Henry Holt, 1954.

9

BODILY CHANGES AND PSYCHOLOGICAL PHENOMENA

THE ORGANISM IN PSYCHOLOGICAL AND SOCIAL PARTICIPATION

If it is assumed that the study of psychology should be kept carefully anchored to the organism, nowhere is such a need more apparent, nor perhaps more feasible and useful at present, than in the study of what has usually been referred to as emotional behavior. In some respects a more relevant headline for the chapter would be "Bodily Changes and Emotions," but this might imply a not altogether desirable limitation. Broadly speaking, there should be no lack of significant relationship between so-called emotional reactivity of the individual and his way of participating in social, political, and economic affairs. In these matters it is perhaps safe to assume that only strongly loaded and emotionally intense opinions, attitudes, and beliefs get translated into action. Yet it must be granted that little more than a beginning has been made in relating bodily changes to any kind of social action. Devices for measuring such changes are often inaccurate and cumbersome, and dependable procedures for determining changes in abstract matters, such as attitudes and beliefs, are difficult to develop. Correlations are consequently not all that could be wished and these may be depressed because better measures are not at hand.

For the most part we must still confine our investigations to studying the rather gross changes, such as those of blood pressure, skin resistance to electric current, muscle tension, temperature, and blood chemistry, as these are brought about by threat to the organisms. Adjustive mechanisms associated with biological survival are more readily observed under threat than is the case where more subtle social adjustments are required. In other words, progress has barely extended beyond the boundaries that are the legitimate domain of biologists and physiologists. In general, experiments have been directed toward the study of responses in muscles and organs that are activated by the autonomic nervous system when the organism is confronted with danger or threat of danger. Thus, most of the reported experimental results that are of interest to psychologists have had to do with the relationship between bodily changes elicited under what are assumed to be rather intense emotion-provoking situations.

There may be bodily changes that relate significantly to psychological phenomena that extend into other areas. For example, it seems to be an implicit assumption of most investigators that there is some kind of neurological change accompanying all learning. Yet, we know little or nothing about the actual modification of structure or function in the nervous system which may result from experience. There could be subtle bodily changes going along with all sensory and perceptual processes. Detecting and measuring these changes, if they extend beyond the more obvious ones associated with autonomic nervous system activation, is largely left for the work of future scientists. It is conceivable that problems having to do with the processes of thinking and imagining can be approached by a study of changes in the organism, but this, of course, remains highly speculative.

In spite of our relative ignorance concerning the relationship between overt behavior, emotions, or thinking and what happens within the organism during the process, many scientists concerned with these problems believe that investigations ultimately will and necessarily must take the direction of studying these basic relationships.

USE OF THE WORD EMOTION

In recent years objections have been raised to the use of the word *emotion* in scientific discourse. The older three-way division of psychology into cognition, volition, and affect (or emotions) is presently seldom used. However, we shall make frequent use of the word "emotion," in part because there is such general use of the word in psychological literature, but mainly because there is not a satisfactory substitute. Nevertheless, there is good ground for thinking that much misunderstanding might be avoided if we could use a more readily definable word that would be acceptable to all those interested in the phenomenon usually discussed under this heading. The classification of behavior into emotional and nonemotional is particularly objectionable. Where this kind of language has been used, the implication has ordinarily been that emotional behavior is on one side and intellectual the other. Sometimes writers have gone a step further and classified people as being either emotional or intellectual. Obviously, we look in vain for an individual totally without emotions. A simple dichotomy of this kind usually has limited usefulness in science.

It might well be that the material usually handled under the heading of emotions could be more effectively presented if we spoke of "level of activity," the "extent of mobilization of energy," or "anticipatory behavior." Even if scientifically more satisfactory descriptive terms are found, the word "emotion" is still going to be widely used in literature and daily conversation. It is not our intention to use the word as though it is the name of a special entity which is either present or absent. Our meaning is more nearly conveyed if we think of emotion *as a descriptive term indicating an energized or highly activated state of the organism.* No present definition of emotions is without objections and this is, of course, one of the reasons for trying to find a better term. Further discussion of general concepts will be found when we deal with theories of emotions. Short definitions that have been used include: (1) an emotion is a stirred-up state of the organism; (2) emotion is awareness of sensation brought about by visceral changes; (3) emotion is a disorganized state and indicates a temporary breakdown in personality; (4) emotion refers to the degree energy is mobilized in a particular situation. It is our preference to think of emotion in terms of a state of the organism in which there is an increased mobilization of energy and especially heightened activity within the autonomic nervous system and the organs supplied by it. Social and psychological threats can certainly provoke such reactions and this is more common in man than is threat of physical danger.

INDEX TO EMOTIONAL REACTIONS

The search for bodily changes that might be used as an index to emotional reactions, or to individual variations in emotionality, has been pursued with great diligence during the last fifty years. There have been published at least three thousand research reports and discussion papers dealing with bodily changes and emotions. Dunbar (8) listed almost this number in a bibliography several years ago. In the end many, if not most, of the investigators have tended to reach the conclusion that their research efforts did not justify much beyond further questions and vague generalities. Some research workers have felt that their work was largely futile. Much of this disillusionment, it is believed, has grown out of the fact that investigators have been asking the wrong kind of questions. It has been indicated before that we must be able to ask vital questions that can be answered by scientific procedure before we have made much progress in a science. Perhaps only recently have very scientifically meaningful questions been asked regarding emotions.

Even though there has been much cause for discouragement in the research area which has bearing upon emotionality, research does continue. The reason for this persistence is obvious—a solution to many knotty problems is needed. The medical profession is concerned with nervous and mental diseases. The part played by emotions in the production of these diseases is not known, but is believed to be of fundamental importance. Physiologists are forced to recognize that the functioning of muscles and endocrine glands is influenced by what is experienced. The adrenal glands, for instance, are activated by a perception of danger. Thus, a thorough knowledge of the functioning of many vital organs of the body requires an understanding of psychological phenomena. If for no other reason, the physiologist must become acquainted with these matters so that he may exercise essential controls when he experiments upon physiological reactions of the glands. Again, psychologists must consider the continuous interaction between physiological processes (many of which may be of a chemical nature) and emotions, perceiving, thinking, believing, and acting. The emotions or feeling tone of the individual, many investigators believe, may affect the entire motivational system and, hence, have direct bearing upon the energy and efficiency with which the individual functions.

There are many practical situations where an index to the emotion-arousing value of various stimuli is desired. The advertiser would make constant use of such a tool in his work. So would all others who wish to know how to effect the beliefs and action of people. Even policemen, lawyers, and the general public have been fascinated by the dramatic possibilities of using bodily changes as a means for lie detection, the underlying assumption being that lying would be accompanied by emotional reactivity and measurable bodily changes within the person being examined, thus enabling the investigator to decide correctly who is lying and who is not.

THEORIES OF EMOTIONS

While methods and experimental techniques are emphasized in a beginning book in experimental psychology, some consideration of theory is not out of place. Unfortunately theories about emotion are rather confusing. Many early writers commented upon the nature of emotions, but possibly we do well to begin with Darwin's idea. Darwin made several critical observations about emotional expression and the role emotions play in actual survival of the animal. He thought that snarling and growling served to warn the enemy, often frightening him away without combat.

Previously in this book, Wundt's tri-dimensional theory of feeling was mentioned, and his terminology is quite suggestive of the language used in discussing the more current activation theory of emotion; however, there are important differences as well. Wundt emphasized introspection and, hence, subjective evaluation was not necessarily supported by experimental recording of bodily changes. It may be recalled that Wundt spoke of feeling as having the dimensions of excitement-calm, pleasantness-unpleasantness, and tension-relaxation. Some writers have taken the position that feeling is a broader term than emotion, and that the words should not be used interchangeably. Wundt usually referred to feelings rather than emotions.

James-Lange Theory

The James-Lange theory of emotion is familiar to almost all who have had a first course in psychology. The essential element in it is that the individual becomes aware of visceral changes (internal bodily process: unstriped muscles and glands) which are brought about by stimuli. The sequence of events is usually emphasized—danger is perceived in the situation and this gives rise to an increased activity of the autonomic nervous system, and, hence, the vital organs of the body are stimulated. When these events occur, the individual becomes aware of viscerally aroused sensations. Thus, consciousness of these internal disturbances constitutes the emotion. There is not necessarily much wrong with the two very similar concepts arrived at independently by James and Lange; the chief objection raised by later writers has to do with the usefulness of the theory since it has not proved to be very fruitful in helping investigators to set up experiments.

Cannon-Bard Theory

The Cannon-Bard theory of emotion is a physiological theory. These investigators, and others who followed their lead, set out to find a "seat" of emotion in the nervous system. Little concern was given to whether the subject was emotional because he became aware of visceral changes. It was determined that lesions in the thalamus or hypothalamus of the brain were associated with deviations in emotional expression. A great amount of experimental and clinical evidence has piled up to support the idea that there is a neurological "seat" of emotion. Whether the individual responds before he becomes aware of fright, let us say, is not considered crucial. The Cannon-Bard theory assumes that when certain neural impulses coming from one of the senses reaches the hypothalamus this gives rise to the emotion. Neural impulses are expected to radiate from this center, some go on to the cortex and then return, completing a reflex arc to a muscle. Still other neural impulses might go to one or more of the vital organs and glands to trip various mechanisms having value in emergencies.

Emotional expression has been obtained when the return fibers from the visceral have been cut. This kind of evidence is used to refute the claims of the James-Lange theory. However, there remains some obscurity as to why one neural impulse arriving at the hypothalamus gives rise to emotional reaction while another does not. In other words, how does discrimination take place without the cortex of the brain having first been activated?

Activation Theory

The activation theory of emotions is to a considerable extent an extension of Cannon's emergency theory, although it differs in that it assumes that activation is a continuum extending from the greatest passivity this side of death, as in deep sleep, to the most extreme agitation. If emotion is thus conceived of as referring to the degree of mobilization of energy, and the participation of the organism in action, we have less trouble making use of a number of indices for emotion. Some of the bothersome questions that have arisen in the past lose most of their significance. For instance, it has long been debated whether or not emotion represented a disorganized state of the organism. It is not difficult to give an example of highly motivated activity that subjectively appears to be quite emotional in nature but which does not lead the individual to display disorganized activity. Leeper (13) has emphasized that it is at least as characteristic of emotional behavior to be organized as disorganized. He goes on to show how all strongly motivated behavior must be emotional in nature. This position is difficult to challenge; however, it is not well to go to the other extreme and assume that all emotional behavior is organized and efficient. It would not be reasonable to argue that the behavior that is descriptive of the individual in panic results without emotion. In this case behavior is not organized or integrated, but surely the individual is emotional. Many psychologists are willing to go along with Leeper in his rejection of the definition of emotion as primarily a disorganized state. The assumption of disorganization had led some writers to speak of emotion as a temporary breakdown in personality. This, it was said, resulted from the lack of an immediate or adequate response to the stimulus situation impinging upon the individual.

That these consequences necessarily took place was what Leeper brought under attack.

An activation theory of emotion would not seem to require an assumption that emotional behavior is either organized or disorganized. There is sufficient evidence that stress may become strong enough to be disruptive. Intellectual efficiency is reduced for all individuals under extreme stress, while relatively mild stress leads to a loss in efficiency for some. Individual differences in this matter are important. There is reason to believe that lower neural level reflexes take over under great stress. The analogy may not be good, but it is a little as though there can be a short-circuiting process. The autonomic nervous system, which regulates the vital organs of the body, temporarily becomes dominant over the central nervous system, which may result in a reduction of efficiency in voluntary behavior. The important centers for intellectual activity are in the cerebral cortex; the centers for emotional reactivity are in the lower portions of the brain. Under great agitation action appears to precede thinking: the individual first makes his response; later he may construct a rational defense of the way he responded. A reflex which involves only the spinal cord, lower brain, or cerebellum, is assumed to be faster than those requiring choice or decision, for these involve cortical activity. The sequence of responses and the time required to respond are of great interest to psychologists. Both are used over and over as indices to behavioral characteristics of the individual.

METHODS OF STUDYING EMOTIONS

There are two general approaches to the study of emotions: the method of impression and the method of expression. Each has certain uses and limitations. Since few experimenters today make primary use of the impression method, attention here will be largely focused on the method of expression.

The Method of Impression

The method of impression was used almost exclusively by early psychologists and close relationship between method and theory is readily seen in their works. Wundt and his students used this method relentlessly. The subject who received the stimulus made a careful description of his experience; thus, much effort was directed toward training the experimentalist to be a careful observer and analyzer of the conscious process. The important scientist was not the one who administered the stimulus but the one who received it.

The James-Lange theory of emotion was based on data derived from the method of impression, but there was a definite hint of transition to the method of expression for studying behavior. In some of his writings James discussed emotion as though the stirred-up state of the organism constituted the emotion. Yet, it was *awareness of that condition* which became the critical point as the theory was formally stated. The advantages and disadvantages of each of the two methods are discussed later.

The Method of Expression

Most recent investigators have used some form of the method of expression in studying emotions. Again, these studies might be conveniently divided into two large classes. There are the studies in which overt evidences of emotion are studied, and those in which recording procedure has been used to detect physiological or chemical changes. This would not be a division without considerable overlap. For example, breathing can be detected fairly well by observing the individual, but recording of breathing is more dependable and has been a regular procedure when breathing rate is to be considered in the investigation.

In a general way, the overt responses that are readily seen or heard are mediated by activity of the central nervous system, while the internal changes are mainly produced by activity of the autonomic nervous system. It is the overt responses, such as physical movements, facial expression, movement of the eyes, and changes in the voice, that we make daily use of when trying to interpret the emotions of those about us. Unfortunately, data derived from these observations have not proved to be very useful for scientific purposes, partly because people are able to control their expression of emotions and may deliberately mislead the observer. Also, there are many individual differences in subjects, and investigators themselves disagree when they attempt to judge the emotion being expressed by any given subject. Limited though the kinds of studies just mentioned may be, they remain the best available for studying patterns of emotional reactivity. We may use this approach reasonably well when the task is to discriminate between the emotions that are felt, such as joy and sorrow.

An analysis of bodily changes has been most useful when attacking problems related to the level or degree of energy mobilization that characterize the individual's participation in a situation. Quantification in terms of changes in blood pressure or galvanic skin resistance is believed by many to be a very useful index to the intensity of the emotion experienced.

It seems clear that the method to be chosen should be determined by the specific problem under study. Most of the problems in emotion can be grouped under two headings: those having to do with differentiation and pattern, and those having to do with intensity or level of participation and energy mobilization.

DIFFERENTIATION AND PATTERN IN EMOTIONS

How emotions become differentiated is a problem more central for the genetic or child psychologist, but the means by which we identify various emotions in ourselves and others and then proceed to describe and predict about them should not be completely avoided by the experimental psychologist. First, it might be said that there are only general patterns of responses associated with emotions at birth such as fear, love, and anger, and the stimuli that are adequate for producing these are limited. Fear may be produced by loss of physical support and perhaps loud noises; pleasantness, or love, is elicited by the touch of warm, soft objects; anger and rage by pain, hunger, or physical restraint. While there is much debate about the relative part played by heredity in laying down emotional patterns for responding, there is good agreement that the infant at a very early date begins to learn or to modify his emotional expressions. Modification no doubt begins to occur within the first days after birth, and is clearly evident within a few weeks. Physical handicaps may delay or prevent the usual course of development in learning to express emotions. For example, those individuals who are blind from birth do not show much facial expression, nor do other motor responses lend themselves as well to classification into recognized patterns as is the case with those who see.

Subjectively there is little difficulty in recognizing that anger, fear, and love are different emotions, but when the investigator tries to communicate this information to others he may bog down. The highly individual nature of such an experience is one barrier to a better scientific use of the material, but semantic difficulties are also encountered. The method of impression is very promising when research is initiated on emotions and personality, but then experimenters are usually forced to study overt expressions in others before they can obtain data that lend themselves well to objectivity and the type of generalizations desired in science.

There have been many investigations in which an attempt has been made to determine the accuracy of judgment of emotions in others. Photographs of various facial expressions have been the most popular stimulus material. A frequent criticism has been that the pictures have not been genuine and that the relatively poor agreement among judges did not reflect the true significance that can be attached to facial expressions. The pictures can be obtained by having an actor pose for them. The actor attempts to express each emotion as requested—smiles, looks angry, frightened, etc. Naturally, something depends upon the skill of the actor in revealing the intended emotion. However, it must also be granted that judgment for different individuals would have to be based upon commonality in the culture if all were to agree that a particular expression showed anger. The villain in a motion picture may be directed to smile before he commits some act of cruelty, the intention being either to portray the villain's enjoyment of the act of violence by the pleasant expression, or again to show how perverted the individual is, so that he completely misleads those around him. The smile may be interpreted by the intended victim as friendly behavior when the villain really intends to indulge in a cruel act.

Pictures have often been taken of individuals who were being exposed to stimuli which are expected to provoke particular kinds of emotion. Thus, a picture in which horror is depicted might be the stimulus intended to get the subject to show the facial expression of horror when posing for the photograph. There have even been attempts to get pictures in the natural situation or to obtain them from files of pictures obtained by magazines or newspaper photographers at the scene of some situation judged to be adequate to produce the experimentally desired emotion. Drawings have sometimes been used. It will be seen that getting completely satisfactory stimulus material for judging facial expressions has not been easy. It is believed by the writer that no procedure for getting facial expressions for judgmental studies has been without some kind of legitimate objection.

The results of the many investigations show clearly that agreement in judgment depends greatly upon the technique used. Not only is the stimulus important but even greater variability may result from the method of scaling. Is the judge going to divide the expression of emotion into no more than a half dozen categories or is he to place them on a scale of twenty? Gates (9) found that children at the age of ten gave 100 percent correct identifications for laughing. On the other hand, *surprise* or *contempt* remained well under 50 percent at that age. If there is a long list of emotions to be judged, there will be many close misses, but in the usual analysis right responses are thrown together and all wrong responses thrown into another category with no provision made for the distance of the estimate or error from the correct position.

Attacking the problem of scaling and a method of analyzing, Schlosberg (18) worked out a scale for judgment of facial expression and later experimented with placing the more common expressions on a circular surface (see Fig. 9-1). There appear to be advantages in such an arrangement. The lack of clear opposites on any scaling procedure offers dif-

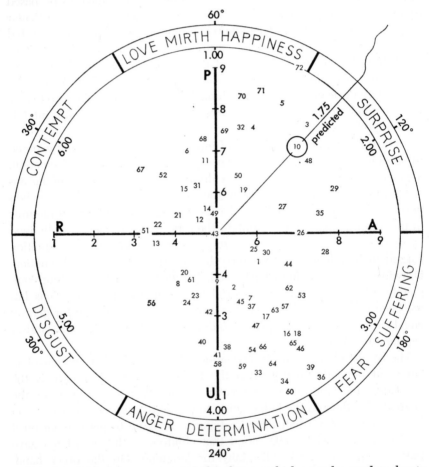

Fig. 9.1. Schlosberg constructed this figure, which may be used to locate, scale, and analyze facial expression. P = pleasant, U = unpleasant, R = rejection, A = attention. A given picture can be placed or located by a dot wherever the judge believes appropriate. (From Woodworth, Robert S., and Schlosberg, Harold, *Experimental Psychology*. New York: Henry Holt & Co., 1954.

ficulty in either making statistical analysis or in diagrammatic presentation.

CULTURE AND THE EXPRESSION OF EMOTIONS

It does not seem possible to set up practical criteria for emotional expression independently of cultural patterns. After birth, learning comes to play an important, and eventually a dominant, role in emotional expression. Even in the more elementary emotions, modification in expression is considerable. Learning is of particular importance in both the expression and recognition in other people of the milder and more subtle emotional reactions. Skill in both are of great importance in maintaining smooth social relationships. People may be taught ways of expressing emotions, but to an even greater extent in most cultures they learn to suppress and to modify reactions that were originally spontaneous. If a person tries to judge emotions in strange individuals of his own culture he is in difficulty enough, but he will encounter still greater confusion if he tries to judge the feelings and emotions of those from a different cultural background. It is the regular course of development for the spontaneous crying of the child to give way to more sophisticated restraint. The extreme in deception is undertaken by the practiced actor who must make his living by his skill in submerging his own personality for the time and conveying the feelings presumed to be felt by the fictitious character of the play.

It is recognized that the study of emotional expression or judgment about emotion demands rather complex controls and certainly must be carried into the social situation before much progress can be made in establishing validity or for producing results of practical use. A chapter is devoted to these problems and suggestions for experiments in the social field occurs later in this book. Yet, there remains much basic research that might be done in the laboratory to build up a satisfactory background of theory and principle in preparation for field studies.

EXPERIMENTAL APPROACHES TO BODILY CHANGES

We now turn from methods that may ultimately prove to be useful in the broader fields of social science to those more closely associated with laboratory work. Although, as we have suggested earlier, progress may eventually be made toward relating bodily changes to imagination, thinking, beliefs, or even attitudes, it is difficult enough at present to relate strong emotions to bodily changes. It has already been indicated that some progress has been made in determining that there is a neural center that controls emotional reactivity about which a number of interesting, if false, beliefs previously had been set forth. Ancients considered the pit of the stomach to be the seat of the emotions, and even now we occasionally hear the expression "bowels of mercy." Some awareness of the vital part that the heart played in helping the organism to keep alive gave rise to the belief in ancient and medieval times that the heart might be the seat of emotions. There remains in our everyday speech a vestige of these ideas. We speak of a "sweetheart," or of being "heartsick," or that someone is "hardhearted." It is only in relatively recent times that the nervous system and the integrating functions of the brain have been recognized as the center most vital to both intellectual and emotional behavior.

Through the years, bodily changes associated with visceral reflexes have been studied for the possible light they might throw not only upon our emotional behavior but also upon the general characteristics of personality. While personality is complex and involved, different aspects of the individual's feelings, emotions, and temperament are among the most fundamental. We must know more about the affective life and the mechanism involved in emotions if we are to learn much about the basis of personality.

So varied and complex are the mechanisms that are set into operation by emotion-arousing perceptions that many investigators question whether we can ever understand them. It is interesting to know, even though the knowledge is frustrating, that the organism is so responsive that a spoken word may alter breathing, change blood pressure and the heating and cooling mechanism of the body, or even set into motion endocrine responses sometimes of long-range consequences. Thus, an individual who has become, for some reason, over-reactive to his surroundings is making such continuous demands upon these systems that the result is often a general fatigue and exhaustion. What is called emotional fatigue may exist in terms of the capacity of the individual to continue to respond appropriately to emotional or social stimulation. The occurrence of cold sweat, sweaty palms, burning skin, and so forth are common complaints among people who have become known as neurotics.

We now turn to the various recordable bodily changes partly because they have engaged the attention of many investigators, but also because spectacular or dramatic results seemingly have been obtained. This approach is thought by some to be the most promising for the long range study of certain aspects of the intensely motivated activities of man.

GALVANIC SKIN RESISTANCE AND EMOTIONAL REACTIONS

First, and possibly most important for the various indices to emotional changes, is research that has been done on the galvanic skin reflex.* Research dealing with galvanic phenomena is abundant. Sometimes the reports have referred to the phenomenon as galvanic skin response, sometimes the words "conductance" or "resistance of the skin" have been used instead of either "reflex" or "response." Some confusion with regard to terminology usage is almost inevitable. A rigid consistency on our part when reviewing the contributions of others would require translating the terms used by different investigators and might constitute an indefensible liberty. There are certainly some advantages in speaking of this phenomenon as changes in skin resistance to the passage of a constant electric current. This at once enables us to refer directly to changes in ohms without any implication as to interpretation of the cause of such change.

The two fundamental procedures used in galvanic studies were both discovered before the beginning of this century. By passing a weak electric current over a circuit in which some part of the body, such as the hand, constituted part of the completed circuit, Féré observed that the flow of electricity changed from minute to minute. It was especially apparent that the fluctuations in transmission were greater and more frequent when the subject was alternately placed first in a stress situation, and then one in which he could be relaxed and calm. Since emotional or intellectual stimulation could be administered and, to a degree, the experimenter could produce at will resistance changes, the name "psychogalvanic reflex" was given to the reaction. That is, as a result of presenting a psychological stimulus, such as a loud noise, an emotionally loaded word, the sight of a snake, or in some way threatening the subject, marked changes in the reading of the galvanometer occur.

The other means of studying galvanic phenomena is known as the Tarchanoff method. Tarchanoff noted that there was a change in the reading of the galvanometer if two electrodes were attached to the body without sending any external current over the circuit. Probably this result is brought about by chemical reactivity in the body so that the electrical potential at one point differs from that at another point. However, the sudden and transitory changes in current flow following psychological

---

* NOTE: It will be recalled by most readers that the galvanometer is a device for indicating the flow of an electric current and takes its name from Galvani, who contributed to the invention.

or physiological stress are assumed to be due to changes in the skin resistance.

The methods of both Féré and Tarchanoff were being studied around 1890. They have certain similarities and differences. It should be remembered that an outside current is used in only the Féré method. In both methods skin is considered the barrier to the passage of electric current. Any stimulus that activates the sweat glands should increase conductivity through the circuit since sweat is a saline solution and this is an excellent conductor of electricity. There is reason to believe that the preparation for secretion is a factor. At least conductivity is improved before sweat appears on the outer surface of the skin. We might visualize the skin as a sieve through which there are numerous holes. Once the sweat glands are activated the holes (sweat pores) are filled with the salty solution which readily conducts the electric current. A dry skin serves as a thin but fairly effective insulator to resist current flow. If the skin is punctured and electrodes inserted beneath the skin, the sudden galvanic changes do not occur.

The sweat glands are activated by the sympathetic division of the autonomic nervous system, and associated with this segment of the nervous system are the various emergency mechanisms of the body which are activated by threat to the organism.

CORRELATIONS OF RESULTS WITH OTHER REACTIONS

Galvanic skin resistance has been correlated with a great many physiological and psychological reactions. There seems to be consistency between decreased resistance and physiological reactions that occur during emergencies where the energy of the body is mobilized for a crisis. The more relaxed and calm the individual, the greater the skin resistance. Thus, during sound sleep the resistance is at a maximum—at least through the palm of the hand. It was found by Waller (21) and Wechsler (23), who measured palmar resistance at various waking hours of the day, that resistance was high at the time of rising, decreased during the day, and became high again late in the evening. Of course, the activity that the subject is engaged in is pertinent and often reverses this general trend.

There is little doubt that the general metabolism and body temperature follow a regular cycle through the day—low temperature and metabolism rate in the morning and high rate about six o'clock in the evening—and that each has some relationship to conductivity of the skin. These diurnal changes are quite persistent and probably represent biological adaptation. This cycle is found for animals that habitually stir during the day and sleep at night. The tendency persists to some extent in man even though he shifts his working hours to night and sleeps through the day. Many individuals find it unpleasant to take a nap during the day because of profuse sweating, which would suggest that the sleeping room should be kept cooler during the latter part of the day or else the bed covering reduced as countermeasures to rising body temperature. Also, workers

Fig. 9.2. Apparatus that may be used to demonstrate galvanic changes under emotional stress. Changes in the dial reading occur with application to the subject of various stimuli. (Courtesy Lafayette Instrument Co.)

are said to tend to be less efficient if they must work during the hours when the temperature and metabolism rates are declining, say from ten at night to six in the morning. It is not unreasonable to suppose that part of the results and attitudes found in these various matters are socially determined, since habits are likely to be disturbed. Again, many variables are involved and more systematic studies are needed. Those just indicated complicate the psychologist's work, mainly because a "drift" may prevent him from establishing a stable base line from which he may determine deviations.

Most investigators report high skin resistance during sleep. Davis and Kantor (7) performed an experiment in which hypnotized subjects were told that they would now go into a deep sleep. The skin resistance increased. Upon receiving suggestions that they were alert, resistance decreased again. These findings were used to support the contention by the authors that hypnosis is a sleep-like state, although they did not assert that hypnosis is nothing more than sleep. Actually, recent investigations have revealed that some of the bodily reflexes and other characteristic responses do not follow too similar a pattern under hypnosis and sleep.

ADEQUATE STIMULI FOR GSR

It is considered that all intense sensory stimuli give rise to decreased skin resistance. Loud noises, flashing lights, a pinch, the prick of a pin, tickling, strong odors, etc., are all accompanied by decreased skin resistance. It has even been shown that an electric shock presented to an animal under deep anesthesia gives rise to a decreased skin resistance.

One of the early studies of GSR made by Peterson and Jung (16) in 1907 revealed a clear difference between words in their effectiveness in producing galvanic responses. Such words as "kiss" or "love" were found to produce a deflection of the galvanometer three or four times as great as words like "pencil" or "table." While it may be assumed that some words when heard under particular circumstances may have emotion-provoking potential, it is noteworthy that their affect-producing value can be measured in the laboratory situation so that differentiation between these relatively mild words can be reliably determined.

In general, later studies have been consistent with these early findings. It will be essential to discuss further the relationship between meaningful stimuli and situations and GSR when dealing with learning. Probably no other technique is easier to use in demonstrating conditioning than the GSR. By giving an individual an electric shock at the same instant that a word is uttered, the subject will later quickly respond with a galvanic change upon hearing only the word without the shock. Once established, this response will be repeated without reinforcement by the shock but will eventually become extinguished in the way usual for a conditioned response.

DIFFERENTIATION OF EMOTIONS BY GSR

While there is satisfactory agreement among investigators that any strong stimuli or assumed intense emotional reaction will be accompanied by a decrease of skin resistance, there is very meager evidence for predicting what kind of stimulus is being used to provoke the response, or what kind of an emotional experience will be reported later by the subject. At present, we are forced to conclude that the GSR furnishes little information that will help to differentiate between emotions. Landis and Hunt (10) presented various stimuli intended to arouse fear, amusement, sex emotion, pleasantness, and unpleasantness. Their results did reveal what was interpreted to be evidence that tension, startle, and confusion give rise to greater GSR changes than do pleasantness. But the intensity level of the stimulus appears to be more readily estimated than the kind of stimulus used or the emotion felt. These findings lend support to the idea that it may be profitable to think of emotion in terms of the *energy level* or *degree of activation* that has been provoked in the organism.

GSR AND INTELLECTUAL WORK

A result very interesting, although not surprising, to those familiar with learning phenomena, is found by repeating GSR provoking stimuli. This is illustrated by Davis (6). He measured the magnitude of ohms resistance for successive presentation of a flashing neon light. The decreased resistance on three successive trials were 1099, 268, 190 ohms, representing an extremely rapid change. The evidence indicates that change in this direction can be depended upon although the amount in many instances may be less. On successive days, Seward and Seward (19) gave electric shock to adult subjects while taking GSR readings. They found consistent evidence for adaptation. Taking the first resistance change as a base of 100, then on the second shock the change for several subjects averaged 78, third 71, and fourth 69. This would give a curved line of decline which is quite typical of many results in psychology where adaptation or fatigue are assumed to take place. Some of the psychological conditions, such as the surprise element, are almost entirely removed after the first presentation. This may account for the big gap between the first and second readings in the study mentioned above, and this too, is not unusual in similar experiments.

TIME FOR GSR

While there is a great variation in resistance brought about by intensity differences of stimuli, ranging from zero to several thousand ohms, there is little variation in the time between stimulus presentation and beginning of the GSR. Whatever the nature or the intensity level of the stimulus, response usually can be expected within the range of one to three seconds after the stimulus. This is so dependable that GSR changes occurring after several seconds are not considered to be due to the intended stimulus but to some random condition such as other external stimuli, or to thought processes and associations beyond the experimenter's control. Davis (6) found the latent period to average 1.7 seconds for sound and 2.1 seconds for light. Neither period was much affected by intensity. This is suggestive of the findings in regard to simple reaction time for visual stimuli which is longer than for auditory stimuli. It will be noted that the response time is many times greater than simple reaction time, which is in the order of one-tenth or two-tenths second. The central nervous system and the striped muscles activated by the stimulus can be expected to respond much more quickly than is the case where the autonomic nervous system and smooth muscles are involved. Other investigators have also found that intensity differences may give rise to changes in GSR of several hundred ohms but that variations in time of onset are quite limited.

SUMMARY

We are led to believe that GSR is a valuable index to the mobilization of energy resulting from sensory or perceptual arousal in the organism. The resistance to the passage of an electric current by the skin is reduced under stress conditions of all kinds. This is true when either psychological demands or a greater physical effort are involved. We are at some loss to fix sequence of events and certainly must be guarded in making claims about causes. Relationships have been established between changes in GSR and muscular work, mental work, blood pressure changes, breathing rate, and the secretion of several endocrine glands. Certain drugs decrease skin resistance while some increase it. There appears to be some orderliness to these conditions, for, in general, those drugs which relax the muscles are accompanied by increased resistance and those causing muscular tension by decreased resistance. We must consider GSR a phenomenon of great generality and that differentiation by analysis of emotions, attitudes, or mental states is scarcely possible at present and may remain beyond the scope of this technique. These findings begin to give a somewhat clearer idea of the kind of questions that might be answered by studying galvanic phenomenon.

It is now well established that GSR is associated with visceral reactivity. The sympathetic division of the autonomic nervous system is considered the mediating agent for making available, in emergencies, the energies of the organism. Severing of the nerves of the autonomic nervous system that extend to sweat glands practically eliminates changes in electrical resistance. The use or more liberal burning of energy by the body requires that the cooling mechanism, of which sweating is the most important, must quickly be brought into activity. The self-regulating or autonomic nature of the vegetative functions of the body become operative without the necessity of conscious effort. Hence, GSR may prove increasingly valuable as a means of studying reactivity in which conscious control or manipulation by the subject may be misleading. It appears that at present the GSR is the most sensitive and reliable index to those responses that are labeled "emotional."

CIRCULATORY CHANGES AND EMOTION

Unlike galvanic changes, which could not be observed until necessary apparatus was invented, there is little doubt that changes in pulse rate and force had been noticed long ago by laymen when under emotional stress. Primitive man could scarcely have been unaware of the pounding and racing of the heart when he was experiencing great fear or rage. While these general observations have been common, and no one questions that there is some relationship between such physiological reactions and the subjective experience of emotions, yet reducing these acceptable observations to systematic description and scientific validation has been very difficult. Not only are there instrument problems, but there remain theoretical difficulties.

EARLY EXPERIMENTS

In 1917 Marston introduced the use of blood pressure as a test of lying. His work was followed by that of Larson, who wrote in 1923 reporting results of polygraph recording of blood pressure changes. In the early studies nearly all the essential factors involved were stated. It was seen that an individual who was confronted with the stress of telling an untrue story in a straightforward manner, and one that might have to be repeated under variable approaches, usually led to increased systolic blood pressure. It was also recognized that false positive results might occur; that is, embarrassing questions could be asked which would produce increased blood pressure. Any highly emotionally loaded associations could give rise to the same results. However, under skilled usage remarkably accurate detection of lying was possible. Marston (15) reported correct detection in 103 judgments out of 107 attempts. While witnesses telling the truth often showed rises of blood pressure up to 5 mm. of mercury, liars under questioning generally revealed increases of 10 to 15 mm. It became a kind of rule of thumb that any change below 10 mm. should be scrutinized carefully before interpreting the results as indicative of guilt. Later investigation of both "laboratory lying" and lying by those under court trial have not yielded quite as dependable results as those reported by Marston. Most investigators think correct detection is possible in only about three-fourths of the cases.

The results reported by Chappel (4) and Larson (12) were in general agreement with those of Marston. They used improved recording devices. It may well be that only modest improvement remains as a possibility in lie detection even by use of the most accurate apparatus. In 1932 Larson summarized the information available on apparatus, techniques, and procedures and went into a critical evaluation of the limitations and possible abuses of lie detection. Continued research reinforces the evidence indicating that investigators should proceed with caution. There is considerable variation in accuracy of results because of the varying degrees of skill in the persons who do the questioning. Much is necessarily left to the judgment of the examiner in interpreting the recordings. If testing has not been done under strictly standard conditions, any strong sensory stimulation, such as incidental noises, flashing lights, etc., may badly contaminate the recordings. Thus, superficially convincing but actually false conclusions may be drawn by the nonanalytic or the uninformed. Individual differences may be enhanced under the excitement generated during questioning, so this must be taken into account. Needless to say, if an unscrupulous investigator is left to his own devices when quizzing the subject, he has ample opportunity to make it appear that the individual is guilty. It is not our purpose here to present a complete evaluation of lie detection apparatus or results. However, attention is given to this work because the techniques used in lie detection are the same as those used for studying general emotional reactivity and trying to measure bodily changes that may be used as indices to emotional states. The research problems confronting the psychologist who would study emotions are very similar to some of the practical problems involved in lie detection in so far as methods and tools are concerned.

APPARATUS FOR RECORDING BLOOD PRESSURE

Accurate measurement of blood pressure changes is by no means an easy task. The physician takes blood pressure by use of a stethoscope and sphygmometer, or sphygmomanometer, as it is often called. This is a rubber sleeve enclosed in strong cloth or leather and is then wrapped around the arm. This can be inflated with air to the point at which the arteries become collapsed, preventing any blood flow. There is a gauge attachment to indicate the amount of pressure being used. The stethoscope is a listening device so the physician may detect at what pressure the blood begins to flow again as air is gradually let out of the sphygmomanometer. The best that can be done with this instrument, as used by the physician, is to take a series of readings and each reading may require several seconds of time. Important changes might not be detected if they were of only a few seconds in duration. Another problem is the possible disturbing effects on the subject that are brought about by manipulating the apparatus. These variables are probably of no great importance in making a medical diagnosis, but might give rise to errors that should not be ignored in research.

For research purposes a permanent record of the blood pressure changes is needed. Then changes may be induced by application of the stimulus, which is designated as the independent variable. A completely satisfactory recording device remains to be invented. It is possible to get a very good record of blood pressure changes by tapping the arteries and having apparatus attached so that the height of the blood is both visible in a tube and can be recorded at the same time. However, such procedure is very traumatizing to the subject, either human or lower animal, and this is not practical in studies of mild emotions. This technique is widely used by physiologists in doing animal studies, but even here some investigators think the experimental results having bearing upon endocrine functions and other physiological processes are seriously distorted by the procedure.

In spite of the objections or limitations of the procedure, most investigators of blood pressure changes as related to emotional behavior have made use of the blood pressure apparatus borrowed from physicians and have then connected this in with a polygraph for continuous recording. This involves the use of an enclosed air circuit extending from the rubber sleeve to a tambour, which activates a stylus that writes. Any change in the volume of air in the sleeve surrounding the arm will be indicated by an excursion of the stylus. Some kind of a mechanical device must be used to draw the paper under the stylus at a constant speed.

It is to be remembered that volume change, as reflected in the movement of the stylus, is actually what is being recorded. Since this is true, any type of plethysmograph may be used as the pick-up device with more or less comparable results. A plethysmograph is a tightly enclosed system, usually made at least partially of rubber, that fits over a finger, hand, or arm. Again, the enclosed air circuit can be led off through a rubber tube to a tambour and attached stylus. Volume change for some portion of the body, as the hand or arm, which is due to pressure exerted from outside, is presumed to be a satisfactory index to blood pressure changes. However, evidence has not always supported the claim of a direct relationship between volume changes and pressure changes when the sphygmomanometer is used for recording pick-up and the results then compared with those obtained in the way physicians use a stethoscope.

Several kinds of writing devices have been used. A smoked drum and stylus was once most often used by both physiologists and psychologists. The stylus here was a metal arm that lightly touched the smoked drum. Later the paper could be removed from the drum and shellacked so that it could be handled and stored. In more recent years, either ink recording or the use of waxed paper and metal stylus, the point being heated by a small electric wire, have been more popular. The ideal recording device possesses a high degree of sensitivity and durability; unfortunately, there is a lack of completely satisfactory apparatus.

Some investigators have preferred to measure blood pressure by attaching the rubber sleeve around the ankle because subjects often complain of pain produced by the inflated sleeve, if recording is continued for more than a few minutes. This complaint is reduced by using the ankle instead of the arm. In all cases the pressure in the rubber sleeve is kept well below systolic blood pressure so that blood flow can continue. Usually a good record of both pulse and blood pressure changes is obtainable when the pressure is held at about 90 mm. of mercury.

Electrical potential changes produced by muscular contraction of the heart furnishes a usable index to blood pressure changes, but this method is indirect, since it initially involves a comparison with the blood pressure reading by another technique. This procedure may eventually prove to be a very satisfactory approach to energy mobilization, but it has not yet been widely used for this purpose. It is possible that an entirely different technique for studying energy mobilization might be used. Investigators may have an unnecessary mental set to translate data into terms of blood pressure changes. Eventually, electrocardiograph recording, for example, or some other index to energy mobilization, may be used directly. At present there is inadequate knowledge about norms of such changes that are to be expected under stress. However, it may be pertinent to question the tendency of investigators to cling so determinedly to measure of blood pressure changes as an indicator of emotional stress.

Blood pressure changes and changes in pulse rate are thought to be almost entirely controlled by the autonomic nervous system. Increases in both result from the neural stimulation of the heart muscles and the walls of the blood vessels through increased activity in the sympathetic division of the autonomic nervous system. There is not a perfect relationship between pulse changes and changes in blood pressure, but they do correspond very closely in a given individual when he is subjected to variable intensity of stimuli within a short period of time. All stress situations are expected to call into play the emergency mechanisms of the organism, and this involves an increase in pulse rate and blood pressure. These changes have been found to relate rather closely to changes in galvanic skin resistance. Changes in GSR and blood pressure (or perhaps better still, pulse rate) are generally considered the best indices to emotional reactivity at the present time. Neither is very useful in differentiating between emotions. Since they are rather highly correlated, the use of both simultaneously does not much increase predictability over the use of either alone.

RESPIRATION IN EMOTION

As early as 1906 Störring (18) suggested that there was a change in inspiration-expiration during speech and perhaps during emotional experiences with or without speech. He noted a change in speed, rhythm, and ratio of the inspiration to expiration. No doubt the rather obvious subjective awareness of breathing changes under surprise or startle had previously been noted by laymen. Many people reveal rather conspicuously the taking of a deep breath after encountering some unusual stimulus. Certainly, writers in works of fiction have frequently commented upon such reaction when describing the behavior of their characters. However, we like to differentiate between the casual descriptions and those following more systematic observations in which the methodology of science has been attempted. Störring perhaps deserves credit as much as any single individual for initiating the latter procedure. He made a systematic attempt to measure the time used in both inspiration and expiration, and then tried to calculate the ratio.

In 1914 Benussi (3) was quite successful in detecting laboratory lying by use of the IE ratio. Other investigators in varying degrees have been successful in detecting deception while some have reported no significant results. An important limitation of breathing, of course, is that the subject has some voluntary control over his breathing. The continuous use of this procedure would certainly be expected to produce a degree of sophistication in many people and, consequently, a decreasing dependability of the technique for lie detection. To some extent, defensive measures may be used by subjects against most of the techniques for revealing emotionality.

In 1911 Rehwoldt (17) demonstrated that subjects tended to increase their rate of breathing when imagining exciting experiences. Shallow, rapid breathing during intense pain is frequently seen by the physician, and he is likely to make use of this observation in determining the condition of his patient. He will become concerned for the life of his patient when the change from normal breathing becomes extreme.

Breathing rate and depth may be increased in preparation for muscular exercise before there is an actual oxygen dearth. Expectation of greater energy need may set to work various mechanisms in anticipation of physiological disequilibrium. This kind of psychological reaction may be bothersome even in certain sports, such as swimming. Many individuals when in a swimming race find it extremely difficult to breathe properly and some of this seems to grow out of the threat that they will not be able to get sufficient oxygen. In the end they may overventilate by breathing too fast and too deeply. An active and vivid imagination may be quite sufficient to trigger these mechanisms and give rise to a prolonged overactivity of breathing, or on the other hand, possibly too little oxygen intake by the extremely anxious person. The individual under stress seems incapable of continuing to breathe at normal rate and thus allow the reflex mechanism to maintain the proper balance in the organism. Possibly all people have experienced some degree of uncertainty when told, "now breathe naturally." Hyperventilation is found to characterize certain individuals, as, for example, some epileptic victims. It is conceivable that dizziness and confusion reported by neurotic and psychotic individuals may be attributed, at least in part, to an imbalance in the organism because of changes in breathing. It is not assumed that such an explanation applies to all patients who experience these symptoms.

It is not unreasonable to suppose that breathing ratio might be more dependable as an index to the energy mobilization process, or what might be otherwise called emotional reactivity, in lower animals than in man. In lower animals we could assume that there would be no voluntary control such as that anticipated for human subjects.

There is not an accurate way of arriving at oxygen consumption changes by means of recording breathing rate. If a good measure of rapid changes in oxygen usage could be obtained without undue experimental disturbance of the subject, it should be a very valuable index to emotions. Oxygen consumption is often taken as an index to metabolism rate. Here again, highly accurate measure of temporary changes in metabolism, obtained by any device, should prove useful, but there is no very satisfactory technique for obtaining this over a short period of time. Better recording, then, is needed if we are to relate these changes to variable stimuli and over short intervals of time. It is known that several endocrine disturbances have important correlates in behavior. Comprehension of these facts involve consideration of body chemistry and psychological phenomena. However, the study of physiological chemistry would necessarily call into use the methods and techniques of the chemist, and this goes beyond a reasonable range for our discussion.

TEMPERATURE CHANGES AND EMOTIONS

Attempts have been made to relate emotional reactivity to both internal body temperature changes and to skin temperature changes. Literary references to the relationship between body temperature and emotionality predates by centuries systematic studies of this phenomenon. There is no intention to defend such statements as having scientific validity, but they may have served to stimulate research upon the problem.

Experiments reveal that animals kept under stress that is assumed to provoke fear maintain body temperature above normal over a period of several hours. It is common belief among physicians that excitement is harmful to the physically ill, partly because the temperature tends to increase; hence the prevention of excessive visiting in the hospital with the critically ill.

In recent years there has been some effort directed toward improving apparatus for taking and recording skin temperature changes (Baker and Csapo, 1). In order that temperature changes be utilized in studying transitory emotional reactions, it is necessary that the temperature pick-up be highly sensitive and prompt to respond. Thermometers have not proved to be very satisfactory and adaptations have usually been made in which thermocouples or thermistors have been used as pick-ups. Sensitivity must be in terms of one one-hundredth of a degree or less. When investigating mild emotional responses of the kind that may be elicited by emotionally loaded words, temperature changes need to be recorded second by second. It will be recalled that galvanic responses usually come within the first three seconds after presentation of the stimulus. Thus, recording apparatus that is not responsive enough to reveal changes of short duration may allow emotional reactions to occur and fade away without this fact being revealed by the recordings.

In an exploratory experiment performed by Baker and Taylor (2), evidence was obtained that skin temperature changes were positively correlated with pulse rate changes and negatively correlated with skin resistance. The temperature pick-up was from the palm of the hand and the stimuli were judged to be fairly provocative of emotional behavior. One stimulus was a jumping electric spark which came as a surprise to the subject. Some of the subjects were probably frightened to a considerable extent.

Most investigators seem to assume that transitory skin temperature changes are brought about by changes in blood circulation through the capillaries. If this proves to be an adequate explanation, there might be advantages in using skin temperature changes over most of the other indices to emotional responses. Remarkable refinement in the measurement of temperature to less than a thousandth of a degree is readily possible. Blood-pressure changes and GSR have rather serious disadvantages for use as indicators of emotional responses; the first because it is so difficult to record, the latter because skin resistance seems to be determined by several factors.

It has generally been accepted that the distribution of blood is changed under varying conditions of the organism. Under stress the sympathetic division of the autonomic nervous system is thought to become more active and this sometimes results in withdrawal of blood from the surface capillaries and some of the vital organs, such as the stomach. Withdrawal of blood from the surface of the body should result in a decrease in skin temperature, but this is contrary to the findings referred to above. However, it may well be that surface temperature changes vary with location on the body. There is little doubt that the embarrassed individual who blushes freely will have a temperature increase about the face and neck. The victim of blushing is even conscious of the glowing skin. On the other hand individuals sometimes turn pale or blanch under terror. Always where there is more blood at one point of the body this condition must be brought about by withdrawal from some other point.

Skin coloration has sometimes been used as an index to blood circulation through a particular portion of the body. Physiologists have often used color changes in the rabbit's ear for this purpose.

OTHER INDICES TO EMOTION

There are a number of indices of emotional reactivity that may have some usefulness. Cannon (5) investigated many bodily changes that were thought to vary with emotions. In a recent review, Lindsey (14) undertook to present a brief outline of the several current approaches to the problem. One of the most widely quoted studies by Cannon was one in which he determined that there was a complete cessation of digestion under intense emotional disturbance. This was demonstrated first in dogs and later in human subjects. Here we see that the emergency function of the autonomic nervous system under some conditions has priority over the other two segments. The digestion of food under temporary

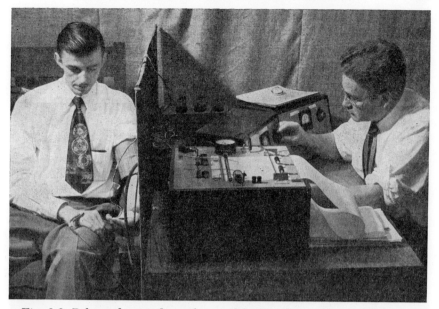

Fig. 9.3. Polygraph recording of several bodily changes being made simultaneously. (Purdue Psychological Laboratory.)

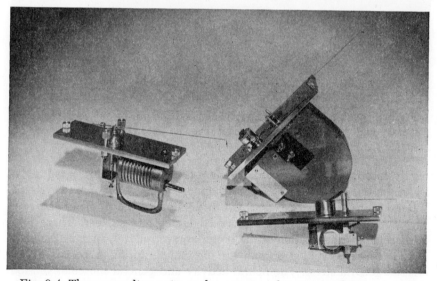

Fig. 9.4. Three recording units as they appear when removed from the Polygraph in the nearby picture. (Courtesy Lafayette Instrument Co.)

emergency may not be as important in the survival of the organism as the immediate release of energy previously stored in the body.

A great variety of apparatus has been used to pick up general body movements, tremors, muscular contraction, eye blink, and shifting eye movements. In each of these measures we usually get some evidence that

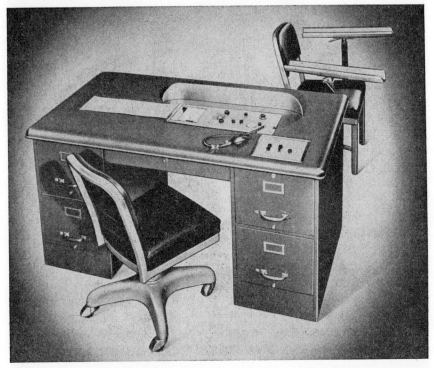

Fig. 9.5. Desk model deceptograph intended for use by police department. Galvanic and blood pressure changes can be recorded. (Courtesy C. H. Stoelting Co.)

highly emotionally loaded situations are associated with increased activity of the body. Some of the reflexes appear to be changed under stress. Intense pain is known to give rise to dilation of the pupil of the eye. The same response has been observed under intense fear. There is a fairly regular exaggeration of the better known reflexes, such as the knee jerk, if reflex-provoking stimuli are presented during a period of increased general stress. The neural activity and general muscular tension thought to accompany all emotional reactivity lead to expectation of such responses.

Decrease in steadiness of the hands or other portions of the body have long been used as evidence of emotional disturbance by those outside scientific circles. The hunter becomes too "nervous" to aim his gun well when suddenly confronted with the wild animal; the soldier loses his skill in marksmanship when going into battle; the musician finds it difficult to exercise skill before the large audience. Previous training and development of great skill under practice conditions may still not insure proficiency under the pressure of the situation.

A very promising technique for studying neural activity under varying levels of activity of the organism is electroencephalography. It is possible to record "brain waves," and these have been shown to vary with the intensity of stimuli that play upon the organism. Bright lights and loud noises are associated with much activity in the neural tissue of the brain as recorded by a suitable instrument. Also, it is believed that the presentation of any kind of meaningful emotionally loaded material gives rise to increased amplitude of the brain waves.

CONCLUDING REMARKS

We do not seem to be ready to attack some of the oldest problems regarding emotion with much hope of success at the present time. There is almost no recent scientific progress that can be pointed to in the matter of differentiating between emotions. Yet, the demands placed upon psychologists to discriminate between such emotions as fear, rage, jealousy, hate, and love continue. Simply asking the individual about his feelings is still a widely used procedure. Studies of bodily changes cannot be said to be very promising at present if we work toward a solution to these particular problems. On the other hand if we make a different approach and look upon emotion as a descriptive term used to denote level of energy mobilization, an aspect of motivation and organization of behavior, we may be able to ask a different set of meaningful questions. Skill in describing and predicting what can be expected of the individual under varying circumstances may in time emerge.

While it is readily conceded that studying emotions by cataloging bodily changes is not a highly effective one, this approach is defended because it appears that we have nothing better at present. To take a defeatist position that we can never understand, predict, or control the phenomenon that has been referred to as emotional or affective behavior in man remains unjustified. Closely tied in with the patterns of emotional complexities are the goals toward which we work in all scientific endeavor. It may well be that part of the difficulty has grown out of the segmenting of emotions into a small part of psychology when the subject matter really permeates all psychological problems. Furthermore, the separation of some of these problems from the general objectives of science and the philosophy of living might be a doubtful procedure. To abandon attempts to comprehend the problems of emotion and motivation is dangerously close to accepting the idea that we can do no better than to proceed blindly toward many of the basic goals which man, for better or worse, is forever setting up for himself.

However frustrating or futile our attempts to study emotion may seem to be, a decision to abandon all effort in this vital area is unthinkable. Only animals without imagination can live without participating in the events of the past and the future; man can be expected to press toward desired goals, endeavoring to control or to avoid those situations, whether physical or psychological in nature, that threaten his survival or well-being. Intermingled with these strivings are the sensations, feelings, and behavior that have been referred to as emotional, and man will keep trying to understand them.

SUGGESTED READINGS

Munn, Norman L. *Psychology: The Fundamentals of Human Adjustment*, pp. 109-135, 136-159. Boston: Houghton Mifflin, 1956.

Morgan, Clifford T. *Introduction to Psychology*, pp. 56-85, 86-106, 248-274. New York: McGraw-Hill, 1956.

Postman, Leo, and Egan, James P. *Experimental Psychology*, pp. 445-462. New York: Harper, 1949.

Garrett, Henry E. *Great Experiments in Psychology*, pp. 148-170. New York: Appleton-Century-Crofts, 1951.

Dennis, Wayne. *Readings in General Psychology*. "Emotion," pp. 111-173; "Motivation," pp. 174-224. New York: Prentice Hall, 1949.

Underwood, Benton J. *Experimental Psychology*. "Motivation," pp. 156-199; "Frustration," pp. 200-240; "Conflict," 241-280. New York: Appleton-Century-Crofts, 1949.

Woodworth, Robert S., and Schlosberg, Harold. *Experimental Psychology*, pp. 107-191. New York: Henry Holt, 1954.

Cannon, Walter B. *Bodily Changes in Pain, Hunger, Fear and Rage*. Boston: Charles T. Branford, 1953.

Stevens, S. S. (ed.). *Handbook of Experimental Psychology*. Lindsley: "Emotions," pp. 473-516. New York: John Wiley, 1951.

Wittkower, Eric, and Russell, Brian. *Emotional Factors in Skin Diseases*. New York: Paul B. Hoehler, 1953.

Best, Charles, and Taylor, Norman B.*The Physiological Basis of Medical Prac-

tice. "The Dynamics of the Circulation," pp. 138-145; "The Mechanics of Respiration," pp. 344-360. Baltimore: Williams and Wilkins, 1950.

REFERENCES

1. Baker, Lawrence M., and Csapo, Geza A. "An improved device for recording changes in skin-temperature," *Amer. J. Psychol.,* 68 (1955), 474-475.
2. Baker, Lawrence M., and Taylor, William M. "The relationships under stress between changes in skin temperature, electrical skin resistance, and pulse rate," *J. Exp. Psychol.* (1954), 361-366.
3. Benussi, V. "Die Atmungssymptome der Lüge," *Arch. Ges. Psy.,* 3 (1914), 244-273.
4. Chappel, M. N. "Blood pressure changes in deception," *Arch. Psychol.,* No. 105 (1929), New York.
5. Cannon, W. B. *Bodily Changes in Pain, Hunger, Fear, and Rage.* (rev. ed.). New York: Appleton-Century-Crofts, 1929.
6. Davis, R. C. "Factors affecting the galvanic reflex," *Arch. Psychol.,* No. 115 (1930), New York.
7. Davis, R. C., and Kantor, J. R. "Skin resistance during hypnotic states," *J. Gen. Psychol.,* 13 (1935), 62-81.
8. Dunbar, Flanders. *Emotions and Bodily Changes* (3rd ed.), pp. 435-568. New York: Columbia University Press, 1947.
9. Gates, G. S. "An experimental study of the growth of social perception," *J. Educ. Psychol.,* 14 (1923), 449-461.
10. Landis, C., and Hunt, W. A. "The conscious correlates of the galvanic skin response," *J. Exp. Psychol.,* 18 (1935), 505-529.
11. Larson, J. A. *Lying and Its Detection.* Chicago: Chicago Univ. Press, 1932.
12. Larson, J. A. "The cardio-pneumo-psychogram in deception," *J. Exp. Psychol.,* 6 (1923), 420-454.
13. Leeper, R. W. "A motivational theory of emotion to replace 'emotion as a disorganized response,'" *Psychol. Rev.,* 55 (1948), 5-21.
14. Lindsey, D. Chapter 6, pp. 473-516, in Stevens, S. S. *Handbook of Experimental Psychology.* New York: John Wiley, 1951.
15. Marston, W. M. "Systolic blood pressure symptoms of deception," *J. Exp. Psychol.,* 2 (1917), 117-163.
16. Peterson, F., and Jung, C. G. "Psychophysiological investigations with the galvanometer and pneumograph in normal and insane individuals," *Brain,* 30 (1907), 153-218.
17. Rehwoldt, F. "Ueber respiratorische Affekt-Symptome." Mit Atlas von 25 Tafeln. *Psy. St.,* 7 (1911), 141-195.
18. Schlosberg, Harold. "A scale for judgment of facial expression," *J. Exp. Psychol.,* 29 (1941), 497-510.
19. Seward, J. P., and Seward, G. H. "The effect of repetition on reaction to electric shock," *Arch. Psychol.,* No. 168 (1934), New York.

20. Störring, G. "Experimentelle Beiträge zur Lehre vom Gefühl," *Arch. Ges. Psychol.*, 6 (1906), 316-356.
21. Waller, A. D. "Concerning emotive phenomena. I. Periodic variations of conductance of the palm of the human hand. II. The influence of drugs upon the electrical conductivity of the palm of the hand." *R. Soc. Lond. Proc. B.*, 91 (1919), 17-31, 32-43.
22. Wang, C. H., Pan, J. G., and Lu, T. W. "The galvanic skin reflex in normal thalamic, decerebrated, and spinal cats under anesthesia," *Chinese J. Phys.*, 3 (1929), 109-122.
23. Wechsler, D. "The measurement of emotional reactions," *Arch. Psychol.*, No. 76 (1925), New York.

10 | THE PROCESS OF ATTENDING: TEMPORARY SET

INTRODUCTION

The content or material that might be included in this chapter is less well defined than that for most of the other chapters. Conventionally, and in the layman's mind, attention has been set off in opposition to distraction. The word has been used almost synonymously with concentration when referring to study habits, except there is a more prolonged time suggested by the latter term. In earlier periods, philosophers were likely to discuss attention as though this implied something very much akin to "will." The individual who could attend under distracting conditions was the person with a strong determination or "will" to keep on with his task. The word "will" has practically disappeared from books on psychology except in historical notes. Currently research and discussion is more likely to be presented in terms of "set." Obviously, motivation is implied and those studies that focus upon the more transient motives and temporary set are most like those of an earlier period that dealt with attention.

While no definition of attention seems to be free from uncomfortable vagueness, the meaning of the word is easiest to grasp, according to what Woodworth once said, by dividing it into two parts: "at tension." The implication is that attention involves a state of readiness—better still, refers to at least minimal muscular response. Muscular tonus, which might be thought of as continuous, is not quite the same thing. Nevertheless, if muscles are kept in a state of good tonus this requires stimulation by the nerves, for tonus tends to decrease if either sensory or motor nerves are damaged. Woodworth seemed to be talking about muscular tension that arose from particular sensory experience and this would be somewhat transitory in nature.

In spite of the vagueness of what is meant by attention, there remain

229

good reasons for devoting time and space to this topic. The first reason is primarily historical and convenience in dealing with published research. Many experiments have been conducted and the reports written within a framework of attention. Thus there is a considerable body of knowledge organized about this subject. These studies include: (1) those in which an attempt was made to determine why the organism is selective in responding to competing stimuli; (2) those directed to a study of shifting sensory reception, as in retinal rivalry and dominance; (3) those concerned with oscillation in perception of ambiguous figures; (4) those dealing with the span of apprehension; (5) those in which an attempt was made to determine the number of activities that could be carried on simultaneously; (6) those revealing a loss of efficiency because of distractors in work or study. While we might write a different and possibly more appropriate heading than "attention," or again organize the material under several different topics, we could scarcely afford to neglect so much research bearing upon transition-like problems standing at the critical junction between sensory-perceptual processes and response psychology.

Those using the introspection method in psychology approach problems of attention with some uneasiness. This was a borderland for psychologists and would remain so, they thought, until more was known about the elements that made up conscious processes. The extreme functionalists who called themselves behaviorists tried to bypass attention in their hurry to get on with the study of observable and recordable behavior. However, it might be supposed that here was the very beginning of response psychology. The adjustment of sensory equipment by use of muscles, the setting up of tensions in the muscles, even minimal responses such as those of the vocal organs during the brief period of readiness and anticipation, or again, those made during silent reading might well have been brought under the scrutiny of the most extreme behaviorists. The last named reaction, movement of the vocal organs during silent reading, was carefully studied, but of course as an example of motor behavior.

WHY THE CURRENT INTEREST IN ATTENTION?

Beyond the historical reason for a chapter on attention are urgent practical uses for guidance in helping a variety of people with everyday problems which are readily discussed by use of the terminology associated with the word "attention." Psychologists have been pushed by people in other occupations and professions to answer many questions like the following: How can the advertiser attract the attention of his prospective customers? Once he has attracted attention how does he hold it until he can get his message across and persuade him to buy? What will neutralize the attention-getting stunts of the competitor? How does the school teacher attract the attention of the daydreaming child who may stare at her but attends to something far away? How does she deal with the distractible child who is forever looking out the window to see what is going on? She may have to compete with the ever-changing interests of a busy street. School buildings have even been constructed with high windows as a means of helping teachers to "hold the attention" of students. Is this a good, or, at any rate, the best solution to her problem?

In the practical everyday situation it might be asked: What can be done to give advantage to the stimulus that is to be received and acted upon. In order to be able to answer such a question it becomes necessary to have a basic understanding of the factors that give advantage or disadvantage to the environmental world which is filled with a multitude of stimuli that are always in competition for the attention. Nor can the ever-changing conditions of the organism propelled by drives and motives be neglected. Attending means that the organism is interacting and responding to the surrounding stimuli.

Everyone who must influence the thinking, the feelings, the beliefs, and the actions of others as a part of his daily work must inevitably deal with attention-getting problems. The politician must first attract his audience before he has a chance to persuade the voter. Those with a strong intellectual interest and who are capable of attending to abstract issues may be offended by the politician's antics at attracting crowds, by wearing peculiar clothes such as a coon-skin cap, or red galluses. Again, they may dislike his use of loud-speakers or a hill-billy band. The road-sign painter must attract the traveler's attention before he can hope to sell or warn; the newspaper headline writer must choose attention-getting words and type; the composer of music or the painter of pictures wants to interest people and to focus their attention upon certain aspects of his creation. In the techniques employed to attract and hold attention the intellectually oriented individual may see more of an appeal to the so-called instincts than he likes to find.

ATTENTION AND ACTION

In some occupations success depends upon attention being quickly followed by action. The gas station operator, who gets but a split-second opportunity at the passing tourists, is a good example of this. On the other hand, the work of the minister, while requiring that his efforts receive attention, wants to hold that attention and interest and to produce patterns of behavior that continue over a lifetime and which may involve not only adhering to certain codes but may also lead to pleasurable participation in rituals that distinguish his particular religious group.

We have tried to indicate that these are vital problems to many people, and psychologists cannot very well avoid such issues. They are distinctly psychological in nature. What can experimental psychology contribute to solutions to such problems? Not as much as might be desired, but it would be a false modesty to say "nothing." There is a considerable amount of relevant scientific information that can be brought to bear upon these everyday problems. One of the greatest difficulties is to transmit this knowledge by the use of terms having meaning for the layman. Too often the potential consumers of psychological information are confronted with a discouraging array of abstractions that get and hold the attention of the professional psychologists, but fail to attract and sustain the interests of the intermediary consumer that would like to make use of the information. Examples of these terms and concepts are: "sensory discrimination," "perceptual selection," "perceptual defense," "incidental learning," "involuntary attention," "mental sets," "tissue needs"; perchance we might even include "attention" and "distraction" as psychologists use the terms!

While we should not insist that existing psychological knowledge is adequate, what we are able to stress is that methods and techniques exist for obtaining much better solutions to these problems than those generally in use. Not a small amount of this information is scattered through the literature and presented under headings that might not seem to have any relevance to those not familiar with the psychologists' approaches to these problems or with what must seem to the nonprofessional psychologist as esoteric jargon.

VOLUNTARY AND INVOLUNTARY ATTENTION

Without intentionally invoking an argument over "free will" or the degree of "choice" that a person may have, we should like to discuss voluntary and involuntary attention. When the observer attends to the content of a lesson, that is voluntary attention. Then attention is deliberately directed to a task according to the dictates of a previous decision. A sudden loud noise like a thunderclap forces its way upon the individual. He responds here by involuntary attention. Under ordinary circumstances attention will be given to intense stimuli whether there is a desire to attend or not. It is not meant to imply that there is a totally different process involved in voluntary and involuntary attention. Perhaps a more sensible view is one in which a single continuum is conceptualized with internally forced attention at one extreme, and externally forced attention at the other. Then individuals would be found distributed according to their ability to attend; ability greatly influenced by bodily needs and learned self-discipline that may enable the individual to resist distractions and to shift attention systematically or in a controlled fashion as stimuli arise in the immediate environment. There would still be a level of external stimuli that would break through for each individual and this would be classified as a distractor. The story of Archimedes who was so lost in his mathematical calculations that he failed to hear the Roman soldiers' command, and was slain, is an example of how amazingly high the threshold for distracting stimuli may be for some people and under some circumstances.

Those who shift attention rapidly are not necessarily less well adjusted than others. Looking at it in this way one may actually find that those at each extreme—the highly distractable and the rigidly controlled—are badly adjusted individuals, even psychotic persons. The individual who seems to be an extreme example of a person whose threshold for external stimuli is so low that he rapidly shifts from one thing to another is like a "manic" individual. Rapid flight of ideas and quick translation from thought to overt behavior is a characteristic of the manic person. On the other hand, the person best able to shut out the influence of surrounding stimuli might be found to typify the "catatonic schizophrenic" individuals. There remains a question about the latter individual—whether or not he deliberately means to attend to his own thoughts. He may hallucinate, and this is assumed to be under little or no voluntary control. He may sit around in a stuporous state, seemingly indifferent to all that goes on about him, while deeply engrossed with his imaginings. Perhaps he is attending to his own problems to the exclusion of the surrounding physical environment and on a voluntary basis. If so, his motivational system must have become very different from that of a "normal" person.

Needless to say, a given stimulus might give rise to voluntary attention upon the part of one individual, and be an unwelcome intrusion for the next person. The noise coming to the classroom may be a welcome relief to the bored student, but the teacher probably sees it as an unpleasant distractor that temporarily forces her attention, as well as that of the students, away from the task at hand. Again, timing is important, for a man may deliberately attend to a business problem during the day, only to have it force itself upon him when he wants to indulge in recreation or sleep. Then he has become the victim of a "distractor."

The investigators of a century ago were still much under the influence of what is now called "faculty psychology." Actually faculty psychology had its roots in phrenology, which goes back still another century. According to the ideas held a hundred years ago, when the first experiments were attempted upon attention, the individual's abilities (or faculties) to discriminate, memorize, imagine, or reason might all be improved by direct training. It was not then appreciated as thoroughly as it is today that training often needs to be specific and concrete. These writers were not aware of a basic principle—that when attention is centered upon one thing it is necessarily taken away from something else. However, we shall not now go into the broad problems of transfer of training or the facts and principles of inhibition and facilitation, as these topics are more appropriately discussed along with learning phenomena. It is sufficient to point out that the individual who is attending to the stars may neglect the people about him; that the botanist who is preoccupied with the leaves of the trees may not see the stones over which he stumbles. If a botanist walks with a geologist, the two scientists may observe and remember different things. It is certain that selectivity is an important aspect of attention and when there is gain in one area it may be at the expense of loss in another. However, it might be presumed that alertness operates at different levels, and it is conceivable that the highly motivated individual shifts rapidly from one situation to another and that heightened attention is at the expense of what would otherwise be passive drifting or daydreaming.

Darwin is quoted as saying that he regretted that his attention had been so completely devoted to the limited observations that were ultimately systematized in his theory of evolution that he lost all interest and appreciation for music and other subjects that gave him pleasure as a young man. Nevertheless, many of the early experiments in psychology were motivated by the belief that man could be taught so that the broad abilities that have been mentioned would be strengthened and usable in general ways. Thus, it was once believed that the individual's general ability to attend could be improved. In order to evaluate the instruction directed to this goal some measure of attention was needed.

SPAN OF ATTENTION OR APPREHENSION

In 1859, Sir William Hamilton (2) used a demonstration before his students to show the span of apprehension. By throwing a handful of marbles upon the floor and taking a quick glance at them it was shown that only six or seven marbles could be clearly perceived. He further pointed out that, by grouping the marbles into units of two or three marbles, five to seven groups could be apprehended. A few years later, Jevons (5) used a more systematic procedure to study the span of apprehension. He was of the opinion that here was "one of the very few points in psychology which can, as far as we yet see, be submitted to experiment." He used a small tray and dropped a handful of beans upon it so that a few were caught. It was the subject's task to make a quick estimate, and this was later compared with the actual number caught. Thousands of trials were given to different subjects and 100 percent accuracy was achieved when no more than four beans were caught. Accuracy declined systematically as the number of beans became larger,

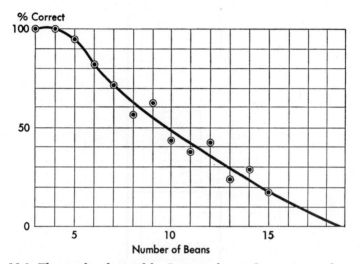

Fig. 10.1. The results obtained by Jevon as he tried to estimate the number of beans exposed briefly by dropping them in a pan. The median span is seen to be approximately 10 beans. Accuracy was very poor when the number was 15 or more. (From Woodworth, Robert S., *Experimental Psychology*. New York: Henry Holt & Co., 1938.)

until less than one estimate in five trials was correct if the actual number of beans was fifteen or more.

The present-day student is too steeped in acceptable scientific procedure to miss the point that many controls were not feasible or even possible in such an experiment. How long was the subject allowed to look at the beans? What kind of subjects were used? Were they a cross section of the total population? Would much time have been saved and more dependable results achieved by exercising better controls and doing with fewer observations?

THE TACHISTOSCOPE

The need for an answer to many of these questions was immediately apparent to psychologists. The search for a more adequate technique for measuring the span of apprehension lead to the invention of the tachisto-scope. The first tachistoscope was a crude instrument. Stimulus material such as dots, letters, or printed words was attached to a piece of wood and this was dropped across a small open window before the subject. An attachment was added that made it possible to catch the falling object

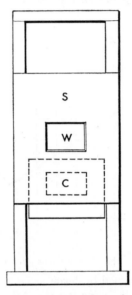

Fig. 10.2. Early fall tachistoscope. In many of the early experiments upon span of apprehension, a simple apparatus like the design shown above was used. S is a stationary screen; W is a window; C is to indicate a card behind the screen. The card (C), upon which material is printed or drawn, was fastened to a board which was fitted into slots cut in the upright timbers on the sides. Then exposure was achieved by dropping the board containing the material past the window (W).

for a brief period before it fell out of sight again. Manipulation was by hand and the use of a mechanical device. Timing depended upon the judgment and motor skill of the experimenter. More accurate controls were still needed but here was a beginning.

The accurate measure of the span of apprehension may be of less sci-entific significance than the by-product—the development of refined devices for controlling the time of exposure of stimulus material. While it is certainly worth-while to know about the span of apprehension, early stress placed upon this ability now seems to be another example of over-enthusiasm.

Many kinds of tachistoscopes have come into use. In the most desirable ones there is a constant field of illumination, movement of the stimulus material is avoided during exposure, and noise and other distractors are reduced to a minimum. Of course, the point of fundamental importance is that there be a way to measure accurately and to make systematic variations in the exposure time. The invention of the camera brought into use

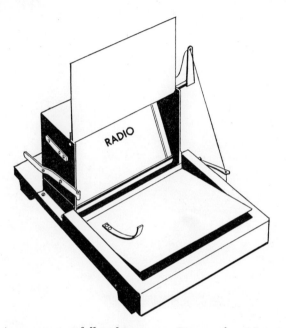

Fig. 10.3. A more recent fall tachistoscope. By use of a string and a tripping mechanism, the screen is quickly opened and closed again. (Courtesy C. H. Stoelting Co., who furnished the picture because of its historical significance.)

the projector and shutter. This was an excellent apparatus for classroom demonstrations but had important limitations for research work. It tended to be long on convenience and short on accuracy and certain important controls.

VARIATIONS IN THE SPAN OF APPREHENSION

The experimental results obtained by the use of tachistoscopes leads to the following conclusions about the span of apprehension: First of all, it appears that the span of apprehension or attention is no more fixed than is the threshold level for a stimulus. It varies from moment to moment. Beyond this variation, under assumed constant conditions, it is found that grouping determined by both the arrangement of the stimuli and the subjective effort of the subject makes a difference much as Hamilton suggested about increasing the number of items by grouping. Span increases to some extent with practice, but there is no such great improve-

Fig. 10.4. Projectors that allow for timed exposures are now frequently used for tachistoscopic presentation of material. Timing is possible in terms of exposure as short as 1/100 or even 1/1000 of a second. (Courtesy C. H. Stoelting Co.)

ment even with prolonged and strenuous effort as some of the earlier investigators had hoped. Soon the subject reaches a physiological or psychological barrier, which is broken only by grouping or some such technique.

In recent years (1940), Hunter and Sigler (3) set out to see the effects of illumination and time upon the span of apprehension. Both were assumed to have effect, but the problem was to establish how much variation might be produced by changing each one from zero up to the maximum. It was shown that an average number of items, say five, could be achieved by a given subject when holding the illumination constant and systematically varying the time. Again, the time could be held constant and an average of five achieved by varying the illumination. However, this result could be obtained only within the middle range of the span. A span of twelve items was achieved by exposure of only such length as permitted the subject to count or to group items.

Fig. 10.5. A constant illumination tachistoscope allowing control over time of presenting material on a screen. Slides are used with the projectors. Constant illumination is achieved by a mechanism that automatically turns one projector off when the other is turned on. (Courtesy Lafayette Instrument Co.)

There is an interesting relationship between the number of items presented tachistoscopically and the time that the subject will render his report. The more items there are, the slower the subject will be in giving his report. While it might be of little scientific significance, there is a close correlation between the length of time the subject used in giving his report and the mistakes he makes. Accuracy is almost 100 percent for three or four items and these are given in less time than the reports on longer numbers. Such correlations might lead to unwarranted conclusions. The inexperienced investigator might conclude that the mistakes were due to slow judgment. Forcing a quick decision for the large number of items certainly cannot be expected to eliminate the progressive number of mistakes as the number of items is increased.

GENERAL DETERMINERS OF ATTENTION

There is a close parallel between some of the factors of advantage in perceptional organization and the determiners of attention. It is difficult to say which proceed in time, and possibly there are inconsistencies here. Certainly, perceptual organization may emerge following voluntary attention. This is the expected sequence in difficult tasks of a visual kind and would probably be the regular course of events in dealing with intellectual problems. The creative artist keeps forcing his attention to a central theme in the hope that he may ultimately achieve an original organization. If this does not come to him after sustained effort, he may choose to turn his attention to a new theme rather than to submit to the obvious. On the other hand, it is unquestionably true that some patterns of perception, even fairly complex ones on rare occasions, may leap out seemingly instantaneously under just the right circumstances.

Factors having attention-getting value are sometimes divided into those associated with the sensory equipment and the conditions of the organism, while others are assumed to be dependent upon external conditions or the stimulus itself. There can be no question but that such factors as size, intensity, color, and movement serve to attract attention. Always there is to be expected an interaction between these so that size is not independent in its value of the others and so on. However, there is further complexity, for the interaction also involves factors primarily of the organism and of previous experience, such as familiarity, emotional appeal, and promise of need gratification. This last would include food, warmth, security, and many others. A further group of factors exist, not easily identified with either external or internal, but perhaps involve some of both. Such factors include repetition, change, and novelty.

Assessment of the relative attention-getting value of a particular factor has been attempted in ways similar to that for studying the strength of motives. The two are likely to be overlapping phenomena. This is especially true for the more sustained motives. What are adequate controls? The investigator is deprived of opportunity to retain 100 percent constancy of all factors save the one independent variable. At present, it is not seen how this ideal kind of experimental control will ever be possible on these problems because of having to use a subject that is assumed never to be exactly the same again after he has experienced an event.

One way that intensity of stimuli has been studied is by having the subject fixate a point between two light spots of slightly different intensity and then ask him to report which light is more vivid to him. The result, of course, favors the more highly illuminated spot if there is a threshold difference. However, it is possible to get a different and contrary response from the expected one if some special and vital meaning is given to the stimulus of the weaker intensity.

Advertisers have often tried to determine the attention-getting value of different advertisements in magazines. They have sometimes systematically arranged advertisements of larger and smaller size, with color and no color, and with saturated and nonsaturated colors. The measure of attention can be in terms of recall or recognition—making sure that there has been equal opportunity to observe in the first place. This might be controlled by use of a large number of subjects, with greater safety in assuming that chance would operate to equalize exposure opportunity for both frequency and time for the group as a whole.

Another index to the power of a stimulus to get and to hold attention is obtained by photographing eye movements of the subject while he thumbs through a magazine. The subject must not know the purpose of the experiment. It is better still if the photographing can be done without the subject's awareness of it, and when he is in a usual reading situation. This is not as impossible a procedure as might be supposed if expense is not too limiting a factor. Concealed photographic equipment with magnifying devices should enable the investigator to make very satisfactory records in a general library reading room.

The advertiser always wants to answer such questions as whether a full-sized page is worth twice as much as a half page, whether the extra cost for color gives good return for his money, and how much of his space should be left white—without picture or print. Here, if he decides to leave more white space around his message, he may trade opportunity to persuade in order to obtain greater attention-getting possibilities.

It is expected that the advertiser will place his main confidence in the more persistent and stronger motives and drives. Thus, he will hope to appeal to the customer through bridging an association of his product with hunger, sex, security, safety, prestige, or curiosity. Where the product has little logical relationship to these drives and a gimmick is used that tends to force such an association, the gimmick may become a distractor. Who knows whether the advertiser who pictures a beautiful girl draped over the car that he is trying to sell succeeds better in selling the car or the girl? While there is an obvious attempt to use sex appeal to sell the car, it may be that the girl becomes an effective "distractor" from the intended message. It is possible that a staggering and useless cost has been borne by inadequately informed buyers of advertising. The evidence is strong that advertising is often ineffectual, but it is also true that research is becoming a useful tool in the hands of the more progressive advertising agencies.

FLUCTUATION OF ATTENTION

It was known by ancient man that a dim star was visible and in the next moment gone. Threshold level stimuli can be expected to fluctuate in this way. It is no doubt true that the disappearing and reappearing star is due, in part, to the stimulus. The atmosphere through which the light must travel is partially responsible for the phenomenon. The bright stars may not twinkle and it is said that the dim ones do not twinkle as much if the observer is above most of the atmosphere. However, the organism in responding must vary also, for there is some generality to the phenomenon of fluctuating sensory reception for different sense modalities and for a variety of stimuli. Thus, the process of attending (or temporary set) becomes involved in all studies of threshold discrimination.

Shift of attention is of major importance in perceiving ambiguous figures. The speed of such shifts can be changed by voluntary attention, and by shifting, or forcing the eyes upon certain parts of a visually presented figure. At the same time, the observer is unable to prevent all fluctuation of the perception when observing figures. Some regularity in the shifts of attention has been noted and there have been repeated attempts to associate these shifts with physical changes such as blood pressure or blood supply to the brain. Early experiments were believed to reveal a dependable relationship, but there is little confidence at the present time in the reliability of some of the reported relationships.

MULTIPLE SIMULTANEOUS ACTIVITIES

The number of activities that can be carried on at one time is a subject of much debate and is probably more appropriately handled under a chapter on attention than elsewhere in psychology. There is some doubt that this is a problem of great psychological significance, but it claimed considerable space in earlier books. There are perhaps important theoretical implications.

There is no question that two or more things may be pursued with continuity as far as motor responses are concerned. People are observed every day who do not have to stop walking in order to talk. The individual may be aware of several kinds of sensory experiences which are all continuing, and during this time he might busy himself with a number of muscular activities. It is legitimate to ask whether he is really "attending" to all of these. It may be that a more correct description is that he turns rapidly from one to the other and so proceeds in a circle or spiral from one stimulus to another. At any rate there may be no conspicuous loss of continuity as the subject attends simultaneously to several sensory demands and he may also coordinate satisfactorily when making complicated motor responses. Many habits are reduced to a routine and they continue to reel off once he has initiated the beginning response. It must be granted that investigators have not been able to quantify the amount of time that must be allowed as a minimum for a single act of attending. If an absolute minimum of time for attending a single stimulus could be determined, it might be revealed that several things could be attended to within a second. It is suspected by many experimenters that attention may shift several times within one second.

DISTRACTORS

Distractors are thought of as sensations or motor responses which are inconsistent with the task at hand. The individual may resist their intrusion with varying degrees of success. There are several ways of evaluating distractors. Data may be gathered to determine the loss of efficiency in performance, i.e., quality and quantity of work done; the ratio of work done to energy used; or subjective reports of the subject's reactions and beliefs concerning the effects of a distractor. In an early study upon the influence of distractors, Morgan (6) introduced a variety of startling noises while subjects were typing. The attempt to type while bells were ringing, buzzers sounding, and phonograph records playing resulted in a greater amount of time per correct letter typed. There was also a tendency to strike the keys harder. The net change, while at first detrimental, did not last. There was a rather quick reversal of speed and strength of stroke back toward the characteristic performance before the introduction of the distractor.

This tendency to "get used to" new and irrelevant stimulus conditions is a part of general adaptability or way of adjusting. The older generation is amazed by the way the younger generation has learned to study while the radio goes full blast. In effect, the radio has lost most, if not all, of its distracting quality. The child does not attend to it enough to prevent him from learning his lesson. It has even been suggested that a child who works habitually in this noisy environment may be greatly disturbed if required to work in a quiet room.

The carrying on of more than one activity may not necessarily result in a loss of efficiency for any of them. Much depends upon how well activities may be woven into a pattern. As early as 1887 Paulham (7) found that he could learn to recite one poem while he was writing another. The tendency to mix words was soon overcome. A number of studies have been made to see how much interference or facilitation might follow when subjects are required to carry on muscular activity while learning. Bills (1) as well as others, found that there was a statistically dependable increase in learning during induced muscular tension over the more relaxed period. These studies were initiated by the observations that increased muscular tension regularly accompanied learning effort for most subjects. There is not as yet convincing evidence that the muscular tension of itself contributes directly to better learning.

Jacobson (4) was of the opinion that much of the muscular activity that accompanied learning effort was due to a general neural spread and he speculated that this was very likely an unnecessary waste of energy. Thus he set about training subjects in differential relaxation. His contention was that the student should be able to keep those muscles which were not essential to the task in a relaxed state. This would result in a saving of energy that could better be expended upon some essential part of the learning. It is readily seen from the studies upon distractors that we may easily get involved in problems of learning when discussing attention. Subsequent chapters are devoted to learning. We shall still have occasion to refer to attention and to develop further concepts that relate closely to this subject.

SUMMARY

The wide use of concepts and techniques among school teachers, advertisers, and other people who hope to attract attention and influence behavior seems to justify the presentation of material of the kind found in this chapter. Beyond this general material, not infrequently presented under other headings by psychologists, are a few rather specific and unique problems that do not readily and logically fall under a title that excludes the word "attention." The studies of the span of apprehension fit conveniently into a chapter like this one. Shifts and fluctuations in attention are phenomena that must be related to perception and sensory threshold changes. There are a number of principles and theoretical concepts that have their historical roots in studies that were reported in terms of problems of attracting and distracting the individual. Many of these results are applicable to a variety of everyday psychological problems, but the consumers of psychological research are almost certain to need help in utilizing this material to the best advantage.

The student may become aware that this chapter serves to bridge a gap between sensory-perceptual psychology and response psychology as perhaps no other chapter does or could. In a way the words "at tension" imply a rather elementary response. Attending is a state of sensory alertness and muscular readiness. It is hoped that there will be no temptation to feel that we are preparing to drop completely certain aspects of psychology in order to take up entirely new material. A more appropriate attitude is one in which the student deliberately carries along his background of information and understanding so that he can bring previous learning to bear upon the new problems in psychology. The rest of the book is focused upon response psychology, with emphasis upon learning, and the way what is learned finds expression in social and scientific pursuits.

SUGGESTED READINGS

Asher, E. J., Tiffin, Joseph, and Knight, F. B. *Introduction to General Psychology*, pp. 267-296. Boston: D. C. Heath, 1953.

Dashiell, John Frederick. *Fundamentals of General Psychology*, pp. 342-363, Boston: Houghton Mifflin, 1949.

Woodworth, Robert S., and Schlosberg, Harold. *Experimental Psychology*, pp. 72-106. New York: Henry Holt, 1954.

McClelland, David C. (ed.). *Studies in Motivation*. Wendt: "Motivation, Effort, and Performance," pp. 448-459. New York: Appleton-Century-Crofts, 1955.

Hebb, D. O. *The Organization of Behavior*, pp. 6-11. New York: John Wiley, 1949.

REFERENCES

1. Bills, A. G. "The influence of muscular tension on efficiency of mental work," *Amer. J. Psychol.*, 38 (1927), 227-251.
2. Hamilton, Sir Wm. *Lectures on Metaphysics and Logic*. Vol. 1, Lec. XIV. Edinburgh: Blackwood, 1859.
3. Hunter, W. S., and Sigler, M. "The span of visual discrimination as a function of time and intensity of stimulation," *J. Exp. Psychol.*, 26 (1940), 160-179.
4. Jacobson, Edmund S. *Progressive Relocation*. Chicago: University of Chicago Press, 1938.
5. Jevons, W. S. "The power of numerical discrimination," *Nature*, 3 (1871), 281-292.
6. Morgan, J. J. B. "The overcoming of distraction and other resistances," *Arch. Psychol.*, No. 35 (1916).
7. Paulham, F. "La Simultaneité des Actes Psychiques," *Rev. Scient.*, 39 (1887), 684-689.

11 | STUDIES OF ASSOCIATION: RELATING AND ORGANIZING

INTRODUCTION

The richness and significance of the philosophical and psychological writing upon association in many ways exceeds that upon any other topic that is the subject matter of a chapter in this book. Broadly conceived, and in one way or another, some aspect of the associative process permeates nearly all the thinking and experimenting in psychology. This is especially striking when we turn to problems of learning, perceiving, thinking, and personal or social adjustments. On historical grounds, argument could be presented for making "association" the first chapter in a book on experimental psychology. However, the material seems more useful at this stage when we are about to turn to the technical problems of learning. Furthermore, there was a delay until relatively recent times in the use of scientific methodology in the study of association. It is somewhat paradoxical that associationism and/or empiricism should have been so important in fostering scientific methodology and the inductive reasoning approach, while deduction remained so long the approach to the study of the associative process itself. We usually think of Galton's (3) studies which were made about 1880 as being the first systematic and scientific investigations of association.

Serious "armchair" attempts to explain how events and objects become associated together go back to the time of the Greeks and probably much earlier. Aristotle formulated what have become known as the primary laws of association: (1) similarity, (2) contrast, and (3) nearness in time and space. Most of the European scholars and scientists of the seventeenth and eighteenth centuries believed that all mental operations could be explained as a process of association. Many of them believed that all the laws of association could be reduced to one—contiguity of experience. It was customary for them to explain complex concepts as the product of compounding of simple associations and images drawn from past experience.

While there are good reasons for abandoning much of the older philosophical terminology and rejecting for scientific purposes the "armchair" method of the early associationists, we are much indebted to these early approaches and contributions. In many ways psychologists are still preoccupied with the same problems that the associationists worked upon, and they are too often blocked by the same difficulties. The language has changed, but the substance has remained much the same. One might imagine how rapidly the well-informed associationist living in 1800 could have incorporated the methods and findings of current psychology into his system. None of the main psychological schools or systems would have appeared too strange in broad outline. He might easily have seen the roots of behaviorism with its stress upon environment and the conditioned response in his own system. The associationists were the first writers to lay great stress upon environmental factors in the production of the total individual and it would certainly have seemed appropriate to him that events must happen together in time for conditioning to take place. There are those who consider an explanation of learning which rests upon conditioning as being little different from explanations based upon associations, except that description may be more specific if the conditioning concept is used. Also, along with studies of conditioning, there have been implications that a reflex arc is brought into operation and hence a close correlation with neurological structure and function.

At first the associationist might feel that he is in a strange world when trying to understand the concept of the gestaltist, for here is found severe criticism of some of the implications in associationism. There is more conflict than harmony found between associationists and gestaltists when they attempt to show how meanings arise. However, in the end the gestaltist accepts the idea that much learning and perceiving takes place in the way associationists claimed, but he reserves the right to deny that *all* development is well explained in that way. The gestaltists object especially to the notion that wholes are slowly put together by the use of small parts. Rather they view the process as often being the exact opposite—the whole emerges first and the parts are fitted in later.

The psychoanalysts, and others working primarily in the area of clinical psychology, would present a formidable new terminology, but then the very essence of the analytic system rests upon assumptions about associations that are made in early childhood—how taboo materials become suppressed and forgotten but retain affect potential which may later lead to perceptual selection, distortion, and eventually maladjustive behavior.

The idea that traumatic emotional experiences of childhood would leave disturbing residue in memory traces, conscious or unconscious, would not have appeared very new to a nineteenth-century associationist.

ASSOCIATION AND LEARNING THEORY

Many modern psychologists consider that sound learning theory must be the cornerstone for building a science of psychology. A quick comparison of the general concepts of learning may fail to impress the nonexpert in the learning field as being very different from the views held a century and a half ago. There is a great body of technical information, but most of it relates to the same central problems concerning the importance of time, space, and effect. Because there is a lack of sufficient evidence to formulate complete theories, or laws of learning, psychologists must still debate about the part played by contiguity of experience and reinforcement in learning. To be sure, it would not, at this stage of the development of psychology, be recommended that research upon learning use association as the starting point. Perhaps association is late in the learning process, for it can be considered that associative connections are the end products of learning or the evidence that learning has taken place. At any rate, somewhat more precise terms are found today in the description of how learning takes place than could be found in the vocabulary of early associationism.

CURRENT PROBLEMS INVOLVING ASSOCIATIVE PHENOMENA

It is not our purpose to give a review of most of the material that might be assembled under the heading of association. The great bulk of writing on the subject would have a strong philosophical tinge. It would have to do with a particular philosophical system and teleology—it would almost certainly bore current psychology students. We want to give a much more limited presentation and to concentrate upon research which has helped to lay a groundwork for studying thought processes, emotional reactivity, and the rather practical problems involved in developing personality tests. One would not be far wrong if he should conclude that nearly all personality tests are merely association tests in which variable types of stimuli are used. What associations will an individual make when he is given words, questions, statements, ambiguous pictures, or ink-blots? If the examiner uses the same stimulus material for all individuals in a group, he can identify those who deviate. He can determine the degree of communality that exists and then he is in a position to evaluate a person upon the amount of agreement or disagreement with others that is found in thinking or in his emotional responding. Once standards are obtained the investigator can use the norms to differentiate between the normal and the abnormal and to determine the relative position or distances a given individual stands from the average or median. Not only may associations be used as a means to diagnose maladjustment, but clinicians go beyond that and use the associative content to plan and administer therapy. Reviving old associations and resynthesizing these in the light of subsequent experience and newly gained insights is a cornerstone in present-day psychotherapy.

EARLY EXPERIMENTS UPON ASSOCIATION

We have indicated that the first systematic studies of association were by Galton. While they were lacking in experimental refinement, they served very well to indicate the possibilities of experimenting in this area and helped to initiate a number of investigations. Galton was both experimenter and subject. It may also be remembered that Ebbinghaus, who began work on his important experiments upon learning about the same time, was also experimenter and subject. Galton went about the problem of experimenting upon the associative process by making a list of words and putting each on a separate sheet of paper and then laying these aside for several days. At the later session he uncovered the words one by one and made two associations to each as rapidly as possible. He wrote the words down for later evaluation and introspecting. By use of a stop watch, he made a record of the time taken for the associations. The association process was repeated at four sessions held about a month apart. When he had finished collecting his data, Galton was able to total the number of associations that he had been able to revive, calculate the average associative reaction time, and to study the content material, which was then categorized into several groups.

At the time Galton was working, great stress was placed upon imagery. He struck upon the idea that people might be classified according to imagery types. He thought that some individuals might be essentially visual-minded, others auditorly-minded, and others might make predominate use of a still different sense. In the end Galton failed to find that there were clear groups according to sense modality and imagery. However, he did find that more ideas could be grouped with visual origin than with any one of the other senses and this result has been supported by later investigations. Later studies have seemed to support Galton's conclusion about the relatively great use of vision in acquiring knowledge. Galton's experiments had importance beyond the actual findings about associations. They helped to initiate interest in the psychology of individual differences as perhaps no other work did.

While it would be easy to find fault with the way Galton controlled his experiment, it is, nevertheless, true that he was able to observe and to anticipate a number of things about association that have since become important in psychological research. He found that some ideas were frequently repeated and these turned out to be related largely to child-hood experiences. He wrote enthusiastically about the possibility of using this technique to learn about the thought process. He must have grasped something of the significance that could be placed upon well-established norms once they were obtained and the meaning that could be attached to marked deviations. In commenting upon his results he said, " . . . it would be too absurd to print one's own words or ideas singly. They lay bare the foundations of a man's thoughts with a curious distinctness, and exhibit his mental anatomy with more vividness and truth than he would probably care to publish to the world." It was not a great many years until word association tests became a regular part to lie detection, although it is doubtful that Galton had this kind of application in mind. He was probably thinking of emotionally loaded material, consciously or at first not fully consciously related by the subject, that might be of an embarrassing nature once it is revealed and interpreted. Such material has become very useful in the hands of clinicians trained in the use of projective tests or the therapeutic process.

It will be seen that Galton (3) was very conscious of the importance of quantification in science. He was able to quantify his data in three ways: (1) associative reaction time for a given word or for the total words, which made it possible to obtain an average; (2) a frequency table; (3) classification of the responses and the number in each group. It should be remembered that at the time Galton worked, research data in all sciences were much less frequently subjected to statistical analysis than is the case today. Introspection was the chief method for making an analysis of psychological phenomena.

Shortly after Galton's studies, Tauscholdt, working in Wundt's Leipzig laboratory in Germany, had the experimenter say the words and the subject respond verbally. This procedure became more widely accepted than that used by Galton. Cattell soon made a further improvement by using a chronoscope for timing and a voice key which was more precise in recording the beginning of the response. While Cattell had been a student under Wundt, in many ways he was much influenced by the leadership of Galton. His interests shifted to the study of individual differences and he combined reaction time and word association in a number of experiments.

VARIATIONS IN ASSOCIATIVE CONTROLS

It is now common knowledge that experiments upon association may be set up with varying degrees of control or direction about how associations may be made. Freud was the first important clinician to make wide use of association and he structured the situation for the greatest freedom. He placed his patient upon a couch and asked him to start talking. The patient was to relate ideas just as they occurred with no thought of making a logical sequence or of producing complete sentences. On occasions, and especially in his earlier works, Freud hypnotized the subject in the hope of getting more vital associations and to reduce the inhibition which the patient might exercise over the expression of embarrassing materials or events that had been rather completely suppressed. Some word might be used to initiate the chain of associations, but this was of little more use than to get the patient started, since it was assumed that the words that were used by the subject would soon carry him away from the original one and that each of these would in succession furnish the stimulus for the new words and ideas.

In various early experiments a number of devices were used to get the kinds of associations wanted and study was made of the influence of restrictions. Sometimes the subject would be required to give only opposites, synonyms, coordinates, supraordinates, etc. Many of these controls were used as a means of studying how these directions influenced reaction time. The facility with which the child can make associations or give words has been shown, for one thing, to be related to intelligence. Thus, one item in the Stanford Revision of the Binet Test requires that the child say as many words as he can within a given time limit.

Between the extremes of highly structured directions and easy freedom in which the individual is allowed to talk as he will are found a number of techniques, each thought to lend itself to some particular purpose. If timing is important, provision for this must be made. Timing in the completely free association technique must be done by continuous recording. The time factor can then be studied later, including analysis of the interval between words and that between shifts in ideas. In the undirected association procedure, content material becomes relatively more important, for the subject is expected to keep returning to content material that reflects preoccupations or anxiety-laden subjects.

Another way of studying the individual's tendency to return to a theme is to use a chain association procedure. Here the subject may be given a word to which he makes ten or more associations. When this is done, another word is given to initiate a new series. Delays and blocking between words can be studied if recordings are made.

RESULTS FROM INVESTIGATIONS ON ASSOCIATION

Results from association experiments might be discussed conveniently under six headings. Only illustrative examples can be given but these will serve to suggest the type and range of studies that have been made. The underlying assumptions about association that are important in the interpretation of results rest mainly upon the idea that strong associations will occur more frequently than weak ones. It is further assumed that a delay in giving a response has significance. This is a very widely used index in a great variety of test items. This index remains less well validated than could be wished, since it is so widely accepted. The factors thought to produce slow reaction time are rather numerous, and for a given subject responding to predetermined stimuli, it may remain uncertain as to which one is operating. Again, it cannot be absolutely determined that slow reaction time is the result of any disturbance produced by the material itself. There remains the possibility that an association is inhibited by the subject because of embarrassment or emotional unpleasantness which is not due to content material of the experiment but to some irrelevant factor in the whole situation. However, in general, the assumption seems justified that emotional reactivity gives rise to blocking and hence slower associative reactions.

In these investigations the experimenter must contend with problems of frequency in past experience, intensity of the previous and present stimuli, recency of the association, nature of previous responses, condition of the organism, and temporary sets. In regard to this last it has been demonstrated that surprise stimuli require longer for an association to come than if the stimulus material is anticipated. For example, if a given word is presented as a surprise, the RT will be longer than if the word is presented as a word belonging to a list concerning which the S has knowledge or expectancy. By this it is meant that *oak* might be responded to more quickly if the subject is told in advance that he is to respond to words in a list containing the names of trees.

Due to all of the possible variables, the careful investigator hesitates to give dogmatic answers about what associations mean. Nor is he quick to accept as final the associative data when required to attach diagnostic labels. Nevertheless, association procedures remain the best means for attacking certain kinds of problems and neither research workers nor clinical practitioners can very well afford to dispense with this technique.

The six aspects of association that become a convenient framework for discussion are: (1) associative reaction time; (2) communality or frequency of occurrence; (3) content; (4) clinical applications; (5) industrial applications or associative tests, including aptitudes and achievements; (6) legal, or investigative uses. A brief discussion of each is presented as follows:

ASSOCIATIVE REACTION TIME

It was necessary to say something about association under the chapter on reaction time and this has been touched upon previously in the present chapter. There have been several experiments performed with the specific intention of having reaction time the dependent variable. Cattell's experiments were among the first and remain important. One of the rather surprising findings by Cattell was that a single letter or a word of considerable length resulted in little difference for reaction time. This discovery was made when it was common practice to have children learn reading by giving careful study to the spelling and thus look at each separate letter. One of the implications of his findings is that it is not easier to give an association with a letter than a word; in fact, it may be harder.

Reaction time for continuous association such as naming trees, flowers, cities, or any class of objects tends to be rapid at first and then to slow down. It may be that several factors operate to give the typical decelerated or convex curve revealed by this procedure. It is likely that there is a tendency for the most familiar to be named first. Certainly, as the remaining list of items known by the subject becomes smaller and smaller a limitation is placed upon the subject in making added associations. No doubt interference phenomena also arise. Presumably the individual becomes increasingly concerned with each additional association for fear he has given it previously and will be repeating himself. Repetitions may occur often for some subjects. As the subject works there may be interesting spurts or changes in tempo. This seems to occur when there is a new group of associations which cluster around some particular core. For example, in naming cities there may be a spurt if the individual suddenly associates and recalls the cities of a given state or region. He may give several midwestern cities in rapid succession then slow down and move to another group, as, for instance, those found on the Pacific Coast.

Associative reaction time has been related to age of subjects. Anderson (1) found that children were considerably slower in RT in free association than are adults. Children under 6 or 8 years of age may require almost twice as long to make responses as adults. Obviously the content would be of importance and this might be so selected as to give advantage in the other direction. In one study, at least, it was found that boys in the age range of 7 to 10 were faster in reacting than were girls.

Several experiments upon RT for different parts of speech produced fairly consistent results. Concrete and familiar nouns result in quick associations. Adjectives and verbs require more time. It is unknown whether this is no more than a matter of familiarity and the number of associations available. Knowledge of these results might be useful in guiding the teacher in making her assignments in language lessons. An understanding of these matters might also indicate something about the precautions that should be exercised in selecting language material for age groups or for matching material with intelligence level of the students.

COMMUNALITY IN ASSOCIATION

Before trying to set up criteria of normality or abnormality, it is a regular procedure for psychologists to try to determine first what people do characteristically. An act that is normal for an individual living in one culture might be an evidence of abnormality in another culture. It is not implied that other criteria of normality are without usefulness. Psychologists, usually, define behavior as normal or abnormal in terms of frequency of occurrence. Thus, if a man repeatedly indulges in behavior that has not been observed among other men, his behavior is taken as evidence for abnormality. In the broad aspect, psychologists operate upon the assumption that what is acceptable or "normal" behavior for one animal might not be for a different animal. While barking by a dog is normal for a dog, if persisted in by a man it is abnormal behavior. This may seem to be far-fetched as an illustration of a human deviation in behavior; nevertheless, it will be the exception if, in a large mental hospital, no person can be found who insists that he is some lower animal and who persists in imitating that animal.

In the early experiments upon association, it became apparent that responses in a given population would be distributed around a central mode or norm. *Chair* is associated with *table; door* with *window; grass* with *green,* etc. Then trailing off into less and less frequent associations will be an extended list of words If *father* is the stimulus word, then *mother* may be the associated response as much as fifty percent of the time; then *son, daughter, grandfather,* and other relatives will perhaps be given less frequently as the relationship becomes farther removed. With repeated administrations and the use of large numbers of individuals, it becomes possible to obtain a very stable word list of frequencies. Prediction becomes possible so that the investigator is able to speak with confidence regarding the expectancy of words that will be associated with the given stimulus words.

Building upon the findings of Galton, Cattell, Bryant, Marbe, and others, an attempt was made in 1910 by Kent and Rosanoff (4) to construct a table of word frequencies that might be referred to by other investigators. They took 100 familiar English nouns and adjectives and gave them to 1,000 subjects. The subjects were presumably from a normal adult population varying in age, occupation, and education, and including both sexes. The subjects were to respond by giving the first word that came to mind, the presentation and response both being given verbally. From these responses frequency tables were made for each of the one hundred words.

The underlying assumption of the Kent-Rosanoff study was that the completely conventional—in a sense the perfectly "normal" individual—will give the response word for each stimulus word that is the mode for the whole group. This is hypothetical, for no individual is likely ever to be found who will actually give as many as one hundred responses that would follow the mode. However, each of the subjects might be arranged according to how well he did agree with the total distribution for the group. It would be an additional bit of refinement to use standard scores reflecting the distance from the average for each word presented. Thus if subject X gave the fifth most frequent one, this would be taken into account in deciding whether X or Y was in closer agreement with the total responses. The subject who deviated most would have few popular words among his responses, and perhaps a number of associations would occur that no one else had given at all.

The number of different words given to a particular stimulus word might be great or small. Very common words having closely associated antonyms or synonyms like long, big, dark, or high might reveal that more than fifty of the one hundred subjects gave the same word in associative response. Then the rest of the words might be limited to five or ten altogether. On the other hand, some words of a more abstract nature could stimulate as many as fifty different response words from one hundred subjects. It has been demonstrated that badly disturbed individuals, such as those suffering from psychosis, give many highly individualistic response words. Thus it may be that one fourth or even one half of a badly disoriented psychotic individual's response words are not to be found in the Kent-Rosanoff frequency table at all.

A word of caution must be given in regard to the use of the Kent-Rosanoff tables for diagnostic purposes. It is necessary to standardize the list for people who do not come from a similar population as the original. Important changes in vocabulary usage have taken place since the Kent-Rosanoff list was made in 1910, so revision would be desirable even if the population used happened to be geographically similar. Those coming from a very different culture would be expected to deviate more than usual. Results reveal that if there is a marked difference in educational level or in occupational specialization, close agreement with the norms should not be expected. Thus it is not wise to conclude hastily that the individual is a serious deviant simply because the response words he gives do not agree very consistently with the tables.

The Kent-Rosanoff table has not actually been widely used for diagnosis. However, the concept that there is communality in thinking is basic in diagnostic work. Those who deviate markedly are suspected of abnormality. This concept seems to be basic in all acceptable psychological tests of personality. In a number of diagnostic tools there is a lack of clearly stated norms; these may not be in concrete and specific terms and the investigator may be tempted to resort to impressions about the degree of consistency. Beck (2) uses the concept of frequency of responses on the Rorschach ink-blot test in constructing his lists of so-called popular responses as well as those percepts said to have "good" form. Responses that are said to have good form or poor form are determined by how often normal people have given the same or very similar responses to the figures. In this test, as well as in other personality tests where the individual must elect to give responses of his own rather than by checking an answer to presented questions or statements, allowance is made for individualistic responses. Thus there is opportunity for extremely rare responses that may be classified as bizarre.

Responses that would occur less often than once in a hundred or a thousand records have the quality of rarity that is one of the primary qualities of bizarreness. Several bizarre responses on almost any test may cause the examiner to raise a question of sanity in the subject, since they would indicate a marked deviation. The experienced psychologist realizes that any criterion for bizarreness is not wholly satisfactory, since by definition occurrence is not frequent. Thus the conclusion of bizarreness is necessarily arrived at in a negative sort of way. There is often great difficulty in discriminating between highly original and creative ideas and those that should be considered as bizarre. Beyond rarity the latter term is used to indicate a lack of logic, or strangeness and inappropriateness. Original and creative associations are examples of deviations from the average, but they do not indicate poor mental health.

CONTENT

Content analysis has been used by clinicians for more than fifty years, but the possible usefulness of studying content is not limited to this purpose. Associative responses can be classified as to the closeness of meaning between stimulus and response. They can then be further scaled in a variety of ways. This procedure is not strange to the psychologist and "scaling" enables him to "measure" and to evaluate most abstractions. Woodworth (6) suggested that responses might be placed into four categories as follows: (1) definition, including synonyms and supra-ordinates, (2) completions and predication, (3) coordinates and contrasts, and (4) valuation and personal associations.

The first three classes of associations may be turned to uses in testing for information, even by direction to the subject to make associations for a given word that can be placed in each category as indicated and according to his judgment. For example, if the subject is instructed to associate to a word like *needle* with terms that fit into each class, a very searching examination procedure is at hand. The responses will reveal how the individual stands with regard to others at various levels of knowledge and sophistication. Woodworth and Schlosberg (8) illustrate how the results might turn out by grouping responses into the four classes using the stimulus word *needle:*

Class 1: instrument, implement, tool, article, and perhaps sewing.
Class 2: sharp, steel, point, eye, work.
Class 3: thread, pin, thimble, cotton, cloth.
Class 4: hurt, pricking, sting, blood, and perhaps useful.

Each class might be broken down further. It will be recognized that some of these associations are very easy and simple ones that could characterize the responses of a child or an intellectually dull adult. It is well known that definitions or associations in terms of use, i.e., a needle is "used to sew" is characteristic of the way a child responds. On the other hand, difficult words or abstractions come only from the intelligent, the educated, the widely experienced individual. Thus to describe and to elaborate upon a needle as "a sharp steel implement with an eye in one end through which a thread may be drawn so the thread is then carried for the purpose of sewing cloth," immediately tells the astute examiner many things about the person who made the association.

The fourth class of associations obviously contains the type that has greatest usefulness for the purposes of the clinician, or the investigator concerned with problems of personal adjustment. Here *needle* becomes a means for inflicting injury and pain. A further step can sometimes be taken through associative procedure or by obtaining case history material that will enable the examiner to determine that the subject has identified himself as the one who is the victim of aggression by others or the one who desires to inflict (or does inflict) injury to others. If such a conclusion can be drawn, then very vital information in understanding the subject has been uncovered.

Often workers combine scientific procedure with a common-sense approach. Few deny that something can be learned about what is worrying an individual—his preoccupations, his fears, and his areas of conflict —by examining the content of associations. Suppose that an individual returns again and again to similar fear-content material when talking or engaging in free association; then certain inferences may be drawn from this with reasonable confidence. If it is found that ten words in the Kent-Rosanoff list of words have caused the patient to respond with "mother," it seems reasonable to conclude that this is an area of conflict. It can scarcely be questioned that such a result reflects preoccupation; it is more speculative that intense and unresolved emotional conflicts have been tapped. Yet if this is not the case why would the subject be held in such associative bondage? The response word in this case might not be extremely deviant or inappropriate, but significance is determined by the repetition and piling up of the same content material. Even though trouble is indicated, the nature of the problem between the subject and his mother might not be clear and the examiner can still stumble into wrong interpretations and speculations.

CLINICAL APPLICATIONS

The clinical applications of association technique will not be discussed in detail, for we have already indicated some of the uses. All of the aspects of association discussed in the last three sections are combined for clinical use. In studying a given patient, an examination may be made of the reaction for the different material, a careful study made of how well it matches that obtained from known subjects, and the presence or absence of highly individualistic content noted. The important point for consideration here is that experimentation is essential before the psychologist is ready to proceed with interpretations and predictions. Because of the urgency to deal with practical problems, there is great temptation to move toward solution of painful personal problems without regard to basing decisions upon the best scientific practices.

The lack of better validation for many of the testing tools used in clinical work should mean that investigators ought to continue to ask such questions as the following: How dependable is reaction time in revealing emotional disturbance? Is the unique association sure evidence for undesirable deviations or does it instead represent wholesome creativity and originality? If the individual is preoccupied with economic insecurity, death, or sex, is he different from others and by how much? All too frequently it may be discovered that the so-called disturbed individual worries about a given situation in which there is a total lack of knowledge as to whether the circumstances under which he must operate are such that his worry is more than average, or is, indeed, the usual thing. If so, is he not really responding adequately to his environment? To interpret behavior and to draw conclusions as to the extent of an individual's maladjustment in total disregard of the situation under which he operates might easily lead to superficial thinking and even to gross injustice in handling the individual involved. While there has been a great amount of talk lately about experimental-clinical psychology, the accumulated results of relevant investigations upon many clinical problems is not very impressive. Answers have yet to be forced for many crucial questions in this area of research.

ASSOCIATION IN INDUSTRIAL APPLICATIONS

In one sense it would be exceedingly difficult to construct a test that would discriminate between individuals without the use of some element of the associative process in either assembling the items or as required by subjects who take the tests. Perhaps this implies a concept of association that is too wide to be of much practical use to the industrial psychologist. In a more restricted sense the psychologist regularly examines for speed and frequency of certain associative responses as a means of determining how familiar an individual may be with the material demanded in doing a particular job. Instead of asking an applicant if he knows what a special wrench is used for, he may be given the name of the wrench and asked to associate to it. The greater familiarity he has with the wrench the sooner and more freely he should be able to respond. The use of pictures of tools or situations may call for associations that become revealing. An applicant may have a work situation structured for him and then he is required to make appropriate associations.

While the usual paper-pencil kind of test items requires association, it is possible to broaden the use of the associative process by more indirect procedures. By use of the less structured approach it becomes much harder for a job applicant to do superficial *cramming* and so provide himself with a few correct answers. It is well known that a short period of coaching by a friend can sometimes supply the individual with the answers that are of a short and objective kind. Thus the applicant may be able to give a better impression of familiarity with a job than the true situation justifies.

Essay type questions are much like free association in that a minimum of cues may be furnished to the individual. There are so many disadvantages to this kind of test that it is rarely used for selecting personnel. However, a variety of semi-objective associative items may be used that gain many of the advantages of both the objective and subjective types of tests.

The testing of special aptitudes and achievement within particular areas of specialization is of primary importance to those who work in business and industry and who have the responsibility of selecting and training personnel. Consequently, a thorough knowledge of the processes of associating, relating, and organizing may be of great use to those who would go about constructing reliable and valid tests.

LEGAL AND INVESTIGATIVE USES OF ASSOCIATION

One of the oldest approaches to the detection of guilt was based upon association. The subject would be given words and required to make a quick association. Selected words assumed to have critical meaning for the individual suspected of the crime under investigation would be presented. If the words brought unusual associations that would have been connected with the crime, this might be used as evidence of guilt. The more expected reaction was that the accused person would become confused, hesitate to make an association, or make overt movements indicating restlessness. Bodily changes which are expected under the increased emotionality believed to be associated with guilt in such situations have already been discussed.

It has been supposed that the demand of associations includes elements of surprise and that guilt can thus be detected by subtle reactions of the subject more readily than would be the case if direct questioning is used. The way the examiner may proceed is illustrated in the following: Suppose that a robbery has been committed in which a window has been broken, a safe blown open, and money and jewelry taken. It might be that the robber left evidence that he had cut himself on the broken glass. A list of critical words can be made that would include window, glass, blood, safe, money, jewelry, etc. It is usual to mix the critical words in with neutral words in order to see if there is a difference in the way the subject responds to the loaded and neutral words.

It is obvious that some of the words used in the list and assumed to be critical may not be emotionally loaded because they revive associations made during the act under investigation. For example, blood is emotionally loaded for almost everyone and the examiner must use caution that he does not assume guilt erroneously. Several such loaded words included in testing might give a false impression. Thus the selection of the stimulus material should be as specific to the criminal act as possible and some discount might be required for terms known to be more generally emotionally loaded.

CONCLUDING REMARKS

What was called psychology a century and a half ago was mostly devoted to a discussion of association and the associative process. Psychology has come a long way since then and psychologists may discuss their subject a long time without ever mentioning the term "association." New and different terminology has often displaced the older words and concepts. Yet, psychologists must still work with the problem of how things become associated, how they become more or less bonded together, and must be concerned with how events are retained in memory and kept in an orderly sequence for later use. Word association tests are still widely used and there is no evidence that this procedure has been entirely exploited. The recent sentence completion tests are very similar in concept and these have been found useful for diagnostic testing. All the projective tests might with some justification be described as tests of association in that unstructured or ambiguous stimuli are expected to provoke associations that are uppermost in the mind of the subject. Tests that are to be used for all purposes, from the simplest ones intended to reveal the subject's knowledge of facts to the most complicated ones in which information must be carried from older situations and circumstances to solving new problems, are based upon the general foundation of association. The experimental psychologist does both direct and indirect experiments upon association.

In the area of association the experimental psychologist and the clinical psychologist have mutual ground for research exploration. It is perhaps realistic to suppose that here there is mutual dependency and that neither group is quite justified in refusing both to contribute and to accept from the other.

SUGGESTED READINGS

Postman, Leo, and Egan, James P. *Experimental Psychology: An Introduction,* pp. 239-274. New York: Harper, 1949.

Dennis, Wayne. *Readings in General Psychology.* Cattell: "The Time It Takes to Think," pp. 282-286. New York: Prentice-Hall, 1949.

Boring, Edwin S. *A History of Experimental Psychology.* "Beginnings of Modern Psychology," pp. 157-178; "British Associationism," pp. 219-245. New York: Appleton-Century-Crofts, 1950.

Woodworth, Robert S., and Schlosberg, Harold. *Experimental Psychology,* pp. 43-71. New York: Henry Holt, 1954.

Hebb, D. O. *The Organization of Behavior,* ch. XI-XIX, pp. 1-59. New York: John Wiley, 1949.

REFERENCES

1. Anderson, M. "An investigation into the rate of mental association," *J. Educ. Psychol.,* 8 (1917), 97-102.

2. Beck, Samuel. *Rorschach's Test I: Basic Processes,* pp. 16, 196. New York: Grune & Stratton, 1949.

3. Galton, F. "Psychometric experiments," *Brain,* 2 (1879-1880), 149-162.

4. Kent, G. H., and Rosanoff, A. J. "A study of association in insanity," *Amer. J. Insan.,* 67 (1910), 37-96, 317-390.

5. McGehee, W. "The free word associations of elementary school children," *J. Genet. Psychol.,* 50 (1937), 441-455.

6. Woodworth, Robert S. *Experimental Psychology,* p. 352. New York: Henry Holt, 1938.

7. Woodworth, Robert S., and Schlosberg, Harold. *Experimental Psychology,* p. 45. New York: Henry Holt, 1954.

8. *Ibid.,* p. 52.

12 | GENERAL LEARNING PROBLEMS AND EXPERIMENTS

SIGNIFICANCE OF LEARNING

There is reason to believe that some learning takes place before birth. At any rate, the phenomenon of learning is readily observable shortly after birth and the rate appears to accelerate and to continue with an upward sweep until at least the adolescent period of life. Even though learning may decrease in rate as the individual grows older it continues to be one of the major activities of man throughout most of his life.

There have been periods in the history of psychology during which reports upon learning experiments may account for more than half of the publications in all psychological journals. So broad is the topic, and so intensively have psychologists studied learning phenomena that some aspect of the learning process is rarely lacking in psychological experiments. This situation is scarcely amazing when consideration is given to how much time a civilized man, during his lifetime, devotes to learning, "relearning," and "unlearning." There is every prospect that one of the prices that is paid for continuing civilization is that an ever increasingly higher percentage of time and energy must be devoted to the effort of learning. Or, to put the matter a different way, while the individual may reveal an inevitable decelerating learning curve as he grows older, all evidence points to an ever-increasing demand for more total learning to be required of the individual as mankind moves into the future. Automation of machinery shows great promise of reducing routines in factory work so that man may become a caretaker of "robots" but there is little to suggest that he is to become a robot himself. There is too much to learn concerning the manufacturing, operating, and repairing of the machinery for this to be the prospect. What was seen as a great threat to the destiny of man by science fiction writers, and even many social scientists, a few years ago does not now appear to be as serious as was at first thought.

LEARNING AND AGING

While general learning and development curves clearly indicate that new learning is not much indulged in by the average old individual, yet what exists typically is not too well tolerated. In western culture there is little comfort for the "old dog that will not learn new tricks." Few attitudes are more deplored than the one revealing an unwillingness to learn. Here is a great cleavage, one of the most unreconcilable difference between the older and younger generation. No one seems ever to learn enough or become the possessor of sufficient knowledge and wisdom that he is willingly excused from further effort to learn. Older people seem to find it difficult to accept this dictum from society, or perhaps they lack the necessary energy to do anything about it. The individual who refuses to continue to learn gradually becomes isolated and ignored. Thus it is that each individual appears to be saddled with a heavy responsibility to keep learning from the cradle to the grave! But it does not have to be assumed that the process is necessarily unpleasant or burdensome.

The "problem of aging," psychologically speaking, then, means to a considerable extent that the individual's learning is gradually decreasing with the prospect that it will eventually become negligible. There is said to be an army of research workers being assembled that plan to go about probing and prodding older people so they will continue to "have something to live for." The effort of these investigators promises to rival the effort of research workers who have already been so successful in staying the eventuality of death. An ever-increasing number of years has been added to the life of the average individual and thus the problem of what older people will do becomes of great concern. No one seems to be in the mood to leave aging people to quiet meditation and idleness, especially, when their years are expected to be so many. This seems to be the attitude, regardless of how well a given individual may have produced, or, if taken from a social viewpoint, how well he might have earned his rest.

We have gone to some length in relating what seems to be an increasingly important problem and so far relatively little research has been done upon it. Attention has been focused upon the young when trying out principles of learning and the subjects in experiments have almost never been aged ones. It may well be that the current generation of aging people have already felt the impact of things to come. They probably retain curiosity about the world as few generations of older people have. Many of them look forward to retirement only if this promises to enable them to devote time and attention to learning more about something that has been inaccessible to them for lack of resources or time, or because of other duties and obligations. If the testimony of aging people is to be believed, they do not seek a static world with the likely correlate that it is also an empty world. It may well be that their eagerness to participate in current affairs is due in part to a rapidly changing and stimulating world. It is pleasant to imagine that education may have succeeded better than the present energetic critics would have us believe. Could it be that a high percentage of people have been infected with positive and lasting attitudes concerning the joys of experimentation and exploration? For better or worse, the scientific attitude seems to be inconsistent with a philosophy of *nirvana*. The quest for knowledge tends to persist among scientists.

It is an intriguing thought that much greater attention may have to be devoted to "unlearning" or breaking down the effects of previous learning if older people are to be efficient. The problems of teaching people new things, when they have had little exposure to life experiences, must be very different from teaching those who have established well-fixed notions and ideas. The evidence is strong that older people can still learn very well under sufficient motivation. However, there are also indications that becoming once again flexible, after having once become rigid, is no easy task. That sets can become a hindrance is readily explainable upon the basis of motivation alone. Again, there might be physiological conditions in the aged that are unfavorable. Nevertheless, it is conceivable that these might be overcome by good nutrition and a proper use of modern chemistry. There is no good reason to suppose that principles of learning that have been worked out almost exclusively by use of young subjects will be entirely adequate and appropriate when applied to old subjects.

DEFINITION OF LEARNING

This is a brief but workable definition: learning includes all modifications of behavior resulting from experience. Usually those who define learning hope to exclude patterns of response that can be identified as inborn reflexes or so-called instincts. Furthermore, behavioral changes that are brought about primarily by growth and maturation of tissues are ordinarily excluded. Changes in behavior of a transitory sort and brought about by fatigue, reflex action resulting from intense stimulation, or reactions under the influence of strong drugs are ordinarily excluded as examples of pure learning.

It is necessary to turn from one aspect to another concerning learning and then to pursue many details if a complete picture of the whole learning process is to be obtained. However, it is well to keep continuously in mind that attention is focused primarily upon the process of acquiring knowledge and the development of skills. Learning takes place by the exposure of the organism to the environment and the interaction that follows between the organism and environmental conditions and forces.

TRADITIONAL APPROACHES TO LEARNING

Much of the material in this chapter will not be entirely new to the student. Emphasis will be given to a number of technical problems that baffle and thwart the experimentalist. In no area of psychology has more energy been expended upon trying to evolve theory and to reconcile facts and theory into meaningful relationship. Consequently we shall try to set forth some of the theoretical framework within which investigators have operated. An attempt will be made to approach these positions objectively and without bias. We assume that the student is not ready to join a group holding a particular systematic position in psychology, a hazardous procedure for a scientist as a rule, but certainly not to be recommended until the individual becomes well saturated with factual information and has been able to examine and to organize those facts into some sort of meaningful whole. Yet, it is scarcely possible to avoid some theorizing even though effort is made to take no particular side. The necessities of thinking lead to the mental manipulation of information and this almost inevitably gives rise to assumptions that furnish the foundation for theory.

It is not intended that the more controversial material be presented. Nevertheless, total avoidance of debatable points need not be expected. This is true because the principal advocates of most of the so-called "schools" of psychology that have arisen during the past half century have found it necessary to set forth a theory of learning that served as the primary foundation for their system. In fact, there are several splinter groups who hold to the general premises of behaviorism, but each takes its point of departure upon some variation in learning theory.

It might be argued that Freud, with his psychoanalytic approach, came nearest to erecting a complete psychological system without basing it upon a stated theory of learning. To some psychologists this becomes a serious indictment and they are quick to dismiss the psychoanalytic system as generally inadequate. As may be remembered, Wundt considered psychologists not yet ready to attack problems involving "higher mental processes." This appears to have included learning. Titchener accepted a similar viewpoint and he became a leading figure among those who persisted in experimenting in psychology by primary use of the introspection method and this method was at its best when sensation and perception were being studied.

We cannot review the work of all the psychologists who made notable contributions to the psychology of learning before 1900. The work of two psychologists, Ebbinghaus and Thorndike, and one physiologist, Pavlov, have since been recognized as initiating major challenges to the limitations of traditional psychology of that time and all were diligent in experimenting upon learning. Garrett, in his book "Great Experiments in Psychology," devotes a chapter to each of these men and covers more detail than we can attempt. His book is among the recommended readings listed at the end of the chapter.

The three experimenters referred to above refused to accept the dictum that learning was any longer inaccessible as a topic for scientific investigation and experimentation. These three investigators began to fashion in rough outline the road signs that were later to mark the way for much experimenting and theorizing about the learning process. The impact of the work of each extended much beyond learning problems, if this is narrowly conceived, for they helped to modify and redirect the whole course of development in psychology. They were the pioneers that initiated research programs that became the subject-matter that is elaborated upon in the next three chapters. In those chapters the work of later contributors along with modified methods and techniques that have evolved is discussed. In this chapter we shall undertake to sketch briefly the contributions of Ebbinghaus to *verbal learning;* Thorndike to *problem-solving* and *exploratory learning;* and Pavlov to *conditioning.* Ebbinghaus used human subjects and this was not new; Thorndike and Pavlov used lower animals as subjects, and gave impetus to making animal and comparative psychology respectable. Altogether the work of these three men expanded immensely the boundaries of what was soon to be considered legitimate psychology.

EBBINGHAUS AND VERBAL LEARNING

The publication of Ebbinghaus' book, *Ueber das Gedachtnis,* in 1885 was an important landmark in the history of learning experiments. As previously indicated, neither Fechner nor Wundt had done much with the whole topic of learning. They and the men associated with them, in general, represented the new science of psychology not only in Germany but to a great extent throughout the world. Ebbinghaus, by publishing in book form, was giving notice that there had come into existence a considerable body of knowledge in an area not heretofore given much attention. He was proposing to incorporate this material into the science of psychology.

QUANTIFICATION IN LEARNING

Ebbinghaus used the number of repetitions required to learn a list of material to a given criterion as his means of quantification. No doubt he was taking inspiration for the necessity of quantifying from the contributions made by Fechner, and he was borrowing methodology in still other ways from the same source. It is probable that Ebbinghaus' interest in problems of learning was stimulated by the English associationists. Prior to his experiments upon the learning process he had spent some time in England and the nature of his experiments, while still very different from Galton's studies of association, are enough like them for it to be supposed that both were intrigued by similar psychological problems. Thus, he was drawing from two sources: The *methodology* developed in Germany was brought to bear effectively upon the *problems of learning* that had become explicit with associationism in England.

EXPERIMENTER AND SUBJECT

In many of the experiments Ebbinghaus himself was both experimenter and subject. This is a respectable methodology among those using introspection but leaves the experimentalist vulnerable to criticism about how his own motivations and attitudes may influence his observations. However, in spite of the objections (and they are sound) that may be raised among those who would make psychology as objective as possible, the general procedure used by Ebbinghaus and the interpretations placed upon his results have both stood the test of time remarkably well.

Ebbinghaus more than any other early investigator determined the general pattern for experiments in human learning. While he had set out to study what was then considered one of the more complex and inaccessible mental problems, usually referred to as memory, he recognized that the general problem of memory could be separated into three major but closely interdependent divisions. He deals with specific problems that might be grouped under (1) acquisition of information, (2) retention of what was learned, (3) later use that could be made of what was remembered.

Detailed discussion of these aspects of learning is deferred since all approaches to learning could be dealt with to some extent by listing them under one or another of the above broad divisions. Briefly, and incompletely, *acquisition* encompasses such problems as sensory avenues to be used in learning, discrimination of sensory stimuli, and perhaps motivational influences; *retention* has to do with storage and thus involves factual and conceptual consideration of functional and structural modifications in the organism resulting from the learning experience, plus the many influences exerted upon the organism by intervening experiences between original acquisition and usage; *use* involves not only recall and recognition, but also all modified performance of the organism as this reflects influence of the previous learning. Use in one form or another and up to the present time is left with the unique role of providing, if not entire and complete at least the most convincing, evidence that learning did, in fact, take place. It is important to keep this in mind, for psychologists must resort to some aspect of "use" in a broad sense for all criteria of learning. Consequently, theorizing and practical considerations are based upon uses that can be demonstrated in terms of *recognition, recall,* and *utilization* of the earlier experience. Possibly the layman is less bothered by the limitations implicit in this situation, for his orientation is already in the direction of the practical significance of the end product of learning.

THE EXPERIMENTAL APPROACH USED BY EBBINGHAUS

The experimental approach used by Ebbinghaus brought within range of attack a wide variety of problems of vast importance to all who would improve their learning or who would teach others. His contributions were eagerly seized upon by those interested in practical applications and thus he laid much of the groundwork for such fields as child and educational psychology. While the problems he attacked were thought by some to be excessively complex—and they were and remain complex—his methodology is classically simple. A brief outline of how he went about experimenting should enable almost anyone to perform a successful imitative experiment. Well-established principles, improved techniques, and refinements in statistical treatment of data remove the probability that one might today make a very important scientific contribution by this imitation. At the same time, perhaps there is not a better way for the beginner in experimental psychology to get a clear perception of the basic steps to be taken in performing an experiment than to follow Ebbinghaus' example.

Although the complete reproduction of a typical Ebbinghaus (2) experiment would scarcely be wasteful of time and space, we shall confine ourselves to condensing and paraphrasing one of his classical experiments in order to place emphasis upon the bare necessities and to present running comments. We shall take the liberty of using our own format and language, but hope to cover the essentials in the following manner:

Purpose

To determine the effort required to learn lists of material varying in length or number of items. It will be seen that this is a clear statement of a simple problem. Ebbinghaus could safely go to work without much concern for studying the literature. Since he was pioneering in studies of learning there was little chance that he had chosen a problem already solved and reported in a journal. It is true that he might have been, and probably was, challenged for bothering to prove what must have seemed to many rather obvious. Surely everyone already knew that it required more effort to learn a long list of items than a short list. Of course Ebbinghaus was interested in something beyond this broad and safe generalization.

The problem could have been stated in a formal but not necessarily very useful hypothesis: *To learn a long list of items will require more effort than to learn a short list.* It could also be stated in a more sophisticated hypothesis that might have sounded safe enough but which would have been found lacking in support: *There will be a direct relationship between the length of a list of items and the effort required to memorize it.* Actually, it is found that Ebbinghaus was very much of an empiricist and he did not always bother to state a formal hypothesis. Upon recognizing a problem the solution to which he could see possible usefulness, he might ask a question and proceed to try to answer it by setting up an experiment and going about the task of collecting pertinent data. He would assume the existence of some sort of law in the relationship between the independent and the dependent variables.

The statement of an hypothesis implies that the experimenter thinks that he knows enough about the problem to risk a prediction. While Ebbinghaus rapidly gained enough knowledge about the learning process to make a number of predictions that would have had a good chance of being supported by the evidence he was about to collect, it should be remembered that not enough experimenting had been done with learning at that time to enable anyone to formulate very much sound theory. Ebbinghaus was busy contributing evidence that was first used inductively for making generalizations, after which he could proceed to theory building. Then eventually the later investigators would be in position to deduct hypotheses from the theories.

Procedure

In working with the problem that we have indicated Ebbinghaus set out to vary systematically the number of items in a list of learning material. However, he would need to exercise a number of controls in order to be able to say something definite about his results should it be found that there was some sort of consistent relationship between the length of the list and the repetitions or the effort required to learn the list. Careful controls would be essential in order to isolate the single independent variable of length of list so that the dependent variable (effort, or number of repetitions) could be analyzed in meaningful ways.

Invention of Nonsense Syllables

In order to improve control over several bothersome factors, Ebbinghaus revealed remarkable ingenuity by inventing nonsense syllables. Nonsense syllables have been described as consisting of a vowel letter flanked by two consonants. Meaningful words were, of course, excluded. The value of this learning material was thought to rest upon the assumption that it would be relatively uniform in difficulty; that it would be entirely new and hence not previously learned to different levels, as all known material would be; that unintentional or incidental review would not take place; that logical associations would not complicate the interpretations that might be possible.

In passing, it might be said that Ebbinghaus may have expected too much of his nonsense syllables, for they do not prove to be perfect controls for any of the purposes intended. Yet, later investigators have possibly dealt more harshly with this brain child of Ebbinghaus than is fair. Nonsense syllables did indeed serve Ebbinghaus well as he set about the task of investigating rote memorizing. There can be little doubt that learning experimentation has been greatly facilitated and enriched because of the invention of nonsense syllables and paralogs—a closely similar form, made by adding more letters.

There are important limitations and justifiable objections to their use, not the least of which is the problem of maintaining interest and motivation in the subject who is to learn them. However, Ebbinghaus, acting as subject for his own experiments, could hardly have been expected to be particularly sensitive to this deficiency in nonsense syllables. He was not lacking in motivation, for he must have spent many long hours in learning them while doing his many experiments. Experimenters who are interested in rote memorizing still make use of nonsense syllables. Everything considered, and when studying certain problems, better material is not necessarily available.

Other Controls

Several controls used by Ebbinghaus would today have to be rated as relatively crude. For example, memory drums of the type now available had not been invented so that timing in the presentation of material may not have been very exact. Again, a variety of objections may be raised because the experimenter was using himself as subject. Even if his intellectual integrity is not challenged there remain questions of the influence of unconscious attitudes, wishes, needs, and so forth. These may enter to distort the results when the experimenter has come to expect or to hope for particular findings. Because of the general lack of theory concerning learning phenomena, Ebbinghaus would have been better off than would be the case for current investigators who would almost inevitably have many preconceived ideas about how the results should come out. In spite of the difficulties and inadequacies, one might still defend Ebbinghaus' use of himself as subject. He was no doubt able to move along rapidly without wasting time and effort with reluctant subjects while he planned his broad explorations and roughed out gross principles about learning not previously established. He was an ardent combination—experimentalist-subject—and he was able to cover much experimental ground in a short time. The work of the experimental psychologist is now somewhat different, often more detailed, so that those who would make a contribution by experimenting upon learning are expected to use more refined techniques.

Learning was to the criterion of one errorless reproduction and the attempt was made immediately after reading the list. While other criteria might be used, there is not likely to be difficulty here so long as the criterion that is used is adequately described and uniformly applied within a given experiment.

Results

Ordinarily the results were presented in numbers just about as collected or else after the simplest kind of mathematical treatment such as in terms of averages or percentages. The data collected in the experiment that we are using as an example are given in the table on the following page.

It will be seen in the table that the list of seven nonsense syllables is in a class by itself. It may be safe to assume that a single reading of this kind of material, and by the subject, Ebbinghaus himself, was regularly sufficient for one hundred percent accuracy for a list up to seven items. In other words, Ebbinghaus had a memory span of at least seven nonsense

TABLE 12-1

Length of Lists	No. of Readings	Time for Lists, Secs.	Average Time per Syllable, Secs.
7	1	3	.4
10	13	52	5.2
12	17	82	6.8
16	30	196	12.0
24	44	422	17.6
36	55	792	22.0

syllables. Since no data are found to bear upon the point, his maximum memory span is unknown. It might have been eight, or nine. We can only be sure that it did not reach ten for the material he used.

There is a very big jump for both the number of readings required and the time used between the list of seven and ten. It should be noted that Ebbinghaus did not use a regular progression (as reported in the experiment) from shorter lists to longer lists by either using a direct and consistent increase of a given number or a proportional increase. Why he chose to use lists of these particular lengths is not known. Hence his procedure means that statistical analysis of his results would be complicated and in the end might not add too much to their meaning anyway. By inspection, it is clear that the number of readings increased faster than did the length of the lists. The average time required to learn each item in the longer lists is much greater. It will be seen that it required more than four times as long, on an average, to memorize each item in a list of thirty-six as in a list of ten.

Conclusions

While there were several things that might have been concluded from these findings, the major contribution that Ebbinghaus made rests primarily upon the fact that he showed that learning could be systematically studied; the results could be quantified, and he obtained evidence that a law did exist in the relationship between the length of a list and the effort required to memorize it. This statement should not be interpreted to mean that he established a formula that could be applied under varying conditions. Actually, the exact nature of the relationship that may exist remains to this time insufficiently explored for it to be clearly and absolutely stated.

The observations that produced the results related above, along with those of several other experiments, initiated a long and energetic search for explanations. It was an intriguing question that arose at once as to why more time would have to be used to learn each item in the longer lists. For example, would the subject get around this difficulty by the simple expedient of breaking the longer lists into three or four parts? Subsequent studies reveal that such a procedure does not enable the learner to avoid the greater proportional effort demanded by the longer lists. Out of need for explanation for the results obtained, a multitude of experiments have been performed. It was reasoned by most investigators that there must be some sort of interference operating. An answer to the nature of such interference might help experimenters to understand a wide range of experimental results and lead to a better understanding of the general nature of learning phenomena. Eventually it was postulated that retroactive inhibition operated to make recall of the items that stood early in the list difficult to recall after the later ones had been studied. Then, in a converse manner, proactive inhibition was believed to operate to make the learning of the later items more difficult because of the forward interference induced by learning the earlier items. More will be said about these phenomena in the chapter dealing with verbal learning.

THE IMPACT OF EBBINGHAUS' EXPERIMENTS

While Ebbinghaus seems to have assumed that what he found when using himself as a subject would be true for other individuals and for the population as a whole, he was too sophisticated an experimentalist to indulge in many glib or unfounded generalizations. It may be assumed that he was looking for principles in learning phenomena that had more or less universal application. However, this view was consistent with that held by other psychologists, for the study of individual differences was still in its early or beginning stage. Little thought had been given to extending the study of behavior to include animals other than man. Yet almost immediately a variety of important studies of learning were initiated in which animals were used as the subjects. Thus, while Ebbinghaus' contributions apply primarily to verbal learning, the impact of his work was felt in a wide range of studies using many methods and different kinds of subjects. He established some of the important general landmarks in human learning and there were clear implications for practical ways by which memorizing might be made more efficient. The interpretations that he and others who experimented upon learning made produced a tremendous influence upon educational procedures. How could the curriculum best be built so that advantage could be taken of the new findings? How could the child be taught so that his efficiency in learning was raised to the maximum? Some of the experimental results had bearing upon the length of class periods, the frequency of practice, sequence of classes, distribution of practice, whole and part presentation, and a variety of other practical educational problems.

THORNDIKE AND EXPLORATORY LEARNING

There was already some interest in animal behavior prior to the publication of Thorndike's book, *Animal Intelligence,* in 1898, but for the most part the observations had not been made under controlled conditions and the reports were often made by untrained individuals who resorted to the anecdotal method. It is not meant to imply that no useful contributions had been made. A considerable knowledge of animal behavior had been set forth in the writings of Lloyd Morgan, Romanes, and others. Unfortunately, a great deal of attention had been focused upon the rather fruitless debate as to whether animals could think or reason. Whereas not all efforts to become enlightened in this matter are deplored, the fact remains that the problem was usually attacked by subjective analysis, or, at best, by the marshalling of anecdotal stories intended to prove that animals could reason. It was clear enough that lower animals could learn, but reasoning was usually held to be a characteristic that distinguished man from lower animals. It is now assumed that the question as to whether animals reason or not is to be answered upon grounds of semantics. If reasoning is defined broadly enough to include any use of symbols (and it is frequently defined in this way), then reasoning can scarcely be denied among animals below man.

ANIMAL BEHAVIOR AND PSYCHOLOGY

Possibly no one deserves more credit for bringing animal behavior within the accepted scope of psychology than Thorndike. He performed a large number of simple experiments in which a variety of animals were used. The subjects included monkeys, dogs, cats, chickens, and even fishes. Most of these experiments consisted of setting up a problem situation for the animal and then observing and describing behavior leading to a solution. An example of such problems was escape from a cage in which the animal was confined in order to leave the cage for greater freedom or to get food.

In many of the experiments, Thorndike used food deprivation as a means of motivating the animal and thus speeding up activity. The hunger drive could be depended upon to lead to exploratory and manipulative activity by the animal. These somewhat crude early experiments by

Thorndike were the forerunners of many subsequent problem-solving experiments. They helped to bring into experimental range the more complicated and so-called higher mental processes. Even though he was using lower animals for subjects, the implications were clear: here was an approach to problem-solving and this could not be satisfactorily segregated from thinking, reasoning, and imagining. There was, and remains, resistance to accepting the findings where animals are used as subjects.

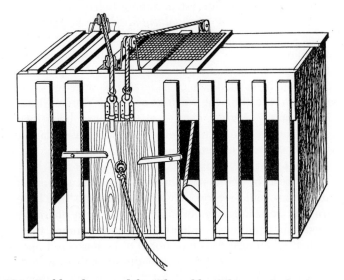

Fig. 12.1. Problem-box used by Thorndike. This particular box was used when studying the problem-solving ability of cats. (From Garrett, Henry E., *Great Experiments in Psychology*. New York: Appleton-Century-Crofts, 1951.)

The method and techniques used with human subjects are, nevertheless, essentially of the same general nature.

EXPLORATORY BEHAVIOR IN ANIMALS AND MAN

There are interesting comparisons between what the psychologist or any scientist is trying to do when he experiments and what Thorndike's animals were forced into doing in order to get out of the problem box. While it is hoped that there might be less random behavior displayed by the human experimentalist, there is likely to be similar exploratory and manipulative behavior before a satisfactory solution is found. Whenever quick insights to relationships are within the capacity of animal or man, whenever great skill can be brought to bear in dealing with the solution such abilities are greatly treasured. However, Thorndike considered it all too typical of human subjects that they revealed trial and error behavior not unlike that characteristic of lower animals. Man might demonstrate trial and error behavior very clearly but he did profit more by his mistakes. Furthermore, he is able to find solutions to problems that are out of the range of difficulty that can be handled by animals.

While it now appears inevitable that animal behavior was soon to come under the scrutiny of psychologists, Thorndike deserves credit for hastening the movement and for displaying ingenuity, originality, and boldness in attacking the type of problems that he chose. There is a kind of simplicity and ease in experimenting upon rote memorizing in the tradition set by Ebbinghaus. Animals are less useful subjects than humans in such experiments. On the other hand, and as surprising as this may be, very complex psychological problems involved in exploration, manipulation, and inventiveness are sometimes more readily approached by use of lower animals as subjects.

TRIAL AND ERROR LEARNING THEORY

Thorndike placed great emphasis upon random behavior as an important and general characteristic of learning. His name is prominent among those associated with the *trial and error theory of learning* and perhaps he deserves priority in the formulation of that theory. Later investigators who have made use of his concepts have sometimes preferred to speak of trial-and-chance success. Obviously there is a lack of completion in the learning process as long as *error* is the end product. It was after chance success that the animal would begin to narrow down its responses to a particular position and to the manipulation of a specific object. Gradually there was an association or connection established between some kind of manipulation of an object and the attainment of the goal sought by the animal.

Following the lead of Thorndike, there have been hundreds of experiments upon learning in which animals at various phylogenetic levels have been used as subjects and then comparisons have been made of the results. Investigators have been interested in speed, accuracy, and complexity of learning that could be obtained from animals standing at the different levels of the phylogenetic scale.

DESCRIPTION OF A THORNDIKE LEARNING EXPERIMENT

It will serve our purpose well in presenting an experiment typical of those performed by Thorndike if we quote from Garrett (3) as he described the behavior of chicks in a simple maze: "In his experiments with chicks, Thorndike used a number of pens or mazes, one of which is illustrated in Figure 12-2. When a chick is placed in section A of the maze, there are four possible exits as shown in the drawing. If the opening on the extreme right is followed by the chick to the second turn, it leads out of the maze and into an enclosure in which there are other chicks and food. The other three exits are blind alleys. The problem is to see how long it will take a chick to select the pathway which will carry it out of the maze. The behavior of a chick when first placed in the pen resembles closely that of a fish when trying to get out of the sunlight. Taken away from the other chicks and from food, and cripped into the pen at A,

Fig. 12.2. Pen used by Thorndike to study behavior of the chick. The shape of the maze does not lend itself well to counting errors but it should be remembered that Thorndike was pioneering in these experiments.

the chick runs back and forth, in and out of the blind alleys, peeps loudly, tries to jump out of the pen and to squeeze through any available opening. At length, 'by accident,' it picks the right exit and gets out. Put back again and again, however, it begins to eliminate useless movements, such as repeatedly entering the blind alleys, until finally it runs directly to the right exit."

ANIMAL LEARNING AND PHYSICAL STRUCTURE

The chicken is usually considered a rather stupid animal. It cannot learn a very complex maze without a great many trials and may wear the experimenter out before accomplishing the feat. Thorndike worked long enough with such primitive vertebrates as the fish and the chicken to determine that they could profit by experience but on the whole that their behavior was characteristically trial and error in nature. Cats and dogs used trial and error procedure in getting out of their problem boxes, but it seemed to Thorndike obvious that they learned more complex problems than the fish or chicken and that fewer trials were required if they attacked the same type of problem in future trials. He was also able to see that the animal's physical structure had some correlation with the speed of learning when the problem demanded certain types of manipulation. The cat was able to manipulate objects better with its paws than could the dog, yet the dog appeared to be more intelligent in handling certain kinds of tasks. These ideas have been amply borne out by later investigators. Consequently, it is often not too meaningful to speak of one animal being more intelligent than another. Conclusions may be biased because of the kind of manipulation required and the physical characteristics of the animal. The white rat does very well in learning a maze, but poorly in releasing itself from a problem box of the kind quickly solved by the cat. The raccoon displays skill in manipulating objects with its front paws and can therefore make good use of this skill in certain performances. It is not exceptionally good in learning to run a maze and if compared with the white rat in maze learning its relative intelligence is likely to be underrated.

QUANTIFICATION AND LEARNING CURVES

Thorndike was interested in doing more than to demonstrate the obvious—that animals can learn. He was addressing himself to the task of showing which animals can learn particular kinds of problems. In most of these early studies, time required was used as the quantified result. His broad purpose was to investigate the nature of learning phenomena so that he could apply the principles to human learning. He was able to present many learning curves constructed from quantified data in terms of time or number of trials required. His methods and techniques have been widely imitated. There have been improvements of apparatus and refinements made in the controls. Thorndike was criticized for overstressing trial and error. It is true that many of the learning curves that he constructed show a very rapid change in time required after one or two initial trials and these learning curves have been interpreted by others as showing evidence of "insight" in learning.

LAWS OF LEARNING FORMULATED

Eventually Thorndike formulated several "laws" of learning. In spite of the fact that these were often under attack by other psychologists, they have greatly influenced thinking about learning phenomena. The two fundamental laws were stated as the *law of exercise* and the *law of effect*. The first concerns the strengthening that results from repetition and weakening that occurs with disuse. The second law has to do with changes brought about by a pleasant or painful outcome following or associated with a response. The *law of readiness* was a forerunner of many theoretical formulations about motivation and "set." Several corollaries to these laws were stated as following from the basic ones. Among these were *frequency, recency,* and *vividness.*

While many writers have viewed Thorndike's so-called *laws of learning* as premature and inadequate, few will deny that the broad principles set forth were closer approximations to the truth about learning than had yet been formulated and that he had extended the scope of psychological investigations to encompass animal behavior so effectively that later investigators scarcely found it necessary to defend their use of animals as suitable subjects for experiments. Their use extends to many types of behavior investigations where it would be well near impossible to get human subjects. The pattern of Thorndike's experiments became the inspiration for a multitude of experiments in which a different species of animal might be used as subjects in an almost endless variety of learning tasks. There remain scores of additional investigations in which animals up and down the phylum might be studied with some profit. It is relatively easy for the near novice to do some of these experiments. The value to psychology in general is somewhat comparable to the value in biology where yet another animal or insect has its life history traced.

PAVLOV AND CONDITIONING

It is now more than a half century since the Russian scientist, Ivan Pavlov, was awarded (1904) the Nobel prize in Medicine for his contributions in an area then considered to be physiology. Discovery of the *conditioned reflex* and subsequent experiments upon conditioning plus the elaborations and interpretations made upon this phenomenon became the chief basis for world recognition of this versatile scientist. In some respects his contributions, or at any rate the impact made upon the two fields, tend to make Pavlov more definitely identified with psychology than physiology. When this is said, account is taken of the way psychology is viewed today. Pavlov (6) continued to think of himself as a physiologist although some of the men working in that field thought that he had strayed away from the central issues of his science.

The problem of placing Pavlov's discovery in proper perspective remains an exceedingly difficult one. Certainly many of the ideas that he used, perhaps the essential ones concerning how things becoming associated together because of their occurrence together in time and place, were by no means new, as indicated in the discussion of the associative process. Literally hundreds of illustrations of how things become associated are to be found in the writings of the associationist dating from John Locke's *Essay Concerning Human Understanding* published in 1690. Yet some would rate Pavlov's work to be the most basic and important contribution to psychology that has yet been made.

SCIENTIFIC VALIDATION OF AN IDEA

If the ideas used by Pavlov were not new, then it is not unreasonable to ask why such great importance is placed upon his work. The answer seems to be that he took what had remained very largely philosophical speculations and opinions and gave them scientific validation. In a sense Newton's discovery of the law of gravitation might be subjected to the same kind of questioning concerning originality. The observation that objects fall to the ground certainly became commonplace before the apple (if this story is authentic) fell upon Newton's head. William James (4), writing in 1890, had ventured an opinion upon neural processes and how the nerves operated when people make associations. In his book *Principles of Psychology,* James had this to say: "When two elementary brain processes have been active together or in immediate succession, one of them, on recurring, tends to propagate its excitement into the other." This gives a degree of specificity to neural functioning that goes beyond anything that Pavlov really demonstrated—or that has been clearly demonstrated to the present, for that matter. It was a logical speculation that may very well be true. Perhaps a way will be invented to demonstrate it some day. However, it was an opinion, an educated guess at best, when James stated it.

Let us state as briefly and clearly as we are able why Pavlov has claim to greatness for his work on conditioning. The original observation or experiment itself is too familiar to need detailed review. However, description of conditioning experiments will be found in a later chapter of this book. Pavlov observed that saliva flowed upon sight of food by the dog. He was able to demonstrate the same response by the ringing of a bell if this was done immediately before food was given to the dog. The auditory stimulus of a ringing bell is not an adequate stimulus to elicit the reflex response of salivation until after learning has taken place. It became clear that by presenting an organism with an entirely new sensory stimulus, nearly simultaneously with a stimulus that was adequate to produce a response, the new stimulus alone soon comes to be sufficient to elicit the same type of response. It can be argued that the response is not exactly the same, and this is true. However, this is an argument that can be used in a similar fashion to say that there are never two exact reproductions of structure or behavior in nature.

It will be seen that Pavlov was no longer dealing with an idea that remained an abstraction. He had been able to set up a demonstration and to make an objective observation. He could measure the intensity of the stimulus used; describe the type of energy; indicate the sense organ involved. He could be sure of some of the neurological facts for he would know which nerve carried the impulse toward the brain and which led back to the muscle involved. The response could be measured in terms of a known unit—quantity of saliva. He was successful in measuring the

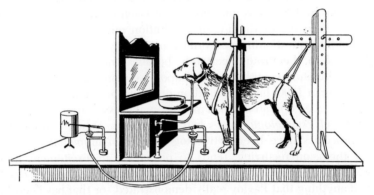

Fig. 12.3. Diagram of Pavlov's apparatus and dog. The saliva flow could be quantified. (From Garrett, Henry E., *Great Experiments in Psychology.* New York: Appleton-Century-Crofts, 1951. After Zerkes and Morgulis 1909.)

variations in the flow of saliva under different stimulus conditions. These several conditions included changes in the stimulus, presentation of the stimulus to the dog following different degrees of food deprivation and hence using a subject with variations in the hunger drive. He systematically made changes in the time interval to see the effect upon the response. With regard to this last, he regularly failed to produce conditioning if the original and adequate stimulus was presented before the stimulus that was intended to serve as a substitute.

The muscles that responded when conditioning occurred could readily be identified and the nerves that activated them indicated. As stated with regard to James's suggestion, there remained a missing link concerning what took place in the nerve centers. Pavlov did not answer all the questions that may be raised concerning the learning process but he showed how experimenters in this field might proceed further on the basis of objective facts before being confronted with the necessity of turning to abstract speculations. He had pushed the boundaries of science deep into the territory once dominated by the uncertainties of speculation and this is the primary function of the working scientist.

PAVLOV AND OBJECTIVE PSYCHOLOGY

For a variety of reasons it has been difficult for investigators to place psychology on a solid foundation among the sciences. In general those who have approached problems in psychology by following the leads furnished by Pavlov have prided themselves upon being the vanguard of those who would abandon all methods that did not meet strict criteria of objectivity. Some have been quick to accuse fellow psychologists of still being subservient to philosophy. These have wanted to cut the strings that bind psychology to philosophy by refusing to use much of the traditional terminology in psychology. Also they have been willing to embrace an entirely new methodology patterned after the physical sciences. Pavlov lived a long life of scientific productivity and few, if any, workers have done more to move psychology into the fold of science and to insure that it should and could stay there.

GENERAL PROBLEMS IN LEARNING

We have already had occasion to indicate some of the general problems of learning. Let us bring together several of the more pressing problems. It is especially desirable to review those that give rise to technical difficulties for the experimentalist.

UNITS OF MEASUREMENT

If we conceive of learning as an act or process whereby something unexperienced and unknown becomes experienced and known, it is easy to recognize the difficulties that confront the experimentalist in establishing suitable units to denote this fact or to represent the resulting modification of behavior. It might be supposed that for Ebbinghaus a nonsense syllable learned, for Pavlov a conditioned response made, for Thorndike a problem solved would each and respectively become a satisfactory and basic unit of learning. In an important sense this is not the case. These units represent end products, but we have seen that quantification was primarily in terms of repetitions required to bring the learning to a certain criterion or the time consumed in reaching this stage of learning. This makes certain comparisons readily feasible but leaves some kinds of considerations difficult to analyze and to state.

Typically, in a school situation the end product is used as evidence that learning has taken place. Hence, the criterion of how much has been learned or again, who has learned most, may be ascertained by the number of relevant questions about the learning material that it is possible for the individual to answer correctly. At best this is likely to be a gross indication of the actual modification of behavior. Some may argue that learning is not really thorough, or perhaps even very meaningful, if a person learns how to answer a question but fails to modify his behavior in a logical way when it comes to making use of his information. Then how do investigators go about collecting evidence that learning has really taken place?

CRITERIA OF LEARNING

Ordinarily evidence that learning has taken place is classified into four categories. These are (a) recall, (b) recogntion, (c) saving in relearning, (d) use. While these criteria are likely to correlate positively, it may well be that a given individual will be much more efficient in meeting one of the criteria than another. Thus in deciding who learns best it may be necessary to be more specific as to what kind of evidence of learning applies. Occasionally an individual is found who becomes known as an idiot-savant. The chances are that such a person can do remarkable feats of recall for some specific kind of information, such as reproducing the numbers on hundreds of automobile license plates, stating the final score for dozens of baseball games, or remembering telephone numbers. The same individual may not be able to modify his behavior so he can make adjustments in his world to the extent of taking care of his own basic needs. It can hardly be denied that learning has taken place, but it may be of a lower order than learning that leads to logical and consistent decisions or to overt action in complex social relationships. The idiot-savant cannot make a sound evaluation of abstract ideas. Better measures of functioning on this level give promise of fruitful scientific investigation of the learning process.

The reader may already appreciate the fact that satisfactory criteria for rote memorizing is much easier to establish than is criteria for meaningfulness or action. Some investigators have marked off ideas in prose, for example, and then the subject is scored upon the basis of how many of the ideas he can recall. This procedure nearly always forces the experimenter into the position of making subjective judgments as to when an idea is actually recalled. Unless the exact words are reproduced—and this becomes rote memory—it is very difficult to decide whether the idea has been adequately indicated or recalled.

Recall

It is not always possible to decide in advance as to which criterion may serve the experimentalist best. This decision will have to be determined by the sort of problem involved. Recall is rarely used in experimental work unless rote memorizing is being investigated. The teacher uses this widely and may combine recall and use. Thus when an essay-type question is given on an examination, the teacher is interested in knowing how many facts are retained by the student and how well those facts may be organized and used in making meaningful statements about a topic. The last is *use* although it may fall short of revealing action beyond that involved in writing or speaking. Recall as indicated above may not serve the experimentalist very well because of the subjective judgment involved in scoring the answers and the low reliability which usually involves both the inconsistent performance of the subject and the examiner.

Recognition

As a criterion of learning, recognition is generally thought to provide for good reliability but may meet less satisfactorily the demands for validity. Most of the objective test items now included in course examinations as well as those found in standardized tests for measuring intelligence or achievement make primary use of recognition. If the subject can recognize a right answer or can distinguish between right and wrong answers when confronted by both, this becomes the evidence that learning has taken place. Obviously in order to be able to distinguish between what one has been exposed to previously and what is an entirely new stimulus, as in the case where a statement is to be evaluated as true or false, is a long ways from insuring that behavior has been modified to any great extent. The modification of behavior might conceivably be limited only to checking one word instead of the other with no other follow through. However, recognition is found to be a sensitive measuring procedure and thus lends itself well to experimental procedure. In the practical situation recognition alone may be rated as too low a level of learning to meet requirements for making sound decisions and taking effective action.

Savings Method

Where sensitivity is of primary importance, experimenters have usually favored the *savings method*. What is meant by this is that the number of repetitions required to bring learning back to an earlier level of achievement is used. It is possible to use time of study in relearning to the established level or criterion. It has been demonstrated that material previously exposed to the individual may leave some trace of evidence that learning took place long after recall or recognition became impossible. One of the best known studies of this kind was that of Burtt (1), who drilled his small son on a Greek poem. Years later he matched the stanzas with others for difficulty and then had the boy memorize both the new material and that previously learned. The son had no recognition of ever having studied or being exposed to the poem, but it was clearly evident, by the difference in the effort required to learn the two sets of material, that the previous exposure had left its trace.

A bothersome problem which pertains to some extent to each of the other methods indicated has to do with the effect produced by the subject's attempt to demonstrate evidence of previous learning. In other words, the act of trying to recall becomes additional practice; test for recognition now becomes an extra exposure, and this is almost certain to be additive in its effect. In the savings method no renewed effort can be made, so the subject reveals the presence of the former learning or fails to do this. Even though there is a failure to get positive evidence that any learning has taken place, it is not safe to deny that nothing happened to the organism or the behavior of the organism. All that can be asserted is that the criterion that was chosen failed to reveal positive evidence and this always has the chance of merely reflecting the sensitivity of the testing instrument.

Use

The *use* that a subject can make of what he has learned probably has the greatest face validity of any of the measures that may be chosen. However, this is rarely employed in experimental work because of the difficulties of quantifying and objectifying the results. Nevertheless, this is a criterion of learning that must not be dismissed because of the important practical implications. To a considerable extent the validity of an education must be determined by the use that the individual can later make of it. It is rare that direct recall or recognition will be of practical usefulness to the individual but he will often be trying to make decisions and take action that should follow what he has learned. Awareness of how events turned out for others does not necessarily rest upon specific memory or detailed memory at the moment of decision or action. To a considerable extent, formal education is an attempt to convey information to an individual so that he does not have to live through painful failures; it is supposed to help him to avoid unnecessary trial and error procedure. Much of the educational task is to learn vicariously. This means more than anything else that guiding principles become operative and enable the individual to form sound judgments from recorded experiences of others; he makes cultural experiences the basis for his behavior.

GETTING SUBJECTS

Since the time that the study of animal behavior upon learning became respectable, a relatively high percentage of the experiments upon learning have been performed by use of lower animals. There are practical difficulties in obtaining some animals and it is frequently the case that expense becomes a prohibitive factor. White rats have been by far the most popular subjects. There are several reasons for their use. These include, at present, great advantage because so much is known about the performance of the rats. There is a wealth of experimental literature to be utilized in making comparisons and drawing conclusions and this is a consideration not to be dismissed lightly. However, there are investigators of animal behavior who deplore the lack of use of a greater variety of animals and they believe that much of the value in using animals in the first place is lost because there is not a systematic literature revealing results from animals at all phylogenetic levels.

White rats are defended as subjects because they are relatively easy to raise, inexpensive to feed and house, readily motivated to work by means of food deprivation or deprivation of one of the other basic drives. The animal is assumed to be largely lacking in memory and hence the belief that the experimenter can exercise relatively satisfactory controls through external environmental manipulation. Again, there is abundant knowledge about the rat's heredity and thus standardization is improved with regard to this factor. Only for the fruit fly might claim be made for the same distinction, but no one has demonstrated that the fruit fly is a very useful subject in psychological experiments.

DEFENSE OF ANIMAL SUBJECTS

It is not believed that psychologists are actually guilty of reasoning that whatever a rat will do the human subject will do also—a criticism frequently leveled at the psychologist who uses rats in his experiments. The purpose in using rats and other animals for subjects is primarily for the purpose of understanding human behavior. There are sometimes good reasons for studying the behavior of some animals for the immediate and direct use that this might have in raising and utilizing the animal. There is surely a wide open field of investigation where domestic animals would be studied for behavioral characteristics. Dogs and cats are wanted largely for the behavior that they display as pets. It is primarily for the behavior or the function they serve that make horses, milk cows, and hens useful to people. In general, attention of animal breeders up to the present has been devoted mainly to improving the physical structure of the animals. This has been done both by controlling genetic factors and by making a favorable environment for the animal. This is only part of the problem, how that structure is used is often important as well. There is not a perfect correlation between structure and function.

Personality may not be a satisfactory term to use with regard to animals, yet there are behavioral characteristics that might be spoken of as differences in disposition or temperament. Every farm boy has had experience in coping with domestic animals that must be cared for under fright or anger. Frightened hens lay fewer eggs; frightened or angered cows can be expected to produce much less milk than otherwise. One race horse may exhaust himself by frantic behavior before the race begins; another may not get sufficiently agitated to run at his greatest speed until the race is over. It is not well known as to how much these characteristics are due to heredity nor how much they might be changed by planned breeding. There can be little doubt that some of the behavior, desirable or undesirable, is determined by experience. Some of it is brought about by deliberate training, other aspects of it may result from unfortunate accidents and incidental learning. Much information about the importance of conditioning in early life is already available to the animal trainer and those who are most competent make considerable use of such knowledge.

It is, of course, the primary business of psychologists to gain understanding of human behavior so they may make a contribution to all those who must predict and control in order to bring about the behavior wanted from people. If the study of animal behavior furthers this objective, then animals should be used as subjects. The botanist may find it easier to maintain motivation when he tries to force the secrets of growth from a beautiful rose, but there is little reason to have confidence that revelations about the laws of nature will come any more readily by studying the rose than a stink weed. Nature no doubt operates upon basic principles common to both plants. It is equally probable that some of the basic principles that govern the behavior of animals is common to all species and there is good reason for studying the behavior of many different animals.

PRESENTATION OF EXPERIMENTAL RESULTS

While it is possible to present the results of experiments on learning in either prose form or in tables, use of learning curves, graphs, and tables have been very effective and these are widely employed. In order for this to be done, the experimental results must be in quantitative form and decision with regard to demands for communicating to others often forces the experimentalist to sharpen and improve his methods and techniques. Learning curves are especially valuable in showing progression of learning in successive practices. Thus a learning curve may be used to indicate the course of learning over a few practices and covering a short interval of time, or it may be used to show development over a lifetime.

It is the general consensus among psychologists that there is not one single curve that can be taken as *the typical* learning curve. We have made primary use of theoretical curves in the accompanying figures,

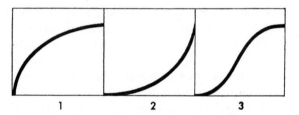

Fig. 12.4. Three learning curves. Learning curves based upon obtained data take different shapes, depending upon several factors. Much depends upon previous learning or the time factor. It can be seen that the third curve could be a composite of curves 1 and 2. The pattern of the first curve is seen if the starting point on the third base line is shifted to about the mid-point.

since this serves our purpose of illustrating what may be expected when data are tabulated and curves drawn to fit these. There is some reason to believe that the S shaped curve best represents the gross or overall progression of learning in man or other organisms. However, we hasten to add that this curve is not very often encountered among learning curves constructed from collected data. It is typical for learning experiments to represent a segment of learning for upon any task there may be much skill and knowledge borrowed from previous experience. All of the factors that have been discussed in this chapter plus some additional ones are likely to be reflected in the shape of any given learning curve. The reader is referred to the explanation and discussion that appears with each figure.

LEARNING EXPERIMENTS AND INTELLIGENCE

It is not our intention to deal with psychological tests as such; however, there have been a number of experiments bearing upon changes in learning that brought about either negative or positive effects upon learning and, of course, if one of these is used over a considerable length of time an increase or decrease in intelligence quotient may be expected. Permanent impairment is clearly in evidence from use of great quantities of morphine, cocaine, opium, and other drugs that act upon nervous tissue. Even alcohol, if used over a long period and in excess, eventually affects adversely the intelligence quotient.

It is found that those test items that demand new learning are most adversely affected by the agencies that have just been mentioned. Old learning seems to be retained better than newly learned material. There is every reason to believe that learning ability is the key element in intelligence. In fact, if a good index to learning rate for a given individual could be furnished at a particular time, this might have advantages for predictive purposes over our present intelligence test. The individual's current ability to learn rapidly may have more relevancy for predictive purposes than does a score that may reflect to a considerable extent what that person did achieve five or ten years ago. A differential loss that indicates a more marked reduction in learning new material than in recalling older material is said to be a useful means of diagnosing organic damage.

Intelligence is often defined in terms of the individual's ability to make adjustments or to engage in abstract thinking. These and most other variations in definitions of intelligence lead to the supposition that those who learn rapidly and well are the same people that are highly intelligent. Feeble-minded individuals gain their label primarily because they cannot learn easily; they do not profit by experience, or, in other words, they fail to learn. Part of the purpose in reviewing the relationship between learning and intelligence is to indicate that those who are concerned with improving intelligence and who believe that this might be brought about through environmental control are likely to approach the problem by trying to find out what leads to better learning. Then they will try to improve the learning with the expectation that a higher intelligence quotient will result. Direct coaching upon the items or ones greatly similar to them in an intelligence test leads to higher scores, but such procedure merely invalidates the test. If the idea is not acceptable that intelligence is 100 percent established by heredity and fixed and static after birth, then improvement in learning rate by administering drugs, proper diet, hormones, or even intellectual stimulation are all to be looked upon with hope that they may improve behavior in ways consistent with what is called intelligent behavior. Most drugs appear to have a negative effect upon learning. Caffeine, when used in small amounts, seems to be an exception. Both temporary and relatively permanent improvement in learning ability is believed to follow from the use of thyroxine by those individuals suffering from a deficiency of secretion by the thyroid glands.

It is improbable that the body chemistry of most people is maintained at optimal balance. Further research is greatly needed before an adequate evaluation can be made of the possibilities for improvement of the individual's functioning by means of nutrition and drugs. Experiments designed to evaluate the assets and liabilities of a given drug are frequently set up so that changes in learning rate become the criteria of the influence exerted by the drug. Thus it is seen that skill in designing learning experiments become a means for studying the usefulness of drug therapy in mental and nervous disease. Indirectly and occasionally such experiments may be used to evaluate the effectiveness of a variety of psychotherapeutic techniques.

CONCLUDING REMARKS

There remain many important problems in the area of learning that have not even been mentioned in this chapter. However, it has been the intention to present the more general problems and procedures with a view to giving the student a broad orientation and overview of the experimental work having to do with learning. The next three chapters deal more specifically with several topics and there more referrals are made to the literature.

SUGGESTED READINGS

Garrett, Henry E. *General Psychology*. New York: American Book Co., 1955.

Munn, Norman L. *Psychology* (3rd ed.), pp. 195-283. Boston: Houghton Mifflin, 1956.

Morgan, Clifford T. *Introduction to Psychology*, pp. 107-134. New York: McGraw-Hill, 1956.

McGeoch, John A., and Irion, Arthur L. *The Psychology of Human Learning*. New York: Longmans, Green, 1952.

Bugelski, B. R. *The Psychology of Learning*, pp. 53-77. New York: Henry Holt, 1956.

Postman, Leo, and Egan, James P. *Experimental Psychology: An Introduction*. "Measurement of Learning," pp. 275-286. New York: Harper, 1949.

Garrett, Henry E. *Great Experiments in Psychology.* "Pavlov and the Conditioned Reflex," pp. 1-19; "Thorndike's Laws of Learning," pp. 40-62; "Ebbinghaus' Studies in Memory and Forgetting," pp. 101-126. New York: Appleton-Century-Crofts, 1951.

Stolurow, Lawrence M. *Readings and Learning.* New York: Prentice-Hall, 1953.

Osgood, Charles E. *Methods and Theories in Experimental Psychology,* pp. 299-600. New York: Oxford University Press, 1953.

Stevens, S. S. (ed.). *Handbook of Experimental Psychology.* Hilgard: "Methods and Procedures in the Study of Learning," pp. 517-569. New York: John Wiley, 1951.

REFERENCES

1. Burtt, H. E. An experimental study of early childhood memory: final report, *J. Genet. Psychol.,* 58, 1941, 435-439.

2. Ebbinghaus, H. *Memory, a Contribution to Experimental Psychology,* 1885. Translated by Ruger, H. A., and Bussenius, C. E. Teachers College, Columbia University, 1913.

3. Garrett, Henry E. *Great Experiments in Psychology,* p. 41. New York: Appleton-Century-Crofts, 1951.

4. James, William. *Principles of Psychology,* Vol. I, p. 566. New York: Henry Holt, 1890.

5. Postman, Leo, and Egan, James P. *Experimental Psychology: An Introduction,* p. 317. New York: Harper, 1949.

6. Pavlov, I. P. *Conditioned Reflexes.* London: Oxford University Press, 1927.

7. Thorndike, E. L. "Animal intelligence: an experimental study of the associative processes in animals," *Psychol. Monogr.,* 8 (1898).

13 | EXPERIMENTING UPON LEARNING: CONDITIONING

The methods and techniques used in conditioning experiments are relatively simple, but the range of these experiments and their use for both theoretical and practical purposes make it desirable to devote a chapter to conditioning. Even though the methods may be simple, the problems and theoretical concepts upon which psychologists work when doing experiments involving conditioning leave nothing wanting in the way of complexity and difficulty.

Pavlov and his experiments have already been mentioned. Conditioning experiments are usually divided into two types. The distinction rests largely upon the procedure used. The first type, including those in the strict Pavlov tradition, is known as *classical* conditioning. The second type has been called *instrumental conditioning,* and is well represented by the experiments performed by Skinner. The majority of experiments that have been performed in recent years and that had as their announced purpose the testing of hypotheses and the establishment of theory in learning have used one or another of these two general procedures. Since theorists in psychology have often gravitated toward the study of learning, it may develop that more will be said about theory in this chapter than in any other in the book. Nevertheless, there are many practical implications associated with conditioning.

CLASSICAL AND INSTRUMENTAL CONDITIONING

It seems impossible to discuss conditioning phenomena without using confusing terminology. This problem was great enough when it was necessary to deal only with so-called classical conditioning, but it has become even more involved since instrumental conditioning has emerged as a partially distinct, but, according to some authorities, a basically similar phenomenon. The reader should be prepared for either apparent or real inconsistency that may be found between writers in their use of terminology when dealing with conditioning. Perhaps even more confusing is the difficulty writers find in remaining consistent at all times with themselves.

Probably most of the confusion arises when the terms *conditioned* and *unconditioned* are used. Woodworth and Schlosberg have advocated that a more appropriate pair of terms to use under most circumstances

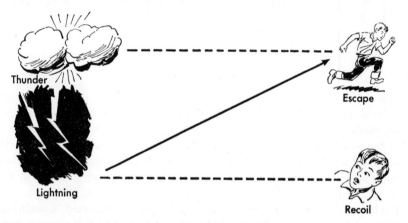

Fig. 13.1. Loud noises produce fear-like reactions in very young children. It can be seen that lightning or dark clouds readily become adequate stimuli for fear responses. (From Garrett, Henry E., *General Psychology*. New York: American Book Co., 1955.)

would be *conditional* and *unconditional*. Whichever pair of terms is used, they must be applied to both the stimulus and the response. There is a "natural" stimulus and a "natural" response and each may be "conditioned."

There appears to be a "natural," or "unconditional," response to every stimulus. By definition, a stimulus is: any form of energy, adequate as to strength and of such a nature as to activate to response one of the senses of the organism. If a ringing bell is spoken of as not being a "natural" stimulus in the activating of a dog's salivary glands, this does not necessarily mean that there is a total lack of some "natural" response to the sound. It may well be difficult to determine what that response is, but it could be a movement of the ears, turning of the eyes, or shifting of the head. It is true that all of these might be examples of conditional response in the dog. Possibly these unconditional responses are limited to activity of a sense organ and the muscles immediately associated with the operation of that sense organ, or to these and the neural impulses that terminate short of reaching and activating remote muscles. The cycling process in the nervous system and the feed-back that occurs from muscular responses, in which the kinesthetic sense becomes involved, is not too well understood. When more adequate information becomes available, it is believed that it will add significantly to the understanding of both conditional and unconditional responses.

It would be helpful in the discussion if it could be safely asserted that all responses necessarily involve muscular action. However, this might place an indefensible limitation upon responding, for it would seem to exclude too much. Presumably, perception does not necessarily require motor responses. Imagining and thinking are rather regularly accompanied by muscular movements, but few would want to argue that neither were at all possible unless involving motor responses. Yet, for the sake of simplicity, muscular activity can be assumed in the discussion that follows. It will, of course, be necessary to include both skeletal and smooth muscles. Pavlov's first observations were made upon the salivation resulting from activity of glandular muscles, which are classified as smooth muscles. Again, some writers draw a sharp distinction between stimuli and responses that involve smooth muscles and those in which striped muscles are used. In the end, this distinction may become the basis for far-reaching theories about learning, such as those set forth by Skinner (13), Mowrer (9), and others. These concepts have led to the formulation of what has been called a dual theory of learning. The basic premise is that distinctly different principles are needed to account for learning, depending upon whether the autonomic or central nervous system is dominately involved.

Classical Conditioning

In order to get before the student the problems so that he may come to understand ways in which classical and instrumental conditioning are alike and different, the following diagram of classical conditioning is presented:

$$Sc\dots\dots\dots\dots\dots\dots\dots\dots\dots\dots\dots\dots\dots\dots R \; (?)$$
(bell)   (movement of ears)

$$Su\dots\dots\dots\dots\dots\dots\dots\dots\dots\dots\dots\dots\dots\dots R$$
(food)   (eating and salivation)

In the interest of economy, the capital letter S for *stimulus* and R for *response* are used. The small letters c or u following either of the capital letters is to be read as *conditional* or *unconditional*, respectively. Thus, *Sc* means stimulus conditional; *Ru* is response unconditional.

The hungry adult dog will salivate upon either the sight or smell of food. It is assumed that both of these stimuli have become conditioned prior to the beginning of the experiment. The ringing of a bell is a less familiar stimulus and the naive dog has not previously experienced it along with the act of eating. This appears to be the only reason that the dog does not at first salivate upon hearing the bell and, therefore, the sound of a bell is a satisfactory stimulus to use when it is desired to observe the whole process of conditioning.

SPECIAL PROBLEMS

While an attempt will be made to avoid going astray by raising irrelevant points, not everything is as beautifully clear as could be wished even in this simple sequence of events. It is reasonable to ask exactly what triggers the response of salivating in the dog in the first place. It might be supposed that food acts upon the taste buds to bring about salivation. Then, does the reflex start with contact of food at the taste buds, or with the perception of food? In other words, what is the "natural" stimulus? When does the experimenter begin to deal with a "conditioned" stimulus? Possibly there exists a response that has been conditioned before the experiment started. Even the young pup salivates when chewing upon a piece of wood; yet this is hardly to be classified as food that should activate the taste buds as a "natural" taste. To suppose that the dog can "think" about food and begin to salivate may be stretching the point. This last may be possible, but at least a clear demonstration is not easy to make. At any rate, if a man is reminded verbally of the delicious taste of sizzling steak under the right conditions of hunger, and, of course, after he has experienced the taste and the word together, so that the word becomes a symbol or revives a memory for the experience, he will salivate.

It has been stressed that, in the process of conditioning, the subject comes to respond to a substitute stimulus for the unconditioned stimulus. For what stimulus, then, does the bell become a substitute? An answer to this question has not been positively and finally determined. Traditionally, writers have tended to avoid giving a specific answer and have merely stated that a substitute stimulus can be used in the place of a previously adequate stimulus. However, a more meaningful statement would seem to be that the bell is merely an extension of a stimulus, adequate enough to call forth the reflex. That a previously adequate stimulus has been eliminated in the process is not evident. In other words, it is no substitute in terms of elimination of the former S.

Instrumental Conditioning

In instrumental conditioning, there is said to be a different chain of events. In his observations, Pavlov noted that a "substitute" stimulus could be used to activate a gland, and, while there may be doubt as to what stimulus was being replaced, it is clear that the gland under observation is controlled by the autonomic nervous system. The most popular experiments in which instrumental conditioning have been used involve a response made by the striped muscles, and this intervenes between the conditional stimulus (say the perception of a lever) and the unconditioned stimulus (food). Now, a better picture of events is gained if a straightforward line is used to diagram what takes place:

$$Sc \ldots \ldots \ldots Rc \ldots \ldots \ldots Su \ldots \ldots \ldots \ldots Ru$$
(lever)   (press)   (food)   (eat and salivate)

Thorndike's problem-box experiments would seem to fit this pattern. If such is the case, without undue stretching of the concept of conditioning, then problem-solving, even abstract thinking, can be based upon this phenomenon. Such an explanation resolves the chief objections raised by critics of Pavlov's early work. They could not see how a bit of "reflexology" could be of much use in explaining the higher intellectual behavior of man. They felt that Pavlov was still working within the realm of physiology and was not yet approaching the complexities of psychology. By combining both classical and instrumental conditioning, various investigators have attempted to validate a theory of learning premised entirely upon conditioning. No one seems to have been able to combine the two types of conditioning under one entirely satisfactory interpretation. The most ambitious approach to making conditioning encompass the whole of learning does not try to reconcile the two procedures entirely. The so-called emotional and other responses made within the autonomic nervous system have been interpreted in terms of classical conditioning, while intellectual learning, it is often assumed, takes place by instrumental conditioning. This is a complicated dualism, set forth by Mowrer and others, but leaves the conditioning process intact to account for all learning.

From what has been said, it should be understood that the subject regularly does something that becomes "instrumental" in attaining his goal, if the term *instrumental conditioning* is to be used. For example, the manipulation of some object by the rat leads to the delivery of food, which is then eaten. Or the situation may be one of confinement, and the animal pulls a string or lifts a latch, after which the door opens and it is able to escape from the cage. Another variation of instrumental learning has to do *not* with a reward, but with the avoidance of pain. Suppose that a rat is placed upon an electric grill that can administer a shock. Then, if a bell is sounded just before the shock is given, the rat will

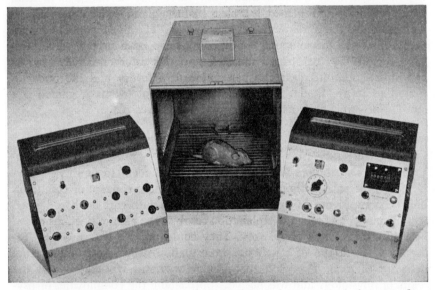

Fig. 13.2. Skinner box equipped with electrical connections for recording responses; also equipped to administer electric shock to the subject. (Courtesy C. H. Stoelting Co., Chicago.)

become restless at the sound of the bell and begin to make avoidance efforts. He may soon learn to climb the sides of the cage in order to avoid the electric shock. In such a case, a *rewarding outcome* must be considered in negative terms, for the reward is such only in that pain has been avoided.

The result just indicated is difficult to reconcile as the same process as tension reduction, such as has ordinarily been claimed for the attainment of a positive goal like food consumption. It appears that tension is generated by the anticipation or presentation of the painful stimulus, and this, at best, would be the only tension reduced by the response. It is not easy to see that over-all relaxation would take place, beyond that immediately induced by the threat. Consequently, it would appear more reasonable that a somewhat prolonged tension state might be generated, not unlike the tension that is associated with anxiety and fear found in people.

Skinner (13), in a series of studies (1932-1938), has been able to demonstrate how animals react under partial reinforcement. By this he means that an animal may learn to run a maze or to operate a lever to get food, when reward comes as a result of only part of the trials. For example, a very hungry rat can be made to press a lever twenty times before getting any food. When the experiment is set up in this way, the rat becomes so busy working the lever that he may not even stop to check whether a pellet has been delivered until after a number of responses have been made. There is no clear evidence that the rat learns how to count. At any rate, if a large number of pressure responses are required before delivery of the food, he does not learn exactly when to stop working and to go for the food. Naturally, a necessary control, if counting ability is to be tested, is that the pellets not fall within his sight. In that case, the rat would be expected to stop working the lever, upon receiving the visual stimulus that indicated the food was to be had. Apparently, strong motivation is required to initiate work when this kind of partial reinforcement is given, but it is interesting to see that extinction is less readily established than when a reward has followed regularly from each response. The animal gets "used to" lack of reward on part of the responses and is not discouraged by these repeated failures. He keeps working for the reward until ultimately it arrives.

CONDITIONING: ADJUSTIVE AND MALADJUSTIVE

In some ways, this topic might be more appropriate for inclusion in the previous chapter. However, unfortunate learning may give the parent or teacher as much, or even more, of a problem with a given individual as does slowness in learning what she wants to teach. Those who work in clinical and abnormal psychology might conclude, with much justification, that "wrong" learning, and the subsequent results, give rise to nearly all of their work with ailing patients. They might also use the implications of learning as a basis for deciding on the patient's area of competence, and for setting limits upon the clinician's field of work. Those problems in nervous and mental illness that have their source in undesirable learning, and the habits premised upon such learning, could be the primary concern of psychologists. Other aspects of mental disease might then be considered as being within the legitimate domain of physicians, psychiatrists, and social workers.

Looked at in the way just suggested, unlearning or relearning becomes a tremendous problem. Thus, it might be concluded that early unintentional, and wrong, conditioning constitutes a misfortune. Psychologists, and apparently all others who deal with people, are at a loss in the practical and effective handling of the problem of unlearning and forgetting. It is not effective, probably not even desirable if effective, to instruct a subject to "forget it." If forgetting is desirable as a goal, workers find it difficult to know exactly how to go about achieving this. Devices to impress the individual with the importance of forgetting seem to be self-defeating. In practice, the usual procedure is to turn the problem around and suggest that all those means that are used to help in retention not be used when trying to forget. This is, of course, a negative approach to the problem. In general, it does not seem to work. Distractions and substitutions are often attempted. These are not feasible in many situations. They have great vogue in the movie industry, forming the theme for many a Western movie, in which the hero occupies himself with capturing wild horses, after being frustrated in one love affair and before finally meeting the real girl of his dreams!

Science is today rather helpless in furnishing theoretical and practical guidance toward effective forgetting. The hospitalized patient, immobilized by regrets and feelings of guilt, whose personality is shattered, presumably because of the emotional traumas he has experienced, is not easily freed from the terror of facing the reality that includes the traumatic events. The businessman, unable to forget a bad investment, becomes exhausted and irritable in his attempts to recoup, and is told to take a vacation during which he is expected to recover his composure. It is not impossible that the vacation serves to give him time to weave even more anxiety-laden fantasies. The "rest" treatment is widely criticized, but a more positive plan has not yet been advanced.

While other theories of learning have been used widely to account for intentional learning, or the acquisition of useful knowledge, scarcely anyone has come forth with an explanation of undesirable learning that is as convincing as conditioning. Hence, the pursuit of an encompassing theory that would account for all learning has been especially attractive, and recruits have been gained by those who make conditioning the basic premise. Here is an approach that will embrace such facts as permanent memory based upon one experience, strengthening by repetition when rewarded, or avoidance when the outcome is painful. It can account for the more abstract consequences, such as the loss of interest following repeated failures, the attitude that all emotional investment leads only to rejection in the end and that the new day and the new experience can only be expected to bring new disaster.

There are many examples in which one experience has been sufficient to influence the attitude and behavior of an individual for the rest of his life. There is no lack of repeated examples of seemingly blind and futile efforts, in which behavior persists over a long period without obvious reinforcement. There has been no reward in these cases; yet the behavior persists and seems to illustrate what happens under experimental partial reinforcement. Altogether, conditioning is to most investigators the phenomenon that most readily explains these diverse results.

CONDITIONING MAY APPEAR CAPRICIOUS

A view of the factors that must be adhered to when performing an experiment on conditioning may lead to a question as to how it is that all of the factors are ever met in a given everyday experience. In fact, investigators often become discouraged with the number of repetitions required before a strong and clear-cut example of a conditioned response, involving one of the well-known reflexes, such as the knee-jerk or eye-wink, is attained. Since these conditioned reflexes are so hard to produce, how is it that learning theories so readily assume that conditioning is not only the best explanation for much learning, but may even explain all of it? Is it only that incidental and accidental learning comes easily? Is it, primarily, that people learn only those things that they *should not* learn without the use of great effort? In other words, it might be supposed that the cards are stacked against desirable learning, that adjustive behavior comes hard and maladjustive behavior with ease! Such a conclusion scarcely makes scientific sense. At any rate, it must be assumed that there is as consistent and regular a relationship in the learning process that leads to a set of habits possessed by the individual who is known as a criminal and whose behavior is judged to be destructive as there is in the proces that leads to an upright citizen who keeps busy with socially beneficial projects. If the one is brought about more readily than the other, some aspect of the situation within the organism or environment under which learning takes place must give advantage.

It is in order to describe and to understand these various matters, to predict outcomes and to control situations in ways expected to bring about wanted behavior, that investigators try to evolve sound learning theory.

KNOWN FACTORS THAT INFLUENCE CONDITIONING

There are a number of factors that make for more rapid conditioning and there are certain limitations within which the subject must operate, or no conditioning will take place. These include both factors within the organism and those applying to the environment. The fact that some of these factors sound like ancient ones, such as the association of events in time and space as indicated by Aristotle and frequently mentioned since, should not obscure the fact that Pavlov and other investigators have advanced these ideas and added useful specific observations concerning them. These factors will be grouped and discussed further under (1) time, (2) intensity, (3) repetition or frequency, (4) outcome or effect: reward and punishment, (5) state of the organism.

Time Factor

Pavlov (12) recognized the time factor as being the most important, or, it might be said, the first essential for conditioning to take place. He had this to say: "The fundamental requisite is that any external stimulus which is to become the signal in a conditioned reflex must overlap in point of time with the action of an unconditioned stimulus. In the experiment which I chose as my example, the unconditioned stimulus was food. Now if the intake of food by the animal takes place simultaneously with the action of a neural stimulus which has been hitherto in no way related to food, the neural stimulus readily acquires the property of eliciting the same reaction in the animal as would food itself. This was the case with the dog employed in our experiment with the metronome. On several occasions this animal had been stimulated by the sound of the metronome and immediately presented with food—i.e., a stimulus which was neutral of itself had been superimposed upon the action of the inborn alimentary reflex. We observe that, after several repetitions of the combined stimulation, the sounds from the metronome had acquired the property of stimulating salivary secretion and of evoking the motor reaction characteristic of the alimentary reflex."

Other investigators have performed experiments with the intention of determining all the limitations that are imposed by the time factor. It was thought for a while by investigators that practically no deviation from simultaneous presentation of the two stimuli could be tolerated. Now, writers usually speak of conditioning taking place under three variations in time: (1) simultaneously, (2) delayed, (3) trace.

It might be supposed that by simultaneously it is meant that the conditional and unconditional stimuli must be initiated at the same instance. However, the usual practice and interpretation is not precisely this, for the term is used if the two come exactly together or if the conditional stimulus is started only a fraction of a second earlier. Actually, conditioning is easier if the conditional stimulus is presented slightly earlier than the unconditional stimulus.

The term *delayed conditional response* is used if the conditional stimulus is initiated first and continued until the unconditional stimulus is presented. There is a bit of vagueness here, for there is no general agreement as to how much of a delay is necessary before this labeling of *delayed* is applied. It is obvious that what is called simultaneous conditioning shades into delayed conditioning. This need not give undue concern, for an arbitrary decision might resolve the problem. Actually, the reason for distinguishing between the two has practical usefulness, and attention has been directed toward determining how long after presentation of the conditional S the experimenter might wait before administering the unconditional S and still obtain conditioning. A number of factors operate here, not the least of which seems to be the intelligence of the animal. Those animals that stand higher in the phylogenetic scale are capable of conditioning if greater delay is used.

The delayed CR and especially the *trace* CR has been used as experimental evidence that lower animals may use symbolic processes. A series of animal studies were carried out by Carr and Hunter in 1913 under what might be thought of as near-ideal conditions, in which the animal was given the Sc over and over with increasing delay. The time interval forces the animal into responding in a way that would seem to depend upon something very close to "memory." Hunter later extended these studies. After the delayed conditioned response had been well established, he would stop the Sc for an interval before allowing the animal to start to the goal. Thus, if a light turned on at a door in front of the rat was the signal that food would appear, the rat was prevented from starting for the food for a period and then allowed to go to it. In the case of the rat and most other animals, it was observed that any disorientation of the body of the animal gave rise to far fewer successes. The "memory trace" does not seem to be strong enough to survive the disorientation plus a very short interval for either the rat or the dog. Hunter found that some of his rats could respond up to 10 seconds and the dogs up to 5 minutes if not turned around before starting for the food. On the other hand, raccoons seemed to be much less disturbed by bodily rotation and they sometimes responded correctly after being turned around and having the delay extended to as long as 15 seconds.

In a study closely parallel, Hunter (7) used children as subjects and found that they could respond by selecting the signaled goal after several minutes. It is noteworthy that, where there were three choices, the child would be able to use language such as "middle," "left," or "right." On the other hand, very young children might be able to select the right goal, but could not or would not use language. Instead, the child might go to the right place or point out which one was the correct goal. In these various studies, the subjects were required to respond upon what has been considered a "trace" within the organism.

In still later studies, Hunter (6) experimented with a child by placing some desired object under a cup and then not allowing the child to retrieve the object until after a time interval. When confronted with a choice between three cups, only one of them covering the object, the child could still go to the correct one after being turned around and waiting several seconds. For one child, he found 80 percent correct responses after a 15-second interval. Chance would account for only a third of the responses being correct.

Tinklepaugh (15) used still a different procedure in studying the delayed response. He used chimpanzees and monkeys as subjects and conditioned them to "multiple delayed reaction" by baiting one of two containers in a series of rooms. The animal was placed in a given spot where it could observe that food was placed in one of the two containers; then, without being allowed to approach either container, it was taken to another room where the process was repeated; and then the experiment was repeated in still other rooms. Later, it would be returned to see if it could still discriminate and make the correct response ruling out chance. The animals were able to perform this task surprisingly well and scored about as well as adult human subjects who were used under approximately the same conditions. In an interesting earlier variation of the single delayed reaction, Tinklepaugh (14) allowed the chimpanzee to observe a banana placed in the container and then secretly he substituted another object, or a less preferred food. The animal's behavior upon discovering no banana, as described by Tinklepaugh, gave the appearance of being that of disappointment!

All investigators of conditioning phenomena have placed great importance upon the time factor and, indeed, there seems to be no escaping the implication that events are bonded together by occurring together in time. It is found that Guthrie (4) denies that delayed, or trace, conditioning should be interpreted as very different from simultaneous conditioning. He states that conditioning can take place only under these circumstances, because the Sc sets up behavior within the organism that continues to operate and to furnish feed-back stimuli until the Su arrives. In other words, the actual conditioning takes place only because the behavior furnishes new stimuli and it is to this that the conditioned response is given. Thus, he stressed that postural adjustments, such as movement of the head, directing the eyes to a particular position, general bodily alertness, and so forth, all meant that there would be a considerable supply of incoming stimuli with sensations arising at the instant the *Su* is presented. Consequently, there might be two major reasons for the difficulty in establishing a conditioned response if there is delay. The first would be that the secondary stimuli would decrease in intensity with the lapse of time, and the second factor would result from competing behavior that would serve to furnish inhibitory stimuli. This last interpretation would seem to fit the observed facts very well in the case of the bodily disorientation that so readily prevents conditioning in lower animals. If the animal is turned around in position, the feed-back stimuli would be weakened or changed and no conditioning would take place.

Pavlov had postulated that within the nervous system there would be opposing tendencies, one of excitation and the other of inhibition. If there was delay during the period between the presentation of the *Sc* and *Su,* there would be a holding-back process. It was noted that salivation might begin only after a slight delay and then become faster as the time approached for presentation of the *Su.* Interesting complications arise if additional and different kinds of stimuli are introduced during the interval between *Sc* and *Su.* Perhaps, for everyday events, and in the learning of people, this is a typical condition of which account must be taken. If conditioning is to be the basic explanation for learning of intellectual tasks, then delayed responses, during which time there is an interplay of symbolic processes, becomes the usual, rather than the exceptional, thing. The organism is never completely passive, nor does it operate in a vacuum where one could introduce the experimental stimulus alone. There can be expected intervening stimuli which are accompanied by associations and imaginings to complicate the situation, and which, therefore, would tend to increase problems of prediction.

Intensity of Stimulus and Degree of Participation

While it is usual to think of the intensity factor as applying primarily to the stimulus, it is, perhaps, not unreasonable to take the response into account. If the muscles brought into play are numerous and if the energy used is great, this might well result in a total effect that differs from minor participation. Many studies have been made in which the responding mechanisms have been interfered with in some way, in order for observations to be made and comparisons drawn, when the organism operates under forced reduction in response. In terms of the results achieved, at least, this is quite similar to what is found when the stimulus is less intense. These two aspects of conditioning will be discussed and certain comparisons made between them. First, the evidence for variation in conditioning that are found when the intensity of the stimulus is manipulated will be reviewed.

Pavlov and others seem to have assumed that conditioning took place more rapidly when an intense stimulus was applied than when the stimulus is weak. While systematic studies of this are not numerous and the evidence somewhat meager, the generalization seems safe enough. However, there may well be important exceptions to the rule. For example, if pain is more than adequate as a signal but is great enough to terrify an animal, any conditioning that is inconsistent with escape or flight might not be easy to establish.

Systematic variation in the stimulus was used by Passey (11) in conditioning the eyelid reflex. He used a puff of air of varying strength as the Su. The Sc was a tone that was repeated without variation in length, frequency, or amplitude. The learning curve is, typically, a negatively accelerated one. Experimental extinction followed the conditioning and then the reverse order was obtained in the way that might be expected. The group that was conditioned more slowly became the first in order of extinction. However, it will be noted that the order for extinction is not consistently reversed for all groups. It is likely that the use of more subjects would have resulted in orderliness here also.

In several experiments in which there is some means of restraining the animal from making a motor response, conditioning is made more difficult or does not occur. Perhaps, it is more accurate to say that the usual response is not elicited, but that some other response is obtained. Suppose that a Su (electric shock) is administered simultaneously with a Sc (buzzer) but the situation has been so arranged that the animal cannot make the usual Ru (escape). Then, does the Rc take place? It appears that only the responses that are brought into play become conditioned, but with the removal of the barriers to escape, new learning is necessary to obtain a conditioned response of escaping at the presentation of the buzzer. The sound of the buzzer may not serve as a signal for escape, this having been impossible previously, but there is restless activity, glandular responses, and probably numerous bodily reactions, such as muscular tension, increased blood pressure, and changes in breathing—all of which may be properly considered as Rc.

The drug, curare, paralyzes muscles, thus preventing responses, but leaves the sensory mechanism intact and functioning. These results have made this drug a popular one when the purpose is to study the part played in conditioning by the cortex, as well as determining whether it is essential that the completed motor response take place before conditioning is possible. There remains some doubt as to where and how curare produces the block. Some have held that the effect is primarily in the brain, while others have indicated a belief that the neuromuscular junction is the critical point for the blocking effect.

Harlow and Stagner (5) were unable to produce conditioning when there was an absence of motor activity. However, they were testing for conditioning after the effects of the curare had worn off. Girden and Culler (3) were able to show that the conditioning that took place under curare did not carry over to the period after the drug's influence was over, but they did get what they considered to be conditioning, as evidenced by a twitching muscle, while the drug was still operative. Furthermore, they obtained evidence to indicate that, if conditioning takes place under the normal state, it may not carry over to the curarized state.

It has been established to the satisfaction of some investigators that conditioning can take place at a subcortical level. Marquis and Hilgard (8) were able to establish conditioning of the eyelid under normal state and this persisted, although it was apparently weakened after removal of the visual cortex area in the brain. Girden and others (3) found that simple avoidance reactions could be learned by decorticated animals. Although conditioning of decorticated animals was found, many, intense stimuli, even for simple avoidance responses, were required. Bromley (1) trained a decorticated dog to make avoidance responses to a tone after a considerable number of repetitions. This study has been given by some writers as an example of "adaptive" behavior in the decorticated animal. It has been recognized that there is an important distinction to be made between the survival of a CR, established before decortication, and the establishment of a CR after the brain modification. An exceedingly difficult problem to deal with in these studies has to do with the spread of brain injury resulting from hemorrhaging following the operation. Usually, autopsies are performed so that the amount of neural tissue damage can be examined more closely. There is, of course, no practical way to restore earlier neural damage in order to ascertain losses in learning. Once a neuron is destroyed, no new ones grow, and recovery must depend upon the functional substitution of other fibers.

After reviewing the literature having to do with conditioning phenomena, in which various brain operations have been used in the study of resulting changes, Osgood (10) summarizes the evidence by saying that cortical participation is not necessary for the formation of conditioned reactions. Subcortical centers are sufficient and it appears probable that spinal integration is capable of mediating associations that may be thought of as CR. There seems to be evidence, according to Osgood, that the cortex may be expected, under different circumstances, to furnish either a facilitating or an inhibiting effect upon subcortical organization involved in the CR process. Lashley concluded, after a great number of studies in which various portions of the brain were removed from white rats, that the ability of the postoperative rat to learn was closely related to the amount of the brain tissue removed. While some qualifications of his broad generalization have been shown to be necessary, the essential truth of Lashley's observations remains. There will be a differential effect with regard to loss that depends upon what part of the brain has been injured and which particular sense modality is involved in reception. Thus, the removal of a small amount of brain tissue from the occipital lobe may increase the difficulty in conditioning the rat if visual discrimination is required. If the discrimination demands the use of hearing, loss of portions of the temporal lobe will be critical.

Repetitions or Frequency of Trials Necessary for Conditioning

The number of trials required to establish a CR varies from a single trial to several hundred. Theoretically, it would appear that the number of repetitions should be highly predictable with optimal situations being reflected by a low number of trials before the CR is well established. However, in practice and without the collection of empirical data, the investigator may encounter surprises. References to simple conditioning may be misleading, for even the simplest CR may actually be a very complex process, subject to influence by many factors not readily identified. For example, the knee-jerk reflex has been frequently used by teachers to demonstrate the conditioning phenomenon to beginning classes in psychology. Yet, much depends upon the lucky choice of the teacher in taking the subject. Reasonable precision can be exercised over timing and intensity so a sharp blow with a rubber hammer strikes the tendon below the knee cap simultaneously with the ringing of a bell, or the presentation of some other stimulus, that is to be the Sc. But sometimes dozens of repetitions have failed to produce the desired conditioning. Presumably, distractions in the social situation, structural differences in the tendon and muscles, failure of a reinforcing outcome, and other factors may account for these failures.

In the chapter dealing with emotional reactions it was pointed out that single intensely emotional experiences are often the source of persistent fears. Such quick results (presumably a CR) are all but unknown in the controlled laboratory situation. Very likely, intensity of the stimulus or experience is insufficient for one-experience conditioning in the usual experiment or demonstration. There are many experiments that might be undertaken after first conditioning the subjects to words of different emotional value, such as socially taboo or approved, pleasant or unpleasant tone, and the like, if quick conditioning were possible as a preliminary to the experiment. Several attempts are known to have been made in which the investigator hoped to establish a *CR* to mild stimuli with such purposes in mind. Most of these experiments have failed, because the experimenters became discouraged before they obtained subjects satisfactorily conditioned to the criteria intended. This does not mean that conditioning within itself is very difficult to demonstrate, but the problem is that of getting uniformity of conditioning from subject to subject and from stimulus to stimulus for the same subject. Uniformity in conditioning, or meeting a stated criterion, may be essential before the experiment can be carried out, and then the results allow for any meaningful interpretation.

Conditioned responses are readily demonstrated in animals if pain is used as the *Su*. The rat rather quickly makes avoidance responses if an electric shock is presented along with almost any clearly presented stimulus.

Reward and Punishment in Conditioning

Much of the literature on learning features the significance of reward and punishment in conditioning. Many comparisons have been made as to the effectiveness of reward in contrast to punishment. Experimental difficulties are relatively obvious. The old problem of how to control for intensity of stimuli arises immediately. What level of pain is to be paired with what level of pleasantness? The type of behavior that is being conditioned makes a difference and it is not easy to bring both reward and punishment to bear in relevant ways to the same behavior. By this, it is meant that the poles tend to be opposite, in that punishment easily leads to avoidance behavior, while reward leads to approach. The differences may transcend the mere factor of direction in space. The practical implications are interesting. For example, a psychologist is known who tried to housebreak a dog by reward, but he was not ingenious enough to set up a rewarding situation that led to the conditioning that would save his rugs. On the other hand, punishment for undesired behavior soon led to escape activity and satisfactory conditioning in the dog. Utilizing conditioning phenomena as a means of achieving educational goals may mean that difficulties of the type encountered by the psychologist must be overcome. There are relatively few educational goals that can be approached by withdrawal, or avoidance activity, hence the advantage is usually on the side of reward for educational achievement.

State of the Organism

It would be an unjustified repetition to labor the point that physiological conditions help to determine the speed and certainty of responses to stimuli at every place in the book in which such information becomes relevant. It will be recognized that, in many of the conditioning experiments, the investigator manipulated the organism so that variable organic states constitute the independent variable. The hungry rat can be conditioned more rapidly than the well-fed rat, if food is the reward; conversely, he may resist conditioning more persistently if the problem is set up so that action must take place spatially in a direction away from the odor of food. A considerable discussion of material relevant to organic states and conditioning is found in the chapter dealing with bodily changes and emotional reactions (Chapter 9).

SUGGESTED READINGS

Morgan, Clifford T. *Introduction to Psychology,* pp. 107-116. New York: McGraw-Hill, 1956.

Postman, Leo, and Egan, James P. *Experimental Psychology,* pp. 287-311. New York: Harper, 1949.

Hilgard, Ernest R. *Introduction to Psychology* (2nd ed.), pp. 233-245. New York: Harcourt, Brace, 1957.

Garrett, Henry E. *Great Experiments in Psychology,* pp. 1-18. New York: Appleton-Century-Crofts, 1951.

Woodworth, Robert S., and Schlosberg, Harold. *Experimental Psychology,* pp. 541-576. New York: Henry Holt, 1954.

Andrews, T. G. *Methods of Psychology,* pp. 23-63. New York: John Wiley, 1948.

Stevens, S. S. (ed.). *Handbook of Experimental Psychology.* Brogden: "Animal Studies of Learning," pp. 568-592. New York: John Wiley, 1951.

REFERENCES

1. Bromley, R. B. "The development of conditioned responses in cats after unilateral decortication," *J. Comp. Physiol. Psychol.,* 41 (1948), 155-164.
2. Garrett, Henry C. *General Psychology,* p. 301. New York: American Book Co., 1955.
3. Girden, E., et al. "Conditioned response in a decorticated dog to acoustic, thermal, and tactile stimulation," *J. Comp. Psychol.,* 21 (1936), 368-85.
4. Guthrie, E. R. "Association as a function of time interval," *Psychol. Rev.,* 4 (1933), 355-367.

5. Harlow, H. F., and Stagner, R. "Effect of complete striate muscle paralysis upon the learning process," *J. Exp. Psychol.*, 16 (1933), 283-94.

6. Hunter, W. S. "Delayed reactions in a child," *Psychol. Rev.*, 24 (1917), 74-87.

7. Hunter, W. S. "The delayed reaction in animals and children," *Behav. Monogr.*, 6 (1913).

8. Marquis, D. G., and Hilgard, E. R. "Conditioned lid response to light in dogs after removal of the visual cortex," *J. Comp. Psychol.*, 22 (1936), 157-98.

9. Mowrer, O. H. "On the dual nature of learning—a reinterpretation of 'conditioning' and 'problem-solving,'" *Harvard Edu. Rev.*, 17 (1947), 102-148.

10. Osgood, Charles S. *Methods and Theory in Experimental Psychology*, p. 481. New York: Oxford University Press, 1953.

11. Passey, G. E. "The influence of intensity of unconditioned stimulus upon the acquisition of a conditioned response," *J. Exp. Psychol.*, 38 (1948), 420-28.

12. Pavlov, I. P. *Conditioned Reflexes*, 26 (trans. by G. V. Aurep). London: Oxford University Press, 1927.

13. Skinner, B. F. *The Behavior of Organisms: an Experimental Analysis*. New York: Appleton-Century-Crofts, 1938.

14. Tinklepaugh, O. L. "An experimental study of representative factors in monkeys," *J. Comp. Psychol.*, 8 (1928), 197-236.

15. Tinklepaugh, O. L. "Multiple delayed reaction with chimpanzees and monkeys," *J. Comp. Psychol.*, 13 (1932), 207-243.

14 | MEMORIZING: EXPERIMENTS IN VERBAL LEARNING

MEMORIZING

We have already indicated that Ebbinghaus was the first to experiment upon verbal learning, or, as he might have preferred, to investigate the process of memorizing. It is our purpose to extend the discussion of experimenting in this area of research and to review the more important principles associated with this kind of learning.

The acquisition and use of an effective language (including symbols that may not be specific to any particular language) are of such fundamental importance to man that it seems justified to include a chapter that focuses upon this topic. There is no intention to labor the point that a sharp distinction separates verbal learning from motor learning, nor, for that matter, is a clear distinction drawn between verbal learning and conditioning. It may be, as some argue, that conditioning furnishes an adequate explanation for the way verbal learning takes place. By verbal learning, then, we mean to refer more to content than to a distinct process.

While exploring, and to some extent manipulating, may certainly apply to lower forms of animal life, verbal learning and thinking are of small consequence except in man. A spoken word can come to serve as the signal, or Sc for a response where the subject is a lower animal, but the process of creating a large repertoire of meaningful signals in this way is a laborious one. In the end only man appears to be able to learn enough symbols and then to relate and to organize them into abstract concepts so that the process becomes of major significance in his behavior.

Formal education (or regular school work) is devoted almost entirely to verbal learning. Almost the whole educational effort is directed toward the acquisition of knowledge and the mastery of skills in communicating. Such learning may include the use of a variety of symbols and is by no means confined to the individual's native language; knowledge and skill in the use of numbers rivals in importance the use that may be made of a particular language of words. This is especially true if the content of the knowledge encompassed happens to be in some field of science.

While words and numbers are the chief media for communicating, there are other means of expression and some of these tend to carry us beyond comfortable limits if we are to focus upon verbal types of learning. A few occupations and professions are to be found that demand special motor skills, which may yet be highly symbolic, but use neither words nor numbers, as the basic skill. These include among others, music (both composing and playing), artistic expression as in painting, sculpture, and dancing. While games and various sports make relatively little use of symbolic processes, there is not always a total absence of these. In athletics, emphasis is placed upon motor skills not involving directly the muscles used in linguistic expression yet organized games, especially, make great use of signals (verbal and signs) that serve as cues for the responses that are to be made. It is not easy for an individual who is badly handicapped in the use of language or other symbols, for whatever reason—low ability, sensory defects, etc.—to become an effective member of a team.

FACTORS INFLUENCING EFFICIENCY IN VERBAL LEARNING

Ebbinghaus was able to state several factors that influenced the efficiency of learning. His attention was focused primarily upon memorizing, but he did not neglect entirely retention and use. Briefly, he noted (1) that distribution of practice sometimes led to more rapid learning; (2) that the amount of material could be so great as to retard the process; (3) that meaningful material was acquired more rapidly than nonsense material; and (4) that the amount of interference varied with materials. These are only part of the observations that he made in a brillant beginning upon the psychology of learning. It will be recognized that these findings readily lend themselves to practical use if the greatest efficiency in learning effort is to be applied.

Factors that influence efficiency in learning are sometimes grouped under three general headings. They include factors having to do (1) with the organism, (2) those primarily related to the nature of the materials, (3) still others belonging to the environment, but not an integral part of the learning material. By first grouping the problems in this manner, it becomes possible to move systematically to further fractioning of the problems involved in the efficiency of learning.

ISOLATING FACTORS

Learning experiments have been designed with a view to tracing out the relative influence of a great number of factors and this is scientifically useful. However, there is always the danger of applying the findings too universally or generalizing too widely. Even the simplest learning takes place under the complexity of many interacting factors and processes. At a given time, one particular factor may become dominant and then it may appear that this is the most crucial factor in learning only to give way under a different set of conditions where this same factor seems to fall into relative insignificance. In other words, there are many factors that may emerge in peculiar circumstances, any one of which may become very conspicuous. Take an example: learning can be decreased at an alarming rate with a temporary deprivation of oxygen. Routines that are greatly overlearned and performed with ease and efficiency may tax the pilot beyond his ability when he gets to altitudes where his supply of oxygen is insufficient. Alertness and skilled performance become impossible for all individuals at high altitudes unless there is some artificial means of getting adequate oxygen into the blood stream. Yet it is not usual, perhaps not actually necessary, to set up a control for oxygen consumption in a typical learning or performance experiment.

Aside from transitory changes in the organism that may have a detrimental influence upon learning rate, it is obvious that there are other more persistent conditions making for variations both between different organisms and for the same individual after basically altered capabilities. Included among variables from person to person are intelligence, general energy and vigor, sex, age, and a number of additional factors having their origin in both heredity and environmental conditions. Then there are sometimes relatively permanent changes for the same individual, unfortunately most of them detrimental ones, such as brain damage resulting from accident or disease, wasting diseases which gradually sap the individual of energy, as well as the slow progression of aging. There is a very considerable knowledge about the effects of drugs upon the organism as reflected in changes in learning rate. Some of the changes may be transitory, while some drugs, if used continuously, produce a permanent loss in efficiency. None is known to have a lasting and beneficial effect save those associated with nutritional needs, which may include minerals, hormones, and vitamins. A few drugs, caffeine being one, seem to lead to a temporary improvement in learning rate. Most of the drugs that give a positive lift for a short time appear to result in a subsequent depressive effect that more than neutralizes the earlier gain. Learning experiments have been widely used upon both lower animals and people as a means of evaluating the effects of therapeutic drugs.

Less tangible, but nevertheless important, factors that are to be identified with the organism are motives, interests, sets, and general attitudes. While it is usually conceded that these should be strong for maximum learning, the problem is more involved than may be thought. It is conceivable that one interest interferes with another; that the possession of one attitude blocks the development of another; that a motive or drive may be so intense as to result in overwhelming anxiety. Under exceptional drive, the slightest threat that the goal will not be achieved may decrease efficiency, especially if strict intellectual controls are essential to the learning task.

The factors that we have been dealing with may have their roots in the environment, although we intended to speak of those that also bring about alterations in the organism. There are many environmental factors making for better or poorer learning that do not appear to leave any definite mark upon the organism. The introduction of guidance, tuition, teaching, and general social stimulation may have positive effects although the good intention of the individual who uses these is not a guarantee that results will not fall to the negative side. Extremely intense stimuli may produce consequences that go beyond the distraction influence and eventually operate to change the organism. For example, heat or cold are at first distractors, but if intensity is increased they may reduce the efficiency of sense organs, neural equipment, and muscles, and can cause permanent impairment.

MANIPULATING MATERIAL TO IMPROVE EFFICIENCY

The direct manipulation of the materials with a view to increasing efficiency includes (1) the way practice is distributed, (2) whole versus part learning, (3) the use of a great variety of mnemonic devices intended to help the individual build associations, (4) the grading of material to match the intellectual level of the subject, (5) arranging material suitable for presentation to a particular sense modality such as visually or auditorily.

In addition to the above procedures there are others, such as arranging material in order of difficulty so that simpler things may be mastered before the individual is confronted with the more complex; logical sequence becomes essential for learning some subjects. For example, in mathematics the student often proceeds step by step and progress is scarcely possible without learning many principles in a given order. While much remains to be learned about interference phenomenon,

enough is known that steps can be taken to reduce retroactive and proactive inhibition. Or to state the matter differently, learning that takes
place before or after a given task may serve either to facilitate or to interfere with the process. The broad problem of transfer of training is of importance in formulating sound educational philosophy and procedures.
Although this is by no means a new research area, challenging studies are
still in prospect.

METHODS AND APPARATUS

The methods and procedures that are used in experimenting upon
verbal learning may call for several kinds of equipment for presenting
the stimulus material and for recording the responses made by the subjects. Mechanical devices may be of use for the convenience and accuracy
of performance of both experimenter and subject. Uniformity with regard
to presentation in materials, timing, and recording by use of apparatus
usually adds up to more refinement in experimental procedure. It is
possible to arrange apparatus so that the subject may receive information about his performance while working, or, again, the outcome can
be rather completely withheld from him. It is appropriate to discuss
methods and apparatus together.

Whole Presentation

The method that is perhaps closest to that used in everyday experience,
or especially in the school situation, is to make all the learning material
available to the subject for a given time, after which testing is done. In
the experimental situation, the subject can be given a printed page, or any
amount desired which is to be studied over a determined length of time.
This means that the subject is free to use whatever procedure he thinks
will bring the best results. He may read over the material rapidly time
after time; skim at first and then read carefully; read the whole carefully once and then concentrate upon the content that is considered to be
important or especially difficult. Some subjects will try to memorize
verbatim while others will search for meaning. Still others will spend
considerable time in trying to recite or review. While instruction to study
in a particular way may lead to greater uniformity in the study method
used, the experimenter is not in good position to enforce a given procedure nor is he usually able to know exactly how the subject went about
the task.

There are certain advantages and disadvantages to experimenting in
the ways indicated above. The experimenter may find it pleasant and
even efficient to be able to begin his experiment without having to pro-

cure apparatus which sometimes proves to be expensive and not readily available. He needs only printed matter, a timing device—a watch will do —questions to ask upon the material to be learned, a piece of paper for the answers, and a pencil. A famous psychologist is reputed to have said that a pencil and a piece of paper could constitute a very effective psychological laboratory! He may have been thinking in particular about their usefulness in experimenting upon learning and especially with the so-called whole method.

While it is not intended to imply that this is the best, or even a very desirable, way to do experimental work, yet it should be kept in mind that it is possible to trade advantages for disadvantages as the experimenter moves from simple and direct methods to those that are more complex. Complexity may give the impression of greater scientific sophistication, but it can be illusory. For example, the method that has been indicated is very likely to result in reasonably good motivation and hence desirable coöperation upon the part of the subject. The subject may try to perform at his maximum level of ability since he does not study under the distracting influence of apparatus nor is he forced into a pattern with regard to tempo or other externally controlled factors that may disorganize and disturb him. At the same time there are disadvantages that may not make it desirable to use the pencil-paper method in studying some problems. Different subjects will use a variety of approaches, so methods of study cannot be satisfactorily compared. It may not be that the abilities of subjects can be safely compared since any difference in performance might well be a reflection of a more or less efficient method instead of reflecting a difference in learning ability. Relatively few experiments are to be found in which this method has been used.

Serial Presentation

By serial presentation it is meant that the material is given item by item and in a controlled sequence of time. The subject ordinarily does not have before him more than one item at a time. It would be possible to present items in serial fashion and then not remove each one before the next item is presented. Experimentalists have generally followed the practice of presenting an item only after the preceding one has been removed. This allows for systematic control over the time devoted to studying each item and review is effectively prevented, at least insofar as going over the stimulus material while it is under sensory observation is concerned. Associations involving memory and imagination for items experienced earlier are still a possibility. The time that can be devoted to this is limited by the rate of presentation.

It is clear that many subjects actively work at incorporating successive items into relationship; thus each item becomes endowed with additional meaning as successive ones appear. This associative process can be reduced if the items come in rapid succession. Even nonsense syllables are quickly organized and these, apparently and inevitably, come to be associated with each other and take on some kind of meaning. Therefore, nonsense syllables soon lose some of the qualities that led Ebbinghaus to consider them valuable for his purposes.

Attention is called to the fact that the sensory avenue that is to be used may force a particular kind of presentation. Some kinds of serial presentation can scarcely be avoided if the material is to be presented auditorially. An attempt to present a large amount of material simultaneously by sound would result in a conglomeration of incomprehensible noises. The whole or complete presentation method is practically limited to use with vision.

There are a number of variations of what is essentially serial presentation and each may have certain advantages and make possible the use of several types of apparatus. It is obvious that presentation for serial learning may be about as simple and uncomplicated as any procedure in learning could be. Words or nonsense syllables can be read to the subject, or again cards having the material written or printed upon them can be flashed manually in front of the subject one by one. Control of the time factor can be reasonably satisfactory if the rate of presentation is practiced before the experiment is started. More sophisticated procedures may involve use of memory drums, tachistoscopic presentation, or film in which material is projected upon a screen.

Anticipation Method

The anticipation method means that an item is presented and the subject is expected to give the next item that is to appear. This is, in a sense, a variation of the serial method. Orderly sequence is, of course, required and assumes somewhat greater significance than in some of the other serial procedures. Evidence of learning is in terms of correct anticipation of the exact item that is to follow. The uniqueness of this method has to do primarily with the way testing is done rather than in the mode of presentation. The testing for the amount that has been learned is carried on continuously as the learning takes place after there has been a single first exposure to all the items. This method is sometimes referred to as the prompting method—each item is to serve as a signal to prompt the subject so he may give the next item in the way that a dramatics coach prompts his actors. Should the actor forget, the first word or two of a passage is spoken to prompt him so he can go ahead with the dialogue.

The director of a drama will naturally be disappointed when performance night comes if each player has not learned his lines well enough so that every speech on the stage is adequate in serving to prompt the right player to say the appropriate next words. The success of the production in the theater is largely determined by the quickness and smoothness that each cue is picked up so an orderly sequence of players and speeches build up to the climax of the play. Accuracy becomes the usual means of measuring the learning in the experiment but promptness may also have some uses in understanding how learning takes place or in understanding the personality of the learner himself.

In a strict sense, the anticipation method is practically limited to rote memorizing. This method is not of much use if the primary goal of the learning is to obtain logical relationships beyond immediate occurrences in time and space. Logical organizing tends to be prevented. Nevertheless, the anticipation method becomes useful in the hands of the experimentalist and has advantages over all other methods in the study of certain problems. The progression of learning is clearly apparent and easily read graphs of learning curves can be constructed. The method lends itself about equally well to short experiments or in those that may be extended over a considerable period of time. The criteria to which the learning is to be brought can be precisely stated and it is clearly manifest when that condition has been met.

In some learning experiments the testing procedure gets badly mixed with the learning process. This may lead to overlearning, or the examiner may think that learning to a given criterion has been met, only to find that the subject must be exposed to the material again after having experienced some advantage, or possibly disturbing influence, growing out of the testing procedure itself.

When other methods have been used, a subject may conclude that he knows a list of fifteen nonsense syllables after having studied them during five presentations, but then he ends up by giving only thirteen correctly. Complications arise about how to proceed next. If it has been desired that subjects learn the list to the criterion of one correct recall, then the subject has opportunity to do some further studying while he has unsuccessfully attempted to give his answer. Another subject may be more cautious and he does not declare his readiness to be tested until he has overlearned. That is, he waits before risking the test until he has studied the list for twelve presentations, whereas he was actually in position to reproduce accurately after the tenth presentation. Obviously confusing variables enter if the purpose is to compare subjects.

The anticipation method is excellent for studying the factor of position in the series. Here again, there is a good record of progression in learning. The number of failures for each trial becomes a matter of record and so is the first trial in which each item has been given correctly. Should the experimenter choose to use a more stringent criterion, say two or three correct successive trials, this too is readily ascertained while the experiment is kept in progress. A test for strength of the learning as revealed by retention and recall can be made at any subsequent time. Nor is review by the subjects, either by intention or accident, likely to be of much importance when the anticipation method is used.

Paired Associates

A similar but slight variation of the anticipation procedure is known as the method of paired associates. Here learning material is presented on the first trial in pairs instead of a running series as described in the anticipation method. Unless the pairs occur in an altered sequence, the net effect is almost identical with the anticipation method, for here the subject will eventually make some connections that are determined by position or sequence. As usually practiced in experimental work the pairs are presented by a previously established random order. A popular procedure is to draw from a table of random numbers after each pair has been assigned a given number. Some experimenters prefer to systematize the positions, arranging in advance the lists so that rotation occurs on each successive trial according to a known pattern. Statisticians seem to prefer randomization because mathematical assumptions concerning probability are more satisfactorily met. The effect of position as well as other possible advantages related to the whole associative process are merely assumed to be unknown. It is certainly conceivable that particular words may be much more easily learned if meaningful associations already exist between them and this can represent an unknown and uncontrollable factor before the experiment starts.

INSTRUMENTATION

It will be recognized that psychological apparatus may be used as an aid to presentation for each of the methods reviewed. However, the advantages to be gained by the use of apparatus are few, if any, in the *complete method*. In the method of *paired associates* some advantage may be possible by use of a mechanical device for presentation, but the task of preparing materials may be great and this may partially offset the advantages. There seem to be distinct advantages gained by use of timed mechanical devices when the usual *anticipation method* is used. Wherever randomization of stimulus material is to be used, adaptation for mechanical presentation is likely to be complicated and may not be worth the effort. If the apparatus used permits manual arrangement of the material between trials, as in rearranging cards upon which the material is printed, it is not necessary to reproduce a complete set of material that is to be used for every new trial or each successive subject.

Four rather common procedures for preparing and presenting learning material are as follows: The first situation in which printed matter, such as a page of a book, may be used needs no elaboration. This can be used only with the complete or whole method. By use of suitable apparatus, the image of a printed page may be projected upon a screen and then used in a group experiment. The second procedure involves the use of cards. After the learning material is properly arranged on cards they can be presented in at least three ways: (1) manually, (2) card flash apparatus, and (3) by use of a projector. Manual presentation is scarcely desirable if great accuracy in timing is essential, and therefore this method is to be avoided in most research efforts. It may be adequate for purposes of class demonstration and for teaching purposes.

An early apparatus for presenting learning material provided for cards with a hole through them being strung on a rod. By mechanical means the rod was withdrawn allowing the cards to drop one by one so the material printed on each was exposed in serial fashion card after card. Accuracy in timing was in gross terms at best and the distracting factor was considerable. The falling cards undoubtedly disturbed the subject and thus may have introduced an anxiety factor that was unsatisfactorily controlled from subject to subject. However, an obvious advantage was that the cards could be arranged in any order for each presentation.

While the use of a projector may enable the experimenter to avoid some of the disadvantages of the card flashing apparatus, other difficulties arise and not too much is gained over the manual procedure. Timing is still handled by the experimenter as successive cards must be placed in the projector. The subject may be less disturbed by the machinery and the experimenter if the learning material is seen on a screen. The subject is not obliged or perhaps in position, in this case, to see any of the manipulations of the experimenter. This procedure may involve the use of fairly expensive equipment, a large and partially darkened room which should also exclude random noises. While these may sound like modest requirements, the use of a projector is, nevertheless, not always very practical. Under crowded conditions a suitable room is not always available, especially if only one or a few subjects are to be run at a time and as a result the room is kept in reserve from other uses while many hours are used in collecting data,

It is possible to make apparatus with mechanical or electronic controls that avoid most of the objections that have been raised in our discussion. Such apparatus seems to be not too readily available commercially. Many types of experiments can be carried out with reasonable convenience if the material is first mounted upon cards for some kind of display. A small enclosed box with a light in it and a slot through which the card can be slipped and with a suitable headpiece that fits the contour of the face and having an opening before each eye can serve very satisfactorily in

Fig. 14.1. Memory drum. (Courtesy C. H. Stoelting Co.)

many experiments. The timing factor is unlikely to be controlled as well as desired. It is possible to have essentially this same equipment but to build a mechanical device for the exposure of the cards with greater timing precision.

Perhaps the most widely used procedure in learning experiments makes use of some type of memory drum. The term *memory drum* seems to encompass several devices that do not involve a drum in any strict sense of the word. Early memory drums were constructed primarily for the purpose of obtaining accuracy in timing. In general, this factor is very well controlled when several of the devices are used since most of them are now electrically driven. This means that they are approximately as reliable in keeping time as an electric clock. One objection to most of the earlier devices—and this still remains a problem with some of the newer ones—is that there may be noise associated with the operation. Convenience and flexibility in the arrangement of material is sometimes awkward. The Ranschburg apparatus permitted the typing or printing of material on a disk. Then the disk was turned so that one item was exposed at a time through a window-like slot. Any new arrangement of material involved a change of disks.

Where a kymograph is used there must be a shield and a slot arranged so that the learning material is exposed with the turning of the drum. A larger amount of material can be arranged on a long roll of paper, which is then rolled off from one drum to another. An auxiliary drum that is placed some distance from the primary drum where the power is applied may be used. Then the learning material is placed upon what becomes a continuous belt that runs around both drums. This has the advantage of allowing for a great variety of material to be arranged in advance and of course makes possible variable arrangement of the same material. Blank space between the materials enables the experimenter to stop the apparatus and start it again when a change in arrangement of material occurs or when a new task is to be given.

BASIC VARIABLES IN HUMAN LEARNING

We shall undertake to discuss only a few of the more important variables in learning, and in this way indicate what have been and remain the primary problems that experimentalists working in this area try to solve. Postman and Egan (5) group variables under three headings having to do with (1) the activities or materials learned, (2) the conditions under which the learning takes place, and (3) the characteristics of the subjects. "Measurable performance depends on *what* is learned, *how* it is learned, and *who* learns it." While we are not trying to follow a scheme strictly consistent with what they suggest, nevertheless, the student might keep continuously in mind that the complicated matters that the experimentalist sets forth are still intended to have bearing upon *what, how,* and *who* in ways not entirely different from what would be the purposes of the journalist who seeks to tell a factual but meaningful story about an incident. It will be immediately apparent (as illustrated in the next paragraph) that we do not discuss material very long without implications about *how* it is used and *who* does the using.

Meaningfulness

Since Ebbinghaus' time meaningful material has been known to be easier to memorize to a given criterion than material having limited or no meaning. It should be kept in mind that meaningfulness is not only a characteristic of the material but must take into account the individual who studies, and to some extent under what conditions or how he studies. While nonsense syllables by definition are without meaning, this is not quite true to the extent of one hundred percent. What is meaningless for one individual is sometimes filled with meaning for the next person. The symbols he uses in complex calculations are filled with meaning to the mathematician but may be so many nonsensical scribbles to someone not trained in mathematics. Furthermore, even nonsense syllables rapidly take on some kind of meaning to all people after they are used. Presumably the highly intelligent and imaginative individual is unable to inhibit associations that are connected with each syllable. Exclusion of meaning does not seem to be a possibility—voluntary control to exclude meaning is not adequate to the purpose for the very attempt to prevent the material from attaining meaning becomes an investment in meaning.

It is no longer a fruitful problem in the psychology of learning to set up an experiment for the purpose of establishing that meaningful material is acquired more rapidly than that without meaning. The task has become one of greater refinement; thus investigators are now interested in how closely meaningfulness is correlated with the learning rate. There remains interest in determining whether greater speed can be expected after an attempt is made to impart richness of content or intensity of affect to the material that is to be learned. In other words, it has become more appropriate to move along to finer experimental discriminations in the hope of establishing more reliable relationships. Then the experimenter is in position to make accurate predictions and to exercise better control procedures.

Affect

There have been many experiments performed with a view to determining how emotionally loaded material may affect learning and forgetting rate. While these studies have usually been in terms of materials classified into pleasant, unpleasant, and neutral as to affective value, there is some doubt that these are safely placed upon a single continuum. The pleasant and unpleasant may not be poles apart, for there are many examples of experiences that hold a little of both. Nor is it likely that this kind of mixture results in a neutral tone midway between the extremes. In fact, some intense emotional experiences give rise to feelings of both happiness and sadness as in almost all great triumphs. Mixed feeling might almost be said to be the rule rather than the exception. Sometimes when confronted with the necessity of action, the person may become a victim of indecision and vacillation.

At one time or another most people have been held in the vise of compulsive doubt—paralyzed when action is needed. It is improbable that an experiment will be set up in which the learning material produces any such strong reactions in the subject. Here again is one of the difficulties in working with the problem, for there is not a consistent and satisfactory relationship between the intensity of emotional loading, presumed to be associated with the material under consideration, and the reaction produced in the subject. Emotional loading as applying to experimental material is likely to produce very mild emotional reactions. It is scarcely feasible to experiment with human reactions that are comparable to the emotionally shocking experiences of the type that all people encounter at some time during life.

It may not come as a surprise that any specific material is difficult to find that is either *pleasant* or *unpleasant* for every subject that is used. The affective tone has been determined primarily by previous experiences, and the variability of experiences from person to person makes it improbable that any word, for example, is responded to pleasantly by all people. Even words such as *flower, love, father, mother* have unpleasant associations for some individuals. The problem of finding words that have only unpleasant associations appears to be somewhat easier. At any rate large numbers of people have voted unanimously that a few words— *vomit, death, crazy*—are unpleasant. However, it might be desirable not only to classify the material as to pleasantness-unpleasantness but also to equate these with regard to intensity. Thus, any advantage in learning rate for pleasant material, and this has been a rather consistent result in experiments, could not be due to intensity differences. The fact seems to be that both pleasant and unpleasant materials are learned faster than materials approaching complete neutrality. It is possible to use material that has already been evaluated for emotional tone (but of course there is some risk that subjects will not concur one hundred percent), or again have the subjects classify the material as to pleasant or unpleasant after exposure. This last choice runs the risk that not all subjects will agree. There is some chance that the learning experience itself may produce a change in the subject's evaluation of the material. Familiarity, complexity, and previous richness of associations are factors having known influence upon the speed with which material may be learned. There are many potential variables that must be taken into account if the experimenter is to place confidence in his results as varying only because of the emotional loading of materials.

In our discussion we have been considering the effects produced by the emotional loading of the material or the reaction in the subject as a consequence of that loading. Closely related, and yet a different problem, has been that in which stress is induced in the subject by some procedure not associated with the materials under study. While some of these experiments are appropriately discussed when dealing with emotions, it should be indicated that learning experiments have been very numerous where performance has been undertaken under imposed stress. This has no doubt been the case because measures of learning have been refined to a reasonably good degree, and also because the experimenter may have wanted to study the relationship between emotions and intellectual functioning, the learning process thus being considered a good one to reflect efficiency of intellectual performance. The disruptive influence of stress growing out of different types of emotions have come in for some study but the results are not easy to interpret. Again, it is difficult to provoke fear, anger, love, rage, and so forth with certainty that the desired emotion and none other actually resulted and that it was also similar to that experienced under ordinary life events.

PSYCHOANALYTIC THEORY ABOUT THE UNPLEASANT

It is an important part of psychoanalytic theory that unpleasant experiences of life may be suppressed. Thus it is consistent with this general concept that greater difficulty will be encountered when learning the unpleasant. Even more crucial to the theory is that forgetting should take place faster and more thoroughly for the unpleasant than for the pleasant. In general, the experimental results seem to support these deductions. Thus the theoretical frame of reference seems to be useful but it remains a problem to determine how these results come about. It should not be concluded that such a phenomenon has found no claim for explanation among those holding to theory that differs from the analytic frame of reference.

One rather unsophisticated way that attempts have been made to verify the psychoanalytic hypothesis concerning forgetfulness has been to ask individuals to write down all their experiences over a given period of life. Then the individual classifies his experiences as to whether they were pleasant or unpleasant. These investigations reveal a clear advantage of pleasant experiences being recalled a greater number of times. However, criticism has been raised that the individual was lacking in criterion as to pleasantness and unpleasantness. Then a given individual might have had many more pleasant experiences in the first place; therefore greater recall would necessarily be expected by chance alone.

SERIAL POSITION

Determination of the influence upon rate of learning that is due to the position of the item in a series has been the purpose of a large number of experiments. These studies may have grown out of concern over practical aspects of the problem, but more important has been the hope that these studies might shed light upon more basic and theoretical problems of learning. The practical problem that arises is obvious to many people since it is rather common knowledge that impressions left from the first and last of events occurring in series tend to be more vivid than the intermediate experiences. Thus a speaker who must perform along with several others may hope to maneuver so he can talk first or last. What has been called the *laws of primacy* and the *law of recency* have to do with the advantage here but do not seem to be an adequate explanation. At any rate, firstness and lastness with regard to time advantage alone can hardly be expected to have much bearing upon the stronger impression that remains if the time interval between learning all items is no more than a few minutes apart.

SERIAL POSITION AND WIDELY SEPARATED EXPERIENCES

The first and last items in a short list of material to be presented for rote memorizing presents a circumstance different from experiences widely separated by time, such as the advantages for memory of childhood experiences over those events that happen during the middle years of life. Yet some of the basic principles may well be operating for each condition. Stated in nontechnical terms, the items in the middle of a series, or the experiences of the middle age of life, appear to get crowded out by those on either side.

It becomes a task to determine whether this is a phenomenon that operates essentially during the learning process or whether the "crowding out" takes place slowly and subtly during the period of retention. The evidence seems to suggest that both processes operate; learning is more difficult for items standing in the middle of a series and retention, as determined by later recall for these items, reveals a still further effect from the ravages of time and events. In the case of a short series or list of items, the differential level of acquisition is largely a reflection of greater ease of learning items at either end of the list. Possibly more widely separated events in time suffer more disadvantage because of interferences subsequent to the learning that operate to modify retention.

From Fig. 14-2 a good picture is obtained of what takes place as learning progresses in learning a list of twelve items by the anticipation method. A skewed curve reveals that those items standing in the third quarter of the list are the most difficult ones to master. All people seem to perform in a similar manner. The item that is most difficult to learn, other factors than position assumed to be under control and equal, stands about two-thirds through the list. There is also stability in this for lists of various lengths extending at least from those as short as five or six items to those of eighteen.

A review of literature reveals remarkably consistent results with regard to the influence of serial position. If subjects are allowed to recall items in any order they please, the last few items are usually given first and then there is a tendency to revert to the first item, after which progression is in the order that the items were presented.

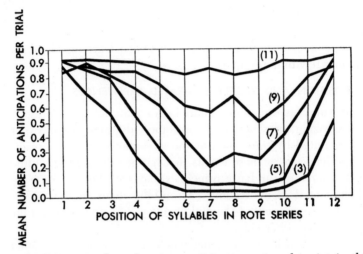

Fig. 14.2. Mean number of correct anticipations at each point in the rote series for five levels of mastery. As learning progresses the U shaped curve is gradually eliminated until the criterion of 100% anticipation is met. (From Ward, L. B., "Reminiscence and rote learning," *Psy. Monogr.* 49 (1937), 220.)

Shanklin (6) derived a formula by logic for predicting about the relative difficulty of learning items standing in each position in lists of various lengths. The formula was $I = 2 \log P(N - P) - 1$ where N equals the number of items and P equals the ordinal position of the item. I represents inhibition of whatever nature. Applying this formula to his own data and to published experimental results he found that correlation between obtained results and prediction ranged between .73 and .99 with all except 9 of 51 correlations standing above .85. Whatever may be the reason for the relative difficulty pertaining to each position there is consistency in it as indicated by the correlations. The regular appearance of the U-shaped learning curve or the bow-shaped curve (depending upon whether correct answers or errors are recorded and graphed) seems to be adequately established as factual. In the next section will be found some of the speculations that have been advanced for explaining the obtained results.

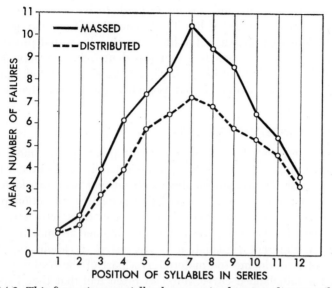

Fig. 14.3. This figure is essentially the same in shape as the one taken from Ward's experiment, except failures are tabulated along the ordinate instead of correct responses. The general shape of the curve is similar for both massed and distributed practice. The relative difficulty of items at each position remains the same. (From Hovland, C. I., "Experimental Studies in rote learning theory," *J. Exp. Psychol.* 23 (1938), 178.)

SERIAL POSITION: RETROACTIVE AND PROACTIVE INHIBITION

The explanation for differential difficulty that results from position in a series has usually been based upon what is labeled as *retroactive* and *proactive* inhibition. Retroactive inhibition means that each item that occurs following exposure of an earlier one acts to reduce the ease with which the former item can be recalled. In other words learning a new item means that recall for older material becomes more difficult. Interference operates backwards over previously learned things. Thus a rest period in which the subject has turned to a very different kind of learning material results in less decay or loss of retention than does a period of equal length devoted to a study of similar materials. The early experiment reported by Jenkins and Dallenbach (4) indicated the relatively good retention during a period of sleep as measured by subsequent recall.

Proactive inhibition operates in the opposite direction. The interference is forward. Exposure to one nonsense syllable becomes a barrier to learning the succeeding one and this effect tends to be accumulative as the subject proceeds through the list. The assumption, if we may judge from the discussions that appear in the literature, has been that proactive and retroactive inhibitions each has an equivalent influence upon learning. Although this idea has not been clearly and definitely stated, apparently earlier investigators assumed that proactive and retroactive inhibition should be equal.

POSITION OF MOST DIFFICULT ITEM

The puzzling and very consistent result points to the most difficult item to learn in a given list as being approximately two-thirds of the way through the list. The reason for this result has not been satisfactorily explained. If it could be demonstrated that proactive inhibition produces a greater adverse influence upon learning than does retroactive inhibition, this could conceivably result in the obtained asymmetrical curve. However, a different explanation is suggested. It might be that the necessity of reproducing the material as a part of the testing procedure leads to the unbalanced curve. Subjects often feel that they know each item in a list after reading them over. Once the necessity of written or oral reproduction is demanded, part of the items may be lost to memory. In this event, a second effect not unlike proactive inhibition again exerts interference in a forward direction.

In Figure 14.4 a schematic diagram is shown of how adjacent and remote associations might operate to increase or decrease the rate of learning for each item. This drawing is taken from Hull (3), who constructed it in an attempt to illustrate how remote items span the items in the central portion of the list and presumably these by-passing associations lead to interference. Another way to look at it would be to conceive of the difficulty in retaining identity of the items in the middle because of the crowding out by items on either side. The items on either side might be said to operate to distract the subject from those in the middle to a greater extent than would be the case of those standing at either end of the list. In this case it would be difficult to conceive of position to right or left having much advantage so that a symmetrical curve should result when undertaking recall.

If subjects are left to their own study habits it was shown by Hornick (2) that more time will be spent in studying items that stand in the middle portion of the series than those items at either first or last position. Presumably this reflects some awareness upon the part of the subject that items in the middle section of the series are more difficult to learn and he compensates by devoting more time to them.

It is assumed that retroactive and proactive inhibition have only detrimental effect. It is noteworthy that Underwood (7), after performing a large number of experiments dealing with rote learning of serially arranged material, was led to conclude that most of the interference giving rise to forgetting was due to proactive inhibition. He raised a question

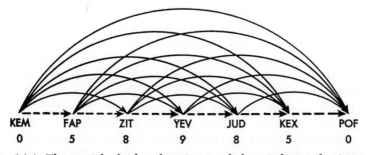

KEM	FAP	ZIT	YEV	JUD	KEX	POF
0	5	8	9	8	5	0

Fig. 14.4. The straight broken line is intended to indicate the immediate excitatory tendency, while the solid lines represent how remote associations may occur. (From Hull, C. L., *Psychological Review* 42 (1935), 502.)

as to whether retroactive inhibition had any significant effect in delayed recall. Underwood and other experimentalists have been attracted to experiments upon serial learning in the hope that in these simplified situations factors might be isolated and investigated so that broad and important descriptive and explanatory principles of learning might be exposed.

TRANSFER OF TRAINING

It is possible that retroactive and proactive inhibitions are of similar general nature as transfer of training. There are, however, differences, and the terms have not been used interchangeably. Transfer effects are said to be both positive and negative—previous learning under some circumstances facilitate the acquisition of new learning material and sometimes the earlier experience seems to furnish a barrier to further learning.

Studies of transfer of training have a long history in the development of psychology. Studies pertaining to this problem were among the earliest performed by experimental psychologists, and we find that William

James set up an experiment to see what the effects would be upon further memorizing if he went through a rigorous period of training. As a pretest he memorized stanzas of a long poem and kept a record of the time required. He then memorized a large number of stanzas after which he timed himself while memorizing stanzas matched with those in the pretest. He found practically no difference, whereupon he was lead to take a skeptical position about the claimed advantages that might be expected from "memory training." This was an important experimental chink in the wall of what was known of as "faculty psychology." It had been common to discuss memory, reasoning, and imagination as though these were special entities or capacities. This ideology appears to have been a hold-over from phrenology, since special localization in the brain for each of these functions was ordinarily implied.

It had been persistently held that courses like mathematics, Latin, Greek, logic, and some others were especially valuable in teaching the student to observe accurately and to reason well. It was assumed that achievement in these subjects would necessarily strengthen the individual in the desirable intellectual traits. A multitude of experiments were performed around the turn of the century intended to test the hypothesis that training in one subject strengthened the student in other subjects. Investigators separated into two camps—some held that only identical elements that were found to be common to the different situations was the best that could be expected from transfer, others held that there was a transfer of general principles, that methods of study, attitudes, habits, and general skills could be developed through studying certain subjects and then made use of in a variety of situations. Thorndike was the spokesman for advocating that the best way to learn a given subject was to study it directly. Thus he was challenging all of the classical courses if the defense made for them was that such study strengthened the student in other fields. Consequently, he would not advise the student to study Latin if his objective was to master the English language. While there might be identical elements in each language, Thorndike held that it would be wasteful of energy to study with a view to profiting by transfer. Judd took the position that many general principles did transfer. To some extent these arguments found expression in the way school curricula were made and the educational philosophy that pervaded the profession of teaching.

The original cause of the argument about transfer gradually dropped out of sight. The position of all the experimenters shifted away from the notion that one subject should be studied because of its value in learning some other subject. Efficiency is lost whenever study is not directly upon the problems to be solved. Yet evidence has not been forthcoming that all subjects have the same transfer value. Rather the facts seem to be that some subjects have more potential for transfer value, either upon the basis of identical elements or upon that of general principles, than do other subjects. Transfer is greatly influenced by both teaching methods

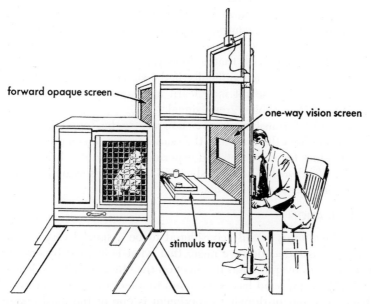

forward opaque screen

one-way vision screen

stimulus tray

Fig. 14.5. The University of Wisconsin apparatus for presenting discrimination problems to monkeys. The food tray is mobile and can be pushed forward so the monkey can reach the food. There are food wells in the tray and these can be covered so the problem is to choose which one to uncover. (From Harlow, H. F., "The formation of learning sets," *Psy. Rev.* 56 (1949), 51-65.)

and the manner of study. It is not believed that psychologists have ever claimed that the mastery of mathematical principles would have no wider usefulness (or transfer value) than the master of some special skill, such as that of playing basketball or using a carpenter's tool. This does not mean that the training of memory or reasoning ability is necessarily a good argument for mastering mathematical principles. It might be supposed that those who believed that some subjects should be taught in school instead of others were right, but they based their arguments upon the wrong premises.

Transfer effects may be in terms of either the stimulus or the response. Wherever a shift is required by the situation and former learning must be suppressed in order that a new habit be formed, the negative effect in transfer becomes noticeable. For example, if a rat learns to reach its goal by turning to the right in a maze, but the alley to the right is closed by a partition and an alley to the left opened so the goal can be reached by making a left turn, the rat is slow to learn the new pathway. The slowness is greater than would have been the case if the rat had never run a maze before. Of course, negative transfer effects extend beyond situations that stand in direct contradiction to earlier situations. If the rat has learned to approach food after being given a green light signal and to flee from an electric shock that follows the flashing of a red light, it is easy to appreciate the rat's difficulty if the signals are reversed. It is not so readily seen that the rat may learn an avoidance response faster if orange is used than a blue-green signal.

Implications of transfer phenomenon are to be found in many discussions throughout the book and the reader is also directed to the recommended reading for more detailed experiments upon this broadly significant topic. Woodworth and Schlosberg (8) devote a section in their book to designs of transfer experiments.

CROSS-EDUCATION

Cross-education is usually considered to be a special case of transfer effects. By cross-education we mean that what is learned by one side of the body crosses over and has its effect on the other side. Thus, learning a skill with the right hand has been found to affect the performance of the left hand. The mirror-drawing experiment is one of the most commonly used in such experiments. First the subject may try to trace a star that can be seen in a mirror and under the circumstance that he cannot see his hand while he works. This first effort becomes the pre-test, after which no further practice is made with the hand first used. Then the subject is given practice with the other hand and this is continued until a degree of skill has been reached. Then the star is traced by using the "untrained" hand and the result compared with the pre-test performance. It is a regular result that some improvement has taken place. Presumably there has been transfer across neural pathways from one side of the body to the other. The nerve centers in the brain that control the left hand are on the opposite side of the brain from those that control the right hand. These studies have been elaborated upon not only for the light assumed to be thrown upon transfer phenomenon and the psychology of learning, but also in the hope that they might lead to a better understanding of the neural processes involved and how learning may give rise to changes in the organism. A variety of similar so-called bilateral experiments can be found in the literature. In these studies comparisons may be made between earlier performances with the left foot, let us say, and later performance following training of the right or left hand.

Fig. 14.6. Mirror drawing is an often-used task in studying transfer effects. A screen must be used to shield the hand from the visual field. (Courtesy Lafayette Instrument Co.)

SUGGESTED READINGS

Hilgard, Ernest R. *Introduction to Psychology*, pp. 281-297. New York: Harcourt, Brace, 1957.

Bugelski, B. R. *The Psychology of Learning*, pp. 382-416, 449-479. New York: Henry Holt, 1956.

Postman, Leo, and Egan, James P. *Experimental Psychology*, pp. 312-444. New York: Harper, 1949.

Underwood, Benton J. *Experimental Psychology*, pp. 281-322, 466-554. New York: Appleton-Century-Crofts, 1949.

Garrett, Henry E. *Great Experiments in Psychology*, pp. 83-100. New York: Appleton-Century-Crofts, 1951.

Andrew, T. G. *Methods of Psychology*. Buxton: "Studying Memory and Thinking," pp. 64-95. New York: John Wiley, 1948.

Woodworth, Robert S., and Schlosberg, Harold. *Experimental Psychology*, pp. 695-732. New York: Henry Holt, 1954.

McGeoch, John A., and Irion, Arthur L. *The Psychology of Human Learning,* pp. 89-137, 299-515. New York: Longmans, Green, 1952.

Stolurow, Lawrence M. *Readings in Learning,* pp. 194-238. New York: Prentice-Hall, 1953.

Stevens, S. S. (ed.). *Handbook of Experimental Psychology.* Hovland: "Human Learning and Retention," pp. 613-689. New York: John Wiley, 1951.

Osgood, Charles E. *Method and Theory in Experimental Psychology,* pp. 495-600. New York: Oxford University Press, 1953.

REFERENCES

1. Burtt, Harold E. "An experimental study of early childhood," in Dennis, Wayne (ed.). *Reading in Child Psychology,* pp. 237-248. New York: Prentice-Hall, 1951.

2. Hornick, Richard J. *Comparison of Rote Learning in Experimentally Regulated and Subject Controlled Speed of Presentation of Material.* (Thesis) Purdue University, West Lafayette, Ind., 1958.

3. Hull, C. L. "The conflicting psychologies of learning—a way out," *Psychol. Rev.,* 42 (1935), 502.

4. Jenkins, J. G., and Dollenbach, K. M. "Oblivescence during sleep and waking," *Amer. J. Psychol.,* 35 (1924), 605-612.

5. Postman, Leo, and Egan, James P. *Experimental Psychology,* p. 317. New York: Harper, 1949.

6. Shanklin, Henry D. *Inhibition as a Factor in Serial Learning.* (Thesis) Purdue University, West Lafayette, Indiana, 1949.

7. Underwood, Burton J. "Interference and forgetting," *Psychol. Rev.,* 64 (1957), 49-60.

8. Woodworth, Robert S., and Schlosberg, Harold. *Experimental Psychology,* p. 735. New York: Henry Holt, 1954.

15 | EXPERIMENTS IN EXPLORING, MANIPULATING, AND THINKING

INTRODUCTORY REMARKS

There have been complaints that little experimental work has been done on the very important problem of thinking. In one sense there is a basis for this view, for not very many experiments have been performed in which the announced purpose was to experiment upon thinking. However, in a different sense it might be said that few problems have received so much attention by psychologists, other scientists, or philosophers. All experiments except the strictest empirical ones, and perhaps to some extent even these, are performed in order to verify the soundness of speculative thinking.

In educational procedure it is not ordinarily true that much time is spent directly in an effort to improve thinking. Emphasis is placed upon collecting facts, mastering skills, and learning how to use those facts and skills. Nevertheless, in the background is the implicit assumption that improved thinking and problem-solving ability is the most important consequence of effective education. The development of skills and the accumulation of facts alone would leave the individual to operate on an inferior level if he remained unable to do good thinking. There have been formal courses offered in colleges that attack the problem of thinking directly but some critics do not believe these to be effective. Courses in logic are usually taught with the idea in mind that studying examples of sound and faulty thinking should enable the individual to imitate the former and avoid the latter. This direct but somewhat abstract approach does not appeal widely, and presumably such courses have not had a great impact upon education if for no other reason than for want of more people being exposed to them.

Perhaps no one questions the validity of an educational goal that includes an attempt to improve thinking. Disagreement arises about how this goal is to be achieved. In earlier years those who taught Greek and Latin were of the opinion that studying those languages was the best way to learn to think. We have already seen that difficulties do arise if too much is expected of formal discipline and transfer effects. The historian defends still a different procedure, for he believes that man learns how to think problems through to a solution by learning about how others succeeded or failed when trying to solve their problems. Semanticists approach the problem of thinking by revealing how symbols, or languages, are never entirely accurate, that the same word does not mean the same thing to different people.

The student of psychology is almost sure to take still a different path to the goal of sound thinking, for he will point out how man's thinking may go askew because of inaccurate information furnished by the sensory equipment, the inhibitions resulting from sets, the quest for closure, and in general because the wish tends to be father to the thought—that desires and needs take precedent over logic. He is especially concerned with the way motivation, stress, and intense emotions may swamp the intellectual process. And so it goes with a variety of people, all of whom agree that sound thinking is an important goal but who follow diverging paths to reach the goal.

To some extent it may well be that all these ways to problem-solving and effective thinking have something to recommend them. As we have seen, it is dangerous to depend too much upon analogy; we may be disappointed if too much dependency is placed upon expecting solutions in one area of problems to carry over to problems of an entirely different sort. The value is greatly dependent upon how well the gap between is bridged by competent teaching or by the insight of the individual involved.

Without meaning to imply that other attempts to deal with the general subject matter of this chapter have been fruitless, it will be necessary for us to limit our discussion to those experiments presumed to be a part of systematic or scientific psychology in which the announced purpose has bearing upon thinking and related phenomena. We wish to focus upon the way exploring leads to discovery, manipulation to invention, and how both relate to problem-solving, thinking, and reasoning. Maze-learning furnishes good illustrations of what takes place when lower animals (or man) explore in search of goals to meet their needs. Manipulative experiments are well represented by problem-box experiments, and these studies are thought to be of use in trying to analyze the process of inventing. Reasoning involves manipulating, organizing, and relating symbols.

Consistent with our procedure in other chapters, a brief review of some of the early attempts to come to grips with these topics seems to be valuable in orienting to the material. Some of the earliest studies, following in the best traditions of experimental psychology of the time, made primary use of the introspective method. However, the contributions that will be referred to included more than subjective or armchair speculation. The procedure was strictly experimental, but involved self-analysis in terms of minute descriptions of each step taken by the subject as he worked upon the solutions to abstract problems.

IMAGELESS THOUGHT

The individuals who became identified with the "Würzburg School" were among the foremost exponents of experimenting upon the process of thinking. They started out, at least, by a strict use of the introspective methods. By use of carefully trained individuals who analyzed the thought process either during or after attempting to solve abstract problems, these investigators came to the conclusion that images derived from sensory experience were not directly essential to thinking. Of the group closely associated with the Würzburg School, Külpe is best known and he was largely responsible for developing the concepts about "imageless thought."

While the method used by Külpe was very consistent with that advocated by Wundt and others of the time, the findings and implications seemed to extend into new psychological territory. The viewpoint of Külpe and others agreeing with his general approach brought into question some of the basic premises held by those who had been working upon sensory and perceptual problems. This new idea became recognized as a serious challenge to sensation. It will be recalled that sensation was then considered elementary—the cornerstone of psychology by most investigators. To advance the notion that such an important process as thinking could be carried on without the use of sensory image was to reduce the significance of what had been considered basic and central to psychology. Psychologists separated into two camps and there has not been a complete reconciliation since.

We shall not dwell upon the work of the Würzburg School, nor try to evaluate the contributions of those associated with this interesting movement in psychology, beyond indicating that it was of considerable historical significance in initiating work that led many psychologists into areas not previously considered as feasible for scientific study. Writers have pointed out that this movement soon led to a shift away from sensory and content psychology and directed attention toward "act" psychology.

Ultimately the new approach led more or less directly to development of what became known as "functionalism." Extremists among the functionalists, in turn, became known as "behaviorists" and those holding to this view hoped to get away from introspection altogether. The behaviorists stressed study of observable activity and they insisted that introspection should be left to philosophers, claiming that it did not, and could not, serve as an effective method in science. Those strongly influenced by this viewpoint still emphasize the importance of using muscular responses as the avenue of approach to an understanding of thinking, and even of personality. Many psychologists continued to regard themselves as "middle-of-the-road," as Woodworth insisted; yet the chasm between structuralism (the traditional viewpoint) and the new functionalism became deep and wide.

BY WAY OF SUMMARY

Members of the Würzburg School had used the traditional introspective method but focused upon new problems in psychology, and it was not long until the revolution (or evolutionary process, if one prefers) that they initiated swept away the methodology as well as the content. In place of using the introspective method, experimentalists turned in ever-increasing numbers to more objective procedures, using recordings and other means that would enable them to obtain data that could be replicated by any careful investigator. (This is a very bothersome problem for the introspectionist, for if two or more experimentalists disagreed—as they often did—who could say which was right?) In this way, psychology made a rapid transition from dealing with material that by nature tended to be subjective and private to objective data that was placed more definitely in the public domain of science. Some topics that had been considered vital to psychologists were almost by necessity avoided, for they did not readily lend themselves to objective study. There was a very strong urge, common to many psychologists, to make the "new" science of psychology objective and more comparable to the other sciences. The behaviorists became the loudest, if not necessarily the most thoughtful, spokesmen for the new doctrine. They made innovations, abandoned older concepts, and eventually developed a system that did not resemble very much either "act" psychology or anything distinctive to the Würzburg School. Logically enough, if proceeding from their premises, they tried to use responses that could be observed or recorded as an index to thinking. Some of them speculated that it might eventually be possible to observe directly what went on in the nervous system while learning or thinking took place. For the time they were content to focus upon minor muscular movements that involved the vocal organs, eyes, lips, and sometimes the grosser bodily movements. They assumed a correlation between thinking and expressive movements and that observable and recordable responses included the only usable indexes to the thought process.

ANIMAL EXPERIMENTS AND THINKING

The approach to problem-solving made by Thorndike required the animals to manipulate objects, but some investigators would contend that thinking does not have to be postulated as essential in the behavior ob-

Fig. 15.1. Using no other reward than manipulation itself or curiosity, it was found that monkeys would unlatch the puzzle over and over and continue this activity for at least 12 days. (From Harlow, H. F. and Meyer, D. R., "Learning motivated by a manipulation drive," *J. Exp. Psychol.* 40 (1950), 228-234.)

served in the animals. Not long after Thorndike's early experiments, maze-learning became popular in experiments with animals. By special adaptation, either by enlarging the alleys or more often by use of one of the several variations of finger mazes, human subjects could be used. Maze-learning is often spoken of as being exploratory in nature. Possibly it is only superficially so, but certainly there seems to be great similarity between maze-learning and the procedure that a man often uses when exploring. Think of the parallel in geographic explorations or even the procedures of the scientists when taking preliminary steps to scientific discoveries.

Observations and experiments indicate clearly that there is much exploratory behavior in animals and that it is found at all phylogenetic levels. The mobile one-celled animal appears to demonstrate such activity. Many wild animals travel extensively and examine as they go. Not only do they search to obtain food, water, or sex, or to gratify other physical needs, but they may investigate strange or unusual objects or situations in a way that will impress the observer as demonstrating a lively curiosity. Trappers sometimes take advantage of this trait and set their traps so the animal will get caught when circling bait or any strange object that is deliberately placed in the animal's habitat. On the other hand, the trapper must display some shrewdness himself if he is to be successful. He finds it necessary to exercise the greatest precaution to prevent the wary animal from somehow detecting danger and avoiding the trap and yet obtaining the bait. The saying is that the "trapper must be smarter than the animal if he expects to be successful," and this evaluation makes psychological sense.

Among animals there may be little capacity for manipulating objects, although it is possible for many to use feet or mouth to perform skilled acts. Structural limitations exclude the possibility for learning many of the delicate skills that can be performed by the human voice or hands. It is not easy to exaggerate the usefulness of hands as an aid to problem-solving and experimenting. There is no disposition to urge that people think with their hands. Yet, the writer has often remarked that the would-be experimentalist needs to use hands and feet more generously than is congenial to the average student.

With the exception of the primates, few animals have physical structure that begins to approach that of the human hands for purposes of manipulating objects. Turning objects over and over at the physical level is often useful just as the same process is helpful at the abstract level. The more serious limitation of animals in problem-solving is, of course, due to neurological inadequacies. The brain has not developed to the point where it is capable of extensive use of symbols and hence memory, imagination, and thinking are activities that remain on a rudimentary level at best. Man explores more than a physical world, for he examines his perceptions, his social relationships, his ideas and concepts. Even so, the usefulness of the hands in placing things in physical relationship is not to be dismissed lightly. Those who have observed the physicist manipulate balls that may be slipped on rods in order to study the relationship between atoms will find it easy to believe that such physical manipulation is useful in both teaching and thinking. Examples of where lower animals approximate the skills of man in exploratory learning are to be found; their skill in the manipulating of objects and symbols that leads to invention does not begin to rival that of man.

EXTREME DEVIATES WITH REGARD TO THINKING

Those who never develop much proficiency in problem-solving or reasoning are thought of as being feebleminded; those who lose effectiveness because of brain damage or who withdraw from participation to an extreme degree may be classified as psychotic. It is characteristic of some psychotic individuals that they are no longer able or willing to test reality with regard to personal or social relationships and to direct their behavior according to what such exploration would indicate to be appropriate. Others cannot accept a given set of facts and organize them to come out with sound conclusions. Historically, and by definition, psychosis is the word used to indicate that the process of thinking has been severely disrupted. The psychotic individual is not held responsible by society if he pursues strange solutions to problems, draws faulty conclusions, or even commits acts of violence against the dictates of society. What might have been considered as premeditated murder if committed by a "normal" individual may be interpreted as the culmination of wrong associations, illogical deductions, and unfortunate acts—all forgivable in the sight of the law if the individual involved is judged to be insane. If a man cannot make his thinking "come out right" he is not legally responsible for his behavior.

A close relationship is assumed between thought processes and overt behavior and this has status in law whatever may be the judgment of psychologists. Psychologists become intrigued with the legal distinction between deviations in behavior believed to result from faulty thinking in contrast to deviations in behavior that stems from emotional maladjustment. The two kinds of behavior are not equally excusable by law. The validity of the distinctions made by law may one day be tested more thoroughly by experimental psychologists, for the problem is clearly within their domain of study.

CURRENT QUESTIONS ABOUT THINKING

As exciting as the ideas about imageless thought may have been for early investigators, it is scarcely possible to generate an argument even among psychologists over this topic any more. Without a completely satisfactory resolution to the problem, investigators have gone on to ask a different kind of question. Provocative questions of the present may have to do with a great variety of situations, many of them having bearing upon everyday practical problems, but there is not neglect of theoretical problems. Experiments upon thinking may be made in order to determine the consequences of limited information, distorted percepts, predetermined prejudices, socially established "sets," influence of group discussions, and a multitude of personality characteristics, such as rigidity or fearfulness. More or less homogenous subjects can be found who possess the traits or characteristic to be brought under experimental study; some of the conditions mentioned can be experimentally established.

Clinical psychologists may try to find ways to break up the "sets" that his patient has in order to help him "think differently" or to act in new and improved ways. The industrial psychologist may conclude that several individuals working together in a "brain-storming" session can break out of a stagnating and confining rut by reviewing known facts, discussing their significance, and organizing and synthesizing available information, and finally come to generate conclusions that by-pass much tedious and needless experimenting. Crucial problems that do not yield in this way become better identified as the ones that require experimental effort.

In a recent book (1957) Maier (10) has been able to assemble a rather formidable amount of evidence and to set forth convincing results that the industrial application of psychological knowledge that is of greatest usefulness has to do with problem-solving. This book carries the title *Supervisory and Executive Development: A Manual for Role Playing.* In this book the theme is pursued that an individual can be given scientific training that will improve his ability to solve problems. Strong emphasis is placed upon simulated situations and problems, which are attacked by individuals who take a particular role, who, along with others who play roles, go through procedure in pursuit of solutions to problems. Careful analysis is later made of how mistakes were made, the way good ideas arose, and the difficulties that were overcome. The great importance of a creative, flexible, experimental attitude upon the part of the participants is highlighted.

In recent years energetic experimenting has been carried on relative to social problems and the way social pressures may influence thinking and the conclusions that are drawn. The several investigations of the so-called "authoritarian personality" are examples of such experiments. The results from these studies reveal how individuals who vary in personality traits tend to solve problems with different techniques and procedures, come to different conclusions when interpreting the obtained data. Attitudes and beliefs find expression in both the methods and the conclusions without any implication of intellectual dishonesty. Jokingly, psychologists sometimes say that even white rats have well identifiable social, economic, and political philosophies; that they reveal national loyalties consistent with that of the experimentalist!

Investigators seem forced to accept the idea that thinking is by no means a purely intellectual matter uninfluenced by emotions and the value system of the person who does the thinking. Pure objectivity is scarcely to be expected in those who search for solutions to problems. Awareness that some sets may be helpful and that others may be harmful in reaching conclusions consistent with what others judge to be objective reality may lead to avoidance of the pitfalls in front of the individual who would improve the accuracy of his thinking. In this matter there is a close similarity between the factors that are associated with efficient learning and those believed to further sound thinking.

In a broad sense, current investigators remain, as in the past, still concerned with how to recognize "good" thinking; how to identify those who are capable of doing good thinking; and how to proceed to train people in the use of better thinking techniques. This requires that criteria be established with regard to both the product of thinking and the characteristics of the person involved. Once the individuals have been identified and selected upon the basis of sound criteria (whether as prospective students for admission to school, or workers for employment in business or industry) there will continue to be need for training, because new problems inevitably arise and increased responsibilities have a way of falling upon the individual as time passes.

The curiosity of psychologists extends beyond these practical purposes of selecting and training people, for they would like to understand more about the process of thinking and how to determine the variables that are important in executing good thinking and then proceed to the usual goals in science of making predictions and exercising controls over phenomena in ways that promise to become beneficial to man.

CLASSIFYING AND LABELING EXPERIMENTS UPON THINKING

A peculiar task arises in choosing illustrative experiments upon *problem-solving* and *thinking*. While several experiments are relevant and serve our purpose well, it is much less clear why some experiments, although described by the experimenters without reference to problem-solving, thinking or reasoning, may not equally well illustrate these phenomena. Almost every well-designated experiment in psychology has important implications for the subject matter of this chapter. These remarks are made in the hope that the student of experimental psychology will not expect to find words in the title of every report telling him that a given experiment is relevant to our present topic when actually this may be the case.

It is doubtful that we can classify the experiments into useful categories. We shall be content to mention experiments, ranging from the simple ones that involve no more than immediate association between concrete objects clearly visible to the animal subject, to those involving abstract and symbolic concepts that tax the ability of highly intelligent people. Even though the basic process may be the same, important specific variations are obvious. This is true if but one subject is involved. The individual attacks the problem of disentangling a puzzling toy in one way, he tries to unravel a scientific problem by another procedure, and he may work in yet a different way if the task is that of putting words of striking imagery together so that a meaningful poem is the result.

MAJOR AREAS OF EXPERIMENTS

In a short but pertinent review of the studies that have been made upon human thinking, Heidbreder (4) discussed first the direct studies that involved the introspective method where the observer reported upon his thinking step by step. Next she took up those studies involving reaction time, giving special attention to those having to do with multiple association and requiring choice. We shall dismiss these experiments without further illustrations at the present, for both types of experiments have been elaborated upon in previous discussions in this book.

Heidbreder proceeded to a discussion of specific experiments that she grouped into rather loose categories. Something of the development of experimenting upon thinking is seen as her general outline was sketched. Problem-solving was viewed as largely overt trial and error by Thorndike. Animal behavior was interpreted as including "mental" trial and error, or insight, as Hobhouse (5) and Köhler (7) preferred to interpret the behavior. Ruger (12) used mechanical puzzles and human subjects and studied problem-solving and thinking process by observing carefully each movement that was made. He recorded the running conversation of his subject and this was later supplemented by having the subject elaborate upon his thought process. Störring (14) and Woodworth were interested in the experimental study of syllogistic reasoning and published results from these experiments in the early years of the present century. In more recent years Woodworth and Sells (19) determined that the conclusion reached in a formal syllogism was readily influenced by the general setting or "atmosphere." By this they meant that a negative premise tended to create a negative attitude and conclusion while the opposite result might be expected from a positive premise. Hull (6) was primarily interested in developing methodology for studying reasoning and concept formation. He tried to show that quantification was possible. Hull and Kuo both made use of Chinese characters as learning material and the subjects were given instruction that was intended to lead them to believe that the task that they worked at was memorizing. The real interest of the experimentalists was focused upon whether or not the subjects would come to use common elements in the written Chinese characters. This was an indirect procedure intended to reveal how concept formation took place.

MEASUREMENTS OF THINKING

In more recent years Hanfmann and Kasanin (2) have developed a test of concept formation and here the subject is required to classify material into logical groups. Presumably the subject's ability to classify material into meaningful categories is an index to accuracy of thought and to capacity for sound concept formation. The test consists of twenty-two blocks. There are five different colors, six shapes, two heights, and two surface sizes. The task is to divide the blocks into four meaningful groups, and this cannot be done on the usual basis of color, form, size, or other ways that can be denoted by a single word. The solution is in terms of a double dichotomy that requires the subject to use an abstract concept. While taking the test, the subject is directed to verbalize his thinking and a record is made of this. The solution that is found along with the steps taken can be compared with standard scores and procedures.

In attempts to study creative thinking, something reminiscent of the anecdotal method has been used with some success. Distinguished scientists and others have sometimes written down their habits of work. There are interesting reports from Helmholtz, Poincare, and others, in which they indicate the steps taken in their progress to a discovery. Wallas (17) collected examples of such reports and after analyzing them concluded that four stages in creative thinking was apparent. These were preparation, incubation, illumination, and verification. It is the assumption that by fractioning the process and then by giving careful attention to each step the individual might improve upon his efforts to think well. The four stages are rather suggestive of those passed through when designing and performing an experiment. The first and last steps, at least, are as relevant in doing an experiment as they are in doing creative thinking.

Some of the most successful investigations of how problems are solved and how conclusions are reached as a result of thinking have been those in which careful consideration has been given to the context under which the thinking was done. Malinowski (11) revealed how there is a close relationship between the language that is used and the cultural patterns that surround the individual. The person's language influences the way he perceives and understands the world about him, both physical and social. Here are to be identified some of the unconscious assumptions that so readily become a part of the individual's conclusions after he has engaged in thinking. Warner and Lunt (18) and others have been able to show by means of opinion surveys that such factors as social and economic status help to determine the prejudices, biases, and convictions of the people living in a particular situation; that conclusions drawn from the same set of data vary from place to place or condition to condition in ways that reflect influences found to exist in the living situation of the subjects involved. Altogether, investigators have become much more alert to how nonrational factors get mixed up in what was once conceived of as primarily an intellectual process. Strong emotional investment becomes a great hazard to a successful outcome of the thinking process.

SPECIFIC EXPERIMENTAL PROBLEMS

Specific experimental problems used by Hobhouse (5) in his experiments were very similar to those Thorndike had used. These included several problem boxes having parts that had to be manipulated in order to obtain food or to open a door for escape. An interesting problem was presented by use of a string which the animal might pull and secure food tied to the distant end of it. Hobhouse complicated the problem by using two or more strings and then observing the animal while it learned which string to chose. Trial and error behavior should have led to random selection of the strings, perhaps, but Hobhouse obtained results that forced him to conclude that various animals could discriminate and perform better than by chance. Later investigators have made use of similar problems to test for color discrimination in animals. This is readily done by tying food to a string of a particular color and then arranging strings of other colors unattached to anything.

Further complications of the string problem is possible by arranging them so they may cross and recross. There is almost no end to the difficulty that can be made by this procedure as anyone knows if he has tried to comprehend the wire connections that constitutes a complicated electrical system. Few animals do well in mastering the string problem with only one crossing. Monkeys are something of an exception for they do rather well as can be seen from the results obtained by Harlow and Settage (3).

Other interesting tasks used by Hobhouse and repeated, sometimes with variations by Köhler and others, involved the use of a stick to draw food to the cage where the animal was confined; use of a short stick to obtain a longer stick which could then be used to reach the food; use of a box that must first be moved in order that the animal could climb upon it to obtain food out of reach from the floor. Hobhouse also made use of the rod and tube which required the animal to insert the smaller rod into the tube after which the spliced tool was long enough to reach food. Köhler was led to conclude that apes used trial and error behavior before accidently inserting a smaller bamboo pole into a larger one, but then once the poles were put together the apes seemed to see the relationship between the longer pole and the food that had been previously placed out of reach.

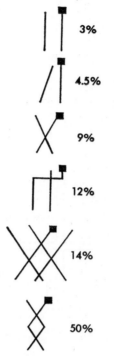

3%

4.5%

9%

12%

14%

50%

Fig. 15.2. The drawings represent the way strings with and without food attached were arranged in order to study behavior of rhesus monkeys. Ten animals were used and each animal made 100 trials with the percent error indicated. (From Harlow, H. F. and Settlage, P. H., "Comparative behavior of primates, VII. Capacity of monkeys to solve pattern string tests," *J. Comp. Psychol.* 18 (1934), 423-435.)

In a study often referred to as an "insight" experiment in learning but one that could have been well described as problem-solving, Tolman and Honzik (16) used an elevated maze over which rats ran in order to get food. First the rats were trained to run the shortest pathway which was directly from starting point to the goal. After the habit had been established a block was placed across this pathway and the rats took a second trail. Finally a block was placed farther along the maze which was a barrier for both the first and second pathways. Now the rats backed out of the closed pathways and elected to use an entirely new pathway, number three, with a frequency much greater than would be produced by chance. This last pathway was the longest one to the goal but it was an open and feasible route. Presumably the rats were able to suppress the older habit patterns and to try a new one which was now the only appropriate one to take to the goal.

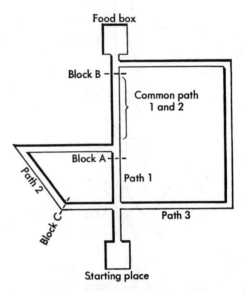

Fig. 15.3. Insight or inferential expectancy have been used to describe the rat's behavior when running this maze, following the use of blocks across earlier learned pathways. (From Tolman, E. C. and Honzik, C. H. "Insight in rats," *University of California Publications in Psychology*, 4 (1930), 215-232.)

Luchins (8) performed a series of "mental set" experiments by use of jars of various capacities which were to be filled with water by systematic pouring from one to another so specified amounts could be measured. Luchins first trained his subjects in a procedure that regularly led to the right solution. After this had been repeated several times an easier and more direct approach was made possible so the right amount of water could be obtained. It was found that most of the subjects (college students) persisted in using the more indirect and complicated procedure. Studies of this kind are performed in the hope of gaining a better understanding of the holding power of well established habits, or of what Luchins spoke of as rigidity. After the individual reduces his responses to a routine, a kind of rigidity seems to set which prevents subsequent flexible and adaptive behavior.

A number of investigators have made interesting use of matches as material; the task is to construct a variety of geometric figures. With a

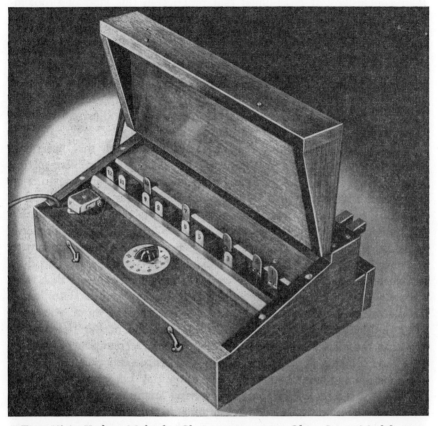

Fig. 15.4. Yerkes Multiple Choice apparatus: Ohio State Modification. Several variations of the Yerkes apparatus have been used in learning studies. By complicating the solution this apparatus can be used in studies of both learning and thinking. (Courtesy C. H. Stoelting Co.)

given number of matches the subject is to construct the maximum number of squares or triangles. The set of subjects usually lead them to try to place all matches on one surface and this does not permit a solution. If the subject is able to break through the more conventional arrangement and make use of the third dimension, the solution is readily at hand.

Szekely (15) presented and discussed a number of problems that he presented to subjects. For example, he asked his subjects to determine in advance what would happen if water is poured into a container where floating objects or heavier-than-water objects are suspended. Then his subjects proceed to carry out experiments in order to verify or to reject their conclusions. It is assumed that practice in this kind of problem-solving will enable students to learn simultaneously how to solve problems and also learn important principles of physics.

CONCLUDING REMARKS

Specific examples of problem-solving experiments might be reviewed at length, for there is much energetic experimenting in this area at present. However, it has been our purpose to give a few examples and to leave the student to pursue further study in the suggested readings.

Attention is called to the remarkable transformation that has taken place with regard to ways and means of teaching for problem-solving and thinking. There is scarcely any dependence placed upon instruction in particular subjects with a view to obtaining transfer effects. Instead of expecting to obtain benefits from certain subjects that will then enable the individual to think and reason in all situations, much more emphasis is placed upon solving problems that have something in common with the ones that are to be solved in science, business, or industry. This does not necessarily reflect negatively upon the academic subjects that were once stressed as having great value because they were said to "teach people to think and to reason." Perhaps the verdict of those who work with problem-solving and thinking *is* against the earlier defense for teaching those subjects. However, there is clear recognition of the fact that good thinking in certain areas of science is scarcely possible without previous training in mathematics, for it is from this source that the student obtains the necessary symbols for solving many scientific problems. Mathematical models are of increasing use in working out experimental designs for study and experimenting. Emphasis has shifted from remote and abstract problems in reasoning to those that more closely simulate the problems in laboratory and in reality situations. Some investigators stress that any would-be problem-solver is likely to improve upon his ability to attack a difficult problem by first attacking similar but simpler problems. He should work out solutions for several of the simplified problems as a preparation for the major attack. The assumption is that many relevant associations and techniques will occur to the worker and that the transfer will be facilitated.

We do not take complete leave of the topics discussed in this chapter, for there is a growing tendency to study problem-solving and thinking as this takes place in small groups. The solution to many problems comes about by an interaction procedure, and therefore improved thinking is one of the important products of group participation. Here, again, it will be seen that a new approach is gradually emerging, for the process of thinking and reasoning was once considered as highly individual, best carried out by the person in isolation. Some problems are resolved much

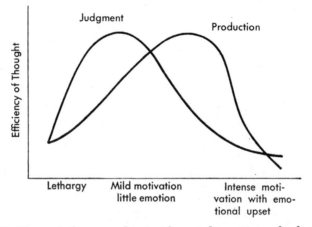

Fig. 15.5. Theoretical curves showing how judgment may be better where motivation is mild but productivity tends to increase with more intense emotional involvement. (Drawn with permission after Johnson, Doland M., *The Psychology of Thought and Judgment.* New York: Harper & Brothers, 1955.)

more rapidly by group participation; others may require a more contemplative attitude and physical isolation of the individual for best results.

SUGGESTED READINGS

Hilgard, Ernest R. *Introduction to Psychology.* "Thinking, language and problem-solving," pp. 304-330. New York: Harcourt, Brace, 1957.

Krech, David, and Crutchfield, Richard S. *Elements of Psychology.* "The world of problems," pp. 359-371; "Creative problem-solving," pp. 372-398. New York: Knopf, 1958.

Woodworth, Robert S., and Schlosberg, Harold. *Experimental Psychology.* "Problem-solving: thinking," pp. 814-841. New York: Henry Holt, 1954.

Vinacke, W. E. *The Psychology of Thinking.* New York: McGraw-Hill, 1952.

Humphrey, G. *Thinking: An Introduction to Its Experimental Psychology.* New York: John Wiley, 1951.

Johnson, Donald M. *Psychology of Thought and Judgment.* New York: Harper, 1955.

Wertheimer, M. *Productive Thinking.* New York: Harper, 1945.

Maier, Norman C. *Supervisory and Executive Development.* New York: John Wiley, 1957.

Hebb, D. O. *The Organization of Behavior,* pp. 140-170. New York: John Wiley, 1949.

REFERENCES

1. Bovard, E. W. J. "Group structure and perception," *J. Abnorm. Soc. Psychol.,* 45 (1951), 398-405.

2. Hanfmann, E., and Kasanin, J. "A method for the study of concept formation," *J. Psychol.,* 3 (1937), 521-540.

3. Harlow, H. F., and Settlage, P. H. "Capacity of monkeys to solve patterned string tests," *J. Comp. Psychol.,* 18 (1934), 423-425.

4. Heidbreder, Edna. "Studying human thinking," p. 121. In Andrews, T. G. (ed.). *Methods of Psychology.* New York: John Wiley, 1948.

5. Hobhouse, L. T. *Mind in Evolution.* London: Macmillan, 1915.

6. Hull, C. L. "Quantitative aspects of the evolution of concepts," *Psychol. Monogr.,* No. 123 (1920).

7. Köhler, W. *The Mentality of Apes.* New York: Harcourt, Brace, 1925.

8. Luchins, A. S. "Mechanization in problem-solving: the effect of *Einstellung,*" *Psychol. Monogr.,* No. 248 (1942), 54.

9. Maier, N. R. F. "Reasoning in humans: I. On direction," *J. Comp. Psychol.,* 10 (1930), 115-144.

10. Maier, Norman R. *Supervisory and Executive Development.* New York: John Wiley, 1957.

11. Malinowski, B. "The problem of learning in primitive languages," pp. 296-336. In Ogden, C. H., and Richards, I. A. (ed.). *The Meaning of Meaning.* New York: Harcourt, Brace, 1938.

12. Ruger, H. A. "The psychology of efficiency," *Arch. Psychol.,* No. 15 (1910).

13. Sherif, M. "A study of some social factors in perception," *Arch. Psychol.,* New York, No. 187 (1935).

14. Störring, G. "Experimentelle Untersuchungen über einfache Schlissprozesse," *Arch. Ges. Psychol.,* 11 (1908), 1-27.

15. Szekely, L. "Knowledge and thinking," *Acta Psychologica,* 7 (1950), 1-24.

16. Tolman, E. C., and Honzik, C. H. *Insight in Rats.* University of California, Publications in Psychology, 4 (1930), 215-232.

17. Wallas, Graham. *The Art of Thought.* New York: Harcourt, Brace, 1926.

18. Warner, W. D., and Lunt, P. S. *The Social Life of a Modern Community.* New Haven: Yale University Press, 1941.

19. Woodworth, R. S., and Sells, S. B. "An atmosphere effect in formal syllogistic reasoning," *J. Exper. Psychol.,* 18 (1935), 451-460.

16 EXPERIMENTING WITH DRIVES, MOTIVES, AND SOCIAL INTERACTION

GENERAL PROBLEMS

"What makes people tick?" is a typical question to be addressed to the psychologist. An answer that is satisfying to the layman is not easy to furnish. While the psychologist is not likely to formulate his question in quite this way, nevertheless he, too, is greatly interested in the drives and motives that initiate and direct action in people. His questions, possibly couched in more sophisticated terminology, but still having to do with "what makes people tick," may be answered with a degree of greater satisfaction. However, experimentation and research remain to be done before he will even approach complete and adequate description and explanation of the forces within the individual—the forces from without, plus the subsequent interactions that make up the dynamic processes which result in the characteristic behavior that is referred to as personality.

Psychologists might as well prepare for continuing and insistent demands for explanation about why a given individual made this choice instead of that; why he commited this criminal act instead of that socially approved one; why he gathered to himself this set of personality traits and characteristics instead of an entirely different set. There are those who accuse psychologists, especially experimental psychologists, of working with the inconsequential and the irrelevant. They complain that psychologists busy themselves with detailed and dull description of all the little wheels that go round and round. These critics are often in a hurry to know about the forces that put the wheels to turning; the structure and function of the balance wheel that, figuratively speaking, regulates man's behavior. Or to use a more modern analogy, not so suggestive of a watch, they want to know about the power that drove Sputnik into the distant sky; the means by which Sputnik was guided and put into orbit, and then especially, about the strange balance of forces that kept it spinning for weeks in outer space without obvious means of support.

The material to be discussed in this chapter has been divided into three parts which follow the general introduction. The first part will focus upon the biological drives and the means of studying these, the second part deals with the more definitely identified cultural and environmental forces that modify and channel the drives, while the third section continues to a discussion of interaction and group dynamics.

There is not often a direct expression of biological drives in people after cultural restrictions and facilitations have operated upon the individual for a few years of life. Thus, we may use the term "motive" more often than "drive," although it will not be found that writers are entirely consistent in this matter. Nor is it likely that we can adhere strictly to a distinction between the two words at all times. It is our intention to use the word "drive" where the implication is that biological factors are of primary importance and "motive" if social forces are clearly predominant. Yet we mean to leave room for the supposition that all human responses are a blend resulting from the mixing of influences from both heredity and environment.

The last part of the chapter is devoted to a discussion of the continuing interaction process, or the interplay of forces as these find expression in individual adjustment and group dynamics. This sounds like an ambitious statement, but we can undertake no more than to indicate briefly what the problems are, to tell something of the methods and techniques that have been used by those who try to experiment in these areas, and to comment upon a few of the newer approaches that give hope for scientific progress. To many investigators there appears to be a fascinating area for research that involves the use of laboratory experimental methods as these may be brought to bear upon problems of human relationships. The psychology of conflict, for example, involves many subtle overtones, but an understanding of conflict and a means of alleviating individual and group conflict short of total war seems to be the future price tag for the survival of mankind.

Forces and Controls

It is recognized that analogies are sometimes misleading, and, therefore, not always a useful means of explaining and imparting knowledge or understanding. Yet the suggestion given by the present preoccupation of mankind is too much for the writer—he cannot resist the temptation to return to the intriguing comparison between the forces that were brought to bear upon Sputnik and those that operate upon the individual.

It is hoped that our illustration, drawn from the uncomfortable proximity of national conflict that threatens world war and disaster, can help give understanding of conflict and, thus, be turned into a constructive use. It is quite probable that Sputnik will be overworked for illustrative purposes long before the student comes to read this chapter. However, it can scarcely be used as frequently as the not entirely apt comparison between the telephone system and man's nervous system that yet gets duty after these many years!

We might think of tissue needs and biological drives as serving the purpose to initiate action in man in a way comparable to the power that forced Sputnik's flight into outerspace. From birth onward, social forces nudge the individual first this way and then that, not unlike the gyroscope and other guiding mechanisms that kept Sputnik on its true course. Finally, when there was an intricate balance of forces, Sputnik was in orbit. Presumably, it is possible for the biological drives and the social regulations to be brought into harmony in such a way that the individual moves forward through life as an integrated and efficient organism. After reaching a particular stage of development, forces become more stabilized and the person should, with minor guiding controls, continue to operate as a comfortable and balanced personality—he is in orbit!

It should be noted that Sputnik did not come to a state of rest nor does the well-motivated and properly adjusted individual become static. It may be supposed that the successful and happy individual, at least, does reach some sort of forward-moving but stabilized state in which opposing desires no longer threaten to rip him apart. If this condition is not brought about and there is waste of energy because of opposing and unbalanced forces, the individual either loses thrust and stalls at a particular level of development, or in the more serious and damaging conflicts, the personality is shattered.

Drives Are Not All Conscious

The continuing dynamic processes that drive the individual, sometimes to positive and creative achievement, sometimes into conflict and dissolution of personality, become important subject matter for the student of psychology. It cannot be assumed that these forces are clearly understood by the individual who is being impelled by them. Unconscious and half-conscious drives and motives undoubtedly play an important role in the lives of all people. As yet there is a baffling lack of knowledge and understanding of these things. While the laboratory psychologists of a few years ago took little interest in these matters, recent investigations, especially those reputed to indicate that a large number of people may simultaneously respond to the same subliminal cue by concerted action, have raised exciting possibilities of rapprochement between the laboratory and the market place. Articles have appeared in the popular press claiming that investigators have flashed subliminal stimuli upon the movie screen during intermission time that gave suggestions for eating popcorn or other foods, with tremendous effectiveness, as reflected by increased buying. Members of the audience were unaware that anything was being projected upon the apparently blank screen. There have been few examples of psychological research that would have, at first thought, seemed to be less promising for practical application than the early studies of subliminal phenomenon. Does this open up a new vista for the advertiser? How much learning can the teacher expect to take place if children are subjected to subliminal cues? What a prospect it is to contemplate that learning might not need to be conscious at all! Those who regard study effort and learning as painful have already become hopeful. They wish to proceed through college by being exposed to the learning material from recordings while asleep at night, or while in a hypnotic trance by day!

The scientific and practical usefulness of these findings remain quite uncertain at present. How much use can be made of subliminal cues in the ever-frustrating process of psychotherapy? Has the psychologist found a scientific approach and a fruitful methodology to the study of the subconscious? Can the domain of the unconscious, reputed by the psychoanalysts to account for nearly all the motivation of mankind, now be explored systematically?

Perceptual Defense and Motives

Recent studies of perceptual defense and perceptual distortion deal with the influences of motivation upon perception, and most of them have made use of threshold stimulation in the experiments. It is believed that unpleasant or socially taboo stimuli must be raised to higher intensity in order that sensations become clear; that perception take place. Distortions of meaning, it has been concluded, are regularly in the direction of biological and social needs that have not been adequately met. The objectionable, the taboo, and the unpleasant cannot be seen or heard as readily as the pleasant; learning takes place more slowly; forgetting is more rapid. There is at least enough supporting evidence to make these generalizations intriguing. Selective learning and forgetting have been proposed from time to time in the past, but greater interest concerning selectivity and distortion has shifted to sensory and perceptual processes in recent years.

Isolating Drives and Motives for Study and Discussion

It seems about as difficult, and probably as hazardous, to isolate studies of drives and motives from other topics in psychology as was the case for emotions. It has already been necessary to say many things about motivation when discussing other subjects, and the writer has some misgivings about including a separate chapter in which it is proposed to present material and to set forth in discussion the part played by drives and motives. The supposition might be made that nothing has yet been said intentionally about them. Implications of the effects of drives and motives are to be found in every chapter. At an earlier period in experimental psychology, there was no lack of intention to bring together research upon learning or motor performance with that upon motivation. It has been somewhat of a concession forced by recent findings that problems in sensory-perceptual psychology may not safely be investigated without using careful controls having to do with tissue needs and social participation. The reported reactions to subliminal cues, previously referred to in this discussion, bear witness to the necessity of this more recent orientation.

It is a working hypothesis, or—perhaps the statement should be put stronger—an irrefutable assumption that all behavior is motivated; that the living organism is never a passive receptacle for stimuli; that the biological and social needs of the organism are ever present and operating as long as there is life. Hence, these needs may influence sensory reception and selectivity; help to determine what and how processes of attending and receiving take place; initiate and channel the infinite number of intellectual, emotional, and motor responses. Thus, an attempt to isolate completely the problems in motivation from the psychological phenomena that have already been related is neither possible nor desirable. However, there remain many useful elaborations to be made concerning findings, methods, techniques, and apparatus.

BIOLOGICAL DRIVES

TISSUE NEEDS AND BEHAVIOR PATTERNS

In this section we shall concentrate upon the physiological needs of the organism. In these urges we should be able to see a close connection between the drive for gratification and the patterns of responses that serve to meet the requirements of the organism. Highly specific responses to particular stimuli are called reflexes. These would not be of as much interest to psychologists as to the physiologists if it were not for the belief that conditioned responses are superimposed upon them and that they become the basis for learning, as presented in an earlier chapter. A less well-defined group of responses, also characterized by more variability in response patterns, are the instincts. Just as instinctive patterns of behavior have been described as elaborations upon reflexes by becoming tied together in linkage (chain-reflexes) or by extension, so has learned behavior been thought of as being determined by modification and elaboration upon the instinctive patterns of behavior which were laid down by hereditary processes. These possibilities are set forth by McDougall in his various works dealing with emergent evolution. The general concept is one in which a parallel was drawn between the way behavior in man has become specialized and complex through the operation of selection and necessity for biological and social survival of the organism, just as structural changes in animals were due to evolutionary processes as described by Darwin.

If we should return to our original question stated at the beginning of the chapter, it might well be that few would question that tissue needs must be postulated as of primary importance. However, more detailed description must be given if we are to have much understanding about how the process operates. It does no harm to suppose that each of the following men started a physical movement some time in his life that was to gratify a physical need, but that somehow there were many intervening variables that prevented complete satiation of the organism until da Vinci painted the *Mona Lisa*, Milton wrote *Paradise Lost*, Livingstone arrived in *Africa* and Einstein discovered the *law of relativity*. It might not be very helpful if the psychologist kept trying to prove that there must be a direct relationship between the tissue needs of the organism and the behavior that finally took place. Somewhere in the remote past the needs of the cells of the body faded into near oblivion and social and psychological needs emerged to direct the behavior. We can be sure that each man made a thousand choices, but a systematic study of all of the variables that entered into those choices is now lost to experimental psychologists. It may be a discouraging come-down to conclude that psychologists must still enter into discussion of a rat's choice at the turning point in a T-maze! Yet, very likely more must be learned about such simple decisions if investigators are to march along toward an understanding of the dramatic decisions upon great issues.

McDOUGALL AND FREUD

Two men, McDougall and Freud, stand out as pioneers who were interested in the dynamic processes that operate to initiate and direct behavior. Both stressed the importance of biological drives and each extended his thinking and theorizing into speculations about the consequence of social controls or cultural prohibitions and deprivations of the basic urges.

Of course, teachers, preachers, and writers down through the ages have had a great many things to say about the impulses of man. We find Rousseau taking the position that man is naturally good; Calvin assuming that man is by nature bad. Rousseau conceived of evil being the outcome of society attempting to modify and to suppress the natural or biological urges. On the other hand, many religious leaders have considered that evil is already present within the biological needs and that "good" behavior can come only with the suppression of the desires to gratify those needs through the dictates of religion or by social controls. Sex has ordinarily been singled out as the biological urge requiring the greatest number of restrictions and taboos. This appears to be the background information from which Freud drew when stressing that blocked gratification of this urge could be expected to underlie all personality deviations. He thought that he found adequate supporting evidence for this belief in fantasy—daydreams and night dreams; in the number and strictness of customs and taboos surrounding sex; in laws and penalties directed to coercive pressures for regulating sexual activity.

The student will already be aware of the many and defensible reasons for using some other word than instinct. However, there is not general agreement about a better word that may be substituted and it is all but impossible to discuss the work of either McDougall or Freud without speaking of instinct. At any rate, no other word can be substituted without risk of distorting what they had to say.

McDougall upon Instinct

McDougall frequently spoke of the instincts as "springs for action." While trying to avoid the implication that there were God-given goals toward which each individual was striving, he kept stressing the significance of the organism being constantly in a goal-seeking state. Many of McDougall's ideas evolved soon after the turn of the present century and he gave expression to them in his books dealing with general, abnormal, and social psychology. He was one of the first writers to use in combination the words "social psychology" and wrote a book entitled *Introduction to Social Psychology* in 1908. In that publication, McDougall (12) listed twelve instincts and with each he paired an accompanying emotional reaction that might be expected with activation of each of these propensities. Few writers have accepted McDougall's list without reservations. Since the list created a great deal of controversy and stimulated research both by those bent upon disproving that the urges cited were instinctive and those hoping to furnish supporting evidence, we believe that the list will interest present-day students who are concerned with understanding the dynamics of behavior.

INSTINCTS	ACCOMPANYING EMOTION
1. To desire food	Appetite or craving
2. To reject certain substances or things	Disgust or repugnance
3. To explore new places or things	Curiosity
4. To escape from danger	Fear
5. To fight when challenged	Anger, rage
6. To have sex desire	Lust or sex excitement
7. To care for the young (mothering)	Tender emotion, love
8. To seek company (gregariousness)	Loneliness, nostalgia
9. To seek to dominate (self-assertion)	Elation, positive self-feeling
10. To accept inferior status (submission)	Humility, negative self-feeling
11. To make things	Feeling of creativity
12. To collect things	Acquisitiveness, pride of possession

Much criticism was leveled at McDougall for his list of instincts. He was attacked to some extent from both sides: those who were strongly influenced by biological findings considered the list too short and in general, inadequate; those who stressed environmental influences did not believe there was justification for all the instincts included. The latter were quick to demonstrate that some of the so-called instincts were at least partially determined by the experiences of the individual. McDougall was not easily turned from his beliefs. In discussing the source for behavior, he had said at the time of publication of the list: "Directly or indirectly the instincts are the prime movers of all human activity." He held that instincts initiated activity, supplied the goals, furnished part of the guiding influences toward those goals. They were considered to have a universal quality, operating in a similar way for all animals, but it was McDougall's idea that higher-level animals tended to be better equipped with instincts than are those standing lower on the evolutionary rung of the ladder.

While McDougall accepted as necessary the idea that theory should be supported by careful observations and by experimentation, he failed to convince most writers that either he, or others who were sympathetic, were able to show convincing experimental results. In spite of this lack,

psychologists have had great difficulty in doing without much that Mc-
Dougall and others of similar views had to say about the prime movers
of behavior. The language used has been modified radically, but the basic
ideas seem to furnish a central theme that persists today. It is as though
the primary principles stand, but that writers and investigators became so
excited when criticizing the details that the ideas that provoked the controversy tended to get lost in the scuffle but nevertheless to survive.

McDougall Summarized Later

After a quarter century of debate, McDougall undertook to restate his
position in summary form in a book carrying the title *Energies of Men*
(13). The sub-title was *A Study of the Fundamentals of Dynamic Psychology*, and we find that his position had not changed greatly, for on
page 9 he had the following to say about energy and psychology:

> The title of this book announces its claim to go beyond mere description
> of our mental life, its aim to explain as far as possible the activity of men.
> So long as any science is content to describe only, it does not require the
> conception of energy. Energy is something that we postulate for the sake
> of introducing order and system into our explanations of the course of
> events, in order that we may formulate dynamic laws of agency, influence,
> or causation. In the physical sciences it has been found extremely useful.
> The biological sciences were for a long period occupied in the main with
> description and classification. But, they are now advancing to the ex-
> planatory stage, concerning themselves with dynamic problems, seeking
> causal explanations in terms of energy and the interplay of energies. Psy-
> chology is no exception. In the past it has been mainly occupied with
> description and classification; but of late years it has become increasingly
> concerned with the dynamic problems of human activity; every year it
> becomes clearer and more generally agreed that the essential task of psy-
> chology is to achieve such understanding of human activity as will make
> possible a more effective guidance and control of the energies of men.

If this was an overstatement of the views of psychologists in 1932—and
there is grounds for believing that it was—it is less of an exaggeration a
quarter of a century later. In terms of sheer numbers of people who devote their professional lives to areas of research and application, a shift
in the direction that McDougall indicated is in clear evidence. The clinical psychologist who tries to arrive at a useful diagnosis or to plan and
execute therapy is charged with giving careful attention to dynamic processes. The people who are working in vocational and educational guidance
focus upon the interplay of abilities and interests; those who work as
industrial psychologists or who consult in industry are not less concerned

with dynamics than with the aptitudes that the man possesses. They are well aware that weak or poorly controlled motives upon the part of an individual in position of management may result in the use of poor judgment and that he may become the instigator of things that lead to unhappy and inefficient workers below him; that men at the lower echelons may pass all the hurdles of abilities and skills, but fail for lack of willingness to use their energy productively.

FREUD AND PSYCHOANALYSIS

Freud, in his analytic and dynamic system, stated many hypotheses about the resulting behavior from society's erection of barriers between the individual (with his biological needs) and the means for gratifying those needs. External forces were seen to operate to prevent freedom in the satisfying of the sex urge, especially, and these restraining conditions were seen as being brought to bear early in childhood. While restraints might continue throughout life, ordinarily long before puberty it could be expected that the process of internalizing would begin to take place for most people. Feelings of guilt about sexual behavior thus comes to the fore to help sustain the external dictates of the culture. Freud emphasized the frequent and disastrous effects of early prohibitive forces and considered that most serious maladjustments could be traced to "suppressed infantile sexuality." Some writers have considered Freud as viewing instincts as a necessary evil—that he took a defeatist or nihilistic position in which he assumed that maladjustment must grow out of frustration. At the same time he assumed that there would be no escaping frustration concerning instinctive drives, since society regularly sets up countermeasures to curb free expression of the drives.

Freud did not set up experiments to validate his numerous hypotheses, but was content to support them by clinical observations. A few individuals, who have been strongly influenced by Freud's ideas, have experimented. Many of Freud's hypotheses, including some of the major ones, do not lend themselves readily to experimental verification. A rather high percentage of individuals who work in the area of treatment have been willing to accept the premises of Freud's analytic system on faith alone. Freud was a most persuasive writer and the faithful accepted his ideas and principles because they believed that they worked in practice.

It is equally true that many critics are to be found who question whether the pragmatic criterion thus advanced by Freud's followers is either sufficiently demonstrated, or, within itself, adequate scientific grounds for accepting some of the ideas advanced. They ask for more careful observations, including both controlled experiments and field or clinical studies. However, the number and richness of hypotheses stated by Freud is unexcelled and his most severe critics cannot ignore them. Under the limitations of present methods and techniques, many of Freud's hypotheses either cannot be studied scientifically or they must be modified and restated. No writer has presented a more fascinating list of hypotheses concerning the broad panorama of dynamic processes than Freud. Further verification and validation is needed for most of his fertile ideas. It is certain that such a chapter as that written by Beach (1) and appearing in Stevens' *Handbook of Experimental Psychology* could not have been written and included in such a book before Freud's time. It was due primarily to Freud's provocative writings that experimental work was carried out upon the previously taboo subject of sex. Beach reviews a massive literature under the title, *Instinctive Behavior: Reproductive Activities,* and much of it is strictly experimental in nature.

TYPICAL METHODS AND TECHNIQUES FOR STUDYING DRIVES

Most of the procedures that have been used in studying the strength of drives can be placed under three headings. These are (1) the barrier that will be overcome in order for the animal to obtain the means of gratifying the need, (2) the pain that will be withstood or suffering involved in reaching the goal, (3) pairing drives to see which choice the animal will make between two goals.

Barriers

In the barrier method, quantification may be in terms of the number of times the animal will climb over a wall in order to gratify a drive. Here a constant treatment must be used with regard to how much gratification can be allowed for each trial in terms of food eaten, let us say, or how much water obtained. Sometimes the height of the wall becomes the independent variable. This may be useful if the wall is gradually raised in height and in which case, the top level represents the relative effort that may be expended in order to get the reward.

Lashley and others have required the rat to jump variable distances in order to get food. The penalty for failure to negotiate the distance is that the rat falls to a net below and must try again before getting food, water, or whatever the desired object may be. This method and the wall-climbing procedure may be extended to the point where great effort is required of the animal. A few investigators have used a water barrier. Here, the animal must enter and swim a distance to obtain his reward. A great variety of physical obstructions have been utilized as barriers.

Pain vs. Drive

The time-honored means of inducing pain by psychologists has been the electric shock. This can be relatively well controlled as to intensity; there is not danger of infections or other undesirable consequences that would follow the mutilation of tissue, yet the pain can be very mild or quite intense. There are several ways that the stimulus may be administered, and these have been used freely in learning experiments. Many of these experiments have been done with the combined purpose of revealing something about both learning and motives. A shock can be given upon touching food or water and, thus, determine how much pain must be used as a deterrent. The intensity level of the shock may be too unpleasant to stand at first. However, if a need like hunger is not met as time goes on, the drive may gradually build up until the animal will withstand great pain in order to obtain food.

Drive vs. Drive

In the procedure for simultaneous presentation of competing objects for drive satisfaction, it becomes essential to control for position of the objects, physical orientation of the animal, and other minor factors that may enter to distort the results. Here the problem begins to resemble that of establishing sensory threshold differences. For example, the animal may be both hungry and thirsty. Then, if comparison is made between these two desires, the experimenter must be careful to have each means of gratification equally available with regard to distance, visibility, and so forth. The T-maze and the Y-maze furnish good controls for the choice point, since the animal approaches down a pathway and then turns either to right or left with nearly equal advantage for each. It is necessary to examine for pre-test preference, as some animals may be expected to reveal a choice for turning one direction. It is known that such a preference is sometimes due to previous learning, but whether this is the basis for the animal's choice under all conditions is not known. Usually the experimenter simply assumes that there may be advantage to either right or left and provides a counterbalanced order to control for this.

Artificial Forms as Stimuli for Instinctive Responses

Among the many interesting attempts to study patterns of behavior that seem to be relatively well fixed by inheritance, and amenable to laboratory methods, are some of the experiments by Tinbergen (18). By passing forms made to resemble the silhouettes of birds of prey over chickens and other birds frequently victimized by particular birds of prey, escape reactions were elicited. The forms to simulate the enemy do not have to have precisely the same dimensions or proportions, since there is either a failure to make fine discriminations or else stimulus generaliza-

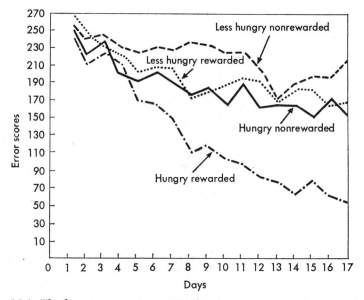

Fig. 16.1. The learning curves suggest that both speed and level of learning vary with motivation and reward. Rats were used as subjects in maze learning. (From Tolman, E. C., and Honzik, C. H., *Degree of Hunger, Reward, and Non-Reward, and Maze Learning in Rats.* University of California Publications in Psychology, Vol. 4 (1930), p. 246.)

tion takes place. To quote Tinbergen, "The domestic cock gives its alarm call, not only when the sparrow hawk is passing, but also as a reaction to sudden appearance of a pigeon or crow."

Movement strengthens the stimulus value of a given form. That is, a quick and typical movement of objects not too closely similar to the bird of prey may cause escape behavior in the fearful bird. Figure 16.2 on p. 368 shows several forms that might be used to release alarm in laboratory studies of these reactions. By use of the several forms, and by passing these over different birds, limits in form and movement can be established within the range of adequacy for producing the withdrawal responses.

Hunger vs. Hoarding

It is not usual that an experiment can be performed in which the gratification of tissue needs operates to the direct exclusion of another

Fig. 16.2. Bird models used by Lorenz and Tinbergen for testing reactions of various birds to birds of prey. Those marked + released escape responses. (From *The Study of Instincts.* Oxford: Clarendon Press, 1951.)

need that appears to have a basis in a biologically determined pattern of behavior. Attention has been directed to the influence of the social situation upon eating and hoarding activity as well as upon what the results may be if the animal is deprived of an adequate diet. It has been held by Morgan, Stellar, and Johnson (14) that food deprivation tends to increase eating and decrease hoarding. A study in which the eating and hoarding activities were studied under group condition and isolation was performed by Denenberg (5). The results indicated that the group situation stimulated eating and depressed hoarding. Studies of this kind appear to have practical implications, not only for human behavior but also for the handling of domestic animals. Increased consumption of food is often desired in animals where the rapid production of body weight is the ob-

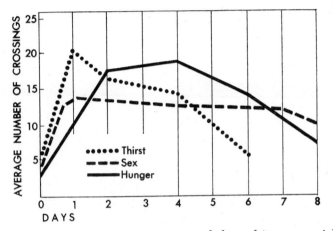

Fig. 16.3. The relative apparent intensity of three drives over eight days, as indicated by studies of rats in crossing a barrier. Conditions surrounding animals will give rises to same variation. (From Garrett, Henry E., *General Psychology*. New York: American Book Co., 1955.)

jective, or, again, the food intake may have direct bearing upon milk production in the cow or egg-laying of the hen.

It is not certain whether the powerful motive for acquisition of wealth in man is very closely parallel to hoarding in animals, but the idea is frequently advanced, and some of the studies have been inspired by the hope that an understanding of hoarding in animals would shed light upon human behavior of this type. The "herd instinct" has also been investigated for the possible value this may have in understanding the social urges in man. Some animals display very strong gregarious traits—buffaloes, wolves, horses, and elephants—while others tend to live and hunt mostly in isolation. Animals of the cat family are said to be less social than those of the dog family. The food that is consumed and the way it must be obtained may very well be related to the relative strength of the gregarious trait.

SECONDARY MOTIVES

Studies of motivation in man are almost entirely concerned with learned motives. This is true because conditioning and social learning begin to affect the individual at an early age and even the biological drives such as hunger and thirst are difficult or impossible to isolate and to study under total exclusion of association, imagination, or modification brought about by social living. Thus, experiments on motivation where human subjects are used are often concerned with preferences,

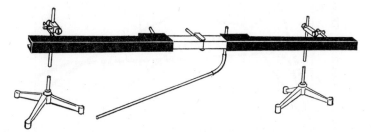

Fig. 16.4. The Galton bar used for length discrimination. A change of incentive results in changes in accuracy of even this simple discrimination. (From Andrews, T. G., *Methods of Psychology.* New York: John Wiley & Sons, 1948.)

tastes in esthetic matters, sentiments, aspirations, ambitions, and attitudes. This does not mean that the biological needs furnish no foundation or that they have an insignificant role.

In a relatively early study (1929) of the influence of incentive upon accuracy of sensory discrimination, Hamilton (7) used a simple and well controlled laboratory experiment that is of interest. He made use of the Galton bar, which allows the subject to adjust two white bars so that they are judged to be of the same length. Hamilton's procedure was to give his subjects an initial trial and the result was then used as the base. Later, each subject worked against his own performance as the standard. After dividing his subjects into seven groups, equated for ability to set the bars accurately as determined by objective scale, he subjected the groups to a training period in which different incentives were used. The column to the left as given below was the systematically changed independent variable. The performance is given in terms of percentage of error calculated against the original performance found and this is to the right and represents the dependent variable.

Group	Percentage of Initial Error
1. Control	127
2. Punishment	24
3. Reward	26
4. Guess-with-punishment	15
5. Told-with-punishment	20
6. Knowledge	45

It will be seen that the control group failed to improve and, in fact, deteriorated. The final score without incentive was not as good as the original. The errors exceeded the number (127%) in the original scores. All the other groups improved, punishment being the condition under which greatest improvement was revealed.

LEVEL OF ASPIRATION EXPERIMENTS

Interest of a number of investigators has centered around the relationship between aspiration and performance. Some have held that important clinical implications may be drawn from these results. Lewin (10) stressed the significance of success and failure in the development of personality. The feeling of failure or success he considered to be dependent upon the relationship between performance and the standard the individual had set for himself. Thus, one student might have a comfortable feeling of success even though his grade might be a C. At the same time, a second student might have a strong feeling of failure and self-blame although his grade is a B. The explanation for the latter reaction is that the student had set his achievement goal at the high level of a grade of A.

Young (20) has made the point that the high-jumper feels no success if he clears the crossbar at a height of one or two feet, nor does he feel failure when he fails to clear the crossbar at eight-foot height. Neither of these settings of height is a particular challenge. The first is too easy and the latter is judged to be impossible. Thus, the experience of success and failure are related to the goal that has been set. The goal must have some resemblance to what is assumed to be reality as related to expectancy. The individual may also take into account his knowledge of how others are able to perform.

A procedure in experimental work sometimes used is that the individual makes a trial and then declares what he hopes or expects to do next time. It is the usual interpretation that a score that is set considerably greater than the actual performance represents a high level of aspiration. Some investigators have assumed that well-adjusted individuals will exercise insight and keep closely together the level of aspiration or expectation, and actual subsequent performance. There remains a question as to how ambiguous the instruction to the subject may be, and exactly what meaning the subject attaches to his estimate. Presumably some individuals may deliberately underestimate in their verbal statement about the next performance so that they may be on the safe side and avoid the appearance of failure. Others may try to be objective and call their shots as closely as possible. Still others may give verbal expression to goals that they know to be unrealistic and beyond their capacity. In spite of all the vagaries, there are intriguing experimental questions raised regarding the relationships between goal-setting, performance, and personality. These different procedures may gradually shed light upon some of them.

SYMBOLIC INCENTIVES IN ANIMALS

Of particular interest to experimental psychologists have been the experiments that have been performed to determine to what extent lower animals can learn to use tokens. These experiments have been assumed to throw light upon such motives as acquisition, generosity, and individual differences. Wolfe (19) demonstrated that chimpanzees could be taught to use poker chips to obtain food. By inserting the chips into machines, not unlike automatic dispensers for food and drinks used by people, the chimps did, in effect, learn to use "money." Following training of this kind both Wolfe and Cowles (3) then put the animals to work to see how much effort they would make to earn the chips that could later be used to obtain the desired food. Either the amount of the work performed or the length of time that the animal can be kept engaged before returning to the dispenser to obtain the desired object can be used as an index to the strength of the incentive.

Examples of sharing tokens have been found. Animals that have unneeded tokens may "loan" them to hungry animals that have none. This kind of experimenting makes it possible to study systematically individual differences among animals with regard to social characteristics. For example, comparisons may be made between physical characteristics and the frequency with which any particular "generous" act may be repeated.

SOCIAL INTERACTION AND GROUP DYNAMICS

The writers of drama and novels have long been concerned with human conflict. By careful delineation of motives and interacting processes writers of the best fiction have given expression to profound conflict between characters. At the peak of Greek civilization some of the world's greatest dramatic plays were written and produced. Many of these had to do with the conflicts encountered by man as his desires and hopes ran counter to the "wills of the gods." The Greeks were often puzzled about solutions to many of the vital problems that confronted man. They conceived of man as being a pawn in the hands of the gods and the wills of the gods were often obscure indeed.

Communication between the Greeks and their many gods was poor at best. It is found that the people frequently sought to learn of the decrees of the gods by consulting oracles and other means, all of which are likely to be thought futile by modern man. In fact, we easily conclude that the Greek gods were a fickle lot. Notwithstanding our ideas about this, the Greeks apparently were strongly convinced that no man's will could stand against the will of even the weakest god. There was no way to circumvent the will of a god unless a stronger god should choose to come to man's rescue. The decree of "fate" was final. Those who are interested enough to examine the relationship will see that Freud drew heavily from the richness of Greek literature when conceiving his analytic system, but of course he did not subscribe to their gods.

In the Elizabethan period of English culture, Shakespeare usually showed his greatest characters in conflict with themselves. If socially disapproved motives such as avarice, jealousy, or overambition took possession of the individual, the setting was one of tragedy. Thus the consequence of ambition without a wise regard for moral codes runs through *Macbeth* and *Julius Caesar;* tragedy results from jealousy and suspicion in *Othello;* compulsive doubting and indecision is basic in *Hamlet.* Some critics consider that in no other place in literature has internal turmoil been more vividly and dramatically drawn than in Hamlet.

There is no lack of examples of forcefully presented characters in conflict in the great novels. We would think of *Les Miserables, Crime and Punishment, War and Peace, A Tale of Two Cities,* along with many others in which the authors trace step by step many subtleties of overpowering conflict in their leading characters. Plot depends primarily upon the author's ability to sketch with skill and logic the operation of powerful drives in the individual. Next, the author must place difficult problems in front of the hero so that suspense is built and sustained. A solution that is satisfying to the hero is found in comedy; there is not an acceptable solution for the hero in tragedy.

The experiments performed by psychologists in which they try to delineate the threads that become entangled in human conflict pale in comparison with the great works of fiction and drama. However, the assumptions that underlie modern science seem to be that by painstaking methods scientists may add little by little to knowledge and understanding of conflict. Ultimately some degree of control over events is assumed to be within man's power. In general, conflict is assumed to be mostly man-made, and therefore subject to control by man. Works of art have as their purpose to reflect life with its struggles, failures, and successes, and perhaps to give an understanding of the causes and effects. Science frequently tries to build upon what is gained from such comprehension. It is believed that more than a minor beginning has been made in the experimental study of conflict as this operates within the individual or as it is found between groups, both small and large. It seems pertinent to review some of the first studies in which intense conflict is induced in a single subject before discussing group conflict and group dynamics.

EXPERIMENTAL NEUROSIS

Toward the end of his long and scientifically fruitful life, Pavlov turned his attention more and more to the study of conflict phenomena and he performed experiments that he referred to as having to do with the production of "experimental neurosis." Pavlov went about his experimental work by first training the animal to expect a particular outcome from a stimulus situation and then doing something to make discrimination difficult or impossible. After conditioning the animal he proceeded by bringing two stimuli, one associated with food the other with pain, into closer proximity so that discrimination finally became impossible and great conflict emerged. An experiment by Pavlov (16) in 1927 will serve to illustrate his technique. First, a dog was conditioned to expect food when a circle was presented, but no food when an ellipse was shown. Gradually the figures were changed in shape so that they became more and more alike until finally the dog could not discriminate between them. At this point the dog was said to suffer a "breakdown." Vacillation between approach and withdrawal characterized the dog's behavior as he struggled for cues to the consequence that would be forthcoming. The behavior became less predictable, varying from passivity to impulsive-like responses. Hunger increased but so did the threat of pain, so the resulting behavior was characterized by whimpering, trembling, and fear-like responses.

RANDOM REWARD AND PUNISHMENT

Since the time of these earlier studies by Pavlov, many experimenters have used essentially the same technique, not only to study discriminating capacity of subjects and their learning ability, but also to produce "experimental neurosis" and "experimental psychosis." A very effective procedure for producing confusion in the animal is to alternate at random reward and punishment—stress is built up by prolonged starvation and by using intensely painful stimuli.

EXPERIMENTALLY INDUCED REGRESSIVE BEHAVIOR

It has long been assumed that regressive behavior is an important characteristic of some psychotic individuals, notably in those suffering from schizophrenia, hebephrenic type. It has been further assumed that regression results from early emotional trauma. By regressive behavior we mean that it becomes more like that which characterized the same individual at an earlier time; that there is no forward development; and that adjustment is attempted on the earlier and more primitive level. Hamilton and Krechevsky obtained interesting results by administering an electric shock to rats at the choice point on a T-maze. This was used to furnish trauma, and then observations were made of how responses that had been established earlier were affected. First the rats had been trained on the maze which had a long arm to the left and a short one to the right. Since the rats could obtain food at either end of the maze they gradually learned to travel the shorter route to B. Then the rats were divided into two groups; one group acted as the control, and in the other, an experimental group, each rat was given a shock. The rats in the experimental group again resorted to their earlier procedure of exploring randomly.

INDIVIDUAL CONFLICT VS. GROUP ACTION

Psychologists take the individual as their center of focus in contrast to social scientists, who are usually concerned with groups and their interactions. Consequently it is not surprising that psychologists, when attacking problems involving small groups, have applied the techniques and the instruments that have evolved in the laboratory, where one individual normally serves as the subject. Only part of the methods and procedures have relevance when a shift is made from the study of the individual to a study of group action. We have deliberately mentioned some of the background material above because it does reflect the tendency of psychologists to view stress, frustration, and conflict as these are found in the individual. Naturally, there are differences between the function of a biological organism and the functioning of any social aggregate. The difficulties that are encountered when reasoning by analogy from biological unit to the body politic are too obvious to need our warning.

Nevertheless, in the study of small groups of people, the hazards may be less if the procedure is something more than armchair speculation and involves making observations and recordings and applying the general procedures of science.

There seems to be no need for biological and social scientists to become alarmed about poaching upon each other's preserves. Perhaps uneasiness in both camps has tended to lead to neglect and a no-man's-land in between where there are some crucial problems needing solution. Obviously, the individual's behavior is not going to be very thoroughly understood until laboratory observations are validated against the way the individual behaves when in his "natural" social environment. It seems equally clear that a thorough understanding of the individual acting as a unit, although never entirely independent of others, is essential to the social scientists. One of the most interesting approaches to these borderline problems having common elements of interest to psychologists and social scientists are the experiments sometimes referred to as having to do with group dynamics. Because of the newness of the work and the relatively small amount of it, we shall not devote much space to this topic. However, there is reason to believe that in future books upon experimental psychology more space will be devoted to group dynamics and experimental social psychology. Such a trend would be a logical sequence to the greater emphasis that has already been seen as developing with regard to studies of motivation, dynamics, and personality at the individual level.

GROUP DYNAMICS

In recent years research workers have become acutely aware of the importance of small groups of people who work together as committees and who seem to make most of the important decisions that deeply influence the lives of all people in modern culture. These small groups include boards of trustees, boards of directors, committees, and sub-committees. There is a long list of committees in most organizations, and these serve a great variety of purposes. They are constituted by appointment from the top level of management and they are elected by vote of those in the lower echelons. Standing committees of more or less permanence and with great power in setting policies are often supported by temporary or *ad hoc* committees set up to do particular jobs, such as fact-finding, investigating, summarizing, and reporting. These special committees rarely make decisions that lead directly to action but their work in assembling material, organizing information, and making recommendations may still be important in the operation of an organization.

Motivation for studying these small dynamic groups is obvious enough. Presumably the complexities of modern society, with each organization having intricate economic, social, and political affairs, prevent very many individuals from having sufficient knowledge to make sound decisions without the aid of both specialists and additional personnel to help integrate, synthesize, and generalize concerning broad situations.

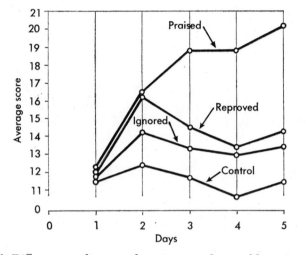

Fig. 16.5. Different results upon learning to solve problems in arithmetic. The four groups were equivalent at the beginning but scores varied with different incentives used. Not all experiments have shown such a striking difference. (Based upon data obtained by Hurlock, E. B., "The evaluation of certain incentives used in school work," *J. Edu. Psychol.* Vol. 16 (1925), page 149. After Munn, Norman L., *Psychology.* New York: Houghton Mifflin Co., 1956.)

Even in nations where there is a dictator there seems to be a great number of problems left to committees; decision and action may be left largely to the hands of the bureaucrats.

Some of the more specific problems that have been attacked in studying small groups include the following: Deutsch (6) set up an experiment to compare the effectiveness of coöperation and competition as these operate in the work of small groups. He divided fifty subjects into groups of five and then presented these groups with problems to solve. In one situation, he promised to reward the individual within each group who contributed the most with an A in the course from which the subjects were recruited. The other situation was structured so the single group that performed the best would be rewarded by having each member of the group receive an A. The results favored coöperation. Effort was coördinated better with a more satisfactory division of labor, motivation was stronger, communication more efficient, and the morale of the group superior. Perhaps there was not less competition but instead of

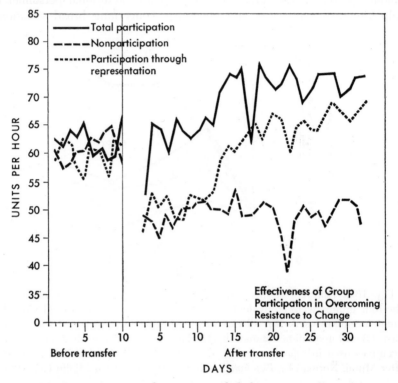

Fig. 16.6. Resistance to a change in work habits is partially a function of participation in discussion of the proposed change. (From Coch, L. and French, J. R. R., Jr., "Overcoming resistance to change," *Human Relat.* 1 (1948), 512-532.)

this resulting in sparring between individuals within the group, there was coördinated and consolidated effort directed toward solving the problem and thus toward competing with the other groups as a whole.

In the industrial situation, a major problem is to get workers to accept a change in work methods. Coch and French (4) decided to use some of the principles that have been advanced as being effective in obtaining coöperation and in getting group action. They used three groups of subjects and each was handled in a different way. Results obtained from each of the groups following the initiation of the changes showed a distinct advantage on the side of full discussion and participation of the individuals in arriving at the decision. While much valuable time may be spent in having individuals at all levels in an industrial firm discuss proposed changes, this is not always wasteful in terms of final net results or time expended. Through careful experimenting it should be possible to arrive at the relative merits of having decisions decreed from above as compared with a more democratic process. To some extent the problem is one of timing—at what point is it best that workers be informed or allowed to participate in decision-making or encouraged to take action when changes are involved? Time that is saved in making and announcing a decision after only a few people have considered an anticipated change may be lost again because of the greater task of persuading those at the lower levels of authority to coöperate and to execute the changes.

Several experiments have been performed in which false information is given each member of a group in order to determine how the members will respond to group pressure. For example, a question may be asked and wrong answers, previously agreed upon, given by all members but one of the group, in order to see how the lone dissenter is influenced. Such experiments are intended to reveal useful information about the force of suggestion and the conflict induced by group pressure.

Several investigators have been interested in the way leadership arises in small groups. While personality characteristics are undoubtedly of great importance, Leavitt (9) was able to show that in one small group leadership fell to the person in position to furnish the most information. He placed each of five subjects in separate cubicles and each held a card with several symbols printed upon it. There was one symbol common to all cards and the task was for the subjects to learn which was the common symbol. A system of switches enabled the subjects to communicate but the arrangement required that one person act as an intermediary. After a large number of trials the subjects were asked to vote for one member of the group as the leader. Leadership was voted largely according to position rather than upon the basis of other possible considerations. The position of the person elected as leader turned out to be at the communication center.

In still other studies of the activity of individual members of small groups, analysis is made of the time each member spends in certain kinds of participation. Some members spend most of their time in giving information, others ask questions, some concentrate upon opposing each proposition, while some are quick to support whatever has been suggested as a possible solution to the problem at hand. While it does not take the members of a group long to recognize these things about each other in a general sort of way, recording the activities and then having the objective data presented to the members has potential for guiding indi-

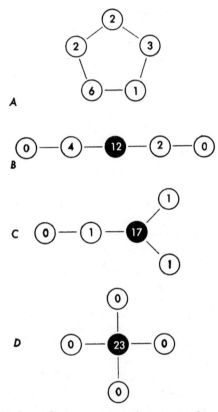

Fig. 16.7. The circles indicate position of various subjects in an experiment upon group leadership. The subject in the center-most position was noted as the leader, presumably because he became the center for communicating or furnishing information. (After Leavitt, H. J. "Some effects of certain communication patterns on group performance," *J. Abn. Soc. Psychol.*, 1951.)

viduals in future participation. This is a good procedure for revealing whether too much time is devoted to certain aspects of a problem to the neglect of more promising or fruitful aspects. For example, it is not infrequent that proposals for a solution to a problem are not timed properly and irrelevant issues may claim too much time. Members may start proposing solutions before all available information has been presented and it is possible that an early weighing of evidence for or against such a proposal may lead to debate and preoccupation of a less desirable solution while no consideration at all is given to a better solution. There has been no time for the effective solution to be proposed.

A variety of other innovations have been injected into the functioning process of small groups with a view to stimulating thoughtfulness and creativity in problem-solving. Sometimes this includes a change of scene or meetingplace of the group in the hope that new surroundings will help to break down old associations and sets that may interfere with the freedom of each member in taking fresh approaches. Again, assignment of various members to roles is sometimes helpful. One way this can be done is to assign a role that is different from the one habitually taken by the individual. The chairman may turn over his position temporarily, or the resistive critic is required to propose solutions instead of objecting to those indicated by others. The accountant may be required to set aside all consideration of cost and concentrate upon human relationships, the systematic and conservative member may be asked to play the role of the gambler or the most progressive and creative member. By practicing on similar but fictitious problems the group is sometimes able to take a much more objective, experimental, and creative attitude. Some of this may then carry over to the reality problem that is to be attacked later. By use of recording devices and later analysis and discussion of all that took place, a close approximation to a laboratory experiment can be carried into effect.

These activities require energy, flexibility, and time, but they are possible in a fluid and dynamic culture. They become means for increasing the tempo of change and at the same time they may furnish certain safeguards to precipitant action that often results from decision-making that is confined to one person. One of the most difficult problems to overcome in the democratic process is to move with greater speed to decision and action. Experiments going on presently that have as their purpose an understanding of group dynamics, and which ultimately furnish guidance and control in decision-making, give promise of producing both scientific and practical results of great worth.

SUGGESTED READINGS

Munn, Norman L. *Psychology*. "The motivation of behavior," pp. 82-108. New York: Houghton Mifflin, 1951.

Underwood, Benton J. *Experimental Psychology*. "Motivation," pp. 156-199; "Conflict," pp. 241-280, New York; Appleton-Century-Crofts, 1949,

Andrews, T. G. (ed.). *Methods of Psychology.* Young: "Motivation, feelings and emotion," pp. 348-390. New York: John Wiley, 1948.

Krech, David, and Crutchfield, Richard S. *Elements of Psychology,* pp. 372-398. New York: Alfred A. Knopf, 1958.

Woodworth, Robert S., and Schlosberg, Harold. *Experimental Psychology.* "Motivation in Learning and Performance," pp. 655-685. New York: Henry Holt, 1954.

McDougall, William. *The Energies of Men.* New York: Charles Scribner, 1932.

Cannon, Walter B. *Bodily Changes in Pain, Hunger, Fear and Rage.* Boston: Charles T. Branford, 1953.

Johnson, Donald M. *The Psychology of Thought and Judgement,* pp. 445-501. New York: Harper, 1955.

Lewin, Kurt. *The Dynamic Theory of Personality.* New York: McGraw-Hill, 1935.

Tolman, Edward Chace. *Purposive Behavior in Animals and Men.* Berkeley, Calif.: University of California Press, 1949.

Stagner, Ross. *Psychology of Industrial Conflict.* New York: John Wiley, 1956.

Hilgard, Ernest R. *Introduction to Psychology* (2nd ed.). "Group dynamics," pp. 500-518. New York: Harcourt, Brace, 1957.

Cartwright, D., and Zander, A. *Group Dynamics: Research and Theory.* Evanston, Ill.: Row, Peterson, 1953.

Hare, A. P., Borgatta, E. F., and Bales, R. F. *Small Groups: Studies in Social Interaction.* New York: Alfred A. Knopf, 1954.

Dennis, Wayne. *Readings in General Psychology.* "Motivation," pp. 174-224. New York: Prentice-Hall, 1949.

Garrett, Henry E. *Great Experiments in Psychology.* "Experimental approaches to personality study," pp. 171-198; "McDougall and social psychology," pp. 199-218. New York: Appleton-Century-Crofts, 1951.

Atkinson, John W. *Motives in Fantasy, Action, and Society: A Method of Assessment and Study.* New York: D. Van Nostrand Co., 1958.

Stacey, Chalmers L., and De Martino, Manfred F. *Understanding Human Motivation.* Cleveland: Howard Allen, 1958.

Bonner, Hubert. *Group Dynamics.* New York: The Ronald Press, 1959.

REFERENCES

1. Beach, Frank A. "Instinctive Behavior: Reproductive Activities," pp. 387-434. In Stevens, S. S. (ed.). *Handbook of Experimental Psychology.* New York: John Wiley, 1951.

2. Bernard, L. L. *Instinct, A Study in Social Psychology.* New York: Henry Holt, 1924.

3. Cowles, J. T. "Food-tokens as incentives for learning by chimpanzees," *Comp. Psychol. Monogr.,* 14, No. 71 (1937).

4. Coch, L., and French, J. R. R., Jr. "Overcoming resistance to change," *Hum. Relat.* 1 (1948), 512-532.

5. Denenberg, V. H. "Hoarding in the white rat under isolation and group conditions," *J. Comp. and Physiol. Psychol.*, 45 (1952), 497-503.

6. Deutsch, M. "The effects of cooperation and competition upon group process." In Cartwright, D., and Zander, A. (eds.). *Group Dynamics.* Evanston, Ill.: Row, Peterson, 1953.

7. Hamilton, H. C. "The effect of incentives on accuracy of discrimination measures on the Galton bar," *Archives Psychol.*, 16, No. 103 (1929).

8. Heyne, R. W. *Functional Analysis of Group Problem-Solving Techniques.* Unpublished report of conference research project, Ann Arbor, University of Michigan, 1948.

9. Leavitt, H. J. "Some effects of certain communication patterns on group performance," *J. Abnorm. Soc. Psychol.*, 46 (1951), 38-50.

10. Lewin, K. T., Dembo, L., Festinger, L., and Sears, P. S. In J. McV. Hunt (ed.). *Personality and Behavior Disorders.*

11. Marquis, D. G., Guetzkan, H., and Heyns, R. W. "A social psychological study of decision-making conference." In Guetzkan, H. (ed.). *Groups, Leadership, and Men.* Pittsburgh: Carnegie Press, 1951.

12. McDougall, William. *Introduction to Social Psychology* (5th ed.), p. 44. London: Methuen, 1908.

13. McDougall, William. *The Energies of Men.* New York: Charles Scribner, 1932.

14. Morgan, C. T., Stellar, E., and Johnson, O. "Food—deprivation and hoarding in rats," *J. Comp. Psychol.*, 35 (1943), 275-296.

15. Murphy, G., Murphy, L. B., and Newcomb, T. M. *Experimental Social Psychology.* New York: Harper, 1937.

16. Pavlov, I. P. *Conditioned Reflexes.* Trans. by Anrep, G. V. London: Oxford University Press, 1927.

17. Smith, H. C., and Dunbar, D. S. "The personality and achievement of classroom participation," *J. Educ. Psychol.* 42 (1951), 65-84.

18. Tinbergen, N. *The Study of Instincts.* London: Oxford University Press, 1951.

19. Wolfe, J. B. "Effectiveness of token-rewards for chimpanzees," *Comp. Psychol. Monogr.*, 12, No. 60 (1936).

20. Young, Paul Thomas. "Motivation, feeling and emotions," pp. 349-551. In Andrew, T. G. (ed.). *Methods of Psychology.* New York: John Wiley, 1948.

17 | DESIGNING AND PERFORMING AN ORIGINAL EXPERIMENT

DIRECTIONS

It is hoped that at least parts of this chapter are worthy of being read twice—once when (or if) the student first plans an individual experiment and again when he has finished all but writing the final report. At the time of the second reading it is suggested that the student also proceed to the final short chapter of the book. That chapter is intended to give the student further orientation as to the scope of science and the part contributed to it by experimentation. Beyond this purpose it is hoped that background information is given in this and the following chapter that will improve the student's ability to set forth his own contributions in a manner so he communicates more effectively with scientists. The second reading might well prove to be more profitable than the first. The student will then be trying to evaluate his work and should be able to determine whether serious mistakes were made in designing or executing the experiment. Careful study of both chapters should provide guidance to help him to present a clear statement of the problem that he has attacked; describe concisely the procedure used; and set down his results in salient form and discuss them so that they become meaningful. Perhaps those readers who have been in the habit of turning to read the outcome in novels before reading the first of the book will feel at home with this procedure! We trust that others will not be too resentful of our rather unorthodox suggestion as to the way this textbook might be used. We shall not defend, at this time, the sequence of chapters used in putting the book together and we do not apologize for asking that some of the material be read more than once.

DEFINITION OF AN EXPERIMENT

While there are many places in the book where the meaning of an experiment has been attempted, let us again review the essential elements.

The reader who is aware of countless studies that have been labeled as experiments, many of which fail to meet very well the requirements of an experiment, may come to believe that repetition of the meaning of an experiment is not wasted effort. Without giving the exact wording, but following Webster's Dictionary closely, we find: *The act of experimenting is undertaken to discover some unknown principle or effect; it is to establish or to illustrate a suggested but unknown truth. The most essential element is to be found in the setting up of effective controls over conditions so that careful observations can be made. Each observation becomes a trial test to confirm or to disprove something held in doubt. The experiment is always undertaken in order to answer a question that has not a fully known or accepted answer.*

Because of the essential truth of the last sentence it becomes clear that the exercises participated in as part of the laboratory work in all beginning science courses require that the meaning be stretched a bit if such exercises are to be spoken of as experiments. More accurately, these activities are provided so that the student may advance by studying examples, then trying to imitate them and in this way become prepared for extensive experimenting.

DIFFICULTY TO OVERCOME

When forced by the necessity of designing an experiment, many if not most beginners suffer some degree of intellectual paralysis. Ideas that initially seemed to be good evaporate the instant the student tries to transmit them to paper. It is easy to become frightened at the prospect that one's ideas (and the methods and techniques intended to prove their soundness) are to come under the scrutiny and probable criticism of others. Thus there is often a rapid transition from quick enthusiasm to growing doubt, and finally to over self-criticism. Ideas or proposed experiments may fall to the wayside one by one as each is analyzed and tested by the several criteria that have been suggested as being useful when evaluating a projected experiment. However, if the student does not panic as a result of this relentless attrition of his precious but embryonic ideas, he may still hammer out a design that will prove to be the beginning of a good experiment.

There is not ordinarily much inspiration involved in setting up each scientifically useful experiment but there can easily be a great deal of perspiration, especially upon the part of a beginner. A long list of rejected ideas and false starts should not lead to alarm. The goal of effective controls over conditions so that careful observations can be made must be kept in mind. The pool of possible research ideas—good, bad, and indifferent—appears to be inexhaustible.

GENERAL APPROACH

Before moving on to the details of planning an experiment it may be well to get a general perspective of the approach that the experimenter makes. In his book, "The Principles of Scientific Research" Freedman (1) begins the chapter devoted to planning research by saying: "The planning of any research should logically be determined by consideration of the nature of the problem, the method which the investigator proposes to apply to its investigation, the thoroughness with which this method is to be applied, the available resources, and the available time."

At once it will be recognized that some of the points raised are relevant to what the student should undertake in an experiment that is intended as only a small part of the total requirements in a college course. There will be little time available, perhaps very limited resources, and while the method to be used should be sound it can scarcely be applied with the thoroughness that will make the study a definitive one. If the student will orient himself to the idea of setting up a pilot study in which the methodology used might be replicated and later applied to a large number of subjects he may be off to a practical start. Seasoned experimenters rarely proceed to the point of freezing their methods, techniques, and procedures without first doing a pilot study, or doing what is often called a "dry run." Execution of this kind of study with a reasonable degree of skill should fulfill the basic purpose in a beginning experimental course. Evidence that the student has been able to fulfill this obligation is necessarily to be found in the report that is submitted. The student will need to be able to report his work with a degree of precision that will enable another person to replicate it. Beyond the objective reporting, he should be able to relate his results to those obtained by other investigators, present meaningful interpretations, and venture generalizations and conclusion consistent with his findings and within the scope and limitations ordinarily considered to be prudent among scientists. In other words, if the student has made progress toward greater scientific knowledge, skill, and sophistication, the individually planned and reported experiment affords good opportunity to demonstrate this. Success of the kind expected here does not have to include the collecting of a great quantity of data. The assumption has been made that research contributions would be a future goal.

FINDING AND STATING A PROBLEM

It is characteristic of beginning research workers to focus attention upon the big problems of the world. It is easy to become overly ambitious and try to hurry on to the great issues. Unfortunately, this is rarely wise at first. Most of the investigators have an uncomfortable feeling about asking small or seemingly trivial questions if they are to use painstaking procedures to answer them. It is natural to hope to avoid wasting effort upon unworthy tasks. While looking forward to scientifically useful results is a sound goal, it is easy to plunge into dangerous pitfalls if over-ambition leads to undertaking too much at first. Questions may readily be asked of such a broad nature that there is little or no chance of forcing an answer. For example, it might be decided that an understanding of human nature was the all-important problem for a person who works in psychology. What question, or questions, concerning human nature can be answered? What hypotheses can be advanced with confidence that proof or disproof will be forthcoming?

Uncertainties and frustrations that generally follow when an attempt is made to solve problems that are too big readily lead to discouragement. Even though the problem may seem to be all-important, a feeling of helplessness may overcome the investigator. How does the psychologist proceed so that he will not be stymied in this way?

Obviously, he cannot afford to withdraw from all the big and difficult problems of human nature. Avoidance of these may serve the purpose of safety but a means of attacking them must somehow be found if significant progress is to be made. Human nature, while broad and perhaps vague, still embraces too much that is vital to permit the psychologist to beat a retreat. It is assumed that "human nature" covers drives and motives, the ways in which sense organs respond when acted upon by energy, processes of perceiving, what has been learned and how this is used, emotional reactions—altogether, the characteristic way man responds to the world about him. The difficulties arise in part, it will be seen, because one general and abstract question is asked instead of many specific and perhaps concrete ones. Human nature encompasses not just one big problem, but many big as well as little problems.

Several years ago Carl E. Seashore (3) set forth nine questions that he said he had become accustomed to ask about a proposed research project. He had wide and useful experience in evaluating problems in various sciences while working in his capacity as the Dean of a Graduate School. One of his duties was to pass judgment as to the probable scientific fruitfulness to be expected from research proposals made by students in all the basic sciences. Confronted with the limitations in teaching staff, apparatus, time, and other resources it was his responsibility to encourage effort in the direction of the greatest usefulness. However, he was mindful that "usefulness" when applied to research must be certain to include long-range objectives best served by an attack being made upon basic problems. Seashore was considered a very successful and stimulating administrator in the scientific field. His influence extended beyond making decisions as to the feasibility of a research proposal, for he was able to furnish research guidance to many students as they pursued their interests in their chosen scientific fields.

While the current number of graduate students would render it totally beyond the capacity of many graduate school deans even to attempt to review all research within a large university, it is believed that Dean Seashore's overview enabled him to produce a useful list of points to be considered by an experimenter working at any educational level. The questions he raised concerning research and experimenting and the discussion of them is applicable to science in general. Perhaps Seashore placed no special significance upon the fact that he came up with nine questions. He saw fit to fraction the problems of research in this way for convenience of discussion. While his questions have bearing upon points that are generally raised after a problem has been settled upon, nevertheless all of them need to be considered before the experimenter proceeds to collecting data. The questions are reproduced as Seashore presented them and our own discussion of each follows:

1. Has the experimenter fractionated his problem so that he can deal with one specific factor at a time and set up an operational definition?
2. Has he isolated the chosen factor for experimentation so that it can be varied under control?
3. Are his findings recordable, countable, and repeatable for verification?
4. Has he kept other factors, subjective and objective, constant?
5. Is the factor measured undistorted by isolation from the total situation, subjective and environmental?
6. Is the factor measured significant?
7. Is the statistical method involved, if any, sound?
8. Does it contribute to some fact that utilizes or has a bearing on systematic science?
9. Are the conclusions after each measurement limited to the role of the factor measured?

Fractioning the Experiment

The problem of human nature, if we are to apply these questions to our earlier illustration, is obviously one that must be fractioned if we can hope to make very much experimental progress. Attempts at fractioning this problem have led to the use of such headings as those standing at the beginning of the chapters in this book. There are, of course, many other aspects of human nature that have been split up and isolated for detailed investigation. Even a literary essay on human nature written by a man of letters might readily be subdivided as a means to orderly and effective presentation.

It is not always necessary in an experiment to fraction a problem so that only one specific factor is investigated at a time. However, this is frequently desirable, and sometimes almost essential, if one is to be sure of the meaning of the results. In modern statistics scientists have a means of mathematical analysis and controls which may permit several experimental variables to operate simultaneously, and yet meaningful interpretations remain possible. In many psychological problems there are advantages to be gained by studying several variables together in order to learn more about interaction processes. Still, it must be said that a considerable degree of research sophistication is required before this kind of experiment should be undertaken. While much progress has been made in applying statistical controls, even since Seashore first set down his list of questions, yet fractioning a problem to the extent that factors can be successfully managed statistically is, and presumably will remain, a scientific necessity. Being able to fraction a problem to the point of successful management is therefore one of the distinctive characteristics of the apt scientist.

Isolating the Chosen Factor for Observation

The second question posed by Seashore scarcely needs further elaboration at this time. Stress has already been placed upon the desirability of isolating a single factor that becomes the independent variable and then systematically manipulating it and observing the effect upon the dependent variables. There are many practical situations in which the investigator wants the quickest and easiest answer concerning the use of one or another commodity. For example, he may want to choose between brands of fertilizer, brands of flour to make a cake, or to determine the best method of presenting material to children who are trying to learn how to spell words.

Measuring and Recording

Some kind of record is obviously required if the experimenter is to transmit accurately his observations to others. There are often several ways that records of findings can be made, but some of the ways may have great advantages over others. For example, pulse rate might be counted by holding the fingers on an artery of the subject while using a stop watch for timing. However, there would be many opportunities for mistakes; the process might be very distracting to the subject; there would not be a running record of the pulse rate that might reveal changes within the observation period—altogether little possibility for checking the results for accuracy later. Repeated performances might reveal a difference which in reality reflected only the unreliability of the experimenter's performance and thus suggest a difference in phenomena that did not exist. Procedures used in the discoveries of most of the truths in nature have been repeated and the results verified literally hundreds of times. Where satisfactory recording is achieved, the effort required to replicate and to verify the results is greatly reduced.

Constancy in Subjective and Objective Factors

It is extremely easy to allow unintended factors to creep into the procedure. A multitude of factors, for the moment not under direct scrutiny, may influence results where a phenomenon is being studied. Temperature, humidity, or lighting conditions, for example, might radically influence the response of an organism, although attention at the time was centered upon the effect of varying some stimulus not related to any of these. The psychologist in particular is familiar with the tricks that may be played upon him through perceptual distortion, selection, and so forth, if he becomes intensely emotionally involved in the problem. When subjective judgment, or even sensory discrimination, plays a prominent part in rendering observations, the experimenter is wise to be especially cautious against being led into error. There is an ever-present threat that he may see what he wants to see. If there is a shift in attitude during the process of experimenting, this can lead to observations that reflect a spurious difference in the data collected during the first and second part of the experiment. The use of the most strenuous objective techniques that are available will help to reduce distortion resulting from attitudes and subjective judgment.

Changing the apparatus during an experiment always presents the possibility that there may be a subsequent difference in the data obtained. The investigator frequently comes to see that he would have done better if he had started with a different apparatus or procedure. The amateur may then succumb to the temptation to make a change while in the middle of an experiment. Nearly always such changes should be made only after all previously collected data are placed in the waste basket! The two sets of data can rarely be combined and scientific integrity maintained. There might be situations where the data collected first should be reported after which the improved plans would be executed in a new experiment. Sound training in any of the sciences helps the individual to exercise better judgment in these disturbing problems.

Distortion and Isolation

While isolation of one or more factors in order to permit systematic variations will usually be essential in an experiment, it is also true that this very isolation presents problems. It could be that isolation is carried so far in the laboratory setting that the findings have little relevance to what may occur in everyday life. The individual always lives in a fluid and dynamic environment where a large number of variables operate simultaneously. It is because of the difficulty in bridging the gap between laboratory findings and everyday events that the layman is often ready to heap scorn (partially deserved, perhaps) upon the "ivory tower" scientists. It is possible that serious mistakes will be made if the reporter upon an experiment glibly generalizes that a response made within the restricted confines of a four-walled laboratory will be the same as a response on a busy street corner. Obviously not all the conditions that may make for variation are the same.

Significance

Seashore raised a question about whether the factors to be measured were significant. The term "significant" is often confusing. The scientifically untrained person is likely to use the word as a synonym for important, meaningful, or vital. There is a more limited and specialized meaning often implied when the term is used by the statistician or psychologist. They may speak of a significant difference between two averages when trying to convey that the difference is a true or dependable one and that repeated observations will still reveal a difference. Thus the word is used to state something about probability, or the chances that repeated observations would still produce results having the same relationships. Analysis of the data may make it possible to conclude that the difference between two averages is significant at the one percent level. That is, repeated measures, if made under approximately the same conditions, will result in the higher average keeping its relative position ninety-nine times in a hundred trials.

While there is obviously a similarity in these two uses of "significance" it is nevertheless true that a difference between the two averages might be "significant" in the statistical sense and yet not be very important in a "practical" sense. Let it be supposed that an educator is concerned with setting up a curriculum for two existing groups of students. These groups might exist because of physical location, income of parents, color of skin, or one of many conditions or circumstances. Now it might be found that a difference for intelligence in the two groups is statistically significant, one group averaging 99 and the other 101. (This small difference could be reliable if a large number of subjects were involved.) Whatever justification there might be for treating the two groups differently in educational procedure, it would scarcely be defensible to use a difference in intelligence as a basis for the decision although factually this exists. There would be much overlapping of the two groups and sensible curricular plans based upon intelligence levels of the individuals would apply about equally well to both groups. So many individuals of the lower group would be more intelligent than the less intelligent in the higher group that the educator would be on doubtful grounds to make different provisions in planning the curriculum. It would usually make more scientific as well as practical sense to divide the students again and start over. Assuming freedom of action and that the primary concern was to plan the curriculum upon the basis of intelligence of the participating students, a better procedure would be to form two new groups by combining the upper half (or more precisely those obtaining a score above 100) of each of the existing groups and letting those who stood below the middle form one group and those above form the other group. The new groupings would almost certainly reveal a greater difference between averages in intelligence than was the case formerly for the two groups. Statistical significance of the difference between the two new groups should be enhanced and might furnish a meaningful basis for a practical decision.

In our discussion we may have included some points that Seashore had in mind when referring to sound statistical methods. However, in raising the question of significance he seemed to be thinking more of the common-sense meaning of the term. He said: "The significance of an experiment can be judged by common sense and logical evaluation of the hypothesis involved." (Ibid., p. 444.) In science, he held, the experiment should always work toward progressive clarification if it is to constitute a significant contribution.

Statistical Methods

We have previously stated that it was not our intention to try to instruct the student in complicated statistical procedures; hence, we shall not elaborate upon this point. However, it is essential to recognize that the first step to sound statistical and scientific procedure is to take measures that are exact, to collect data that are countable, accurate, and relevant to the problem to be solved. "When you can measure what you are speaking about and express it in numbers," says Lord Kelvin, "you know something about it, and when you cannot measure it, when you cannot express it in numbers, your knowledge is of a meagre and unsatisfactory kind. It may be the beginning of knowledge but you have scarcely in your thoughts advanced to the state of a science." (Freedman, 2) There is nothing to prevent the novice from counting. Unless data can be reduced to numbers in some way, there is little chance of determining how reliable and valid they are. The choice and application of the best statistical treatment that is possible in dealing with a given set of data requires knowledge and skill that must remain a challenge for later achievement.

Making a Contribution

Even a simple experiment, and one not far advanced because of insufficient subjects, may still be directed toward answering a question that can be woven into the scientific system of a field of knowledge. A piece of apparatus can be tried to see if it will work dependably; a range of subjects may be used to see if the methods and procedures are equally appropriate. "The merit of experiments is measured by the extent to which they contribute basic and enduring facts toward systematic science," says Seashore. An experiment may be valuable if it merely serves to tell us how to plan a more effective experiment.

Conclusions

There is a great temptation to overgeneralize from a small amount of data. Few people can resist the impulse to conclude that all Chinese are like the one they happen to know, that some event was caused by something that was observed to happen before the event in question. The warning against overgeneralizing needs emphasis. Yet, in drawing conclusions there is also an obligation upon the scientist to try to generalize to events and phenomena beyond those that he has under direct observation. It is the broad purpose in science to discover principles and laws that make possible prediction and control that set into motion events that will bring about new and desired events. Usually conclusions can be divided into two types: first, those that can be derived rather directly from the facts collected; second, those of a more speculative nature that raise new hypotheses for testing and suggestions for further research.

FURTHER PRACTICAL QUESTIONS OF PROCEDURE

Often it becomes reasonably clear during an early stage of data collecting that an experiment is going to be a success or failure. Costly mistakes in methods of procedures may become obvious. Insurmountable problems may arise concerning getting sufficient numbers or the right kinds of subjects. The experimenter may come to realize that his broad theory or the specific hypotheses that he derived from it are defective. Judgment as to what course of action to take must rest upon many considerations. Sometimes it is the part of wisdom to stop and redesign the experiment.

While nearly all the problems of setting up an experiment and carrying it forward to the completed report might be handled appropriately in discussing one or another of Seashore's questions, there remain a few points for discussion that might be useful. Some of these are very practical matters and not infrequently require an arbitrary decision. They include the answers to such questions as: Has someone already performed the experiment? What apparatus is to be used? Could the experiment make better use of lower animals than of people? How are subjects obtained and what is the best way to enlist their coöperation? How many subjects should be used? How much over-all time will be required to complete the experiment? Perhaps most of these questions allow alternate answers, but the situation may indicate that only one solution is feasible.

There is no absolutely certain way to learn whether others have performed the exact experiment or one that is so closely parallel that repetition is worthless. A search through the basic books in experimental psychology is a good way to start. Usually the subject index and references listed will give clues. Reports of those experiments judged to be most like the one proposed should be read in journals and use made of the accompanying bibliography. If the library does not have the journals in which the original articles were reported it is usually an easy task to secure an inter-library loan of the needed references. The expense should not be great, but it is usually paid by the person making the request. Few libraries are extensive enough to provide all needed research materials in any field of knowledge, but reference librarians will ordinarily give willing help.

Apparatus

Within limits the nature of the problem dictates the apparatus that is to be used. Some choice may be possible and, of course, it is only sensible to make use of the most accurate and refined apparatus that is available. However, for the proposals that we have in mind here, the student need not insist upon expensive apparatus merely to get slightly greater accuracy. Again, since learning methodology is the primary objective, relatively simple and rugged apparatus that is within range of the student's manipulative skill is to be preferred over more intricate apparatus that cannot be kept operating.

Subjects

In most colleges subjects are taken from the general or elementary psychology classes. Varying degrees of pressure are likely to be brought to bear under some procedure of making participation in experiments as a requirement of the course. There are hazards in going to dormitories, fraternities, or sororities after subjects, especially if the experiment is moved to the location of the subjects. It is most unlikely that a satisfactory control can be kept over the surrounding situation. Also, there is apparently a greater temptation for the subjects to take the experiment lightly and thus there is the risk of inadequate coöperation. On rare occasions experimenters have paid their subjects. As a rule this is resorted to only when a subject is expected to devote several hours to the task, and of course, some experiments may require repeated visits to the laboratory over weeks or months. Decision regarding the number of subjects to be used will be determined by several factors, with time being an important practical one. In more extensive research, statistical consideration often determines the answer to what is a sufficient number of subjects.

Animal or Human Subjects?

Certain experiments require animals, others people. Some experiments can make use of either. Experiments upon sensory processes become rather complicated if lower animals are used. Nearly always some learning task will be essential as a means of determining whether sensory discrimination has been possible. On the other hand, subjective reports may be admissible in studying sensory or perceptual problems when human subjects are used. If intense pain is a part to the experiment, human subjects may not be obtainable. Severe punishment is rarely necessary in psychological experiments and the dictates of civilization generally prevent experimenters from doing inhumane acts on animals. Experiments in which drugs of unknown potency are to be used are nearly always tested upon animals before being administered to human beings. Most scientists feel that the purposes served justify the means and they do not consider such procedure as wanton cruelty.

Time Factors

Planning an experiment that can be completed within the time limits of a school term is very bothersome to most students. The risk is nearly always in planning an experiment that runs too long to allow sufficient time for the necessary preliminary work and to analyze the data and write a report. The writer's observations include many examples and testimonies to hasty work as the student desperately tries to meet the deadline at the end of the school term. Experience here as elsewhere too often teaches a dear school. Let it be said that the student is off to a good start if he makes a time schedule in the beginning. A workable time schedule might look something like the following: (1) the problem found and background literature read during the first third of a school term. (2) The second third might be devoted to running subjects, tabulating, and analyzing results. (3) Most workers will need about a third of the time to organize and write the report. A considerable portion of the report can and probably should be written in rough form even before the data are collected. If the problem has been clearly stated, background literature reviewed, procedure described, and proposed manner of handling results outlined in advance, the chances are not only that the experiment will be more tightly designed but also that the final reporting will be easier for the writer and more comprehensible to the reader.

Some of the above questions, and others that will arise, have alternate answers. Often there are few guides to the best choice, in which case an early but arbitrary decision may be best. The seasoned experimenter learns that every question that is raised becomes a potential barrier to action. Each affords the compulsive doubter some distress; all afford the procrastinator his excuse. It is not easy to distinguish between the questions that are vital and those that are trivial, between those that must be carefully weighed and answered after thoughtful study and those that should be disposed of by the use of the least possible intellectual energy.

Summary

It is found that there are two general kinds of questions raised in designing an experiment. One set has to do with the purpose of the experiment. Speculation about possible answers may lead us to state one or more hypotheses. These are then to be tested by suitable methods and techniques. The second set of questions has to do with the methods and procedures to be brought to bear upon the general problem under consideration. If these last questions are not properly raised and effectively dealt with in such a way that answers are forced to the original questions, the hypotheses are not tested.

If all the criteria used by Seashore to evaluate an experiment have been met, and if the experimenter has not stumbled upon some lesser problems, meaningful results should be obtained. It is the mark of an amateur if the methods and techniques that are used in an attempt to force a solution to the problem at hand have not been brought to bear effectively in the experiment. In which case the hypothesis remains untested. Occasionally a good problem has been stated, but, for lack of technical advances in methods or apparatus, a definitive experiment remains, at the present, impossible.

The reason for experimenting is that the answer sought is not a foregone conclusion. Consequently, any experiments that are in general well conceived may turn out to be failures in terms of the results sought; that is, if a specific and positive answer is sought beyond the usual scientific goal of discovering the principles or truths of nature. The beginning scientist is badly in need of tolerance for frustration in order that he may accept relative failures. One is reminded of the hundreds of failures, discouragements, and almost new starts that marked the path of Edison to the electric light; Burbank to the seedless orange; Pasteur to an effective vaccine. So-called negative results may serve a very useful scientific purpose. It must be granted that positive results usually produce a more cheerful scientist.

SUGGESTED READINGS

Seashore, Carl E. "Measurement of scientific merit in applied psychology," *The American Psychologist*, 3 (1948), 443-445.

Underwood, Benton J. *Psychological Research*, Chaps. 4, 5, "Research design," pp. 85-173. New York: Appleton-Century-Crofts, 1957.

Bugelski, B. R. *Experimental Psychology*, Chap. 3, "The steps in scientific work," pp. 38-60. New York: Henry Holt, 1951.

REFERENCES

1. Freedman, Paul. *The Principles of Scientific Research,* p. 94. Washington: Public Affairs Press, 1950.
2. *Ibid.,* p. 15.
3. Seashore, Carl E. "Measurement of scientific merit in applied psychology," *The American Psychologist,* 3 (1948), 443-445.
4. *Ibid.,* p. 444.

18 | SCIENCE, RESEARCH, EXPERIMENTATION

PURPOSE

The purpose of this chapter is to orient the student to the broader aspects of experimental psychology as this relates to research and science. While we may repeat ourselves at times, it is intended that the chapter be something more than a summary or review of the material covered in the book. Not much has been said about research previously, but we shall assume that most of the students who elected to take the course in which this book is used intend to become scientists working in the field of psychology. The psychologist, it is believed, must expect to devote a considerable amount of his time to research while in training. Those who are to become recognized as productive scientists are likely to begin research while students, certainly no later than when graduate students, and continue during much of their professional careers. Among psychologists, research usually means experimental research.

Possibly it will seem premature to introduce a discussion of research while the student must still look forward to considerable undergraduate study. However, during the last few years "research" has become the label of a profession or career that interests many people. Furthermore, a career in research gives promise of attracting an ever-increasing number of both men and women. Careful consideration about a career is assumed to claim much of the thought of any college student who has not yet come to a final decision in this matter. Research work on either a part-time basis, or as a full-time job, has expanded rapidly and gives promise of increasing acceleration and scope. Perhaps in no other field of science does research at present claim a higher percentage of the time of qualified professional workers than in psychology.

Possibly it is an undue liberty in the use of the word "research" to use it as the label of this somewhat new profession and to put it alongside medicine, law, or engineering. Nevertheless, if there is a willingness to accept teaching as a profession, research may qualify as well. A high percentage, but by no means all, of those doing research combine it with teaching. Even now it may be that the number of people devoting part or all of their time to research is greater than the number in any of the older recognized professions, excluding teaching alone.

We are not trying to write a job description of research, nor are we primarily concerned with promoting an embryonic profession, as worthy as that cause might be. We do want to discuss the relationship between science, research, and experimenting. Possibly it could be said that all true experimenting is both science and research. It is not true that the statement can be turned around and claim made that all science, or all research, is experimental. In order to speak as concisely as possible concerning these relationships it becomes desirable to elaborate upon the first two terms used in the title of this chapter—*science* and *research*. It is taken for granted that not much more needs to be said about experimenting.

WHAT IS SCIENCE?

A brief statement of the meaning of science was attempted in the introductory chapter. There it was emphasized that the methodology used in acquiring information was the distinguishing characteristic that set off a particular body of knowledge that could be called science. The content or subject matter might enable the reader to make a further discrimination and speak of a particular science. The following definitions of science have sometimes been used:

"Science, as its name implies," says Bertrand Russell (Freedman, 2), "is primarily knowledge; by convention it is knowledge of a certain kind, namely, which seeks general laws connecting a number of particular facts. Gradually, however, the aspect of science as knowledge is being thrust into the background by the aspect of science as the power to manipulate nature." In speaking of the development of science and more particularly of physics, Millikan had this to say: "This perceptual effort to reduce the complexities of the world to simple terms, and to build up infinite variety of objects which present themselves to our senses out of different arrangements of motions of the least possible number of elementary substances" (2). Thus it may be seen that a scientist conceives of his work as being primarily that of isolating elements for study so they may be better understood and then organizing them again into meaningful wholes. Sir William Dampier used a rather short and pithy definition of science: "Ordered knowledge of natural phenomena and the rational study of the relations between the concepts in which these phenomena are expressed" (3). This definition may seem too circular to some, for in effect it says that science is what the scientist works at. If one objects to speaking of science as an activity, a definition closer to that found in a dictionary is that science is an organized body of knowledge. This knowledge comes into existence by the use of a particular methodology; it is the product of deliberate effort of scientists; research is the basic ingredient in the making of a science.

WHAT IS RESEARCH?

Not all research, of course, is confined to the sciences. Nor is all research in the sciences of an experimental nature. There are literary, historical, theological, and many other areas in which research may be done. A large number of workers may never leave the repositories of libraries and museums to complete their research; others may make observations of natural phenomena. The scientist usually finds it necessary to make use of the library as he progresses in his research, but most of his time and effort is likely to be spent in the laboratory. The library may be very useful to him while he searches for ideas and unsolved problems. Investigations continue in the library until it is determined what others have already discovered. Following these efforts, the scientist usually turns to the task of making his own observations in order to collect original data. If the observations are made under controlled conditions, where one (or more) variable is systemically manipulated, he is experimenting. When the data are collected, the investigator must deal with problems of classifying and analyzing his data. If his knowledge and skill are great he may be able to carry through this part of his work with a minimum of referral to the procedures of others. However, once the results are set forth in objective form, the chances are great that the experimentalist must again return to published reports so he may compare his findings with these; enter into discussion of his results, which eventually should enable him to present meaningful interpretations and draw conclusions. An experiment becomes useful to science when the experimenter has been able to communicate his methods and results; relate these to the work of others; and finally incorporate his contribution into the general structure of some science.

The laboratory may, and probably does, claim most of the time of the scientist in contrast to the workplace for research workers in other areas of knowledge. Not infrequently the library work seems to be tedious drudgery to the original and creative scientist; however, he dares not neglect it if he is to become recognized as productive and not wasteful

TABLE 18.1. A FEW PURE SCIENCES AND SOME REPRESENTATIVE
TECHNOLOGICAL APPLICATIONS

Pure Science	Representative Application or Technology
Anatomy	Dentistry, Surgery
Astronomy	Aerial, Marine, and Terrestrial Navigation
Botany	Agronomy, Forestry, Horticulture
Chemistry	Industrial Chemistry (manufacture of paints, plastics, soaps, synthetic fabrics, fertilizers, insecticides, dyes, stain removers, polishes, etc.)
Physics	Aeronautical Engineering, Civil Engineering, Electrical Engineering, Mechanical Engineering (manufacture of automobiles, airplanes, home appliances, industrial tools, etc.; construction of buildings, bridges, electrical generators, etc.)
Physiology	General Medicine
Psychology	Clinical Psychology, Industrial Psychology, Psychiatry, Education
Zoology	Animal Husbandry, Veterinary Medicine
Astronomy, Geology, and Physics	Weather and Climate Forecasting
Botany, Chemistry, and Physiology	Pharmacy
Chemistry and Physics	Metallurgy

From Lachman, Sheldon J. *The Foundations of Science,* p. 19. Detroit: The Hamilton Press, 1956.

of energy in his experimenting and economical and effective in his reporting.

By research, then, we refer to a broad range of investigations calculated to discover new facts and principles, or to permit a revision of interpretations and conclusions previously advanced. Experimenting is a special kind of research which is primarily concerned with answering questions by means of manipulating variables.

HOW SCIENCE IS MADE

By whatever means knowledge may be advanced in some fields, we now come to the point where we wish to propose that the primary building block of science is the product of an experiment. Sometimes the experiment is highly restricted in its scope and importance and contributes a very small brick that is to go into a very large structure. Again, an experiment may be sweeping in its implications and, when successful, is to be compared to a massive cornerstone. If we continue to pursue our analogy, science as a whole is like a great unfinished building having many wings; methodology becomes the structural steel that binds these together into a single structure.

Although we may conceive of the experimenter as molding into shape the building blocks of a given science, the process is not always a straightforward one in which he collects any kind of raw data and proceeds by putting this into the desired shape. It might be that experiment after experiment fails to produce blocks of the quality and shape that can be fitted into the structure of a given building. However, the pile of rejects is not always rubbish. There have been dramatic examples of experiments that came out in unexpected ways, or in which some peculiarity in results was found that did not fit into any known place. Later these odd blocks, so to speak, became recognized as suitable cornerstones for a new room to science. The first observation that specks of mold became small islands surrounded by bacteria-free space on the surface of the growing host was an unexpected, and, for a time, unused observation. It was years after Fleming's observation in 1929 that hundreds of research workers became involved and millions of dollars invested in mold-farming in order to produce penicillin.

It is necessary to test and retest all along the line. Science is sometimes advanced by indulging in the inductive reasoning process and sometimes by deduction. Experimental findings become the basis for speculation and help to generate hypotheses and then again they become the means by which hypotheses are verified or tested. Often facts seem to be well established by repeated everyday observations and experience. Yet, scientific procedures may be necessary to dismiss any remaining doubt, or to further explanations for the known facts. Without scientific verification there is always great danger of confusing facts with fiction, sound interpretations with superstitions. Francis Bacon (1605, Advancement of Learning) quoted Celsus as saying: "That medicine and cures were first found out, and then after the reasons and causes were discoursed; and not the causes first found out, and by light from them the medicine and cures discovered" (Beveridge 1, p. 133).

Again, it is also true that many medicines discovered in this way later proved to be less successful than at first thought. Mistaken belief in a medicine before it has been sufficiently tested has often resulted in great economic waste, prolonged suffering without beneficial treatment, and sad disappointments. Presumably these unfortunate circumstances are not all in the past. A particularly difficult problem is to evaluate all the side-effects of strong medicines so that one condition is not treated with a degree of success only to be accompanied by the individual suffering damage in some other aspect of health. Because of relatively little progress in the use of drugs in treating mental diseases, to take an example in a field important to psychologists, the problem of side-effects of drugs is of no small consequence.

Freedman (4) had this to say about the way science is made: "Scientific research is essentially compounded of two elements—observations by which knowledge of certain facts is obtained through sense-perception, and reasoning by which the meaning of these facts, their interrelations, and their relations to existing body of scientific knowledge, are ascertained as far as existing state of knowledge and the investigator's ability permit." It is seen that science becomes the product of a fortunate blending of thinking, observing and manipulating. If all are not carried on simultaneously, it may be wise to juggle the sequence of these procedures from time to time. In fact, it is typical that the experimenter ranges backwards and forwards through these processes.

NOT ALL PSYCHOLOGY IS EXPERIMENTAL

While primary concern is with the contributions to the general body of psychological knowledge, it should be held in mind that some areas of the field at present lend themselves better to experimenting than do others. It is conceivable that a psychologist working in the area of clinical, child, or social psychology may pursue his task a long way before feeling that it becomes necessary to perform an experiment, either as a means to identifying a problem and generating a hypothesis, or to verify some speculation. While experimenting is possible in all fields of psychology, competent professional psychologists may make important contributions without advancing theories or testing hypotheses by experimentation. A parallel may be seen here between psychology and other sciences. The botanist may pursue his science by describing, classifying, and observing growth processes of the plants; the geologist rarely performs an experiment until he has progressed a long way into describing geological formations and even advancing speculative explanations. Eventually the botanist is likely to want to improve his plants or to develop new types, then he is confronted with the necessity of experimenting. The geologist may be challenged concerning the soundness of his explanations about rock formations and he may well find it necessary to verify his theoretical speculations by making rocks. Then he will be experimenting. Much experimenting and engineering was required before synthetic stones could be produced satisfactorily, but at present even diamonds are manufactured on a commercial scale.

There seems to be some tendency for the so-called natural sciences, such as physics and chemistry, to do their experimenting in an early stage of theorizing. The problems that arise and the hypotheses that they test are highly abstract and theoretical. If principles and laws are discovered, use may be made of these at a later time in very concrete and down-to-earth ways. The time comes when theoretical problems give way to emphasis upon developmental or engineering problems. It might be considered that the gadgets that fill the modern home are the material end-products of basic principles after they have been put to practical use. On the other hand, the social scientists seem to find their problems in the day-by-day living of people. These problems may be quite definite or specific in nature upon first being encountered. The psychologist, social worker, or psychiatrist may find his research dictated because of the need to find solutions to some very immediate and urgent problems in everyday conflict: What factors contribute most to conflict between married couples? Why do parents and children find it so difficult to understand each other and hence indulge in a running battle? Why cannot the child make friends, avoid fighting, or withstand the impulse to withdraw into a world by himself? Why does the adolescent become hostile, run counter to the regulations of society, and become a delinquent?

As progress toward solution to one of the above problems is made, or as investigations proceed, the social scientist may find himself becoming more and more abstract and speculative. Consequently, verification by means of experimentation or daily application of the end-product tends to become increasingly difficult. The social scientist may find himself moving from the simpler to the more complex as he tries to unravel an individual's problem, or in trying to alter some condition in society that he believes contributes to the problems that he is trying to solve.

While it may not always be the case, the physicist or chemist may progress from the abstract to the concrete and specific. If this is the situation, verification may be very clear and leave little doubt as to the consequence of his research. The final court of verification in the social sciences may involve projection into the course of action that will be taken by future generations of people. The social scientist is therefore not often able within a short time-interval to set up an experiment on a vital issue where he predicts that something will happen and then go about the manipulation of variables to force a test or verification of his ideas within the scope of a few days or months. He usually expects to make the final test in the operation of society itself. Traditionally, the problems that psychologists work upon are more closely identified with the social sciences than the natural sciences. However, it has already been indicated that the methods, as distinguished from the purpose and problems, may be more closely identified with the physical sciences.

WHEN IS THE EXPERIMENT INTRODUCED?

While an experiment can be set up as an aid to further progress in a science at almost any stage of development, it may appear to be more feasible and fruitful at certain particular points than at others. Usually a degree of progress has already been made toward a solution to the problem at hand before the experiment can be set up with a good chance of success. Progress has ordinarily advanced to the point where the experimenter is able to venture an hypothesis as to what will be found. In this connection we are reminded of Newton's statement: "No great discovery is ever made without a bold guess."

The urge to make a guess arises from need for an answer to a question that can be clearly stated. At any rate, guesses that are made following good questions are more likely to be borne out later. Fruitful questions themselves can be asked only after a certain amount of information has been acquired. It is not surprising that the relative amount of time and energy devoted to experimenting tends to rise as a particular science matures. The possibility—the demand, in fact—for "educated guesses" increases with the maturity of a science. It is not assumed that psychology is an exception to this generalization.

WHEN SHOULD THE INDIVIDUAL BECOME AN EXPERIMENTALIST?

We have indicated that the experiment may be profitably introduced at different stages of an investigation. It has been an intriguing question to ask when is the best time for the individual to become an experimentalist? The history of science is overwhelming in its verdict that youth is the time to begin experimenting. Most of the basic discoveries of science have been made by young men. A very few men like da Vinci, Franklin, and Pavlov were able to keep the questioning attitude, the energy, and the habits of work that are essential to the experimentalist into ripe old age. To be sure, the individual may turn to experimenting in his advanced years; with greater ease apparently he may continue to experiment if he has been doing that for years; but the evidence is clear as to the importance of learning to experiment early. The chances are great that other activities, such as teaching, administrative work, or the writing of books, will distract older people from research and experimenting. Other pursuits are nearly always more rewarding economically.

It is our thesis that the psychologist-to-be might invest heavily and wisely a great portion of his study time and his energy while in college to becoming an understanding and skilled experimentalist. If a sound beginning has been made by the student, the purposes of this book and the first course in experimental psychology have been realized.

SUGGESTED READINGS

Townsend, John C. *Introduction to Experimental Methods*. New York: Mc-Graw-Hill, 1953.

Underwood, Benton J. *Psychological Research*. New York: Appleton-Century-Crofts, 1957.

Beveridge, W. I. B. *The Art of Scientific Investigation*. New York: W. W. Norton.

Lackman, Sheldon J. *The Foundations of Science*. Detroit: The Hamilton Press, 1956.

Freedman, Paul. *The Principles of Scientific Research*. Washington, 1950.

Editors of Fortune. *The Mighty Force of Research*. New York: McGraw-Hill, 1956.

Foundation for Research. *Human Factors in Research Administration*. Ann Arbor, Mich., 1956.

REFERENCES

1. Beveridge, W. I. B. *The Art of Scientific Investigation*, p. 133. New York: W. W. Norton.

2. Freedman, Paul. *The Principles of Scientific Research*, p. 13. Washington: Public Affairs Press, 1950.

3. *Ibid.*, p. 15.

4. *Ibid.*, p. 13.

5. *Ibid.*, pp. 17-18.

INDEX